P9-EDM-968

Critical Essays on

JERZY KOSINSKI

CRITICAL ESSAYS
ON
AMERICAN LITERATURE

James Nagel, General Editor
University of Georgia, Athens

Critical Essays on
JERZY KOSINSKI

edited by

BARBARA TEPA LUPACK

G. K. Hall & Co.
An Imprint of Simon & Schuster Macmillan
New York

Prentice Hall International
London Mexico City New Delhi Singapore Sydney Toronto

G. K. Hall & Co.
An Imprint of Simon & Schuster Macmillan
1633 Broadway
New York, New York 10019

Library of Congress Cataloging-in-Publication Data

Critical essays on Jerzy Kosinski / edited by Barbara Tepa Lupack.
p. cm. — (Critical essays on American literature)
Includes bibliographical references and index.
ISBN 0-7838-0073-8 (alk. paper)
1. Kosinski, Jerzy N., 1933– —Criticism and interpretation.
I. Lupack, Barbara Tepa. II. Series.
PS3561.O8Z62 1998
813′.54—dc21 97-45948
CIP

This paper meets the requirements of ANSI/NISO Z3948–1992 (Permanence of Paper).

Printed in the United States of America

zdjeto wam z ramion ciezar
jestescie jak ptaki i dzieci
—Tadeusz Rózewicz

In memory of

Jerzy Kosinski
(1933–1991)

and

Jerzy Tepa
(1908–1992)

Contents

General Editor's Note

◆

This series seeks to anthologize the most important criticism on a wide variety of topics and writers in American literature. Our readers will find in various volumes not only a generous selection of reprinted articles and reviews but original essays, bibliographies, manuscript selections, and other materials brought to public attention for the first time. This volume, *Critical Essays on Jerzy Kosinski,* is the most comprehensive gathering of essays ever published on one of the most important modern writers in the United States. It contains both a sizable gathering of early reviews and a broad selection of more modern scholarship. Among the authors of reprinted articles and reviews are Gail Sheehy, Hugh Kenner, Elie Wiesel, Robert Coles, Robert Alter, and Elizabeth Stone. In addition to a substantial introduction by Barbara Tepa Lupack, three original essays were commissioned specifically for publication in this volume, new studies by Thomas S. Gladsky on Kosinski's fiction as history, Jerome Klinkowitz on the nonfiction prose, and Norman Lavers on Kosinski's novel cycle. We are confident that this book will make a permanent and significant contribution to the study of American literature.

JAMES NAGEL
University of Georgia

Publisher's Note

◆

Producing a volume that contains both newly commissioned and reprinted material presents the publisher with the challenge of balancing the desire to achieve stylistic consistency with the need to preserve the integrity of works first published elsewhere. In the Critical Essays series, essays commissioned especially for a particular volume are edited to be consistent with G. K. Hall's house style; reprinted essays appear in the style in which they were first published, with only typographical errors corrected. Consequently, shifts in style from one essay to another are the result of our efforts to be faithful to each text as it was originally published.

Acknowledgments

I would like to thank Jerome Klinkowitz for his advice, support, and encouragement. The excellence of his critical insights into contemporary literature is matched only by the generosity of his spirit. I am deeply grateful not only to Jerome Klinkowitz but also to Thomas S. Gladsky and Norman Lavers for agreeing to write new essays for this collection; their perspectives have enriched my understanding and readings of Kosinski's work. The fine criticism of Kosinski by other scholars, especially Paul R. Lilly Jr., John W. Aldridge, Paul Bruss, Jack Hicks, Ivan Sanders, and Daniel Cahill, has also influenced and challenged my thinking. The Polish Institute and *The Polish Review* have long encouraged my work: I am grateful to Krystyna Olszer and Joseph Wieczerzak, and I am especially indebted to the late Ludwik Krzyzanowski, distinguished scholar and editor. My thanks as well to Gloria L. Cronin and Blaine H. Hall, whose comprehensive bibliography was indispensable; to the University of Rochester's Rush-Rhees Library for various services that facilitated my research; to Impressions Book and Journal Services, for their expert assistance throughout production; and to Bill Henry for his careful reading of the manuscript. My husband, Alan Lupack, continues to offer wise counsel and unconditional support. Finally, I am grateful to James Nagel for giving me the opportunity to undertake this project and for his assistance throughout.

Introduction

Barbara Tepa Lupack

Two decades ago, Jerzy Kosinski's place in American literature seemed assured. His first novel, *The Painted Bird,* was hailed as a masterpiece of both Holocaust literature and modern fiction; translated widely, it won France's Prix du Meilleur Livre Étranger. *Steps,* his innovative second novel, received the prestigious National Book Award. The short but wickedly satiric *Being There* not only reached the best-seller list but also spawned a successful movie adaptation, for which Kosinski wrote the prize-winning screenplay. Subsequent works such as *The Devil Tree* and *Cockpit,* which he touted in interviews as important links in his cycle of novels, were disappointing but forgivable works, slight missteps on the path of what promised to be a long and brilliant literary career.

As fascinating as Kosinski's fiction was Kosinski's life, upon which—he implied—so much of that fiction was based. "To appreciate the cruel, ironic, suspenseful, oddly perverse yet highly moral world" of his novels, he wrote in one version of the biographical essay appended to several of the paperback editions of his novels, "one must first acknowledge the random succession of pain and joy, wealth and poverty, persecution and approbation, that have made [Kosinski's] own life even more eventful than those of his fictional creations."[1] Although in recent years much of his autobiographical account has been disputed or disproved, Kosinski claimed that he was abandoned at the age of six, suspected of being a Jew or a Gypsy, and forced to flee alone from village to village in Nazi-occupied Europe, where he survived by his wits. Traumatized and rendered mute for five years, until a postwar accident caused him to regain his voice, he was eventually reunited with his father, a philologist, and his mother, a concert pianist, and placed in a school for the handicapped. After completing high school in less than a year, he attended universities in Warsaw and Moscow, where he was threatened with expulsion for defying Marxist doctrine. Despite these skirmishes with authority, he rose rapidly within the state-controlled system to become an "associate professor" who spent winters as a ski instructor and summers as a psychological counselor at a seaside resort.

Secretly plotting his escape from Stalinist Poland, he mastered the "bureaucratic judo" and invented four prominent academicians to recommend him for study in the United States under the auspices of a fictitious foundation. With a cyanide capsule in his pocket in case his plan failed, Kosinski arrived in New York in December 1957: he was 24 years old, fluent in many languages but not English, and virtually penniless. While holding a variety of odd jobs, including serving as a chauffeur to a Harlem drug lord, Kosinski taught himself English and soon secured a spot in the graduate program in sociology at Columbia University as well as an actual fellowship from the Ford Foundation. Two and a half years after his arrival, he produced his first book, *The Future Is Ours, Comrade,* a sociopsychological analysis of a totalitarian state. While working on his second book, *No Third Path,* a study of totalitarian behavior, he met and eventually married Mary Hayward Weir, the superrich young widow of the founder of U.S. Steel. In the six years before her death from an incurable illness, Mary introduced Kosinski to the world of the influential and the powerful. During their marriage, he began writing *The Painted Bird,* ostensibly as a way of helping Mary to understand his past. That novel, published to great acclaim in 1965, established his literary career, and other novels quickly followed. It was, to be sure, a compelling life story, which he told spellbindingly and retold often, in interviews and in materials about himself that he circulated among critics and scholars through his own small publishing company, Scientia-Factum.

Kosinski's prominence among the literati was matched only by his ubiquitousness among the glitterati. He moved with equal ease from the campuses of Princeton and Yale Universities, where he held teaching appointments, to the celebrity-studded soirees and the exclusive beaches of the rich and privileged, where he was photographed with such notables as George Harrison, Diane Von Furstenburg, and Zbigniew Brzezinski; from the responsibilities of the presidency of the American Center of PEN, the international organization of writers, a position he held for the maximum two terms, to the late-night irresponsibilities of television talk shows, where he was a regular and popular guest. Much like the protagonists of his novels, Kosinski—it appeared—had survived personal nightmare to achieve the American Dream of wealth, celebrity, and success.

Kosinski's fortunes changed, however, with the publication of a cover story in the *Village Voice* in June 1982. That story, which was carried worldwide, accused him of being a lifelong liar, a CIA stooge, and a literary fraud who employed assistants to write large portions of his fiction. Colleagues rallied to defend him against the charges, many of which were eventually disproved. But Kosinski was convinced that irreparable damage had been done. He spent much of the 1980s "running from the Voice" and rebutting accusations that he had squandered his considerable talents in pursuit of American pop cult status. He published only one more novel, a complicated and convoluted work intended to rehabilitate his reputation by fictionally rebutting the *Voice* charges, before taking his own life on May 3, 1991.

Today Kosinski continues to be read and admired as one of the major forces in the shaping of the contemporary American novel. His works can be found on bookstore shelves as well as on academic reading lists, and he is studied alongside such literary giants as Hemingway and Faulkner. His nine novels have gone through numerous reprintings and reissues in America and have been translated into 40 languages, while his posthumously published volume of essays, the bulk of which he collected before his death, the remainder compiled by his second wife, Katherina von Fraunhofer-Kosinski, reveals his sharp critical eye and reconfirms his position as a leading intellectual and philosophical novelist.

How is it, then, that Kosinski, a man so controlled and so controlling of his public persona, could have come as close as he did to being undone? Is it because—as he often suggested—he was so much like the title metaphor of his acclaimed first novel: a painted bird who circles its flock vainly trying to convince its kin that it is one of them, only to be "forced farther and farther away" until the other birds "peel off [after it] in a fierce attack"? Or is it because he was not so much the victimized bird as the bird painter who seeks to subvert the collective conformity of the flock—a type of the artist himself, who manipulates things and events and embellishes the ordinary with a "spot of rainbow"?[2]

It is possible, as one unquestionably pro-Kosinski article published in the *New York Times* in late 1982 maintained, that the *Voice* exposé that almost ruined him was the culmination of a 17-year-long ideological attack on Kosinski as a cultural target, an attack that reached back to the publication of his "anti-Polish" first novel, continued with Kosinski's rejection of Judaism and his propitious marriage to the staunchly anti-Communist Mary Weir, and found fresh voice in his criticism of the Polish government and his support of Solidarity in the early 1980s. But in fact Kosinski, albeit unwittingly, was complicitous in undermining his own credibility, even in giving the *Voice* writers verifiably false information that they were able to use against him in their article. For years, he had engaged in various deceptions—though not necessarily those cited by the *Voice*—and had enlisted the support of others, including his wives, his friends, even his mother. He concocted wild, conflicting, and often outright misleading stories about himself; those stories, repeated and embellished, became a way to "invent and reinvent" himself, a task he felt was incumbent upon any good writer, and to project a very specific public image at the same time that he protected his most private inner self.[3] "My visibility," he once boasted, "is my ultimate camouflage: nothing hides one better from the public than appearing on the Johnny Carson show, because everyone thinks they know what one is doing and what one is all about—and yet there are 364 other days in the year, when they don't."[4]

Asserting that his motto was *Larvatus Prodeo,* "I go forth disguised," Kosinski publicized his strange penchant for secrecy and concealment to the point of self-exploitation. In interviews and television appearances, he spoke of the weapons he kept hidden and of the disguises he wore when he ventured outside, especially at night, and even allowed himself to be photographed for *New York* magazine wearing various wigs, mustaches, and costumes.[5] He told of eavesdropping on conversations, particularly when people were discussing him, as a way of learning about himself and about how others perceived him. He repeated tales about Plato's Retreat and the various sex clubs he frequented, places in which he felt safe because the patrons were more concerned about self-recognition than the recognition of others. He would regale his friends with well-rehearsed anecdotes about his duplicities, some of which were benign and amusing: on one occasion, he posed as a spastic just to get to the head of the queue at a French post office; on another, he hid under a desk and tickled the ankle of a visiting diplomat, who was so terrified of the tarantulas in the area that he leapt into the air. Other stories were more shocking, such as the blind dates Kosinski claimed to have arranged for macho polo players with beautiful women who turned out to be transsexuals in progress. Those anecdotes, like the many terrifying and horrific incidents of his early life as a child of the Holocaust and as a young man coming of age in Stalinist Poland, found their way into his novels. But the more Kosinski sensationalized his life by his consciously eccentric behavior, the more inseparable his life became from his fiction. Just as the dancer in Yeats's great poem "Among School Children" becomes indistinguishable from the dance, Kosinski's life seemed increasingly to be his fiction, and his fiction seemed to be his life. Kosinski told an interviewer that even during his adolescence in Eastern Europe, "instead of writing fiction, I imagined myself as a fictional character."[6]

Kosinski's tendency to blur the boundaries between life and art, between memory and fiction, initially found a receptive audience among critics, some of whom went so far as to suggest that reinvention of the self was an integral part of the American Dream. Jack Hicks took note of the new wall Kosinski had built from " 'the stones' of his past . . . finally a literal pseudo-life, a mythic carapace first hardened on the pseudonymous Joseph Novak"; that historical self, according to Hicks, created "by the dissimulation of materials selected from his past[,] mirrors the process of self-creation and invokes the same themes and preoccupations undertaken by the protagonists of his fiction." John Corry put it more simply: "Critics say that his works are autobiographical; he says they are novels. Declare that his works are pure fiction, however, and he will say that everything in them is true." Kosinski's friend Barbara Gelb hinted that his inventiveness with facts is "by design—another form of trick or test, to catch you out, part of his social experimenting."[7]

But Kosinski's often contradictory versions of his biography soon began to cast a pall on his artistic and literary practices. Jerome Klinkowitz, the first prominent literary critic to treat Kosinski's work in a substantive way, wrote that he felt obliged to sort out his own experiences with the man and with his writing because of the "conflicting stories that Jerzy himself had been telling me" and the conflicting stories Klinkowitz had heard about Kosinski, both in the United States and in Poland. In an article entitled "Betrayed by Jerzy Kosinski," Klinkowitz wrote that he regrets having endorsed Kosinski's unverifiable biographical material as scholarly fact: "Inventing his own life of fiction is Jerzy Kosinski's most natural act. . . . stories about him rebound as reactions to the sometimes cock-and-bull narratives that he's created about himself or perhaps rumors whose seeds he has planted to spice up the plot [of his life of fiction]." Needing a "myth" to surround his novels, Klinkowitz concluded, Kosinski was careful to keep that mythology consistent with the changes in American political sensibility, from cold-war hostility through détente and back again to rambunctious anti-Communism.[8]

Kosinski's fabrications came back to bite him in an especially vicious way in the front-page *Village Voice* story "Jerzy Kosinski's Tainted Words," in which journalists Eliot Fremont-Smith and Geoffrey Stokes challenged Kosinski's ethics and alleged that his chronic prevarication—a "frantic manufacture of fables, as if to cloak his hollowness"—extended to his novels. By hiring assistants not only to edit but to help compose portions of his novels, Kosinski had effectively "trash[ed the writer's tradition]; by refusing to admit the level of his collaboration with others, he has erected a repugnant wall of denials . . . [and] betrayed his own talent along with his craft." Among Fremont-Smith and Stokes's specific claims were the following: that the editorial help Kosinski hired was so substantial as to amount to coauthorship of at least three novels; that the nonfiction Novak books were actually ghostwritten and financed by the Central Intelligence Agency; that *The Painted Bird* was first written in Polish and then rendered into English by an unnamed translator; and that Kosinski manipulated the facts of his biography to such an extent that "almost *nothing* he says can be relied on."[9] Although many, but not all, of the collaborators cited by the *Voice* soon disavowed the article and although Fremont-Smith and Stokes failed to deliver a follow-up piece exposing more of Kosinski's deliberate deceptions, suspicions about Kosinski's authorship lingered. Appreciating that his relentless self-promotion and distractions with celebrity had made him an easy target, Kosinski tried to defuse the controversy with humorous and parodic accounts of his multiple identities as well as with high-minded arguments about the journalists' First Amendment rights to print their conclusions, no matter how erroneous. But the controversy followed him to his death—and, in fact, found new life in the wake of his suicide.

Ironically, although Kosinski succeeded in convincing others that his fiction was autobiographical, it now seems that one of his best and most sustained fictions was actually his autobiography. In the first and only comprehensive biography of Kosinski to date, James Park Sloan challenges many of the "facts" of Kosinski's life and provides a detailed account of his actual experiences, both in Poland and in the United States.[10] Contrary to

Kosinski's oft-repeated claims that he roamed the villages of Eastern Europe alone as an orphan of war, for instance, Sloan confirms that Kosinski was never abandoned; in fact, his parents, his adopted younger brother, and he spent the war years in relative safety and comfort. Early on, Kosinski's father, Mojzesz (Moses) Lewinkopf, had realized the peril that German occupation would pose for Polish Jews and began making preparations to leave Lodz, where Jerzy had been born. In Sandomierz, the first of several towns in which they eventually resided, the Lewinkopfs—on official identity papers that Mojzesz had been able to arrange—became the more Gentile-sounding Kosinskis. After the war's end, they moved yet again, first to Jelenia Gora and ultimately back to Lodz, where the elder Kosinski's strong ties to the Party helped secure him a large home, a good living, and a measure of influence. Although he dabbled in languages, Mieczyslaw Kosinski (the former Mojzesz Lewinkopf) was neither a philologist nor a professor by profession, as his son later claimed, but rather a businessman involved in the textile and leather trades; to be sure, he was a successful and intelligent man, prescient enough to have dollar reserves, which helped the family to survive the war. Kosinski's mother enjoyed playing the piano but was never a conservatory-trained concert pianist; that too was Kosinski's reinvention—although apparently Mrs. Kosinski later engaged in some reinvention of her own, by supporting her son's story that they had been separated during the war.

As for Kosinski himself: although certainly traumatized by the experience of war in Poland, especially by his need to conceal his real identity, he was never rendered mute (a point Kosinski eventually conceded when he suggested that the boy's muteness was best described as symbolic). And there were numerous other embellishments. The position of "aspirant" that Kosinski held at the university was hardly equal to that of "associate professor," or even to the amended "assistant professor" of his later accounts; an aspirant was the Polish term for a graduate teaching assistant. The secret plot to escape from Stalinist Poland, which he said he refused to discuss with his parents for fear of their safety, was—as Klinkowitz first suggested and Sloan confirmed—anything but clandestine. A Ford Foundation grant to the Institute for International Education in August 1957 had provided funding for an exchange of scholars and specialists between the United States and Poland. Potential Polish graduate students, many of them in the social sciences, were recruited for the pilot program, and a number of Kosinski's fellow students were ultimately selected. Surprisingly, Kosinski did not apply—a decision he quickly regretted and rectified. With the help of his mentors, several of whom had been involved in the original selection process, and with the required pledge of financial assistance—a $500 deposit in a New York bank in Kosinski's name—from his uncle in America, Kosinski soon secured a visa to pursue graduate work in the United States.

When he arrived, he was, according to some of his contemporaries, neither penniless nor unacquainted with the English language. Nor is there any evidence to support his claims that he was the first to break a color barrier by serving as chauffeur to a Harlem drug lord. Such details, however, made for a great story, a story to which he clung, even as revelations about his actual past—that his marriage to his first wife, Mary, had ended in divorce two years before her death, that Mary's "incurable illness" was not cancer of the brain but alcoholism, that he did indeed employ translators and collaborators to assist in his writing—forced him increasingly to equivocate, to qualify earlier statements, and ultimately to spin new tales.

The real reason for Kosinski's obfuscation of biographical fact is unclear. Perhaps it was the vestige of his very real childhood need to mask his identity, as James Park Sloan has suggested; perhaps it was "the almost reflexive desire of a Holocaust survivor for disguise—a habit of continuous self-invention," as Geoffrey Stokes and Eliot Fremont-Smith suggested; or perhaps it was merely another of the deceptions and games that Kosinski played to expand his own perception and the perceptions of others, as Paul Bruss and others have suggested. What is clear, however, is that for Kosinski the melding of fact and fiction was a seminal part of the artistic process. As he explained to George Plimpton and Rocco Landesman in 1972: "What we remember lacks the hard edge of fact. To help us along we create little fictions, highly subtle and individual scenarios which clarify and shape our experience. The remembered event becomes a fiction, a structure to accommodate certain feelings." In an essay written in 1989 and included in *Passing By,* he wondered about the relevance or accuracy of any post-traumatic memory. There was no reason, he felt, to return to the villages he saw during the war because "what I have to say . . . I have already expressed in metaphors. I am not interested in explicit memory because I cannot trust it. In my case memory is always clouded by my desire for inventiveness."[11]

Although the revelations of Kosinski's various deceptions have prompted some scholarly revisionism, in the end, the only true gauge of his literary reputation is his writing. And "happily," as Jerome Klinkowitz reports, despite the gossip about Kosinski's personal life, "his texts survive intact."[12] The novels are intriguing explorations of the self and of the picaresque hero; most are part of a larger fictional cycle; and a handful are by any measure truly extraordinary—so extraordinary that they stand as highly original works of literature, brilliant attempts at new and exceedingly bold effects. Regarding his most innovative novels, *The Painted Bird* and *Steps,* for instance, William Kennedy concludes that "the revisionists can go pack salt."[13]

Kosinski once observed that it is a good thing that novelists die, "because their biographies die with them. So then you just read their books."[14] Although Kosinski's biography has not died, people still read his books, and Kosinski's place in literary history is secure.

I
Reviews

Kosinski's first two books, both nonfiction volumes, were based on notes that he had brought with him when he emigrated to the United States in 1957, notes that he intended to draw on as the basis for his dissertation when he undertook graduate study the following year at Columbia University. Published under the pseudonym Joseph Novak, purportedly to protect Kosinski's parents in Poland from recriminations, the books examined collective behavior as seen through the eyes of various individuals whom Kosinski met during his brief visits to Moscow as a student.

Contemporary readers and reviewers responded quite favorably to Kosinski's candid observations. Joseph G. Harrison called *The Future Is Ours, Comrade,* which was subtitled "Conversations with the Russians," a "grim and fascinating" book worthy of a thoughtful and careful reading. Both Richard C. Hottelet and William J. Jorden praised the important firsthand testimony and abundance of inside information, and Stephen Rosenfeld remarked on the compellingly real and convincing portrayal of the lives of the people Novak encountered. Even Edward Crankshaw, who faulted the lack of humor, the author's lack of judgment concerning the persons he interviewed, and other aspects of the book, admitted that it contributed to an understanding of the mechanics of Soviet society. Perhaps most interesting, however, was the *Times Literary Supplement* review, which claimed that the book "has all the fluency of the best of American journalism."[15]

Published two years later, *No Third Path* afforded another look at the Soviet system; this time, however, Kosinski subtly shifted his focus to the situation of the individual within the collective, which would become a prominent theme in his fiction. Again, the critical response to this "impressionistic record from within" was largely positive: Henry L. Roberts was disturbed by Kosinski's description of the relationship between the individual and the collective, Ernest S. Pisko by the insights into the way that Soviet leaders tried to replace individual reflection with conditioned reflexes. William O'Connor, for whom the "conversations" offered a certain "thrill of discovery," found the book to be a worthy companion to *The Future Is Ours, Comrade* as a portrait of Soviet life. But William Henry Chamberlin felt that the book, admittedly one of the best collections of "raw material" on the Russian mind, could have been improved with more analysis by the author.[16] Kosinski's cold-war message, though, seemed to have lost some of its novelty: unlike *The Future Is Ours, Comrade,* which was serialized in the *Saturday Evening Post* and condensed for *Reader's Digest, No Third Path* was a commercial failure.[17]

In its preliminary explorations of motifs and characters that recur throughout Kosinski's later work, his nonfiction can properly be seen as a kind of apprenticeship. It is, however, in his brilliant first novel about a young boy's odyssey through war-torn Eastern Europe, written in part to preserve the memory of his past, that Kosinski really found his voice. A trip into the world of nightmare, *The Painted Bird* (1965), wrote Anaïs Nin, surpassed "most of the books in which experience of terror and physical cruelty are told."[18]

The reviews, proclaiming Kosinski to be not merely the master of the macabre but an authentic voice of the century, were overwhelmingly positive.[19] Joseph P. Bauke called *The Painted Bird* a novel of terrifying impact replete with scenes of sadism rarely matched in contemporary literature. David Evanier, struck by Kosinski's parallels between the atrocities committed within the concentration camps and the evils occurring outside as well, labeled the novel a deeply moral work. Both Oleg Ivsky and Guy Davenport found it so heartbreaking that they recommended it only to readers with "cast iron stomachs." Andrew Field, who commended the novel for its high literary merit, concurred that its "flame-dark pages" described events that were almost unreadable.[20]

For noted psychiatrist Robert Coles, who had initially expected *The Painted Bird* to be a tender, gentle story suitable for high school students, it was a brilliant and unnerving account of how a boy keeps alive in the face of what emerges finally as hell itself; his story, notes Coles, "tells a million stories," of other exiles and outcasts and suffering people.[21] For Anne Halley, the novel was a survivor's tale crossed with the lost-child genre of children's fairy tales, which contains all the archetypal fairy-tale elements.[22] Calling it "a testament not only to the atrocities of the war but to the failings of human nature," Peter Prescott compared *The Painted Bird* to Anne Frank's diary, a comparison echoed by Harry Overstreet and cited on the paperback edition. As an autobiographical account of the sufferings of a child during the war, *The Painted Bird,* according to Neil Compton, could be grouped with Günter Grass's *The Tin Drum;* its juxtaposition of childish innocence and the most brutal forms of fallen adult experience produces a myth that is uncommonly intense. Charles Poore likened the nightmare world of *The Painted Bird* to Goya's "Disasters of War" and cautioned in his review that "Things Like These Happen to People We Know."

Perhaps the most important review of all was by the prominent scholar and Holocaust survivor Elie Wiesel, who declared that "this poignant first-person account transcends confession and attains in its parts the haunting quality and tone of a quasi-surrealistic tale."[23] The painful and absurd cosmic joke that transforms ordinary people leading ordinary lives into persecutors more brutal than the Nazis, notes Wiesel, is one to which everybody is victim; it not only turns the boy into "Everybody's Victim" but also provides eloquent proof—if ever proof were necessary—that "Auschwitz was more a concept than a name." Wiesel's enthusiastic review certified *The Painted Bird* as a classic and was quoted in promotional copy for the novel alongside playwright Arthur Miller's statement congratulating Kosinski for the "very important and difficult" task of making the "normality" of the Nazi experience so apparent.

Most American reviewers offered only the most effusive praise for the novel. Even those such as Neal Ascherson, who declared it "a suspect document [of the Holocaust] and a dubious novel," saw it as a fable about "the proximity of savagery to innocence and delight, an idea . . . Kosinski shares with Hieronymus Bosch."[24] Yet the novel managed to generate some bitter and outright hostile reviews from Poles, who protested Kosinski's slanderous exaggerations. As Henry Kamm observed, what made the vehement Polish response especially curious was the fact that the book had not even been published in Poland.[25] (It would not appear in Polish translation until 1989.) But the Polish reaction was nonetheless strong enough to cause Kosinski to change some of the specific references: in later editions of the novel, for example, the boy no longer comes from a "large city in central Poland" but from the more generic "Eastern Europe," and he learns to read not in "Polish" but in his "mother tongue."

Whereas *The Painted Bird* described the outrageous cruelties visited upon a young boy attempting to survive the atrocities of World War II, Kosinski's second novel, *Steps,* published in 1968, followed rather logically as a chronicle of the changes, perversions, and deformations in character of that survivor.[26] But the barbarity of *Steps,* no longer attributable—as was the brutality in *The Painted Bird*—to ignorance or poverty, was even more impersonal, technological, and gratuitous. The novel's scenes or vignettes, recounted in the first person and in a simple and deliberately unembellished style, offer little solace or solitude; instead, they comprise a series of sexual acts and aberrations—including defloration, adultery, rape, incest, homosexuality, prostitution, and gang bangs—that, noted John J. McAleer, blend into a kind of erotic symphony.[27] Yet, although *Steps* is a strongly sexual novel, Stanley Kauffmann wrote, "it is also a novel about terror, killing, politics, and the scraping-out of some plateaus of tranquillity in a sliding-climbing existence . . . a book so scorchingly personal that it is unique."[28]

Other reviewers, however, seemed unable to agree whether *Steps* was a jumble of random episodes that read like a "slick and cynically selected" anthology written with an eye on the popular audience or a bold philosophical statement by an intellectual writer with a stark existential vision.[29] Some considered the novel—a Literary Guild Alternate Selection and the eventual winner of the National Book Award for Fiction—to be Kosinski's most significant achievement.[30] Martin Tucker called the novel a tour de force, an impressive tale of the narrator's quest for power and control, in which the brilliant ordering and control of material surpassed even the achievements of *The Painted Bird*. Eliot Fremont-Smith, who was responsible for launching the *Voice* attack against Kosinski almost a decade and a half later, wrote that the novel is profoundly disturbing and powerful, like a serpent coiled to strike, and its language "perfect, efficient, and lucid as a gem." Like D. A. N. Jones, who commended the refreshingly austere language of the novel, Hugh Kenner praised the calm of Kosinski's prose as well as the controlling motif of the narrator's journey "through time and space," which defines the novel's structure.[31] Kenner saw that structure not as steps but as circles—of cruelty, ritual, and restless love—that form still other circles. "Love is restless," he wrote, "because ritualized by cruelty; ritual is cruel because loveless; cruelty is the mode of love because the rituals confine experience."

Kosinski's bold choice of form and content in *Steps* invited comparison, particularly to European modernists. Tucker made the obvious connection to Conrad, Kosinski's fellow Pole; Kauffmann felt that "some of the episodes suggest Babel, some a darker Dinesen, some de Maupassant." Kenner wrote that "Céline and Kafka stand behind this accomplished art," whereas for McAleer, "Camus, Vailland, and Djilas determined [Kosinski's] style, his choice of theme, and his treatment of it." P. N. Furbank declared that *Steps* is written in the tradition of Dostoyevsky, Sade, Camus, Mailer, and the theater of cruelty. For W. B. Hill, the novel evoked Melville and Kafka; for Marvin Felheim, it was Kafka and Conrad as well as Nabokov, Hawthorne, Poe, and Dickens. Bruce Cook detected "an existential pessimism . . . associate[d] with Sartre and the other writers of that school" but felt that ultimately Kosinski's voice was new and "distinctly his own."[32]

Not all the reviews, however, were so laudatory. Many critics commented on the novel's coldness, its contrived and sensational sex scenes, and the indifference of its narrator to the events he experiences and describes.[33] Irving Howe, for instance, praised the style of *Steps* but admitted that he was unsure of the book's meaning; the unnamed spectator is so immoral and detached that he seems to be "from the other side of the moon." Observing that only a fragile barrier separates aesthetics from psychosis, Geoffrey Wolff scored *Steps* for its morbid and salacious contents and its lack of symbolic life or resonance, while the *Time* reviewer thought the novel lacked the "grounding situation, the structure and connective tissue" that could have made it more than the abstract expression of a pathological mind. Even *Kirkus* called *Steps* a failure for not imposing substance on "a slipstream of sensation and movement." Still others commented on the novel's desperation and pretension, lack of moral imagination, witless incoherence, derision of innocence, and convoluted negativity.[34]

In contrast to Roger Baker, who called *Steps* "brilliant, cold, unpleasant" and described its structure as cinematic, Clive Jordan complained that the episodes—a kind of violent, literary *Mondo Cane*—had no underlying progression, a judgment with which others concurred. Katherine Gauss Jackson confessed that she did not know what the steps were or to what they were leading; Paul West described the structural device of Kosinski's "inexplicably flat" novel more as a sort of seesaw tottering between two extremes than as steps generating any power or intensity; and Barbara Bannon concluded that to find a semblance of order in the novel's disconnections, the reader must follow his or her own "steps" rather than the author's.[35] Kosinski, in fact, had anticipated such adverse criticism. As he had done with *Notes of the Author on The Painted Bird*

(1965), he self-published a short essay entitled *The Art of the Self: Essays à Propos Steps* to explain the philosophy of his art—and to call the reviewers' bluff.[36] *Steps,* he wrote, lacked a sense of traditional plot; the episodes, meant to impart "a hint of recognition, an intimation—no more," must be imagined as part of a larger symbolic montage. In this way, the novel's deliberate subversiveness forces readers to uncover its meaning for themselves.

Kosinski's emergence as a humorist and satirist was marked by the publication in 1971 of *Being There*. The story of a simple gardener's chance rise to the pinnacle of American celebrity, the novel was a real change of pace. Some reviewers decried it as slight and derivative, the literary equivalent of soap opera with no discernible moral. The majority, however, hailed the novel as an original, compelling, and deceptively dark fable about the vacuousness and narcissism of contemporary culture.[37] Among those most impressed with it was the distinguished literary critic John W. Aldridge, who wrote in his review essay that *Being There* was a modern parable of contemporary America "raised to the ultimate level of electronic derangement and peopled with creatures who perceive life wholly in terms of the images offered them on the television screen." With its metaphoric and analogical ideas, the novel belongs in the tradition of classic European modernist works that explore "the nature and meaning of the human condition . . . in an essentially amoral and surely anachronistic universe."[38] Novelist William Kennedy described it as mellower and more comical than *Steps,* which he characterized as "trauma perceived as the normal human condition," but he recognized that *Being There* was also a subtle polemic.[39] For Jerome Klinkowitz, the novel was a finely crafted and well-turned practical joke by which Kosinski confirmed his role as an astute observer of the American scene; for Marilyn Gardner, who praised Kosinski for exploring so cleverly the current media mania, it was a major philosophical critique of American affluence and mass culture; and for R. Z. Sheppard, it was simply a "tantalizing knuckle ball of a book delivered with perfectly symmetrical hops and metaphysical flutters."[40]

Reading the novel as myth, Richard Combs compared it to *The Great Gatsby* and *The Magic Christian*. Peter Glassgold called Chance a Candide in reverse, designed by the author to tell us "that we are a passive people, slack-jawed observers of secondhand experience," while Daniel Stern saw Chance as "Candide in the Electronic Age," an existential hero so reduced to essence that he becomes a metaphoric mirror for those around him. For Steven Kroll, *Being There* was "Counter-Alger," the story of a perverse Horatio Alger told in the mode of Ionesco. Martin Tucker described the novel in similar terms of reversal, though for Tucker the reversal lay in the order of the journey: unlike Kosinski's other characters who begin in trauma and end in stasis, Chance starts out in a safe world and ends up in an utterly absurd one. John J. McAleer agreed that *Being There* spoofed the American Dream of success.[41] The fabular qualities of *Being There* also merited mention.[42] V. S. Pritchett pointed to Chance's "gift of nullity," which carries the comedy from scene to scene in Kosinski's ingeniously "neat fable." Irving Howe called *Being There* a "neat literary joke" about the paralyzing mindlessness of television, the dominant styles of American culture, and the loss of innocence, a novel "smaller, fresher, more clever . . . [than] the fable or allegory that some reviewers have supposed." Geoffrey Wolff felt Kosinski was stalking even bigger game than television: "insensibility," he wrote, "is the fable's most ruinous vice."[43]

John Updike, on the other hand, found little to praise. Dismissing *Being There* as a "dim and truncated version of those old Hollywood comedies wherein a handsome bumpkin charms the world and makes good," he called it a "thin, thin, preposterously thin" novel that suffers by comparison to Nabokov's work and reveals little but the portraitist's diffident contempt for the American political and financial establishment. Ronald De Feo labeled it one of the most feeble satires in English in recent years. Anatole Broyard found "banality dressed up as profundity" on every page. Neither realism nor parable, the tale of Chance was scarcely compelling enough to maintain interest for James Farrant, while Lee T. Lemon wondered if anyone could find the protagonist's simplistic answers to problems of inflation and the cold war plausible. Paul Delany noted that *Being There,* Kosinski's first work to have an American setting, scored a few hits but finally failed to convince or convict. Michael Cooke disparaged the novel as slender pseudoallegory. Barton Midwood was even harsher in his indictment: the plot summary, he wrote, is better than the novel, which is simply an unintentional "joke, blown full of tepid air, communicating neither any sense of the ordinary world nor of a cogently realized fantasy."[44] If *Being There* was a joke, however, at least it was a popular and enduring one with audiences, who saw the fruition of Kosinski's vision in the American political process, especially in the come-from-nowhere candidacy of Jimmy Carter and the telegenic success of Ronald Reagan. Scripted as a film by Kosinski, *Being There* scored again, winning awards from the Writers Guild of America and the British Academy of Film and Television Arts.

Kosinski's fourth novel, *The Devil Tree,* the story of Jonathan Whalen, the rich but rootless inheritor of the American Dream if not of the underlying Puritan ethic, followed in 1973. John J. McAleer applauded it, noting that the pure flame of Kosinski's prose burned in his latest novel like a laser beam. Stanley Kauffmann termed Kosinski's method "recrystallization," a resolidifying of the sharp crystals of experience so that "the patterns burn coldly." Peter S. Prescott found *The Devil Tree* to be a difficult, impressive fiction with a disturbing but coherent philosophy, and he predicted that readers who grasp "Kosinski's Deviltry" will find it overwhelming. Marion Simon Garmel praised the ideas and poetic language of the novel; Larry Swindell compared Kosinski to Conrad, Nabokov, and other nonnative writers who had mastered English; and Jerome Klinkowitz suggested that *The Devil Tree* presented an American character's struggle with his unique quotidian.[45] Other reviews were more mixed. Philip Stevick found Kosinski's narrative techniques "marvelously expressive" but considered the book's parts "better than its whole, and its voice greater than its vision."[46] Alan Hislop described the prose as terse and hard-edged but felt that the elements were not fully integrated; the reader finishes the novel with a "sense of unexpectations unfulfilled."[47]

Yet most reviewers concurred with Elliott Anderson, who saw little pattern to the movement and concluded that *The Devil Tree* was simply a thin, bad novel. The very titles of the reviews suggested the critics' disdain: "Stepping Down into Drivel," "Sterile Diversions," "The Ravings of the Rich," "Pulp-Fiction Style, Pop-Psychology Jargon, and a Genuinely Sadistic Imagination," "Bad by Design? Or Just Bad?" It seemed, in fact, that reviewers were competing to outdo each other in ways to describe just how bad the book really was. Pearl K. Bell called it profoundly unforgivable and full of flaccid prose, a lumpy bundle of mindless blather probably written by a tape recorder or Xerox machine; Robert Alter accused it of being self-indulgent, cliché ridden, and derivative; George Stade derided it for having a "weak grip on [contemporary] unrealities" and for being unworthy of the trouble it took to get to the punch line. Phoebe Adams suggested that even if the hero's role is taken as a metaphor for American society, "there is a whiff of roast chestnut about the scheme." Ronald De Feo complained about the book's implausibility and savagery; the disembodied Whalen's shallow, fractured prose amounted to little more than a kind of intellectualized pornography. Susan Knight observed that even if *The Devil Tree* could be considered fashionable, it was merely an emasculated version of *Steps*. For John Kiley, the central character possessed no humor, maturity, or charm; for John Skow, Jonathan's hopeless neuroses were singularly uninteresting and contributed only to the novel's sense of futility. Russell Davies found the novel indistinguishable from the considerable mass of depression literature and likened its flat monotony to the lobotomized dronings of a psychiatrist's couch. The kindest thing Christopher Lehmann-Haupt could say about the work was that it committed the fallacy of imitative form: its structure matched perfectly the hollowness and banality of modern America. Applying a slightly different medical metaphor than Davies did, Lehmann-Haupt called *The Devil Tree* a lethal text that spreads like poisonous effluvia throughout the nervous system. Instead of being art, the novel ends up being another product of the very culture that it is attempting to anatomize; instead of being a prognosis of the disease, it ends up being a symptom.[48]

Even reviewers generally sympathetic to Kosinski found little to like. Phillip Corwin, who attempted to read *The Devil Tree* as a philosophical novel, found its superficiality disappointing, especially because its author was such a talented writer. Theorizing that Kosinski had succumbed to what he was satirizing, Corwin urged him not to be devoured by commercialism—an increasingly common charge.[49] Kosinski too appeared to be disappointed with the book and subsequently revised and expanded it, explaining that at the time he wrote it, he had felt restricted by the proximity of the story to events in his own life. The new edition, published almost a decade later in 1981, was "vastly superior to the original," according to Barbara Tepa Lupack, and an interesting link in the cycle of Kosinski's fiction.[50] But even the revised version received little favorable critical attention—or, for that matter, much critical attention at all.

On the other hand, reviewers reacted strongly to *Cockpit* (1975), Kosinski's fifth novel, a kind of literary confession by its protagonist, a former secret agent named Tarden who had left the "Service." Some found the novel to be "grim and gross," "one dimensional," or "all skill" with little illumination; they complained that it was a flickering sequence of fantasy-violence with no heart and agreed with Frederick Karl that it was "a great anal saga, dominated by a confidence man, capable of great cruelty." For Peter S. Prescott, the "repellent fable" of a man who tries and fails to gain absolute control of his life proved the least tolerable of Kosinski's novels. For Hilton Kramer, the combination of the hateful protagonist, the splintered action full of cruel entrapments, and the detached but erotic relish with which the anecdotes are recounted added up to the sheerest nonsense parading as arcane wisdom. For Lee T. Lemon, *Cockpit* held all the fascination of a "freak show." Charles Deemer felt the novel was so bewildering and horror filled that he called it "Satan's Soap Opera."[51]

But many saw *Cockpit* as Jonathan Baumbach did: an audacious and elaborate return to the seemingly random picaresque mode of earlier, successful works such as *Steps*. Admittedly harsh and enigmatic, wrote Richard R. Lingeman, *Cockpit* was nonetheless profoundly chilling in its vision of contemporary life. Elaine Feinstein noted that it moved forward with the velocity of a thriller, the velocity itself unnerving, while Jane Larkin Crain agreed that readers "devour" with great curiosity its powerful and brutal plot. Gerald Barrett compared it to Melville's *Confidence Man;* Stefan Kanfer, though he found Tarden's need for retribution disturbing, called Kosinski's talent "relentless" and agreed with earlier reviewers that "not since Conrad has an Eastern European found so profound a voice in the English language." In his use of a protagonist more alienated than ever, of adventures more quixotic, and of incidents more bizarre, Kosinski—according to Eric Korn—showed himself to be a superb and enigmatic anecdotalist, a medieval homilist updated for our times, and—according to Ivan Sanders—a writer of the first order.[52] Most important, however, the novel proved to be popular with readers and rose to the 10th spot on the *New York Times* best-seller list, thus confirming Kosinski's belief that he was, to a certain measure, "reviewer-proof."[53]

In contrast to the superspy Tarden of *Cockpit,* George Levanter, the hero of Kosinski's sixth novel, *Blind Date* (1977), is no professional agent but rather a small investor and an idea man who, according to Kosinski, learns that "life is composed of moments, each commencing with one's awareness of its being."[54] A relatively mellow hero, Levanter is the first Kosinski protagonist capable of subordinating his own pleasures to those of another—though, wrote William Plummer, such geniality costs him much of his power.[55]

Loosely structured, thinly plotted, and overly fascinated with celebrity and other aspects of American popular culture, *Blind Date* is a flawed novel, yet it became Kosinski's best-selling hardback and received a number of surprisingly favorable reviews. Anne Knight called it Kosinski's most engaging book to date. At once revolting and stylistically bold, its violence more metaphorical than gratuitous, the novel—wrote Barbara J. Tepa—marked a brilliant return to the style of Kosinski's earlier works. Jerome Klinkowitz commended *Blind Date* for its lessons about survival and described Kosinski as a consummate storyteller deftly stringing together the novel's various events. Judson Hand found those "blind dates" richly wicked and obscene but also horribly honest; John Riley suggested that they allowed readers a chance to experience a whole host of hidden and guiltless pleasures. For Daniel J. Cahill, the episodes, framed in chilling and controlled prose, had an undeniably "powerful effect." For Arnost Lustig, the novel enlarged the borders of the bearable and worked "perfectly and beautifully," like a steam engine whose energy grows to the point at which it explodes or moves forward.[56]

But other reviewers, many of whom admired Kosinski's talent, excoriated what they felt was its misuse. Raymond Sokolov, for instance, saw *Blind Date* as an elegantly concocted cheap thrill that consists largely of encounters with prostitutes, the romancing of cripples, and rape, murder, and extortion, all actions the reader is supposed to accept from a morally neutral position. Having revisited the familiar "shit and gore" of his earlier novels, Kosinski—wrote Geoffrey Wolff—must reach further and further for new curiosities, moral conundrums, and simple abominations.[57] Such narrowness, concluded Lee T. Lemon, was unworthy of a major talent; it turned him into a self-conscious fantasist and a vicious bore who views man as having no moral character, chooses cheap thrills over ideology, and creates scarcely developed characters and scenes. By pandering to grisly popular tastes, noted Michael Mason, Kosinski undoes any possible greatness; he reduces his work to something that is too simple and unconvincing. Anatole Broyard blamed Kosinski's mistrust or dislike of the ordinary for causing him to run "the risk of pretentiousness, the social disease of much current fiction." Kosinski, concluded Broyard, "seems to have lost faith not only in morality but in art as well."[58]

One of the new charges against Kosinski concerned the poor treatment of his female characters. Xana Kaysen called Kosinski a misanthrope who, like most misanthropes, majors in misogyny; the women in the novel are victimized largely in the cause of macho self-realization. And John Leonard recognized that in this book full of victimization and randomness, there are nevertheless some constants: every social relationship involves a corruption of power, and every sexual act combines manipulation, brutishness, and contempt. Once Kosinski learns in his fiction to respect women, wrote Leonard, he will be a fine novelist.[59]

Passion Play, published in 1979, depicted an aging horseman pursuing his dual pleasures: polo and young women. Although it too reached the lower rungs of the best-seller list, the novel did not receive particularly kind reviews. In one of the most favorable, William Kennedy described the protagonist, Fabian, as a poignant middle-aged character who continues the struggles of the boy from *The Painted Bird*.[60] Most critics, however, concurred that in Kosinski's rather pale play of passion, Fabian was a contemporary knight more aberrant than errant.[61] Paul Abelman called him a combination American cowboy-hustler and European hero whose adventures are occasionally powerful but more often silly and irritating.[62] Joshua Gilder described Fabian as full of inward-turning aggression and modulated neurotic self-absorption with sickness and his body; his sexual exploits are the stuff of *Penthouse* or adolescent romance. Peter S. Prescott read *Passion Play* much the same way: as an adolescent erotic fantasy, part myth, part psychological thriller, problematic in its unresolved tone and credibility. Hans Konig believed that because the best hope in Kosinski's loveless, joyless world was to be left alone, Fabian pursues his one-on-one polo instead of seeking a higher Grail. Jerome Klinkowitz commented on the tone of fatigue in the novel as well as its sexism.[63]

Although parts of the novel were admittedly familiar scenes of sex and violence, Barbara Tepa Lupack contended that other parts were stirring, even romantic. Ivan Gold concurred; and though he criticized the novel's "leaden, arbitrary tone," he praised the "virtuoso writing about sex and horsemanship." John S. Reist Jr. noted that Kosinski missed his mark with a failed title metaphor and with inadequate development of women and secondary characters, yet Reist also singled out admirable erotic and evocative polo passages. But Barry Yourgrau suggested that even those sections of the novel are so stiff-necked and conspicuously "fine" that they impede the narrative and reduce it to a series of sloppy, baroque set pieces. Stefan Kanfer likened the novel's prose to that of Harold Robbins and wondered if Kosinski would ever use his keen ear for language and eye for social nuance for some purpose other than exploring the same theme of aimlessness. Novelist D. Keith Mano offered an even more damning assessment: written with painstaking negligence, *Passion Play* is proof of Kosinski's God-given flair for mediocrity. "This is the National Book Awarded Jerzy Kosinski?" he wondered. "I haven't felt so crestfallen since I found out that Salisbury steak was no more than a social climbing quarter-pounder."[64]

Kosinski's eighth novel, *Pinball,* published in 1982, followed Patrick Domostroy, an older classical musician who stopped composing because his talents were no longer valued, as he crossed paths with Goddard, an extraordinarily popular young electronic rock genius—and, in many ways, the mirror image of Domostroy. Although the novel revealed Kosinski's uncommon familiarity with music and the music business, it sounded an almost universally false note among critics. Given Kosinski's obvious musical knowledge and interest, Joseph McLellan was surprised by the lack of intensity in the novel and its objectification of characters; the only persuasive relationship in the book, he observed, was the overly familiar one between victim and victimizer. Lester Bangs thought *Pinball* was an unreadable novel with a ludicrous plot, cartoon characters, and leaden dialogue. Adam Mars-Jones condemned it as flashy and mechanical; Pat Rogers called it totally unsubtle and pointless. Joshua Gilder tried to believe that Kosinski, whom he recognized as an important author, had produced something of importance in *Pinball* but soon realized it was merely a pornographic thriller. Similarly, Christopher Bigsby tried to analyze *Pinball* as a coercively plotted book that celebrates the imagination, but he could point only to the isolation of the characters, the obsessiveness of the themes, and the writing, described as being as cold as a vivisectionist at a lecture. For Benjamin DeMott, *Pinball* was self-indulgently lax, "depressingly flat, [and] ridden with pulpish Grand Guignol," dense clichés, and screaming sex partners—in short, a sadly unrewarding book.

Sally Emerson found *Pinball* entertaining, but only in the most undemanding way: the machinery of the plot, she discovered, was rusty, and the characters forced to creak along familiar paths. Even Doug Fetherling, who saw in *Pinball* the potential for commentary on urban anthropology, felt that Kosinski undermined his own social message with a disintegrating plot so full of silly coincidences that it amounted to an ersatz mystery. Stefan Kanfer seemed to speak for the majority when he concluded that readers must be saying to themselves: " 'What a premise!' 'What a talent!' 'What a waste!' "[65] Although early sales of the book were promising and producer Lee Guber briefly considered staging *Pinball* as a Broadway musical, Kosinski was evidently no longer reviewer-proof. Only a few months after the publication of the novel, "Kosinski's Tainted Words" appeared in the *Village Voice*.

Six years elapsed before Kosinski published his ninth and final novel, *The Hermit of 69th Street* (1988). Wounded by the *Voice* scandal and smarting from the increasingly hostile critical reception of his fiction over the last decade, he was determined to make *The Hermit* an innovative "autofiction" in which his hero, a 55-year-old Polish American Jew named Kosky (Kosinski, as he told interviewers, "without the 'sin' "), attempts to defend himself against accusations of fraud by two local journalists from the *Courier*. But rather than rehabilitating his reputation, as Kosinski had hoped, the novel merely confirmed his obsessive self-involvement.

Although John Calvin Batchelor found fascination in *The Hermit's* original form and narrative, "whose existence we are literally seeing being formed before our eyes," and praised Kosinski's "highly personalized literary response to the charges leveled against him," reviews of the novel were generally devastating. Walter Goodman described the book as self-consciousness cluttered with flotsam, boldfaced quotations, and women as sexual objects, "sex-lit chat" that, despite its intellectual trappings, was unlikely to appeal to readers. While Brett Singer searched for the redeeming aspects of this "dizzying, mystical, word- and world-drunk" book about sin and redemption, "this apologia disguised as a novel," K. N. Richwine suggested that perhaps the attempted Joycean wordplay, sophomoric numbers games, and interlarded quotations might have been a stab at postmodernism. Larry McCaffery commented on the peculiar blending of intimate revelations and abstract musings on the nature of the self and the sources of artistic creativity, and although he saw *The Hermit* as Kosinski's most ambitious, experimental, and nakedly confessional novel, McCaffery too concluded that it is a self-obsessed novel born out of a sense of necessity and compulsion. *Kirkus* called the book an even deeper dead end than the enervating *Pinball* and complained that Kosinski buries the reader under a staggering blanket of boredom. John Blades saw the novel as a chaotic 500-page Hefty bag, full of quasi pornography, numerology, dirty talk, assorted mysticism, coy scraps of autobiography, and unfamiliar quotations.[66] Indeed, the occasionally clever and self-parodic novel was an inside joke that few reviewers or readers were in on and that wasn't really that funny to start with; it was, as McCaffery observed, a book written by Kosinski for himself.

Apart from reviews, some of the earliest and most interesting critical work on Kosinski was in doctoral dissertations—not surprising because Kosinski was, and continues to be, a popular—even cult—author among college students.[67] Sharon Rosenbaum Weinstein's "Comedy and Nightmare: The Fiction of John Hawkes, Kurt Vonnegut, Jr., Jerzy Kosinski, and Ralph Ellison" looked briefly at Kosinski's "nightmare vision," those dark inner forces with which "the self must struggle alone"; Robert Edward Golden's "Violence and Art in Postwar American Literature: A Study of O'Connor, Kosinski, Hawkes, and Pynchon" examined the depersonalized violence of modern warfare in various contemporary works, including *The Painted Bird*. David Joseph Lipani's impeccably researched "Jerzy Kosinski: A Study of His Novels" was an excellent introduction to Kosinski's life, themes, characters, and language, and Sister Ellen Fitzgerald's "World War II in the American Novel: Hawkes, Heller, Kosinski, and Vonnegut," which focused exclusively on "the experience of the second World War [as rendered] in especially nonconventional ways," offered strong and insightful readings of *The Painted Bird* and *Steps*. James D. Hutchinson, in "The Art of the Self: The Quest for Authenticity in the Novels of Jerzy Kosinski," suggested that the unifying element of Kosinski's first four novels is the motif of the psychic quest that "defines each protagonist as a kind of existential man struggling with an existentially-disoriented universe," an effective approach to which Hutchinson returned in a number of later book reviews and essays. Barbara Jane Tepa's "Inside the Kaleidoscope: Kosinski's Polish and American Contexts" raised important issues about Kosinski's Polish influences, including the works of Biegeleisen on peasant behavior and the novels of Reymont and Dolega-Mostowicz. Tepa's research, wrote James Park Sloan, was "indisputably the most thorough and well informed among the critical studies of [Kosinski's] work." It represented one of the greatest challenges to the insulation of Kosinski's past, placed him in "unprecedented peril," and almost added up to a disaster "seven years before the *Village Voice* undertook to disclose and expose" (*Jerzy Kosinski,* 331–32). Mitchell Bernard Bloomfield, in "The Fiction of Jerzy Kosinski: The Perverse in the Modern Imagination," discussed the influence of existentialism, especially of Heidegger and Sartre, in Kosinski's fiction and explored the quest theme, though from a different vantage point than Hutchinson had; Bloomfield concluded that "for Kosinski, the choice of the perverse is a last resort, the final defense of the self" in the face of a lost faith and an indifferent universe.

Kosinski is mentioned or discussed briefly in other doctoral works, including Geoffrey Dennis Green's "Writers in Exile: Chapters in the Critical Examination of Literature and Society," Anthony Raymond DeCurtis's "Contemporary American Fiction and the Process of Fictionalization," Nicki Sahlin's "Manners in the Contemporary American Novel: Studies in John Cheever, John Updike, and Joan Didion," Zita M. McShane's "Functions of the Grotesque in Twentieth-Century American Fiction," Thomas Hale Fick's "An American Dialectic: Power and Innocence from Cooper to Kosinski," Ronald Granofsky's "The Contemporary Symbolic Novel," Melvin Hunt Raff's "This above All: The Challenge of Identity in Modern Literature," John Douglas Kalb's "Articulated Selves: The Attainment of Identity and Personal Voice through Language and Storytelling in Works by Twentieth-Century Authors," Martin Kich's "Everyone Goes Around Acting Crazy: A Study of Recent American Hard-Core Naturalists," and Laura Eileen Ferguson's "American Subdominant: The Collapse of Identity into Image in the Post-War American Novels and Films of European Émigré Writers and Directors." Kosinski's work is treated more prominently in Nicholas John Vitterite Jr.'s "Descants and Pricksongs as a Modality of Postmodernism: A Study of the Works of Robert Coover and Jerzy Kosinski," though largely from the perspective of the Jungian typology of self; in Janice M. Viscomi's "Jerzy Kosinski: Contemporary Novelist as Knight," an examination of "the enigmatic nature of the Kosinski hero" and Kosinski's reliance on the genres of horror and satire, which—respectively—"emphasize the ever-threatening world in which man exists alone" and "detail the futility of institutions and philosophies in such a situation"; and, perhaps most ignominiously, in Barbara Sue Ellis's "Clinical Characteristics of the Narcissistic Personality: The Literature of Jerzy Kosinski," a study of a group of pre-Oedipal disorders in which there is a specific pathological ego structure. And Kosinski is also a subject of several studies of the literature of the Holocaust, including Sara Reva Horowitz's "Linguistic Displacement in Fictional Responses to the Holocaust: Kosinski, Wiesel, Ling, and Tournier," Sheng-Mei Ma's "The Holocaust in Anglo-American Literature: Particularism and Universalism in Relation to Documentary and Fictional Genres," Lea Fridman Hamaoui's "Words and Witness: Narrative and Aesthetic Strategies in the Representation of the Holocaust," and, most recently, Janet Schenk McCord's "A Study of the Suicides of Eight Holocaust Survivor/Writers."

II
Critical Overview

If many of the early critical works on Kosinski, like the biographical entries and accounts, have a familiar ring to them, it is because Kosinski had a hand in shaping them. In addition to the stories that he invented or embellished and then polished by repeated retellings to receptive audiences, he would often serve as his own press agent, even to the point of feeding flattering or supportive material to reviewers and scholars or sending them photocopies of other scholars' work about him, with marginal "corrections" in his own hand. Jeanie Blake, interviewing Kosinski soon after the publication of *Passion Play,* was struck by the fact that "almost absentmindedly" he would open his suitcases to reveal copies of newspaper stories written about him as well as stacks of photographs taken by him, on horseback, a camera strapped to his side, at polo games. Unaware that this was a common ploy, she found "rather charming and a bit disalarming" the fact that Kosinski "hands these articles out to interviewers to be helpful."[68] Such self-promotion, however, went well beyond the need to hustle his work; it was, as Jack Hicks and others have observed, a carefully erected public self that made good use of disguise and performance and was remarkably effective in shaping listener reaction and reader response.

The difficulty in separating the literary merits of Kosinski's novels from Kosinski's chronic tale spinning and celebrity seeking must have proven off-putting to some critics and scholars because, for a writer of Kosinski's popularity and stature, there have been surprisingly few substantive books or longer analyses of his work. The first, and still one of the finest, studies of Kosinski's fiction is Jerome Klinkowitz's *Literary Disruptions* (1975; rev. 1980), a staple of criticism of contemporary literature that focuses on several innovative and therefore "disruptive" fictionists.[69] In a long chapter devoted to Kosinski, Klinkowitz provides an outstanding introduction for both academic and general readers. Klinkowitz outlines Kosinski's biographical background; traces the genesis of Kosinski's themes, particularly his most familiar theme of the survival of the self, to his two Polish master's theses and to the pseudonymous Joseph Novak nonfiction; and offers an excellent, insightful reading of Kosinski's first four novels. (The revised edition includes a "Postlude" that comments on the novels through *Blind Date,* especially on the shift in the novels since *The Painted Bird.*) *Literary Disruptions* is also the first major study to allude to the important questions of the authenticity of the novels themselves and to the relevance of autobiography to fiction, questions Klinkowitz pursued in subsequent essays such as "Betrayed by Jerzy Kosinski," which appeared in his *Literary Subversions,* and in numerous fine reviews.

In 1981 Byron L. Sherwin, a professor of theology at Chicago's Spertus College of Judaica, published *Jerzy Kosinski: Literary Alarmclock,* a slight but highly flattering book that focused on the connection of Kosinski and his work to the Holocaust and to Marxist collectivity.[70] An uncritical admirer, Sherwin accepted without question all of Kosinski's familiar stories, including those about his boyhood in Poland, his arrival in the United States, his quick mastery of English, and his subsequent good fortune. And in so doing, Sherwin imparted a certain scholarly legitimacy to them. The favor was clearly not lost on Kosinski, who later turned to Sherwin as a mentor when, as a way of coming to terms with his own Jewish identity, Kosinski undertook a study of the works of Abraham Joshua Heschel, for whom Sherwin had once served as secretary. Grateful not only for Sherwin's early interest but also for his continued support, especially after the *Voice* scandal, Kosinski eventually appointed Sherwin as coexecutor of his estate, with Spertus College designated as the ultimate site of his papers. *Jerzy Kosinski: Literary Alarmclock* is thus more important as a footnote in Kosinski's personal history than as a serious critical study of his work.

Two other books published in the same year were more substantive and more objective than Sherwin's 52-page appreciation. In "The Romance of Terror and Jerzy Kosinski," a long essay in *In the Singer's Temple* (1981), Jack Hicks proposed that the guiding principle for Kosinski's paradoxical life and work was a particular image introduced in *No Third Path:* "the man on the fence," who suggests "an aloneness, a detachment, a separation of the solitary self from any form of social life" and whose pose between two equally tempting but impossible alternatives implies the "constant dialectic" that underlies Kosinski's fictional world.[71] Hicks examines in detail the psychic, philosophical, political, and artistic aspects of Kosinski's work, fused as they are in one "complex multistranded vision," and pays close attention to the metamorphic nature of the Kosinski protagonist, who sheds various selves as he evolves from victim to victimizer, and to the correspondingly elaborate fashioning of what Hicks calls Kosinski's public self. Particularly interesting are Hicks's analysis of the steps, the cockpit, the levanter, and other symbols in the novels and his reading of *The Painted Bird* not only as Jungian text but also as myth and fairy tale.

Paul Bruss takes a different approach. In *Victims: Textual Strategies in Recent American Fiction* (1981), Bruss observes that despite what seems to be its conventional point of view, Kosinski's fiction, with its deliberate disorientations leaving the reader "with little to build an interpretation upon," is actually radical.[72] The Kosinski text, its language stripped bare, almost falters—to be dismissed by the cursory reader as a shocking, even outrageous, portrayal of the human condition and of the fundamental arbitrariness of human experience, of which all Kosinski's protagonists are conscious. But stripped bare, "a Kosinskian text does recover the dilemma of language that lies at zero—where all structures begin." In his sophisticated and intelligent treatment of Kosinski's textual strategies, Bruss discusses the problem of language in the early fiction, the narrator's acts of demystification and neutralization in *Steps,* Tarden's games and the expansion of perception in *Cockpit,* and the resurgence of relationships in *Blind Date.*

Published in 1982, Norman Lavers's *Jerzy Kosinski,* the first full-length study devoted exclusively to Kosinski, offers a detailed summary of each of the novels, an analysis of some of the major themes and characters, and an extended biographical profile, including a handy chronology of important events.[73] Lavers's aim was to explore "the intricate relationship between life and art, between memory and creation," that is so pervasive in Kosinski's writing, and to that end, Lavers sought Kosinski's help in his ambitious project. But, contends James Park Sloan, although Kosinski did indeed assist by providing new details about his life—many of which were eventually proved to be more fiction than fact—he went so far as to line edit the actual text to make the biography and chronology consistent with his painstakingly crafted public persona. *Jerzy Kosinski* thus became an irrefutable record of Kosinski's reinvention of himself, one that would soon come back to haunt him. At the same time, however, the book was and continues to be—as Lavers had intended—an excellent resource, whose plot summaries and commentaries on characters and symbols are particularly beneficial for readers unacquainted with Kosinski's work.

After the eruption of the *Village Voice* scandal in the summer of 1982, much of the press about Kosinski was concerned with rehashing or refuting the charges against him by Geoffrey Stokes and Eliot Fremont-Smith, authors of "Jerzy Kosinski's Tainted Words." Michele Slung's "The Wounding of Jerzy Kosinski," Jan Herman's "Did He or Didn't He: *Village Voice* Sees Ghosts and CIA Spooks—But Kosinski Says They're Imagining Things," and Dave Smith's "Kosinski Whodunit: Who Ghost There If Not Jerzy?" offered excellent overviews of the scandal.[74] John Corry's "A Case History: 17 Years of Ideological Attack on a Cultural Target," subsequently recollected in Corry's book *My Times,* was an even lengthier rebuttal that discredited Stokes and Fremont-Smith and provided Kosinski's responses to the accusations.[75] William Safire, a columnist for the *New York Times,* claimed in an essay entitled "Suppressing Fire" that the charges stemmed from the liberal establishment but could be traced to Polish propagandists. He called the attack an attempt to destroy "the reputation of a writer who refuses to conform to the prevailing leftist maundering of much of the literary set" by the propagandist who "merely scatters his seeds and waits. Then dupes rush in where agitprop knows better than to tread." Concluding that Kosinski was a "complex and kooky genius," Safire embraced him for "the fierce iconoclasm of his vision."[76]

Others, like Stuart Applebaum from Bantam, Kosinski's "prime contract" publisher for many years, suggested that the attack had another purpose: the *Voice* had a vendetta against the *New York Times,* which a few months earlier had run, as a Sunday *Magazine* cover story, an uncritically adoring—and often inaccurate—profile of Kosinski by Barbara Gelb, wife of deputy managing editor Arthur Gelb. In turn, Charles Kaiser noted in a *Newsweek* article that the two recent *New York Times* "overkill" essays defending Kosinski against plagiarism smacked of "Friends at the Top of the Times," specifically Arthur Gelb and A. M. Rosenthal. "Kosinski's Friends See Red," reported David Schneiderman in a brief *Voice* piece that, although insisting Stokes and Fremont-Smith's charges were essentially true, quoted responses to the article by Kosinski's supporters. In letters to the *Voice,* Austin Olney, editor in chief of Houghton Mifflin, publisher of *The Painted Bird, Blind Date,* and *Cockpit,* admitted that Kosinski could be "difficult and demanding" as well as flamboyant and manipulative, but Olney asserted that references to Kosinski's autobiographical contradictions were merely "a red herring." And Thomas B. Morgan, past editor in chief of the *Voice,* agreed that nothing in the "tissue-thin, self-righteous confusion of the Stokes–Fremont-Smith article comes close to justifying a front page article (or any page article) in any publication, let alone *The Village Voice.*" No argument in the "Tainted Words" article, he added, "has sufficient credibility to prove that Kosinski's reputation is 'in jeopardy.' "[77] But Kosinski, who likened himself to other victims of assassination, knew that damage had been done, and as evidence he pointed to the fact that no one seemed interested anymore in his novels, but only in the charges against him.

The next major studies of Kosinski, in fact, did not appear until 1988. Paul R. Lilly Jr.'s *Words in Search of Victims: The Achievement of Jerzy Kosinski* was a powerful treatment of Kosinski's vision and his use of language, especially as a weapon with which he escapes his own prison at the same time that he imprisons others.[78] Lilly argues convincingly that Kosinski's rejection of his mother tongue and his engagement with a new language do not expose his vulnerability but rather give him an unexpected strength that allows him to victimize his readers. Kosinski's fiction, whose power derives from the narrow rhetorical stance he imposes upon his material, is therefore ultimately about the art of writing fiction. Although generally sympathetic to Kosinski and his work, Lilly does not ignore the controversy: in fact, in a lengthy appendix, he provides an excellent summary of it and offers thoughtful reflections on its effect on Kosinski's literary reputation. "Five years after the *Village Voice* article," he writes, "critical interest in Kosinski has shifted from the nature of the assistance he has asked for in the past to the value of what he has written"—true, perhaps, of more perceptive critics such as Lilly, but not universally so. Published the same year as Lilly's book, Barbara Tepa Lupack's *Plays of Passion, Games of Chance: Jerzy Kosinski and His Fiction,* part of the Rhodes-Fulbright International Library series, provided original and detailed readings of both the nonfiction and the novels through *The Hermit,* synthesized criticism on Kosinski's work, and drew parallels between Kosinski's writing and that of contemporary European, especially Polish, authors.[79]

Welch D. Everman's *Jerzy Kosinski: The Literature of Violation,* a general introduction to Kosinski's work, followed in 1991.[80] The original draft of the book, as Everman notes in his final chapter, was completed in early 1982, almost a decade before the book's publication, which may help to explain why *Pinball* (1982) is covered in an epilogue and why *The Hermit* (1988) is completely ignored. These, however, are serious omissions in a topical study, even a rudimentary one, as is the absence in Everman's secondary bibliography of any Kosinski criticism published after 1980. Reworking the familiar view of Kosinski's protagonists as both victims and victimizers, Everman proposes that Kosinski's novels "constitute a literature of violation" in which "his characters are violators and violated in turn," and he imposes, a little too insistently, the Heidegerrian "I/they" distinction on all of Kosinski's work. Still, the book is a good basic resource, though somewhat dated even on its publication.

Much of the most interesting information about Kosinski and his fiction came out over the years in interviews, and the best are collected by Tom Teicholz in *Conversations with Jerzy Kosinski,* which also appeared in 1993.[81] The volume opens with "Stepmother Tongue" (1965), in which Dick Schapp presciently observes that "there is a fleeting temptation to suggest that there is no Jerzy Kosinski, that he is a figment of his own vivid imagination" (3). The collection ends with "Jerzy Kosinski, the Last Interview," conducted three days before his death, in which Kosinski reveals to Pearl Sheffy Gefen that he is "bored" with himself and with the writing of novels, even though fiction allows him to "invent and reinvent" himself (229, 230). In between are most of the major interviews spanning Kosinski's literary career, including the early but seminal *Paris Review* "Art of Fiction" interview with Rocco Landesman and George Plimpton. In this interview, Kosinski began spinning his own myth with the stories of his escape from Poland and his arrival in the United States and discussed everything from the Polish reception of *The Painted Bird* to the code words he used for his books in progress. Jerome Klinkowitz's important "Jerzy Kosinski: An Interview" explored at length the function of memory as an artistic device as well as Kosinski's use of literary form and language. In Gail Sheehy's widely read "The Psychological Novelist as Portable Man," Kosinski asserted the purpose of his fiction ("to engage the reader in a drama" [126]) and defined his protagonists as "self-appointed reformers of an unjust world" (123).

Conversations is valuable not only for the individual interviews that Teicholz collected, most of which are fascinating in themselves, but also for the evidence they provide of Kosinski's obsession with his public persona. Kosinski tried to control many of his interviews by following a certain formula—a brief biography, with mention of his abandonment during World War II, his muteness, his struggle with authority as a student in Stalinist Poland, and his dramatic escape from Eastern Europe; comments on the necessity of his writing only in English; the notion of himself as an inner émigré; the philosophy of his fiction, often tailored to the particular novel he was promoting at the time; the attacks on television and popular culture—and by extensive "editing" afterward. Indeed, the interviews in *Conversations*—presented chronologically and without abridgment—often repeat the same questions. Yet despite Kosinski's adeptness with the press and with his own public relations, his answers are often filled with discrepancies and contradictions. In several of the interviews, for example, Kosinski comments that he has no children because they would be "yet another fragmentation, another split in the self," and in order to maintain the freedom of his self, "I must depend on no one and no one must depend on me" (20). In another interview, he confesses: "I wanted to [have children] at one time or another, but by then it was too late." A woman once wanted to carry his child, he adds, and "said she would take care of it; but luckily it did not happen, because it would have been an egoistic error on my part" (235). In another interview, conducted more than a decade earlier, he admitted that although he never wanted them, "I *had* two children," the first by a maid in a hostel when he worked as a ski instructor, the second by a law student in Poland. "There was also, I think, one in the United States," a child "promptly—legally—adopted. . . . I know the name of the family" (189).

As *Conversations* demonstrates, Kosinski often manipulated his statements to reflect his shifting positions. Regarding movies and adaptation, for instance, he explains to George Plimpton and Rocco Landesman that film is a lesser medium than fiction; film merely shows a man's emotion, whereas literature, closer to the Aristotelian idea, "*purges* him from his emotion" (35). To Jerome Klinkowitz, Kosinski suggests that he is not a novelist of low culture like Harold Robbins or Jacqueline Susann; unlike their works, Kosinski's do not follow the "easily perceivable pattern" of film (56). To Art Silverman, Kosinski states that he "refuse[s] to sell to the movies" because his novels "are not meant to be films"; filmmaking, he asserts, is a collective situation that corrupts the writer (116). To David Sohn, he remarks that film relieves people of the need to interact and renders them mute, and to Gail Sheehy that film, unlike literature, distracts rather than confronts us. To Tom Zito, Kosinski—after agreeing to the filming of *Being There*—begins to reverse himself: his novel, he says, is ideal for adaptation because it is "completely visual" (160). To Nancy Collins, however, he insists that he never really wanted to film his novel and offers a rather maudlin explanation for why he gave in: watching an ailing Peter Sellers telling an interviewer that the one role he wanted to play before he died was Chance, "I, moved to tears thinking of Peter dying [without realizing his dream], naturally said yes." Conceding that movies aren't so bad after all, he tells Collins that "there will be another film and a book—both called *Autofocus* and both about the same character: a fashion photographer in New York City. Dustin Hoffman will star, Dick Richards will direct, Kosinski will write" (191, 192). To Tom Teicholz, he admits that he is proud of the film *Being There,* which is "very true" to the book (183). To Barbara Leaming, he confesses that he is at work on a screenplay of *Passion Play* and speaks of the enjoyment he felt in bringing to life the character of

Zinoviev on the screen in Warren Beatty's *Reds*. Putting the most positive spin possible on his acting debut, Kosinski notes that as Zinoviev he used dialogue that he wrote himself and was able to "speak for the philosophy that once oppressed me in the first half of my life" (210).

Although a couple of the interviews in Teicholz's book are puff pieces—Cleveland Amory's "Trade Winds," for instance, during which Kosinski demonstrates his ability to hide in his own apartment and challenges Amory to find him—most are important and complex. For readers interested in who Kosinski was—and in who he purported to be—the interviews in *Conversations with Jerzy Kosinski* are essential reading.

The most recent addition to Kosinski scholarship—and, to be sure, one of the most significant—is James Park Sloan's *Jerzy Kosinski: A Biography* (1996). Sloan, a novelist as well as a literary critic, chronicles a story as fascinating, as revelatory, and occasionally as gossipy as Kosinski's novels themselves, a story of Kosinski's half-truths, masks, and other deceptions. Sloan's exhaustive research, especially into Kosinski's childhood and adolescence in Poland, turns up much new information: Sloan locates, for instance, the many houses in which the Lewinkopf/Kosinski family lived together during the war and identifies some of the actual people whom Kosinski later transformed into Lekh, Marta, Ewka, and other memorable characters in *The Painted Bird*. Because Sloan concerns himself with the man, there is, unfortunately, little analysis of the fiction, but the implications of his study are far-reaching nonetheless, especially as a correction to Kosinski's version of his wartime experiences and his life in Stalinist Poland. Also covered in great detail is Kosinski's new life in the United States, including his compulsive sexual adventuring in New York's erotic underground and his unusual relationship with his second wife, Kiki, who provided much of the material about her late husband as well as access to their circle of friends. Certainly the most comprehensive biographical treatment of Kosinski to date, Sloan's *Jerzy Kosinski* promises to remain the definitive biography, particularly of Kosinski's early years.

Although longer, book-length critical studies of Kosinski and his fiction have been relatively few, essays and articles have been more numerous. Daniel J. Cahill's "Jerzy Kosinski: Retreat from Violence" is among the earliest and best. Cahill writes that Kosinski tracks the impact of the brutality of World War II and "of the power of incessant violence to sear the mind" and to distort humanity's power and capacity to restore any moral balance. Kosinski's protagonists—specifically the brutalized boy of *The Painted Bird* and the narrator in *Steps,* whose life is "drained of any meaningful content"—are trapped in a world of dissolving meaning, in which there are few fragments to shore up against their ruin. Yet by retreating, those heroes survive, even triumph over, the landscape of violence that is a constant in Kosinski's fiction as well as in his life. One of the most consistently insightful critics of Kosinski's work, Cahill explored further the nature of Kosinski's protagonists; the themes, methods, and interrelationships of his novels; and the reception of his work in a number of other essays, including "Kosinski and His Critics," as well as in interviews, three of which—on *The Devil Tree, Blind Date,* and *Passion Play*—are collected in Tom Teicholz's *Conversations with Jerzy Kosinski*.[82]

Whereas Cahill noted the significant links between actual events in Kosinski's life and his fiction, Ivan Sanders dismissed the attempts to read Kosinski's works as autobiography.[83] In "The Gifts of Strangeness: Alienation and Creation in Jerzy Kosinski's Fiction," Sanders suggested a different approach to the fiction: the perspective of the alienated outsider. The characters of Kosinski's first four novels, Sanders noted, are "uninvolved, unattached individuals who, either by choice or by necessity, view human interaction as an essentially one-sided affair, where the aim above all is to master a situation, to understand, to control, to *possess* experience—visually, verbally, if not always physically." Their alienation is conveyed not only by language that communicates a sense of estrangement but also by the unconventional form of the novels and by Kosinski's evocation of a time and place at once "cosily familiar and eerily strange." Like Sanders, Elizabeth Stone found Kosinski's fiction to be disquieting.[84] The novels, which she calls an assault on the nerves, pierce the social skin and "recreate the aura of nightmare paranoia, rouse fears of psychic petrification, depersonalization, engulfment"—not simply modern fears but the founding terrors of infancy released by myth and fable. For Stone, the appeal of Kosinski's work is that the protagonists do not succumb but survive by their relentlessness, invention, and industry as "Horatio Algers of the Nightmare." She details the types of psychological defenses they mount, from invisibility to giving voice to their experience, from disguise to careful cultivation of memory, in preserving a sense of their identity.

Preservation of the self recurs as a theme not only in the fiction but also in critical consideration of it. In "The Quest for the Elusive Self: The Fiction of Jerzy Kosinski," Samuel Coale observed that the theft of the self is the greatest evil to Kosinski's protagonists, who must struggle to build an identity out of "bits and pieces which testify only to its inevitable loss and destruction." And in "The Cinematic Self of Jerzy Kosinski," Coale suggested that the protagonists of the novels from *The Painted Bird* to *The Devil Tree* possess a self that is distinct from that of the well-rounded literary characters of earlier fiction, a "cinematic self," which allows them to become their own events despite the "disconnected series of fragments, images, and episodes" that threaten to overwhelm them.[85] In "Jerzy Kosinski: Words in Search of Victims," Paul R. Lilly Jr. uses the notion of self even more effectively than Coale; Lilly analyzes several of Kosinski's novels from the perspective of the transformation of the self from vulnerability to strength, from victim to oppressor, by means of language. In another excellent essay, "Vision and Violence in the Fiction of Jerzy Kosinski," Lilly develops that idea further by suggesting that Kosinski's protagonists, in order to avoid victimization, know they must seize power.[86] Their violence becomes neither an abstraction nor an isolated event without meaning but "the end result of a dynamic flow of power between victim and oppressor." Sometimes planned, sometimes random, sometimes disguised as political, racial, or sexual, violence is always an integral part of Kosinski's vision to "assault" the reader's imagination, to make the writer the aggressor, the reader the victim, and the word the weapon.

Thomas S. Gladsky examines yet another aspect of the quest for identity in "Jerzy Kosinski's East European Self." He argues convincingly that despite the Americanized settings and protagonists, Kosinski's novels are unmistakably informed by an Eastern European presence. Gladsky suggests that Kosinski's fiction falls into three not entirely distinct periods: rejection of the old Eastern European self, the impulse toward accommodation, and the reconciliation of the old- and new-world selves. "The old skin" sloughed off in *The Painted Bird* and *Steps* is replaced in *Being There* and *The Devil Tree* by new selves in the form of typically American protagonists who have no roots at all. In *Cockpit* and *Blind Date,* the survival of the self is directly related to the past, which recreates itself as it is destroyed. The impulse toward reconciliation, faint in those novels, becomes brighter in *Pinball* as Domostroy condemns the hidden self and tends to identify increasingly with Poles. In the Kosinski section of *Princes, Peasants, and Other Polish Selves,* Gladsky's extended study of ethnicity in American literature, he demonstrates that the renunciation of the nonethnic self is even more pronounced in *The Hermit* and suggests that "Kosinski, had he lived to write more, would have stretched ethnicity into yet different shapes."[87]

In "Charting the Abyss," a chapter in his book *The American Novel and the Way We Live Now,* John W. Aldridge focuses on Kosinski's protagonists, all of whom are scarred and lone survivors, modern terrorists, "black knights or agents of retribution—some quite literally secret, double, and/or CIA—wandering up and down a world of the nightmarish landscape of wartime Poland." Exclusively male, they operate alone, relying on subterfuge and technology, in the "immense panorama of futility and anarchy which is contemporary history."[88] Andrew Gordon, in "Fiction as Revenge: The Novels of Jerzy Kosinski," concurs that Kosinski's protagonists are struggling for survival, in "combat against the collective antagonism of the Total State and all its institutions and also against other people, whether enemies or lovers," and Gordon describes in psychological terms the pathology of their revenge.[89] Krystyna Prendowska, on the other hand, rejects the common view of Kosinski's characters as victims, just as she implies that Kosinski, in his later fiction, refused "the victimology inherent in *The Painted Bird*—victims are as evil as criminals." In "Jerzy Kosinski: A Literature of Contortions," Prendowska argues that whereas *The Painted Bird* presented the world of a child-victim mutely asking for compassion, the later novels—*Steps, Being There, The Devil Tree,* and *Cockpit*—"turn to the consistent narrative told by a perpetrator of evil: an addict of violence, a picaro, a sexual outlaw, or a psychopath." The primitive beauty of *The Painted Bird* is thus replaced by tape recorders, electronic doors, needles, and radar, the weapons of modern heaven-hell with which the later protagonists are armed.[90] Prendowska's readings of the novels as "contorted" are interesting, if cursory. Better and more compelling readings and analyses appear in Frederick R. Karl's *American Fictions 1940–1980,* which provides outstanding historical overviews and critical evaluations of contemporary literature.[91]

Individually, Kosinski's novels—especially the early ones—have attracted serious critical attention as well. Perhaps the single best overview of *The Painted Bird* was by Gerald Weales, who, in "Jerzy Kosinski: The Painted Bird and Other Disguises," discusses Kosinski's world, his style, and his thematic concerns. Stanley Corngold offered some perceptive comments on the language and style of the novel, which he described as fictional autobiography that touches the heart of Western poetic consciousness. R. J. Spendal, with an almost mathematical precision, attempted to organize the novel into groups of episodes linked by the principle of parallel with contrast. Michael Skow, Michael Carroll, and David Cassiday viewed *The Painted Bird* as a modern bestiary in which animals serve a thematic function, establish the novel's tenor of violence and terror, and "stipulate a world of viciousness and violence, brutality and baseness, savagery and selfishness"; in Kosinski's world, the authors conclude, human behavior is "at least as bestial as what we would expect from 'mere' animals." Whereas David J. Piwinski, in a short note, traces the source of one particular metaphor—the painted bird—to a biblical verse from Jeremiah, Lawrence L. Langer, in his larger study *The Holocaust and the Literary Imagination,* discusses the technique of metaphor as an instrument of dehumanization in *The Painted Bird,* whose theme he sees as humanity's complicity in evil, a complicity by which people are transformed into beasts. Meta Lale and John Williams, on the other hand, take a more clinical approach to the novel by chronicling the psychopathology of the boy throughout the novel as he develops "ego defense mechanisms of withdrawal, fantasy, and introjection" in order to survive. Thomas H. Landess likens the novel to the genre of the sexually violent pornographic movie and argues that in the narrative, Kosinski achieves a sense of pain-in-sexuality akin to the best of the sadomasochistic pornographer's art. David H. Richter describes the textual variations in the different editions of *The Painted Bird*—the first edition (1965), the paperback (1966), and the revised edition (1970)—and the three different readings based on the endings or denouements; Jerome Klinkowitz points out some bibliographic errors in Richter's essay (and Richter replies to Klinkowitz's "new light") in "Two Bibliographical Questions in Kosinski's *The Painted Bird*."[92]

Criticism of *Steps* focused largely on the novel's language and structure. Robert Boyers, in "Language and Reality in Kosinski's *Steps,*" argued that the structure is neither symbolic nor realistic and claimed that the book can be assessed only in terms of the weight it applies to the reader's sensibilities. For

John Kent von Daler, *Steps* is indeed a series of steps, or flights, connected largely by the masculinity of the narrator; it is up to the reader to impose a larger sense of form on the novel. Byron Petrakis felt the novel was largely cinematic; he argued that Kosinski's own skill as a photographer and his association with Roman Polanski explain the various cinematic techniques—panning, montage, master symbolism—that undergird the book's very visual effects and ally it with the New Wave cinema and the *nouveau roman* described by Robbe-Grillet. In "Literary Disruptions; or, What's Become of American Fiction?" Jerome Klinkowitz offered possibly the best explanation of the novel's strategy: it is an immersion in the heart of the trauma itself.[93] And in "Retrospect: Judging a Book Award," James D. Hutchinson comments on the richness of character and the subtle poetics of the novel as he makes the argument that it is most deserving of the National Book Award.[94]

Critics writing about *Being There* have concentrated largely on its mythic structure and its literary antecedents. In brief notes, both John M. Gogol and Andrew Gordon have drawn parallels between Chance and Narcissus. In other short notes, Raymond B. Murray comments on Chance's Krylovian qualities, and Herbert B. Rothschild Jr. links the political themes of *Being There* to those of *Coriolanus*. Barbara J. Tepa, in "Jerzy Kosinski's Polish Contexts: A Study of *Being There*," demonstrates contextual similarities between Kosinski's satire and Dolega-Mostowicz's popular novel *The Career of Nikodem Dyzma* and other Polish works with which Kosinski was no doubt acquainted. And in "Kosinski's Modern Proposal: The Problem of Satire in the Mid-Twentieth Century," Earl B. Brown proposes that Kosinski found an appropriate voice for satire in his story of Chance because "satire in the mid-twentieth century has emerged as horror."[95] Kosinski's familiar concerns with popular culture and the impact of television on contemporary life are discussed by Patrick Brantlinger in "What Hath TV Wrought: McLuhan's 'Global Village' or Kosinski's 'Village Videot'?" and Nancy Corson Carter in "1970 Images of the Machine and the Garden: Kosinski, Crews, and Pirsig."[96] Gary H. Arlen's "From the TV Viewer's Perspective," Aljean Harmetz's "Book by Kosinski, Film by Ashby," Robert F. Willson Jr.'s "Being There at the End," Mary A. Fischer's "Peter Sellers' Chance of a Lifetime," and Barbara Tepa Lupack's "Hit or Myth: Jerzy Kosinski's *Being There*" focus on the film version of *Being There* and offer interesting insights into the process of film adaptation, especially when the novelist is also the film's screenwriter.[97]

Kosinski's later novels have, on the whole, generated less critical interest than the early ones. James D. Hutchinson's "Authentic Existence and the Puritan Ethic" examines the central symbolic structure of *The Devil Tree* and concludes that Jonathan's entrapment in the baobab, or devil tree, is a symbol of the condition of modern man; Stuart Hirschberg's brief note on "Becoming an Object: The Function of Mirrors and Photographs in Kosinski's *The Devil Tree*" suggests that mirrors and photos are not just a series of static images but serve instead as links between seemingly unrelated episodes of the novel; and Jerome Klinkowitz, in "How Fiction Survives the Seventies," mentions *The Devil Tree* as an example of an innovative novel that synthesizes, organically, fragments of contemporary life.[98]

Ross Wetzsteon, in his essay "Jerzy Kosinski: Existential Cowboy," finds *Cockpit* "fascinating and disconcerting" and feels that it reads like an unacknowledged sequel to *Steps* and *The Devil Tree*. He proposes that readers have a more visceral reaction to it than to Kosinski's other novels because the narrator is less a victim and more a perpetrator of the crimes, a man who, in an "enthralling evocation of moral sadomasochism," can achieve a sense of personal identity only by imprinting his sensibility on others yet must deny others any control whatsoever over his own destiny. John G. Parks, on the other hand, in "Human Destiny and Contemporary Narrative Form," discusses *Cockpit* in terms of its main theme of the individual versus the collective, and John L. Grigsby, in a brief note, suggests *Cockpit* begs comparison as well as contrast with *Gulliver's Travels* and the novels of James Fenimore Cooper.[99]

Unlike Daniel J. Cahill, who demonstrates in "An Interview with Jerzy Kosinski on *Blind Date*" that Kosinski's sixth novel repeats motifs from the earlier works at the same time that it explores new ideas about the randomness of life, violence, and modern society and draws on new influences such as Jacques Monod, Paul Elmen's brief article "Jerzy Kosinski and the Uses of Evil" condemns Kosinski's use of violence and calls *Blind Date* an unpromising book.[100] Ami Shinitzky's "Life Is a Drama—Jerzy Kosinski: The Man and His Work" concentrates largely on the use of polo playing in *Passion Play*. Barry Nass argues in "Androgyny, Transsexuality, and Transgression in Jerzy Kosinski's *Passion Play*" that the transsexuality and androgyny of the novel are not shocking or sensational but incisive: the explorations of gender identity and sexual change conflict with patriarchal values and epitomize Kosinski's concern with the struggle for self-understanding and affirmation of selfhood in a hostile world.[101]

The only extended treatment of *Pinball* is Regina Gorskowska's "*Pinball:* Aspects of Visibility: An Interview with Jerzy Kosinski," in which Kosinski explains how *Pinball* stands outside the cycle of his other novels, discusses the hostile reviews the novel received, and talks about its central metaphor of invisibility.[102] And, apart from Stephen Schiff's excellent essay "The Kosinski Conundrum," which explores the impact of the *Voice* scandal on the themes and methods of Kosinski's final novel, critical consideration of *The Hermit of 69th Street* has been limited to brief notes, "A Note on an Episode in Jerzy Kosinski's *The Hermit of 69th Street*" by Stuart Hirschberg and "Jerzy Kosinski: The Polish Cooper" by Thomas S. Gladsky, who has written perceptively on Polish ethnicity in American literature.[103]

Worth noting as well are the bibliographies and checklists of Kosinski's work, the earliest of which—by Maryann D. Greenstone, Ira Bruce Nadel, and Frederic E. Rusch—are now grossly incomplete.[104] "The Great Jerzy Kosinski Press War: A Bibliography," by Jerome Klinkowitz and Daniel J.

Cahill, offers a useful list of selected regional press articles, mostly from 1982, dealing with the authorship controversy.[105] Thomas P. Walsh and Cameron Northouse's *John Barth, Jerzy Kosinski, and Thomas Pynchon: A Reference Guide* is an excellent resource, but unfortunately it is limited to criticism of Kosinski only from 1960 to 1973.[106] The best and most comprehensive bibliography is Gloria L. Cronin and Blaine H. Hall's *Jerzy Kosinski: An Annotated Bibliography,* which includes more than 450 entries and is divided into useful categories, such as interviews, general criticism, and reviews of and criticism on each of the novels and nonfiction books.[107]

Although much good critical work has already been published, many aspects of both Kosinski's life and his fiction remain to be explored. The three original essays in this volume begin to do just that. Jerome Klinkowitz, in "Jerzy Kosinski in Fact: A Master Fabricator's Nonfiction," provides a new assessment of the themes and purposes of Kosinski's nonfiction and demonstrates how even in his final work, *Passing By,* published posthumously, he was strategically attempting to reframe his public image. In "Is There Any History in It? The Fiction of Jerzy Kosinski," Thomas S. Gladsky offers an interesting and valuable approach to Kosinski's novels: not as traditional or new historical novels but as fiction "very much about history without being historical." And Norman Lavers explores important new links within the cycle of Kosinski's later fiction, particularly in the evolution of the protagonist from *Cockpit* to *Passion Play*.

In his last interview, conducted only three days before his death, Kosinski observed that "a critic is also a writer, and it would be creatively obscene and unwise not to pay attention to what they say." In the same interview, however, he mentioned that in one corner of his small New York City apartment, he keeps a bear trap—"a metaphor for the literary critic."[108] This dual vision of the critic as simultaneously positive and threatening suggests the many dualities that Kosinski grappled with throughout his life and throughout his writing. And it is precisely those dualities—victim and victimizer, public persona and private self, bird catcher and painted bird—that make Jerzy Kosinski so enigmatic, paradoxical, and fascinating as a man and as a novelist.

Notes

1. "On Kosinski," a five-page biographical essay, appears in the Bantam paperback edition of *Blind Date* (1978), immediately following p. 269. Revised versions of "On Kosinski" appear in the Bantam paperback editions of *Passion Play* (1980) and *Pinball* (1983).

2. Jerzy Kosinski, *The Painted Bird* (New York: Pocket Books, 1966), 44.

3. Pearl Sheffy Gefen, "Jerzy Kosinski: The Last Interview," originally published in *Lifestyles* magazine, Winter 1991, 18–24. Reprinted in Tom Teicholz, ed., *Conversations with Jerzy Kosinski* (Jackson: University Press of Mississippi, 1993), 227–37.

4. Barbara Leaming, "Penthouse Interview: Jerzy Kosinski," *Penthouse,* July 1982, 128–30, 167–71.

5. "Revealed: The Real Authors of Jerzy Kosinski's Novels," *New York,* 28 February 1983, 37–39.

6. George A. Plimpton and Rocco Landesman, "The Art of Fiction XLVI—Jerzy Kosinski," *The Paris Review* 14 (Summer 1972): 183–207. Reprinted in Teicholz, ed., *Conversations with Jerzy Kosinski,* 20–36.

7. Jack Hicks, *In the Singer's Temple: Prose Fictions of Barthelme, Gaines, Brautigan, Piercy, Kesey, and Kosinski* (Chapel Hill: University of North Carolina Press, 1981), 177–267; John Corry, "17 Years of Ideological Attack on a Cultural Target," *New York Times,* 7 November 1982, sec. 2, pp. 1, 28–29; Barbara Gelb, "Being Jerzy Kosinski," *New York Times Magazine,* 21 February 1982, 42, 45–46, 49, 52–54, 58.

8. Jerome Klinkowitz, "Betrayed by Jerzy Kosinski," in *Literary Subversions: New American Fiction and the Practice of Criticism* (Carbondale: Southern Illinois University Press, 1985), 127–48.

9. Geoffrey Stokes and Eliot Fremont-Smith, "Jerzy Kosinski's Tainted Words," *Village Voice,* 22 June 1982, 1, 41–43.

10. James Park Sloan, *Jerzy Kosinski: A Biography* (New York: Dutton, 1996).

11. Plimpton and Landesman, in Teicholz, ed., *Conversations with Jerzy Kosinski,* 24–25; Jerzy Kosinski, "Aleksander and André Wat," in *Passing By: Selected Essays, 1960–1991* (New York: Random House, 1992), 8.

12. Klinkowitz, *Literary Subversions,* 128.

13. William Kennedy, "Jerzy Kosinski: On Still Being There," in *Riding the Yellow Trolley Car: Selected Nonfiction* (New York: Viking, 1993), 136.

14. Jerzy Kosinski, "My Twenty-Minute Performance . . . ," in Teicholz, ed., *Conversations with Jerzy Kosinski,* 51.

15. Joseph G. Harrison, "Conversations with the Russians," review of *The Future Is Ours, Comrade,* by Jerzy Kosinski, *Christian Science Monitor,* 25 May 1960, 13; Richard C. Hottelot, "From Collective to Kremlin, It's One Big State of Nerves," review of *The Future Is Ours, Comrade, New York Times Book Review,* 22 May 1960, 3; William J. Jorden, "Collective Way of Being," review of *The Future Is Ours, Comrade, Best Sellers,* 15 June 1960, 113; Stephen Rosenfeld, "Behind the Iron Curtain," review of *The Future Is Ours, Comrade, Washington Post,* 22 May 1960, E6; Edward Crankshaw, "Reporting on Russia," review of *The Future Is Ours, Comrade, Observer,* 30 October 1960, 22; "Soviet Sketches," review of *The Future Is Ours, Comrade, Times Literary Supplement,* 3 February 1961, 75. See also the review of *The Future Is Ours, Comrade, Booklist,* 1 July 1960, 651; W. C. Jaskievicz, review of *The Future Is Ours, Comrade, Best Sellers,* 15 June 1960, 113; Jessie Kitching, review of *The Future Is Ours, Comrade, Publisher's Weekly,* 18 April 1960, 48; Joseph Ruef, review of *The Future Is Ours, Comrade, Library Journal,* 15 April 1960, 1585; Alexander Werth, "America's Friend or African Missionary?" *New Statesman,* 22 October 1960, 620; and E. Litvinoff, "Several Types of Soviet Reality," *Guardian,* 21 October 1960, 8.

16. Henry L. Roberts, "Communism: Two Ways of Looking at It," *New York Herald Tribune Books,* 4 March 1962, 11; Ernest S. Pisko, "A Condition of Super-Integration," review of *No Third Path,* by Jerzy Kosinski, *Christian Science Monitor,* 13 April 1962, 15; William O'Connor, review of *No Third Path, Best Sellers,* 1 March 1962, 479–80; William Henry Chamberlin, "Firsthand Impressions of How the Soviet Mind Works," *Chicago Sunday Tribune,* 25 February 1962, 4. See also Roberts's brief review in *Foreign Affairs,* July 1962, 672.

17. See also George Summent, review of *No Third Path,* by Jerzy Kosinski, *Library Journal,* 15 March 1962, 1146–47; review of *No Third Path, Booklist,* 15 April 1962, 551; and review of *No Third Path, New Yorker,* 17 March 1962, 188.

18. Comments attributed to Luis Buñuel and Anaïs Nin on the flyleaf and cover of the Bantam paperback edition of *The Painted Bird* (1972).

19. See, for example, the following: Trevor Allen, "On Expatriates," *Books and Bookmen,* April 1966, 40; John Arimond, "Engrossing Sociological Novel," *Extension,* March 1966,

47; Richard Kluger, "A Scapegoat in Need," *Harper's,* October 1965, 128–30; F. L. Ryan, review of *The Painted Bird,* by Jerzy Kosinski, *Best Sellers,* 1 November 1965, 299; Chayym Zeldis, "Job, the Child," *Jewish Frontier,* March 1967, 22–26; review of *The Painted Bird, Kirkus,* 1 August 1965, 785–86; review of *The Painted Bird, Choice,* January 1966, 772; Leonore Fleischer, review of *The Painted Bird, Publisher's Weekly,* 12 September 1966, 90; C. Peterson, "Missing the Boat," *Books Today,* 20 November 1966, 9; Irving Wardle, "New Novels," *National Observer,* 6 March 1966, 26; and David Williams, "Childhood's End," *Punch,* 23 March 1966, 432.

20. Joseph P. Bauke, "No Wakening from Nightmare," *Saturday Review,* 13 November 1965, 64; David Evanier, *Commonweal,* 1 July 1966, 422–23; Guy Davenport, "Messages from the Lost," *National Review,* 8 February 1966, 120–21; Oleg Ivsky, review of the *Painted Bird, Library Journal,* 1 October 1965, 4109; Andrew Field, "The Butcher's Helpers," *New York Herald Tribune Book Week,* 17 October 1965, 2–3, 26.

21. Robert Coles, "Book Reviews," *Harvard Educational Review* 37, no. 3 (1967): 493–96. Reprinted as "*The Song of the Painted Bird*" in Robert Coles, *That Red Wheelbarrow: Selected Literary Essays* (Iowa City: University of Iowa Press, 1988), 87–92. Jessie Kitching, review of *The Painted Bird, Publisher's Weekly,* 13 September 1965, 81, also refers to the novel as a "realistic picture of the horrifying life of thousands of abandoned children in Europe in the war years."

22. Anne Halley, "Poor Boy Spreads His Wings," *Nation,* 29 November 1965, 424–26. For a brief review and discussion of the fairy tale qualities of the novel, see also *Times Literary Supplement,* 19 May 1966, 461.

23. Peter Prescott, review of *The Painted Bird, Chicago News,* 6 November 1965; Neil Compton, "Dream of Violence," *Commentary,* June 1966, 92–95; Charles Poore, "Things Like These Happen to People We Know," *New York Times,* 16 October 1965, 25; Elie Wiesel, "Everybody's Victim," *New York Times Book Review,* 31 October 1965, 5.

24. Neal Ascherson, "Chronicles of the Holocaust," *New York Review of Books,* 1 June 1967, 25. The reviewer in *Booklist,* 1 January 1966, 434, also reads the novel as a "fable and indictment of man's inhumanity to man."

25. Henry Kamm, "Poles Are Bitter about Novel Published Abroad," *New York Times,* 12 December 1966, 2.

26. Granville Hicks, "Sadism and Light Hearts," *Saturday Review,* 19 October 1968, 29.

27. John J. McAleer, review of *Steps,* by Jerzy Kosinski, *Best Sellers,* 1 November 1968, 316. F. Yorick Blumenfeld, in "Dark Dreams," *Newsweek,* 21 October 1968, 104, 108, similarly suggests that *Steps* is more than just a novel. For Blumenfeld, it is a collection of erotic reminiscences, held together by a compelling lack of conscience.

28. Stanley Kauffmann, "Out of the Fires," *New Republic,* 26 October 1968, 22, 41.

29. Marvin Mudrick, "Must We Burn Mme. de Beauvoir?" *Hudson Review* 21, no. 4 (1968–1969): 759–60.

30. For particulars of the awards and of Kosinski's acceptance speech, see Margaret Cooley, "National Book Awards—The Winners," *Library Journal,* 1 April 1969, 1476–77; Henry Raymont, "National Book Awards: The Winners," *New York Times,* 11 March 1969, 2; and "Writer Fearful of Nuclear Peril," *New York Times,* 13 March 1969, 44.

31. Martin Tucker, "A Moralist's Journey into the Heart of Darkness," *Commonweal,* 29 November 1968, 319–20; Eliot Fremont-Smith, "Log of Atrocities," *New York Times,* 21 October 1968, 45; D. A. N. Jones, "Lean Creatures," *New York Review of Books,* 27 February 1969, 16; Hugh Kenner, "Keys on a Ring," *New York Times Book Review,* 20 October 1968, 5.

32. P. N. Furbank, "Fiction's Feelingless Man," *The Listener,* 8 May 1969, 655, and W. B. Hill, review of *Steps,* by Jerzy Kosinski, *Choice,* February 1969, 1582. See also Hill, review of *Steps, America,* 3 May 1969, 538; Marvin Felheim, "The Haunted Edges of Consciousness," *Michigan Daily,* 24 November 1968, 6; Bruce Cook, "The Real McCoy," *National Observer,* 28 October 1968, 21.

33. Marvin Mudrick, for example, concludes that reading Kosinski is like reading 3,000 pages of the Marquis de Sade.

34. Irving Howe, "From the Other Side of the Moon," *Harper's,* March 1968, 102–5; Geoffrey Wolff, "Growing Poisonous Flowers," *New Leader,* 7 October 1968, 18–19; "Bird of Prey," *Time,* 18 October 1968, 114; review of *Steps, Kirkus,* 15 August 1968, 927; "Album from Auschwitz," *Times Literary Supplement,* 8 May 1969, 481; Maurice Capitanchik, "Private Lives," *Spectator,* 9 May 1969, 621; Paul Bailey, " 'Stuff' and Nonsense," *London Magazine,* May 1969, 108, 110, 112; Michael O'Malley, *Critic,* April–May 1969, 76; Richard Jones, "Patterns," *Times* (London), 10 May 1969, 21. For another view of *Steps* as failed fiction, see Irwin Stark, "The Agonies of Survival," *Hadassah Magazine,* March 1969, 19.

35. Roger Baker, "Off-Beat Ideas," *Books and Bookmen,* July 1968, 41–42; Clive Jordan, "Big 70," *New Statesman,* 9 May 1969, 665–66; Katherine Gauss Jackson, "Books in Brief," *Harper's,* November 1968, 160; Paul West, "Portrait of a Man Mooning," *Chicago Tribune Book World,* 3 November 1968, 18; Barbara A. Bannon, review of *Steps, Publisher's Weekly,* 5 August 1968, 54.

36. Jerzy Kosinski, *Notes of the Author on "The Painted Bird"* (New York: Scientia-Factum, 1965), and *The Art of the Self: Essays à Propos Steps* (New York: Scientia-Factum, 1968). Both essays are reprinted in the final section of *Passing By: Selected Essays, 1960–1991,* 201–45.

37. See also James Finn, "A Rich Parable," *New Republic,* 26 June 1971, 32–33.

38. John W. Aldridge, "The Fabrication of a Culture Hero," *Saturday Review,* 24 April 1971, 25–27. Reprinted as "Jerzy Kosinski's American Dream," in John W. Aldridge, *The Devil in the Fire* (New York: Harper, 1972), 267–73.

39. William Kennedy, "Who Here Doesn't Know How Good Kosinski Is?" *Look,* 20 April 1971, 12. Reprinted as "Jerzy Kosinski: On Still Being There," in William Kennedy, *Riding the Yellow Trolley Car,* 133–36.

40. Jerome Klinkowitz, review of *Being There, The Falcon* 4 (Spring 1972): 122–25; Marilyn Gardner, "A Lifelong Nobody and a Would-Be Somebody," *Christian Science Monitor,* 27 May 1971, 11; R. Z. Sheppard, "Playing It by Eye," *Time,* 26 April 1971, 93.

41. Richard Combs, "Idiots First," *Sights and Sound* 49, no. 3 (1980): 195; Peter Glassgold, "Taking a Bad Chance," *Nation,* 31 May 1971, 699–700; Daniel Stern, "Candide in the Electronic Age," *Life,* 30 April 1971, 14; Steven Kroll, "Counter-Alger," *Washington Post Book World,* 30 May 1971, 2; Martin Tucker, "Leading the Life of Chance," *Commonweal,* 7 May 1971, 221–23; John J. McAleer, review of *Being There, Best Sellers,* 1 July 1971, 173.

42. Ian Weddle, *London Magazine,* October–November 1971, 150–51, finds the fable chic, a kind of allegory twice removed—an allegorical figure made into a human being rather than a human being made into an allegory. Stephen Wall, "Seeing Is Believing," *Observer,* 23 May 1971, 29, calls *Being There* a fable with agile structure.

43. V. S. Pritchett, "Clowns," *New York Review of Books,* 1 July 1971, 15; Irving Howe, "Books: A Gathering of Good Works," *Harper's,* July 1971, 88–92; Geoffrey Wolff, "The Life of Chance," *Newsweek,* 26 April 1971, 94–96.

44. John Updike, "Bombs Made Out of Leftovers," *New Yorker,* 25 September 1971, 132–34; Ronald De Feo, "Books," *Modern Occasions,* Fall 1971, 622–24; Anatole Broyard, "The High Price of Profundity," *New York Times,* 21 April 1971, 45; James Farrant, *Books and Bookmen,* June 1971, 35; Lee T. Lemon, *Prairie Schooner* 45, no. 4 (1972): 369; Paul Delany, "Chance Learns How from Television," *New York Times Book Review,* 25 April 1971, 7, 55; Michael Cooke, "Recent Fiction," *Yale Review* 61, no. 4 (1972): 603–4; Barton Midwood, "Fiction," *Esquire,* October 1971, 63, 66.

45. John J. McAleer, *Best Sellers,* 15 February 1973, 525–26; Stanley Kauffmann, "A Double View," *Saturday Review,* 27 February 1973, 42–43, 46; Peter S. Prescott, "The Basis of Horror," *Newsweek,* 19 February 1973, 85–86, reprinted as "Kosinski's Deviltry" in Peter S. Prescott, *Never in Doubt: Critical Essays on American Books, 1972–1985* (New York: Arbor, 1986), 155–57; Marion Simon Garmel, "Perfect Freedom Fails Kosinski's Searching Hero,"

National Observer, 10 March 1973, 23; Larry Swindell, "Kosinski's Labyrinth Is No Funny Forest: But Compelling, Yes," *Philadelphia Inquirer,* 18 February 1973, 6H; Jerome Klinkowitz, "Insatiable Art and the Great American Quotidian," *Chicago Review* 25, no. 1 (1973): 175–77. For a brief discussion of the novel's many voices as full of resonance and counterpoint, see "All in the Margins," *Times Literary Supplement,* 6 July 1973, 783.

46. Philip Stevick, "Voices and Vision," *Partisan Review* 41, no. 2 (1974): 305. Duncan Fallowell, in *Books and Bookmen,* September 1973, 89, also comments on Kosinski's talent with narrative and notes the power of the book.

47. Alan Hislop, "Company Men," *Saturday Review of the Arts,* March 1973, 70–71. See also Victor Howes, "Under the Microscope: A Novel in Bits and Pieces," *Christian Science Monitor,* 25 April 1973, 11, and "In Brief," *New Republic,* 10 March 1973, 33–34.

48. Elliott Anderson, "Stepping Down into Drivel," *Chicago Tribune Book World,* 4 March 1973, 5; Pearl K. Bell, "Sterile Diversions," *New Leader,* 19 February 1973, 16–17; Robert Alter, "Pulp-Fiction Style, Pop-Psychology Jargon, and a Genuinely Sadistic Imagination," *New York Times Book Review,* 11 February 1973, 2–3; George Stade, "The Realities of Fiction and the Fiction of Reality," *Harper's,* May 1973, 90, 94; Phoebe Adams, review of *The Devil Tree, Atlantic,* March 1973, 107; Ronald De Feo, "Two Disappointments, One Disaster," *National Review,* 16 March 1973, 322–23; Susan Knight, "Poor Jonathan," *New Statesman,* 13 July 1973, 56–57; John B. Kiley, *Critic,* May–June 1973, 80–81; John Skow, "Strike It Rich," *Time,* 19 February 1973, E5, E7; Russell Davies, "The Ravings of the Rich," *Observer,* 24 June 1973, 33; Christopher Lehmann-Haupt, "Bad by Design? Or Just Bad?" *New York Times,* 13 February 1973, 35. See also Patrick Cruttwell and Faith Westburg, "Fiction Chronicle," *Hudson Review* 26, no. 2 (1973): 419. Cruttwell and Westburg note that even Jonathan realizes it is hard to take his problem of being too rich seriously; how then, they wonder, is it possible to satirize something admittedly unreal?

49. Phillip Corwin, "Evil without Roots," *Nation,* 30 April 1973, 566–68. For other reviews of *The Devil Tree,* see the following: *Library Journal,* 1 November 1972, 3261; *Booklist,* 15 March 1973, 672; *Playboy,* April 1973, 28; *Choice,* 10 June 1973, 620; *Virginia Quarterly Review* 49 (Summer 1973): civ; Valentine Cunningham, "Autogeddon," *Listener,* 28 June 1973, 873; Thomas R. Edwards, "Jonathan, Benny, and Solitude," *New York Review of Books,* 22 March 1973, 29; James D. Hutchinson, "Authentic Existence and the Puritan Ethic," *Denver Quarterly* 7 (Winter 1973): 106–14; Lee T. Lemon, "The Fiction-Gambler," *Prairie Schooner* 47 (Summer 1973): 183–85; Mark Taylor, review of *The Devil Tree, Commonweal,* 2 November 1973, 119.

50. Barbara Tepa Lupack, "New Tree, Old Roots," *Polish Review* 29, nos. 1–2 (1984): 147–53.

51. Adrian Ayres, "*Cockpit:* Gray, Gloomy, Grim, and Gross," *Chicago Illini,* 8 November 1976, 10; Bud Foote, "Kosinski," *National Observer,* 6 September 1975, 17; Edmund Fuller, "Playing Tricks on a Sordid World," *Wall Street Journal,* 6 August 1975, 8; Christopher Ricks, "Lost Allusions," *New York Review of Books,* 27 November 1975, 44–45; Frederick R. Karl, *American Fictions 1940–1980: A Comprehensive History and Critical Evaluation* (New York: Harper, 1983), 504; Peter S. Prescott, "Superboy," *Newsweek,* 11 August 1975, 76; Hilton Kramer, "Lonely Rituals," *Commentary,* December 1975, 78–80; Lee T. Lemon, "Freak Show," *Prairie Schooner* 50, no. 2 (1976): 172–73; Charles Deemer, "Satan's Soap Opera," *New Leader,* 24 November 1975, 45.

52. Jonathan Baumbach, "Jerzy Kosinski Working Out Past Imperfections," *New York Times Book Review,* 10 August 1975, 3; Richard R. Lingeman, "Fables Ending in Riddles," *New York Times,* 15 August 1975, 33; Elaine Feinstein, "Defectors," *New Statesman,* 12 September 1975, 313; Jane Larkin Crain, "New Books," *Saturday Review,* 23 August 1975, 45; Gerald Barrett, "Montage," *Michigan Quarterly Review* 15, no. 3 (1976): 356–59; Stefan Kanfer, "Corrupt Conquistador," *Time,* 4 August 1975, 63; Eric Korn, "Alienation Effects," *Times Literary Supplement,* 29 August 1975, 961; Ivan Sanders, *Commonweal,* 29 August 1975, 373–74.

53. James Park Sloan (333–34) observes that with *Cockpit,* "an interesting phenomenon had arisen in the reception of Kosinski's books." Even when reviewers found his work "flawed and less fresh in what it had to say," Kosinski had a loyal following of readers. "The combination of violent and sexual content, accessible language, and the suggestion of profound philosophical depths," concludes Sloan, made *Cockpit* "a book that could be read by individuals far removed from the influence of the literary epicenter."

54. Daniel J. Cahill, "An Interview with Jerzy Kosinski on *Blind Date,*" *Contemporary Literature* 19 (Spring 1978): 133–42. Reprinted in Teicholz, ed., *Conversations with Jerzy Kosinski,* 150–58.

55. William Plummer, "In His Steps: The Mellowing of Jerzy Kosinski," *Village Voice,* 31 October 1977, 77–79. For other reviews of *Blind Date,* see J. F. Desmond, *World Literature Today* 52, no. 3 (1978): 472; E. S. Duvall, *Atlantic,* December 1977, 108–9; and Peter F. Michelson, *American Book Review,* April 1978, 4–7.

56. Anne Knight, "Jerzy Kosinski, Self-Searcher," *Horizon,* November 1977, 96; Barbara J. Tepa, "Kosinski Takes Another Chance," *Polish Review* 23, no. 3 (1978): 104–8; Jerome Klinkowitz, "Jerzy Kosinski: Puppetmaster," *Chicago Daily News Panorama,* 22 October 1977, 16, 22; Judson Hand, "Down Depravity Lane," *New York Daily News,* 30 October 1977, 18; John Riley, "Kosinski's Banquet of Forbidden Delights," *Los Angeles Times Book Review,* 27 November 1977, 4; Daniel J. Cahill, review of *Blind Date, New Republic,* 11 March 1978, 34–35; Arnost Lustig, "Love and Death in New Jerzy," *Washington Post Book World,* 27 November 1977, E3.

57. Raymond Sokolov, "Clockwork Blue," *Newsweek,* 21 November 1977, 121–22; Geoffrey Wolff, "Kosinski's Killing Ground," *New Times,* 9 December 1977, 86–87. In "Prurience," *Spectator,* 11 February 1978, 20, Peter Ackroyd similarly accuses the novel of name-dropping, cheap romance, and precious fictionalizing. Levanter, writes Ackroyd, "is a creature of fantasy, and like all fantasies, he becomes quickly and irredeemably boring."

58. Lee T. Lemon, review of *Blind Date, Prairie Schooner* 52, no. 3 (1978): 305; Tom Paulin, "Guilty Dreams," *New Statesman,* 10 February 1978, 193–94; Carole Cook, "Books in Brief," *Saturday Review,* 12 November 1977, 27; J. F. Desmond, *World Literature Today* 52, no. 3 (1978): 472; Michael Mason, "A Sense of Achievement," *Times Literary Supplement,* 10 February 1978, 157; Paul Gray, "Dead End," *Time,* 31 October 1977, 104, 106; Jay L. Halio Jr., "Violence and After," *Southern Review* 15, no. 3 (1979): 703–4; Anatole Broyard, "Casual Lust, Occasional Journalism," *New York Times Book Review,* 6 November 1977, 14.

59. Xana Kaysen, "Kosinski: Rapist as Moralist," *New Boston Review* (Spring 1978): 18, 22; John Leonard, "Death Is the Blind Date," *New York Times,* 7 November 1977, 33.

60. William Kennedy, "Kosinski's Hero Rides On," *Washington Post Book World,* 16 September 1979, 1, 11. Another reviewer who saw Fabian as following in the usual steps of other Kosinski protagonists was Alan Cheuse, "Books in Brief," *Saturday Review,* 19 January 1980, 52–53.

61. For other commentaries on and reviews of *Passion Play,* see Carol Lawson, "Behind the Best Sellers," *New York Times Book Review,* 21 October 1979, 58, and Valentine Cunningham, "Let It Bleed," *Times Literary Supplement,* 25 April 1980, 470.

62. Paul Abelman, "The Champ," *Spectator,* 19 April 1980, 19–20. See also "Fiction," *World Literature Today* 54, no. 2 (1980): 282, in which Marvin J. LaHood suggests that Kosinski's writing skill ultimately lacks profundity or loftiness and that in this novel, the hollow din of life is too superficial to be interesting.

63. Joshua Gilder, "Existential Cowboy Gone Astray," *New Leader,* 19 November 1979, 19–20; Peter S. Prescott, "A Horse Story for Grown-Ups," *Newsweek,* 10 September 1979, 73; Hans Konig, "Missions Impossible," *Nation,* 15 September 1979, 216–18; Jerome Klinkowitz, "The Aging Kosinski Knight, Questing on the Polo Field," *Chicago Sun-Times,* 2 September 1979, sec. 3 ("Show"), p. 9.

64. Barbara Tepa Lupack, review of *Passion Play,* by Jerzy Kosinski, *Polish Review* 25, nos. 3–4 (1980): 116–17; Ivan Gold, "Picaresque Sport," *New York Times Book Review,* 30 September 1979, 9, 18; John S. Reist Jr., "A Mere 'Picaro,' " *Christian Century,* 30 January 1980, 112–24; Barry Yourgrau, "Short Circuits," *Village Voice,* 24 September 1979, 48; Stefan Kanfer, "When Going Is the Goal," *Time,* 17 September 1979, 105; D. Keith Mano, "Big Reject," *National Review,* 12 October 1979, 1312–13.

65. Joseph McLellan, "Playing at Life," *Washington Post Book World,* 7 March 1982, 7; Lester Bangs, "Brief Encounters," *Village Voice,* 16 March 1982, 43; Adam Mars-Jones, "Rolling over Chopin," *Times Literary Supplement,* 28 May 1982, 579; Pat Rogers, "Ambassadors," *London Review of Books,* 3–16 June 1982, 18–19; Joshua Gilder, review of *Pinball,* by Jerzy Kosinski, *Saturday Review,* March 1982, 63–64; Christopher Bigsby, "Coercive Plots," *Times Educational Supplement,* 6 August 1982, 17; Benjamin DeMott, "Grand Guignol with Music," *New York Times Book Review,* 7 March 1982, 8; Sally Emerson, "Recent Fiction," *Illustrated London News,* July 1982, 61; Doug Fetherling, "Sex and Dreams and Rock'n'Roll," *MacLean's,* 8 March 1982, 64–65; Stefan Kanfer, "Trebles," *Time,* 22 March 1982, 84, 87.

66. John Calvin Batchelor, "The Annotated 'Roman à Tease,' " *New York Times Book Review,* 3 July 1988, 11; Walter Goodman, "Jerzy Kosinski's World of Parallels," *New York Times,* 20 June 1988, C17; Brett Singer, "Kosinski Minus the Sins," *Los Angeles Times Book Review,* 25 September 1988, 3, 12; K. N. Richwine, review of *The Hermit of 69th Street,* by Jerzy Kosinski, *Choice,* December 1988, 646; Larry McCaffery, "Kosinski's Mask behind the Mask," *Washington Post Book World,* 10 July 1988, 1, 9; review of *The Hermit of 69th Street, Kirkus Reviews,* 1 May 1988, 645–46; John Blades, "Jerzy Kosinski's *Hermit* Drives Critic to 'Murder,' " *Chicago Tribune Books,* 15 May 1988, 3.

67. Sharon Rosenbaum Weinstein, "Comedy and Nightmare: The Fiction of John Hawkes, Kurt Vonnegut Jr., Jerzy Kosinski, and Ralph Ellison" (Ph.D. diss., University of Utah, 1971); Robert Edward Golden, "Violence and Art in Postwar American Literature: A Study of O'Connor, Kosinski, Hawkes, and Pynchon" (Ph.D. diss., University of Rochester, 1972); David Joseph Lipani, "Jerzy Kosinski: A Study of His Novels" (Ph.D. diss., Bowling Green State University, 1973); Sister Ellen Fitzgerald, "World War II in the American Novel: Hawkes, Heller, Kosinski, and Vonnegut" (Ph.D. diss., University of Notre Dame, 1974); James D. Hutchinson, "The Art of the Self: The Quest for Authenticity in the Novels of Jerzy Kosinski" (Ph.D. diss., University of Denver, 1974); Barbara Jane Tepa, "Inside the Kaleidoscope: Kosinski's Polish and American Contexts" (Ph.D. diss., St. John's University, 1975); Mitchell Bernard Bloomfield, "The Fiction of Jerzy Kosinski: The Perverse in the Modern Imagination" (Ph.D. diss., Michigan State University, 1975); Geoffrey Dennis Green, "Writers in Exile: Chapters in the Critical Examination of Literature and Society" (Ph.D. diss., SUNY at Buffalo, 1977); Anthony Raymond DeCurtis, "Contemporary American Fiction and the Process of Fictionalization" (Ph.D. diss., Indiana University, 1980); Nicki Sahlin, "Manners in the Contemporary American Novel: Studies in John Cheever, John Updike, and Joan Didion" (Ph.D. diss., Brown University, 1980); Zita M. McShane, "Functions of the Grotesque in Twentieth-Century American Fiction" (Ph.D. diss., Case Western Reserve University, 1983); Thomas Hale Fick, "An American Dialectic: Power and Innocence from Cooper to Kosinski" (Ph.D. diss., Indiana University, 1985); Ronald Granofsky, "The Contemporary Symbolic Novel" (Ph.D. diss., Queen's University at Kingston, 1986); Melvin Hunt Raff, "This above All: The Challenge of Identity in Modern Literature" (Ph.D. diss., University of Maryland, 1989); John Douglas Kalb, "Articulated Selves: The Attainment of Identity and Personal Voice through Language and Storytelling in Works by Twentieth-Century Authors" (Ph.D. diss., Michigan State University, 1989); Martin Kich, "Everyone Goes Around Acting Crazy: A Study of Recent American Hard-Core Naturalists" (Ph.D. diss., Lehigh University, 1989); Laura Eileen Ferguson, "American Subdominant: The Collapse of Identity into Image in the Post-War American Novels and Films of European Émigré Writers and Directors" (Ph.D. diss.,

UCLA, 1992); Nicholas John Vitterite Jr., "Descants and Pricksongs as a Modality of Postmodernism: A Study of the Works of Robert Coover and Jerzy Kosinski" (Ph.D. diss., Emory University, 1984); Janice M. Viscomi, "Jerzy Kosinski: Contemporary Novelist as Knight" (Ph.D. diss., University of North Carolina at Chapel Hill, 1986); Barbara Sue Ellis, "Clinical Characteristics of the Narcissistic Personality: The Literature of Jerzy Kosinski" (Ph.D. diss., Widener University, 1991); Sara Reva Horowitz, "Linguistic Displacement in Fictional Responses to the Holocaust: Kosinski, Wiesel, Ling, and Tournier" (Ph.D. diss., Brandeis University, 1985); Sheng-Mei Ma, "The Holocaust in Anglo-American Literature: Particularism and Universalism in Relation to Documentary and Fictional Genres" (Ph.D. diss., Indiana University, 1990); Lea Fridman Hamaoui, "Words and Witness: Narrative and Aesthetic Strategies in the Representation of the Holocaust" (Ph.D. diss., City University of New York, 1991); and Janet Schenk McCord, "A Study of the Suicides of Eight Holocaust Survivor/Writers" (Ph.D. diss., Boston University, 1995).

68. Jeanie Blake, "Old Man River Lures Literary Giant to City," in Teicholz, ed., *Conversations with Jerzy Kosinski,* 178.

69. Jerome Klinkowitz, *Literary Disruptions: The Making of a Post-contemporary American Fiction* (Urbana: University of Illinois Press, 1975; 2d ed., 1980).

70. Byron L. Sherwin, *Jerzy Kosinski: Literary Alarmclock* (Chicago: Cabala Press, 1981).

71. Jack Hicks, "The Romance of Terror and Jerzy Kosinski," in *In the Singer's Temple: Prose Fictions of Barthelme, Gaines, Brautigan, Piercy, Kesey, and Kosinski* (Chapel Hill: University of North Carolina Press, 1981), 177–267.

72. Paul Bruss, *Victims: Textual Strategies in Recent American Fiction* (Lewisburg: Bucknell University Press, 1981).

73. Norman Lavers, *Jerzy Kosinski* (Boston: Twayne, 1982).

74. Michele Slung, "The Wounding of Jerzy Kosinski," *Washington Post Book World,* 11 July 1982, 15; Jan Herman, "Did He or Didn't He: *Village Voice* Sees Ghosts and CIA Spooks—But Kosinski Says They're Imagining Things," *Chicago Sun-Times,* 25 July 1982, Book Week section, 25; and Dave Smith, "Kosinski Whodunit: Who Ghost There If Not Jerzy?" *Los Angeles Times,* 1 August 1982, 3–5. See also Sarah Spankie, "Top Novelist Exorcises His Ghosts," *Times,* 27 March 1983, 12.

75. John Corry, "A Case History: 17 Years of Ideological Attack on a Cultural Target," *New York Times,* 7 November 1982, Arts and Leisure section, 1, 28–29. See also John Corry, *My Times: Adventures in the News Trade* (New York: Grosset/Putnam, 1993).

76. William Safire, "Suppressing Fire," *New York Times,* 18 November 1982, 27.

77. Charles Kaiser, "Friends at the Top of the Times," *Newsweek,* 22 November 1982, 125–26; David Schneiderman, "Kosinski's Friends See Red," *Village Voice,* 16 November 1982, 3; Austin Olney, Letters to the Editor, *Village Voice,* 6 July 1982; Thomas B. Morgan, Letters to the Editor, *Village Voice,* 6 July 1982.

78. Paul R. Lilly Jr., *Words in Search of Victims: The Achievement of Jerzy Kosinski* (Kent, Ohio: Kent State University Press, 1988).

79. Barbara Tepa Lupack, *Plays of Passion, Games of Chance: Jerzy Kosinski and His Fiction* (Bristol: Wyndham Hall/Rhodes-Fulbright International Library, 1988).

80. Welch D. Everman, *Jerzy Kosinski: The Literature of Violation,* Milford Popular Writers of Today, vol. 47 (San Bernardino: Borgo, 1989).

81. Some interesting interviews not included in *Conversations* are Geoffrey Movius, "A Conversation with Jerzy Kosinski," *New Boston Review* 1, no. 3 (Winter 1975): 3–4; Martin L. Gross, "Conversation with an Author: Jerzy Kosinski," *Book Digest,* November 1980, 19–27; R. E. Nowicki, "An Interview with Jerzy Kosinski," *San Francisco Review of Books* 3, no. 1 (1978): 10–13; and Benedict Giamo and Jeffrey Grunberg, "Chance Beings," in *Beyond Homelessness: Frames of Reference* (Iowa City: University of Iowa Press, 1992), 31–49.

82. Daniel J. Cahill, "Retreat from Violence," *Twentieth Century Literature* 18, no. 2 (1972): 121–32, and "Kosinski and His Critics," *The North American Review* 265 (Spring 1980):

66–68. The three interviews that appear in Tom Teicholz's *Conversations with Jerzy Kosinski* are "*The Devil Tree*: An Interview with Jerzy Kosinski" (66–87), "An Interview with Jerzy Kosinski on *Blind Date*" (150–58), and "Life at a Gallop" (162–66).

83. Ivan Sanders, "The Gifts of Strangeness: Alienation and Creation in Jerzy Kosinski's Fiction," *Polish Review* 19, nos. 3–4 (1974): 171–89.

84. Elizabeth Stone, "Horatio Algers of the Nightmare," *Psychology Today,* December 1977, 50–60, 63–64.

85. Samuel Coale, "The Quest for the Elusive Self: The Fiction of Jerzy Kosinski," *Critique* 14, no. 3 (1973): 25–37, and "The Cinematic Self of Jerzy Kosinski," *Modern Fiction Studies* 20, no. 3 (1974): 359–70.

86. Paul R. Lilly Jr., "Jerzy Kosinski: Words in Search of Victims," *Critique* 22, no. 2 (1980): 69–82, and "Vision and Violence in the Fiction of Jerzy Kosinski," *Literary Review* 25, no. 3 (1982): 389–400.

87. Thomas S. Gladsky, "Jerzy Kosinski's East European Self," *Critique* 29, no. 2 (1988): 121–32, and *Princes, Peasants, and Other Polish Selves: Ethnicity in American Literature* (Amherst: University of Massachusetts Press, 1992).

88. John W. Aldridge, "Charting the Abyss," in *The American Novel and the Way We Live Now* (New York: Oxford University Press, 1983), 53–64.

89. Andrew Gordon, "Fiction as Revenge: The Novels of Jerzy Kosinski," in *Third Force Psychology and the Study of Literature,* ed. Bernard J. Paris (Rutherford: Fairleigh Dickinson University Press, 1986), 280–90.

90. Krystyna Prendowska, "Jerzy Kosinski: A Literature of Contortions," *Journal of Narrative Technique* 8, no. 1 (1978): 11–25.

91. Frederick R. Karl, *American Fictions 1940–1980: A Comprehensive History and Critical Evaluation* (New York: Harper, 1983).

92. Gerald Weales, "Jerzy Kosinski: The Painted Bird and Other Disguises," *Hollins Critic* 9, no. 3 (1972): 1–12; Stanley Corngold, "Jerzy Kosinski's *The Painted Bird:* Language Lost and Regained," *Mosaic* 6, no. 4 (1973): 153–67; R. J. Spendal, "The Structure of *The Painted Bird," Journal of Narrative Technique* 6, no. 1 (1976): 132–36; Michael Skau, Michael Carroll, and David Cassiday, "Jerzy Kosinski's *The Painted Bird:* A Modern Bestiary," *Polish Review* 27, nos. 3–4 (1982): 45–54; David J. Piwinski, "Kosinski's *The Painted Bird," Explicator* 40, no. 1 (1981): 62–63; Lawrence L. Langer, "Men into Beasts," in *The Holocaust and the Literary Imagination* (New Haven: Yale University Press, 1975), 167–91; Meta Lale and John Williams, "The Narrator of *The Painted Bird:* A Case Study," *Renascence* 24, no. 4 (1972): 198–206; Thomas H. Landess, "The 'Snuff Film' and the Limits of Modern Aesthetics," in Suzanne Ferguson and Barbara Groselclose, *Literature and the Visual Arts in Contemporary Society* (Columbus: Ohio State University Press, 1985), 197–210; David H. Richter, "The Reader as Ironic Victim," *Novel: A Forum on Fiction* 14, no. 2 (1981): 135–51; "The Three Denouements of Jerzy Kosinski's *The Painted Bird," Contemporary Literature* 15, no. 3 (1974): 370–85; and Jerome Klinkowitz and David H. Richter, "Two Bibliographical Questions in Kosinski's *The Painted Bird," Contemporary Literature* 16, no. 1 (1975): 126–29.

93. Robert Boyers, "Language and Reality in Kosinski's *Steps," Centennial Review* 16, no. 1 (1972): 41–61; John Kent von Daler, "An Introduction to Jerzy Kosinski's *Steps," Language and Literature* 1, no. 1 (1971): 43–49; Byron Petrakis, "Jerzy Kosinski's *Steps* and the Cinematic Novel," *Comparatist* 2 (1978): 16–22; Jerome Klinkowitz, "Literary Disruptions: Or, What's Become of American Fiction?" *Partisan Review* 40, no. 3 (1973): 433–44.

94. James D. Hutchinson, "Retrospect: Judging a Book Award," *Denver Quarterly* 4, no. 3 (1969): 128–35. For a different perspective, see Chuck Ross, "Rejected," *New West,* 12 February 1979, 39–42. Ross describes his experiment in sending an unsolicited manuscript, which in fact was a typescript copy of the National Book Award-winning *Steps,* to publishers; all rejected it, including the book's original publisher.

95. John M. Gogol, "Kosinski's Chance: McLuhan Age Narcissus," *Notes on Contemporary Literature,* September 1971, 8–10; Andrew Gordon, "Jerzy Kosinski's *Being There* and the 'Oral Triad,' " *Notes on Contemporary Literature,* September 1987, 6–8; Raymond B. Murray, " 'That Certain Krylovian Touch': An Insight into Jerzy Kosinski's *Being There,*" *Notes on Contemporary Literature* 19, no. 2 (1989): 6–8; Herbert B. Rothschild, "Jerzy Kosinski's *Being There:* Coriolanus in Postmodern Dress," *Contemporary Literature* 29, no. 1 (1988): 49–63; Barbara J. Tepa, "Jerzy Kosinski's Polish Contexts: A Study of *Being There,*" *Polish Review* 22, no. 2 (1977): 52–61; Earl B. Brown Jr., "Kosinski's Modern Proposal: The Problem of Satire in the Mid-Twentieth Century," *Critique* 22, no. 2 (1980): 83–87.

96. Patrick Brantlinger, "What Hath TV Wrought: McLuhan's 'Global Village' or Kosinski's 'Village Videot?' " *Media and Methods,* April 1978, 36–41, 89–91; Nancy Corson Carter, "1970 Images of the Machine and the Garden: Kosinski, Crews, and Pirsig," *Soundings* 61, no. 1 (1978): 105–22.

97. Gary H. Arlen, "From the TV Viewer's Perspective," *Watch Magazine,* March 1980, 54–57; Aljean Harmetz, "Book by Kosinski, Film by Ashby," *New York Times,* 23 December 1979, B1, B19; Robert F. Willson Jr., "Being There at the End," *Literature/Film Quarterly* 9, no. 11 (1981): 59–62; Barbara Tepa Lupack, "Hit or Myth: Jerzy Kosinski's *Being There,*" *New Orleans Review* 13, no. 2 (1986): 58–68.

98. James D. Hutchinson, "Authentic Existence and the Puritan Ethic," *Denver Quarterly* 7, no. 4 (1973): 106–14; Stuart Hirschberg, "Becoming an Object: The Function of Mirrors and Photographs in Kosinski's *The Devil Tree,*" *Notes on Contemporary Literature,* March 1974, 14–15; Jerome Klinkowitz, "How Fiction Survives the Seventies," *North American Review* 258, no. 3 (1973): 69–73. See also Daniel J. Cahill, "*The Devil Tree:* An Interview With Jerzy Kosinski," *North American Review* 258, no. 1 (1973): 56–66, reprinted in Teicholz, ed., *Conversations with Jerzy Kosinski,* 66–87.

99. Ross Wetzsteon, "Jerzy Kosinski: Existential Cowboy," *Village Voice,* 11 August 1975, back page, 37–38; John G. Parks, "Human Destiny and Contemporary Narrative Form," *Western Humanities Review* 38, no. 2 (1984): 99–107; John L. Grigsby, "Jerzy Kosinski's *Cockpit:* A Twentieth Century *Gulliver's Travels?*" *Notes on Contemporary Literature* 19, no. 2 (1989): 8–10.

100. Daniel J. Cahill, "An Interview with Jerzy Kosinski on *Blind Date,*" *Contemporary Literature* 19, no. 2 (1978): 133–42, reprinted in Teicholz, *Conversations with Jerzy Kosinski,* 150–58; Paul Elmen, "Jerzy Kosinski and the Uses of Evil," *Christian Century,* 17 May 1978, 530–32.

101. Ami Shinitzky, "Life Is a Drama—Jerzy Kosinski: The Man and His Work," *Polo,* December 1979, 21–23, 44; Barry Nass, "Androgyny, Transsexuality, and Transgression in Jerzy Kosinski's *Passion Play,*" *Contemporary Literature* 31, no. 1 (1990): 37–57. See also Daniel J. Cahill, "Life at a Gallop," *Washington Post Book World,* 16 September 1979, 10, reprinted in Teicholz, ed., *Conversations with Jerzy Kosinski,* 162–66.

102. Regina Gorskowska, "*Pinball:* Aspects of Visibility: An Interview with Jerzy Kosinski," *Society for the Fine Arts Review* 4, no. 2 (1982): 3–4.

103. Stephen Schiff, "The Kosinski Conundrum," *Vanity Fair,* June 1988, 114–19, 166–70; Stuart Hirschberg, "A Note on an Episode in Jerzy Kosinski's *The Hermit of 69th Street,*" *Notes on Contemporary Literature* 19, no. 2 (1989): 5–6; Thomas S. Gladsky, "Jerzy Kosinski: The Polish Cooper," *Notes on Contemporary Literature* 19, no. 2 (1989): 11–12.

104. Maryann D. Greenstone, "Jerzy Kosinski: Chronicler of the Jewish Experience," *Studies in Bibliography and Booklore* 10 (Winter 1971–1972): 53–56; Ira Bruce Nadel, "Jerzy Kosinski [Joseph Novak], 1933– ," *Jewish Writers of North America: A Guide to Information Sources,* American Studies Information Guide Series 8 (Detroit: Gale, 1981), 241–43; Frederic E. Rusch, "Jerzy Kosinski: A Checklist," *Bulletin of Bibliography and Magazine Notes* 31, no. 1 (1974): 6–9.

105. Jerome Klinkowitz and Daniel J. Cahill, "The Great Kosinski Press War: A Bibliography," *Missouri Review* 6, no. 3 (1983): 171–75.

106. Thomas P. Walsh and Cameron Northouse, *John Barth, Jerzy Kosinski, and Thomas Pynchon: A Reference Guide* (Boston: G. K. Hall, 1977), 55–89.

107. Gloria L. Cronin and Blaine H. Hall, *Jerzy Kosinski: An Annotated Bibliography,* Bibliographies and Indexes in American Literature, no. 15 (New York: Greenwood Press, 1991).

108. Gefen, in Teicholz, ed., *Conversations with Jerzy Kosinski,* 229.

REVIEWS

◆

The Painted Bird

Everybody's Victim

ELIE WIESEL

The flow of scholarly essays and personal memoirs dealing with the manifold impact of the Nazi era on man and his vision of himself has not diminished in the last 20 years. Quite the contrary, it has increased. As always when a mystery is confronted, knowledge becomes a handicap. The more facts we accumulate, the less we understand their texture. Thus, most attempts by scientists, psychologists, moralists and even novelists to come to grips with the phenomenon of men's mass-extermination by man have ended in failure.

The task of the chronicler seems somehow easier. He writes not to reach conclusions and be rewarded for them; all he asks is to be heard, to be believed. For he knows what to say and what to omit, when to commit blasphemy with word or prayer, and also when to remain silent. His purpose then is not to bring forth new grandiloquent ideas or to exercise death or guilt, but simply to bear witness in behalf of himself and of those whose voices can no longer be heard.

It is as a chronicle that "The Painted Bird," Jerzy Kosinski's third book (but his first on this subject), achieves its unusual power. It is the story of a little boy and his experience in exile. Whether he wants it or not and despite his willingness to forgive, he serves as witness for the prosecution. One of the best. Written with deep sincerity and sensitivity, this poignant first-person account transcends confession and attains in parts the haunting quality and the tone of a quasi-surrealistic tale. One cannot read it without fear, shame and sadness.

Much has been published about what was done during the war to children in Eastern Europe. They were always the first to be sacrificed. The hero of this novel was 6 when his agony began. Because of their prewar anti-Nazi activities, his parents chose to send him away to relative safety in some remote Polish village for the duration of the German occupation. But the old

Reprinted from *New York Times Book Review,* 31 October 1965, 5, 46.

woman who was to take care of him died two months after his arrival. The child found himself homeless and alone in a distorted world; he had lost contact with his parents and his childhood as well. In more than one sense he became a wanderer, a fugitive, a painted bird trying desperately to acquire new colors in order to melt into his surroundings, only to discover that everywhere he had become everybody's victim.

Being dark-haired and black-eyed in a region where all peasants are fair-skinned and superstitious, he was accused of being a gypsy and forced to expiate the fear he inspired in his tormentors. Hounded from village to village, on the run for his life, he was drawn deeper and deeper into a nightmare of grim violence and near-insanity. Some scenes of rape and murder have the breath of a Malaparte, or the touch of a Goya. Buried alive with only his head visible, he was defenseless against a concerted attack of ravens seeking to peck out his eyes. Another time a drunkard let him hang by his arms for hours every night, with a dog in the hut trained to kill him if he came within its reach. One old woman taught him local practices of witchcraft. A young girl used him to satisfy her perverted desires. Later he saw her being forced by her father and brother to take a ram as her mate. As before, wounded and humiliated, he fled again, but wherever he went he was faced with the same primitive brutality. Devout Christians, come to church, would there, within their holy sanctuary, beat him unconscious. Even children had but one passion: to make him bleed and shout in pain. Eventually he survived the war, but not without losing his voice and his innocence as well. Driven to hate, he was saved by it.

The liberation found him prematurely hardened and revengeful. He had tried everything else before: he had prayed to God and even to the devil; he had dreamt of becoming saint or brute made in anybody's image, no matter whose. But prayers and dreams were useless weapons. Self-preservation and salvation were to be obtained neither through faith nor through submission. In order to remain alive he had to gain the will and the power to counter evil with evil, to leave no cruelty unpunished, to provoke the death of a murderer and hit back at his enemies with their own cruel methods. Hate and hate alone proved its efficiency as an instrument of survival.

Rendered with economy, skill and insight, this metamorphosis of the boy's mind and heart constitutes one of the terrifying elements of the narrative. Equally terrifying is the realization that what it describes took place in ordinary villages where ordinary men, women and children led ordinary lives and to whom the war, more abstraction than reality, brought inconveniences but not serious upheavals. Their brutality had nothing to do with political decisions taken in Berlin; it was homebred, eternal. And their victim was neither Jew nor gypsy, but a forlorn Christian child of good Christian parents. His dark complexion was his misfortune. Had his hair been blond and his eyes blue, this memoir would not have been written. And this is precisely what makes it so significant and so tragic: it was due to a joke, painful and absurd as it may sound. It could as easily not have happened at all. Or, which is the same, it could have happened to anybody, anywhere.

If we ever needed proof that Auschwitz was more a concept than a name, it is given to us here with shattering eloquence in "The Painted Bird," a moving but frightening tale in which man is indicted and proven guilty, with no extenuating circumstances.

Poor Boy Spreads His Wings

Anne Halley

A survivor's story, *The Painted Bird* belongs to that 20th-century genre which teaches us that our daily and clear, comforting separation of "real" experience from nightmare, of objective event from the sequestered madman's fantasy is neither natural nor enduring; human life under the rule of reason, of something like charity and love, is life under a special dispensation, a lucky historical accident, limited, a luxury. From the survivor out of the Polish villages we can learn again what—drifting down aisles in a mass-discount-comfort culture and in spite of riots and demonstrations—we may try to forget; human life, the cheapest thing there is, can be maintained and has been for centuries in the midst of chaos, brutality, organized and disorganized ill will.

The other genre to which this survivor's tale must, I think, be linked is a good deal older. We know this story and these actors, have them in our bones, although we have usually met them in symbolic, more bearable, differently fictionalized and selected detail: Hansel and Gretel in the witch's hut; "The Poor Boy in the Grave"; "Jorinda and Joringel." The peasants, the millers and blacksmiths, the bird catcher, soldiers, toothless crones, priests and plowboys, among whom the narrator spent the war years—the abandoned child himself—are deep in our consciousness: not only Grimm's *Fairy Tales,* but *fabliaux,* Chapbooks and *Volksbücher,* the *Simplicissimus* Thirty Years' War chronicle, superstitions and customs brought by our grandparents out of old-country villages, are random examples only of where we have met both the actions and characters in this book.

Thus, a dark-haired, olive-skinned boy of 6—a child who looks like a Jew or gypsy—is sent in 1939 to stay out the war with a peasant woman. After the foster mother's sudden death, the story becomes a nightmarish, blow-by-blow account of the child's partly passive, learning-to-struggle survival: the blows are literal, of course, for clubs and whips and switches and cudgels and flails are the ordinary implements of peasant life. The child wanders, dodging and fleeing from village to village, from cruel master to master, and must usually watch the occasional kindly host meet a violent end. The peasants fear the boy's black eyes, his Jewish or gypsy "otherness"; he is thought to be a kind of changeling or child of darkness. Defined by his darkness alone, and powerless without goods or protectors, he is tolerated, exploited, tortured, not quite murdered, forgotten in good seasons, but blamed for bad.

The various episodes, no doubt based on experience, seem to embody and play on recognizable folk-tale motifs, always with that "realistic" twist, or reversal, which shows that there is neither justice, nor reason, nor black or white magic to help one in extremity. Only chance. When the foster mother, a passable witch, burns with her hut, the child is *not* restored to joyful parents—though here, in the first episode, he fully expects to be. Foundlings and strangers are not given bed and board by the poor because they are our Lord in disguise, or may have three wishes to dispense. They are Jews to be misused and turned over to the German ovens. The bird catcher and his beloved are not noble youth and maid but aging, half-mad outcasts who—instead of turning into birds or a flowering bush—are ultimately kicked to death by the other peasants; goats do not turn into princes although peasant girls may love them; the crucifix does not speak, miraculously, for the innocent; to be held under ice or to be thrown into and nearly drowned in a manure pit does not, like the fairy-tale fall-down-the-well, lead to a gentler, magic country but only to the hero's emergence into more cruel trials; the huntsman who is ordered to perform the ritual killing is, interestingly enough, a German soldier who allows the boy to escape. The narrator does not marry the king's daughter after his trials: for a while at least he "marries" the Red Army, whose soldiers rescue him. With the Russian soldiers he is given the change of clothing so important in folk tales for change of identity: not princely garments, but a uniform and a Red Star. Finally, restored by means of the traditional identifying birthmark to his parents, the boy encounters not the "happily ever after," but that complex disorganized postwar society, in which ultimately even the saving hagiography of Stalin as protective, hard-working Father, and the ideal of a rational Collective will turn out disproved fairy tales.

The book's epilogue, however, attempts to reverse the bitterly ironic anti-fairy-tale pattern: in what seems to me an odd reversal, Mr. Kosinski finds that the freedom and independence, which he learned among the peasants, were subject only to "the limits of his own determination and skill." He implies that America today may be a comparable, fit habitat for the man determined to survive and spread his wings. We may nevertheless hope for a world less natural, less governed by accident, inherited fear, superstition and the brutality that is no one's fault because it has always existed: I mean, a society less traditional, perhaps, in which even those of the wrong color can survive with a less heroic effort of skill and determination, and with less reliance on their luck.

[Review of] *The Painted Bird*

ROBERT COLES

I suppose in fifty years or so some sensitive social historian will pick up *Centuries of Childhood* by Philippe Ariès and realize how urgently it needs an epilogue—a long and frank account of what the most recent of centuries has seen fit to do with children. It will be a sad moment for us all, because the "progress" we have made has not kept us from unprecedented murder, of children among others. Germany, whose citizens believed strongly in science and contributed significantly to medicine, emerged as the Anti-Christ, ready to take the world to hell and laugh as we all burned. To the east we saw further irony. A socialist revolution committed to economic justice fell into the hands of a vulgar, suspicious tyrant who ordered people (and associates) killed for the most gratuitous and arbitrary reasons.

If Germany and Russia have furnished us naked totalitarianism at its worst, I need not remind anyone who has lived through these past few decades how persistently we have had to face the presence of war. There was Spain and the innocent families killed by both sides. There was Korea, only a few years after the *second* World War was over. Today there is Vietnam. Not for long in this century have we been spared the faces of terrorized children, made homeless or orphans by bombs, injured by fires and bullets, hungry and cold because soldiers have orders to kill one another and destroy whatever cannot be killed. For those of us in America, it is and has been far off. We may be asked to give a few dollars to "save the children" or to this or that rescue committee, but the boys and girls have belonged to other people.

A year or two ago a book appeared with the inviting but mysterious title *The Painted Bird.* From the literary viewpoint alone it was of interest: the author, Jerzy Kosinski, was a young Polish emigré who seemed in surprising control of the English language, and though we have had that kind of thing happen once before, the likelihood of a recurrence has always been considered small. Moreover, the form of the book was as unusual as its content. In it a boy narrates his experiences from age five or six to age twelve—though not the way it is done in a children's book. The book concerns itself with what

Reprinted from Robert Coles, book review of *The Painted Bird,* by Jerzy Kosinski, *Harvard Educational Review* 37, no. 3 (1967): 493–96, with permission of the journal.

must be one of the most sordid moments in man's entire history, and the child who lived through those moments—now to tell us about them—presumably is not talking to his age-mates but to *us,* who still murder and otherwise torment children.

In any event, *The Painted Bird* startled its reviewers, who could only say again and again how awful and terrifying yet haunting its pages turn out to be. They didn't have to give the plot much of a summary; we have learned to be unsurprised when mention is made of the Nazis and, in general, the Europe of a few years ago. One point was unusual though: the child is described as living in eastern Europe, and his experiences are not those inflicted upon inmates of concentration camps or prisoners of the German or Russian armies; rather, the boy moves from village to village, presumably in Poland, or Hungary, or thereabouts, so that the disasters he experiences could only be called the result of Hitler's war.

The sad facts of history make Hitler and Stalin mere successors to a long line of tyrants and exploiters whose benighted rule has kept countries like Poland incredibly backward for centuries. In 1782, a French nobleman and priest, Hubert Vautrin, came back to Lorraine after five years in Poland and Lithuania, full of somber and disheartening experiences and observations. In 1807, he published *L'Observateur en Pologne,* a book very much like de Tocqueville's *Democratie en Amérique.* Much of what the boy in *The Painted Bird* comes to experience is described by Vautrin: the coarse, violent men; the fearful, superstitious women; the extreme poverty, the extreme ignorance, the extreme suspiciousness; and side by side, the isolated centers of wealth and privilege shared by the nobility and, of all people, the bishops of the Church.

It is safe to say that the Eastern Europe of *The Painted Bird* would not surprise Vautrin. The nameless boy in Kosinski's novel—if that is the word for the book—takes us from village to village amid that squalid backwater of European civilization. At six he learns of war, and thereafter there is nothing to face but hate, punishment, hunger, fear, and death. He is dark but not Jewish. Because they have been anti-Fascists, his parents, city people, fear he will be killed on sight by the Nazis. Thus they surrender him to a man who promises to find foster parents for him in a distant village. As the Germans approach, the parents themselves flee. Within two months of his arrival, the boy's foster mother dies; and from then on, for years and years, the boy has to wander from village to village, as if hounded by God himself.

What is one to say about this book? When I first started reading it, I thought I would find a tender and gentle story, suited for a certain kind of high-school student who was near enough the age of the book's narrator to feel very much a part of his mind, if not of his experiences. That is one of the book's most brilliant and unnerving characteristics: it only gradually confronts the reader with the full dimensions of the evil it means to describe. In so doing, the author is true to life and perhaps enables us to understand how this boy—and others like him—kept alive in the face of what emerges finally as hell itself.

What else, after all, can people like us do but speculate intellectually on the implications—psychological, educational, moral, and theological—of such a book? As the pages became increasingly impossible to face—the brutality and violence, the monstrous, horrible injustice—I found myself more and more thoughtful, to the point that the book became rather stimulating by the end. That is, I had a dozen things to dwell on, all of them large and weighty issues.

In contrast, the boy's survival clearly had very little to do with his inability to speculate and analyze. Humiliated and degraded again and again, he becomes like his brutish oppressors and stubbornly holds on, even as they have for centuries. He does not fight them—that would mean certain death—but learns to crawl, to cling tenaciously to whatever miserable, wretched half-promise is available. Home is where you find it, and survival does not require mental health.

What, in fact, does happen to the boy's mind as he sees the darkest side of any moon that ever was? As do other exiles and outcasts, he develops a shrewd knowledge of the moods and susceptibilities of the powerful. If they are crudely sensual people, perverse and deceitful, he can be shrewdly disarming, cooperative, or evasive. Desperate fear and paralytic anxiety are perhaps luxuries of the comfortable or expressions of some last-ditch, impossible situation. The long, slow grind of most suffering and persecution exacts quite another order of adaptation frum the victim. It is to this book's credit that the boy rather briskly sets about his business: accommodation in the interests of life. Let the middle-class American intellectuals fight over the morality of such behavior—when a Hannah Arendt exposes its banality, as she did in Eichmann in Jerusalem. Nor should the reader fall back upon the child's age. The author rather obviously sees him as a representative of all refugees, all outcasts, all suffering and debased people. His desire to persist, to live no matter what, can be found unbelievable or wrong—but only by those who cannot know how absurd it is for them even to try to comprehend the kind of choices that so-called civilized Europe presented to millions in our time.

The worst part of this book, this story that tells a million stories, comes at the end, when miraculously the child is found by his parents. For years he has escaped the instant death the Germans threatened and somehow had lived through a succession of inhuman and savage experiences: torture and hunger; sexual perversions of one sort or another, including the bestiality that Krafft-Ebing attributed to "rustic" people; assault and, worse, comfort offered, then withdrawn; bizarre, mystifying encounters with an assortment of witches, idiots, and mad people. All this becomes if not second nature then life itself, world without end; until, that is, the world catches up with its own lunacy and confronts its bewildered prisoners with the fact that now all is well. To your feet—Jews, Negroes, gypsies, indeed poor people everywhere! We are through for a while. Thirty million died, and rest assured that in a few years there will be more bombs; but for the moment pause—and go back to your old ways. We will stop the firing squads, end the hangings, empty the prisons, and give orders that no more ovens be stoked. You, all of you, return to one another. Accept our retribution. Receive your rights, your vote, if that is what you want, and some bread. And be sensible, be mature. Forget the past, the broken twisted past—that some of you persist in seeing still at work, still around to exploit and murder in the name, always, of God and country. Look to the future, to what you can have, can be—that is, some of you. (Don't ask how many; that is something we shall have to learn in time.)

I suppose we too will have to wait and see how this boy and all the others manage. Fortunately, the author at least allows him the dignity of his own past, his own circumstances. He does not need guidance or "treatment." It is not a neurosis or psychosis that threatens him. Words like *rehabilitation* or *help*—with all their gratuitous, naive, and sometimes absurd implications—are not summoned. The boy had become mute, and his parents, whatever their love, cannot draw him out. He is back with them, but he prefers the company of night people, those who for a variety of reasons live on the edge of the law. His parents are worried and hurt, but the suffering they have in common with him prevents them from becoming moralistic. They do not find him full of "problems"; they see him naturally and appropriately reluctant to deal with any world except the brutal one he has learned to deal with and indeed now possesses.

Eventually he talks. He has gone off to ski, sent by his parents in the hope that hills and snow would be neutral territory. In a fierce blizzard, he again struggles for life, for action and yet another victory. Again the direction is downward; but now the struggle is different and weighted in his favor. In a hospital room, after sustaining injuries on the ski slopes, he hears a telephone and can answer it. That is the end of the book.

I note that in the original hardcover edition the author adds something more. The boy will find eastern Europe under the Communists as hard and oppressive as the life he experienced in the villages during the war. In point of fact, Jerzy Kosinski is a pen name for Joseph Novak, who wrote *The Future Is Ours, Comrade,* and *No Third Path* before *The Painted Bird* was published. Fortunately, the paperback edition eliminates the author's desire to harness the power and originality of this story with a political sermon. Nothing in the book has prepared the reader for propaganda, and if Joseph Novak had to intrude on Jerzy Kosinski, he did it in the right way, with an obvious and expendable afterthought.

As for the world that presumably now has that boy as one of its men, the evil, hate, and murder continue. The title of *The Painted Bird* comes from an incident in the book. The boy meets up with Lekh, a birdcatcher who sadly and grimly paints birds and then releases them to be killed by their own kind. The boy is, of course, a painted bird, different in one or another respect from the majority. Yet I fear things are even worse these days. So many birds are hunting down so many other birds that the individual tragedies created by one birdcatcher seem almost exceptional. In our world, majorities not only persecute minorities; the strong not only persecute the weak; but the powerful set themselves against the powerful, and the earth itself must live in fear.

Steps

Keys on a Ring

Hugh Kenner

These Steps trace a circle. On the first page the narrator is "traveling farther south," brandishing before a girl in a whitewashed village the credit cards of awing affluence. (She has little to offer but vulnerable youthfulness. He'll abandon her.) It's on the last page, having made it in America, that he sets out on that journey, abandoning a different girl. Like keys arrayed on a ring, his recollections imply sequence but not beginning; behind his American memories are his European memories; behind these, the exile in America remembering. And he stays on the move.

From the calm of his prose (everything composed in memory, the sentences pellucid) we judge that his journeying through time and space is not a distraction but a learning. His memories are what he knows, implying three categories: cruelty, ritual, restless love. There's another circle here: love is restless because ritualized by cruelty; ritual is cruel because loveless; cruelty is the mode of love because the rituals confine experience. One can't say where such a process commences, and it doesn't end. One keeps moving, and there's all the earth to move around on.

Some of the rituals are amatory, but the harshest ones are political. "I remember one occasion when the professor asked him to comment upon a political doctrine recently implemented by the Party. He rose, pale and sweating, yet trying to look impersonal; he answered that certain aspects of the doctrine seemed to mirror perfectly the many oppressive aspects of the total state, and for this reason it lacked all humanity. . . . We knew he was doomed. One of the University officials told me afterward that the man was no longer alive. He almost sneered as he recounted the sordid circumstances of his suicide in a lavatory."

And the word "lavatory" completes a circle; these sentences conclude a quiet 800-word sequence about the privacy this doomed student had found

Reprinted from the *New York Times Book Review,* 20 October 1968, 5.

(pursuing a ritual of his own) only in lavatories. To justify the time he spent in them he pretended his purpose was to erase disloyal graffiti.

Are we to suppose that the texture of life was wryed when the party moved in? It's a meaningless question: our narrator belongs to the generation for which the party has always been there. And when, at 24, he flies to America forever ("I felt cheated and robbed: so many years had led to nothing more than a seat on a plane") are we to suppose that a new life begins? Another meaningless question: the texture of experience alters, not its nature.

In Europe, during military training, he had watched a trigger-happy sniper. "The soldier's rifle kicked twice and muffled shots cut into the silence. When I looked toward the couple again, they lay in the swaying grass like two surfers suddenly swept off their boards by an unpredictable wave." In America, during a game played with fast autos, a man stepping from a parked car is no less gratuitously slaughtered. "In that instant a competing car rammed into the door, slamming it closed. The body disappeared. Only the head remained outside, as if balanced on the knife-edge of the door; then it rolled down and hit the asphalt like one more book that had been struck off."

The struck-off book is a brilliant symbol: it's a counter in the game, the rite of which is to dislodge at high speed books taped to the sides of cars parked along the street. ("I slipped a stereo tape into the car's player, and as the music heightened my tension I accelerated; my nerves gauged the steering, the speed and the distance. I sensed I was knocking off one book after another. I won.")

The Use of Books, we think wryly. Yet we don't choke on the symbol. Symbols repel when they seem thought up. This one doesn't. We can imagine that game perfectly well, just as we can imagine—and believe in—the woman kept suspended in a cage in a barn, to assuage village lusts, or the affluent man who has girls to offer ("Of course, he added, they wouldn't entertain us spontaneously") and seems not to feel he need comment when the substance of his offer proves to be an empty room plastered with lewd photographs. ("He asked me whether I had enjoyed myself, and he pressed me to return soon to meet his other friends.")

Low-keyed, efficient, controlled, the prose of "Steps" encompasses the banal, the picturesque, the monstrous, with never a flicker of surprise. Scene illuminates adjacent scene; vignette after vignette stays in the memory. Céline and Kafka stand behind this accomplished art, and it doesn't diminish their achievement to remark that by contrast with the voice Mr. Kosinski's ring of fables implies, their voices seem often to grow taut or to insist. Beneath "The Trial's" poised narration we can detect the banked outrage of a man who had read Dickens. Beneath the economical fictions in "Steps" we are allowed to detect only the leisure of unlettered fictive memory, as though—it is one of Mr. Kosinski's many feats—we were detained forever with a consciousness for which the world of "The Trial" and "Journey to the End of Night" seems a tranquil norm: as, the reader may reflect with enlightening surprise, it nowadays is.

Out of the Fires

STANLEY KAUFFMANN

One measure of Jerzy Kosinski's quality is that he arrived in the US in 1957 without a word of English and by 1968 he has written four books in English: two works of non-fiction, published under the pen-name Joseph Novak, and two novels, *The Painted Bird* (1965) and now *Steps*. A better measure of his quality is that this achievement is irrelevant. Both his novels (I haven't read the Novak books) are admirable in themselves, and the second one pushes into extraordinary inner chambers, echoing and appalling. These days any impatient juvenile can show his impatience with the traditional novel by giving us loose pages in a box or omitting description or omitting everything else. In *Steps* Kosinski breaks with the traditional novel in a traditional way: he makes his book so scorchingly personal that it is unique. It's possible to make comparisons (as I shall) because no artwork is completely new, but *Steps* is a "new" novel because it is so utterly Kosinski's, wrought in memories and understanding of himself, his own fierce fight to find breathing-space in the welter of overwhelming experience.

In a pamphlet about *The Painted Bird,* he described that book as "the author's vision of himself as a child, a *vision,* not . . . a revisitation of childhood . . . the result of the slow unfreezing of a mind long gripped by fear. . . ." It is a series of short chapters about a homeless Jewish child in Eastern Europe during the Second War whose experiences with peasants and soldiers are so icily brutal that they justify the quotation from Artaud in Kosinski's pamphlet: "Cruelty is above all lucid, a kind of rigid control and submission to necessity." The inner coil of the book slackens somewhat toward the end, but it is one of the best works of literature to come out of the European horror. The author says that *The Painted Bird* is organized "in little dramas, in spurts of experience, with the links largely omitted, as is the case with memory." In *Steps* this method is further refined, with a greater admixture of imagination to experience.

The new book, only 148 pages, consists of some 50 episodes arranged in eight unnumbered sections. Many of the episodes are linked in content; all of them are unified in vision. It would be too bald to say that *Steps* is about the

Reprinted from *New Republic,* 26 October 1968, 22, 41. Reprinted by permission.

boy-protagonist of *The Painted Bird* as a man. The arrangement is no longer chronological, and the settings now sometimes seem metaphorical, as does some of the action. The real relation with the first book is in the mosaic method and in the fact that *Steps* derives from the world of *The Painted Bird*.

There is no attempt here to tell a sequential story; the individual stories construct a cosmos. A few of the episodes, the only ones with dialogue, are snatches of conversation in the "present" between the narrator and his mistress. Almost all of them are stories about the narrator, self-contained but thematically cumulative. Some of them suggest Babel, some a darker Dinesen, some De Maupassant. All are touched with sexuality or violence or both, all share the quality of an author who insists on forcing one foot in front of another into the irrational maze of his life. It is a life that epitomizes in thousandfold intensity the questions and fears of most contemporary men. The author calls up his experience for examination, for *adjustment;* he is saying, "I cannot make life rational or humane, but I can record that some rational and humane men live it, knowing what they pay in reason and humaneness."

Each of the episodes can be described, but by describing any one of them, I throw the book out of balance. For instance, in the first episode the narrator, traveling in an unnamed country, persuades a simple village girl to come away with him by demonstrating the power of his credit cards. The episode, a small latter-day Dinesen tale, is complete but unfinished until one reads the next episode—which is about the narrator stranded on an (Aegean?) island without money, sleeping with some gross women just for food. There is obviously a reverse relation between the affluent man seducing a girl with implied wealth and the impoverished man servicing the gross women who have trifling wealth. In the next episode the narrator is a ski instructor having an affair with a girl in a nearby tuberculosis sanitarium who wants to make love to his naked image in a mirror. The next episode goes from this sexual abstraction to bestial sex, in the milieu of *The Painted Bird,* in which the narrator watches a girl performing before peasants with an (unspecified) animal. In the next episode the narrator has a rendezvous with a svelte woman, finds that his organ will not rise, goes out and picks up a whore who turns out to be a transvestite (thus with a male organ). And the next episode is the narrator's reminiscence of an army game involving male organs. . . .

Many of the episodes "star" the male organ, in fact and as symbol. In this, *Steps* resembles another fine novel by a survivor of the European holocaust, *Blood from the Sky,* by Piotr Rawicz (published by Harcourt, Brace & World in 1964, well reviewed, and disgracefully neglected). Perhaps this is because the fact of circumcision often made the lives of the Jews depend, in no facetious way at all, on their penises; transformed sex into a function of the organ that could have meant their deaths. (Kosinski has an episode about circumcision.) Even more than for most males, for some surviving Jews the virile member certified not only virility but triumph. There are some "present" scenes in which the narrator explains to his mistress why he has certain sexual predilections. The explanations seem mere rationalizations for his urge to prove that he is alive, *still* alive, and wants to do everything he can with his penis to glory in that fact.

But, as I feared, descriptions of individual episodes give a one-sided image of the book. It *is* a strongly sexual novel; it is also a novel about terror, killing, fear, politics, and the scraping-out of some little plateaus of tranquillity in a sliding-climbing existence. Large terrors of the past get transmuted into pragmatic applications: the narrator (in New York?) practices gangsterism on fellow-immigrants; or the narrator saves himself by posing as a deaf-mute in a Near Eastern city. (The boy in *The Painted Bird* was mute for years.) In another episode, probably a dream, he finds himself a guard over condemned prisoners, in a situation like that of a guard in one of the German death camps.

> I glanced around me: the armed men, tense and ready, stood at my sides and behind me. Only then did I realize that the prisoners were about to be beheaded. My refusal to obey orders would mean my being executed with those who stood in front of me. I could no longer see their faces, but their shirts were only a few inches from the blade of my knife.
>
> It was inconceivable, I thought, that I would have to slash the neck of another man simply because events had placed me behind his back.

The oppressed man has come to understand the accidentality of much oppression, the circumstantial basis of much morality.

The quotation above is typical of Kosinski's style: simple and precise, not overtly emotional. Sentences are generally short and direct. It is a style made of small, deceptively plain, exploding capsules. Except for the narrator, there are no characters, only figures who perform clarifying functions. The steady coolness of the book and its very brevity—which heightens the sense of tremendous distillation—add to its power. The book has a last irony. In the closing episode the viewpoint shifts to the "present" mistress and shows her as victim of the narrator. The world has done its hardening work on him.

In *The Painted Bird* I felt the author pulling himself free of his past as out of a quagmire, each page a knot on the rope by which he climbed upward. Not so here. *Steps,* a superior work, more subtly conceived, is a piercing view of that past as part of the world's present. For me, the title does not signify progress from one place to another or from one state to another but simply action about experience: steps taken to accommodate experience and continuing reality to the possibility of remaining alive.

A few of the episodes show the bones of contrivance, like one about a contest with cars to knock books off other cars' fenders. A few of them, even after a second or third reading, yield insufficient resonance. But in the main, *more* than the main, this small book is a very large achievement. Through all its smoke and fire and pain, a curious pride persists. The book says finally: "Hell. Horror. Lust. Cruelty. Ego. But *my* hell and horror and lust and cruelty and ego. Life is—just possibly—worth living if at last we are able to *see* what we do, if we can imagine it better and imagine it worse."

A Moralist's Journey into the Heart of Darkness

MARTIN TUCKER

In Kosinski's first novel, *The Painted Bird,* a six-year-old boy was forced over a number of years to take giant steps into an awareness of man's potentiality for gratuitous evil and rooted indifference. In his second novel, the hero, now a young man, takes smaller steps, and they are all on the same level, but the totality of his journey is as profound as the one experienced in the earlier novel.

And the presentation of that journey is an amazing *tour de force.* Kosinski takes the reader along a series of steps, or experiences, which do not go up or down, and yet move to the center of a vast, unknowable depth.

The hero in this unconventional novel is a nameless "I" person who narrates a number of experiences; records several dialogues with his nameless mistress, usually while they are in bed and just before or after their sexual encounters; and expresses his feelings about people and events he has been, like a naturalist, coolly observing. The hero makes no judgments; he records, watches, waits. It is significant that not one character in the novel is given a name, and yet the novel is about the naming of people, or rather the putting into words and names the perceptions the hero has studiously cultivated. In this sense the novel is about the identity—and identities—of human beings; conversely it is about the significance most people deny to another's identity. Perhaps this is the reason so many of the episodes concern characters stripped naked of their clothes. Yet—and this is one of the brilliant ways in which Kosinski conveys his ideas—it is not nakedness which reveals the identity but the clothing which the character has subsumed into his personality.

Thus in one episode the hero sneaks away from an army drill march, and with three other soldiers runs through the woods. Each of the men disrobes, and frolics in a clearing. When the company of marching soldiers approach, the other men run away, but the hero is caught before the advancing corps. Responding intuitively—Kosinski puts it, in a "reflex" action—he stands erect, every part of him, and salutes the commanding officer. Or, in another

Reprinted from *Commonweal,* 29 November 1968, 319–20.

episode, the hero arranges a proxy assignation. The encounter is made possible by a friend with whom the woman has fallen in love. The friend blindfolds the woman, leaves her bed at a propitious moment, and beckons the hero in. After leaving the woman, the hero cannot envisage her naked; she has not acknowledged him, and he, in turn, is "unable to recall the shape or movement of her body, but vividly remembers the smallest detail of her clothes."

In another sense the novel is about control. Kosinski's preface is a quote from *The Bhagavadgita:* "For the uncontrolled there is no wisdom, nor for the uncontrolled is there the power of concentration; and for him without concentration there is no peace." Kosinski's hero tests his control of the situation by gauging how much cruelty, love, sadism he is able to will into his experiences. The experience is the measure of his control, and thus the limit, and limitation, of his ability to learn. Motivation, in the conventional sense most readers understand, is absent. In its place is a naturalistic awareness of the progression of a situation. In one episode the hero, from a hidden vantage point, hurls bottles at a night watchman on the grounds of a factory. The hero as sniper bears no grudge against the watchman; he is intent on observing the watchman's reactions. The watchman, who earlier in his life had deserted from the army, now refuses to flee or take cover in the building a few feet away. He keeps hitting out at the bottles. One of them finally strikes him dead.

In still another episode the hero arranges for a mass rape of a girlfriend who has become tiresome to him. He does not stay for the finale; once having controlled the situation, he departs. With another girlfriend he has different, but related, thoughts: "It occurred to me then that if I introduced her to drugs of a certain kind, and if she became addicted, she might free herself from what she had been. . . . she would acquire new desires and new habits and liberate herself from what she thought of me, from what she felt for me. . . . Like a polyp she would expand and develop in unpredictable directions."

Kosinski's pure, shorn style fits perfectly with his material. He is not after the grotesque or macabre; he is a moralist who prefers the recording of man's potentiality for evil above the construction of feeble excuses for its being. His technique in his second novel is even more impressive than in his first, which relied occasionally on exotic details and a pat conclusion. In *Steps* he forgoes chronology and conventional methods of characterization. The pattern emerges from an association of ideas. One experience leads to the retelling of another experience because of thematic parallels, or a similarity of content. Motifs keep reappearing to give the work a haunting concentration of impressions. In the first episode in the novel the hero picks up a girl and promises her the world through his credit card. In the final episode the hero's mistress is left alone, swimming, a small rotten brown leaf brushing her lips. In the first episode the girl lived with her illusion and paid the price of it; in the last episode the mistress is under the shadow of a wet leaf, but it is a shade of reality, and it has its meaning, a source that never runs dry.

Through his hard, brilliant ordering of material Kosinski has achieved a testament about our times. Like Joseph Conrad, another Pole who learned English as a second language and made it his chief means of literary communication, Kosinski has created a literature indisputably his own and not soon forgotten. Like Conrad, Kosinski shows that man is whatever he *can* be; only he can be much more than he is.

Being There

Jerzy Kosinski: On Still Being There

WILLIAM KENNEDY

Jerzy (pronounced Yair-zheh) Kosinski is a supreme artist of The Con, which I define as the art of survival in hopeless climates. "Con" is "confidence" in the traditional definition, but for Kosinski, I would add "control," "confound," "connive" and more. The enemy is any collective that denies individuality and thereby encourages death of the self; a brutal peasantry perhaps, a totalitarian bureaucracy, a mindless television audience, even the cancerous accumulations of a man's own past, which might erode his ability to survive the present. The key survival words are "Endure," "Manipulate." The aim is subversion of the enemy.

To Kosinski, life is relentlessly hostile, and so The Con requires perpetual vigilance. There is no such thing as success, only a benign interlude between failures. Love is the destruction of any love partner's independence, a deep joy at having dominated the other. He writes of existential man, but while the nameless protagonist of his second novel, *Steps,* might admire the arrogant individuality of Meursault, another existential figure from Camus's *The Stranger,* he would really think Meursault naive for not understanding his situation before it became deadly.

Kosinski's education in The Con began in his own childhood in Poland, wildly fictionalized in his first novel, *The Painted Bird,* a masterpiece of horror. A boy, perhaps Jewish or gypsy or neither, is sent by his parents to a rural village to avoid death by the Nazis. He suffers through demons, sadistic abuse, starvation, bestiality, genocide, bodily immersion in water, fire, earth, excrement, all this the work of the peasants for whom harboring Jews or gypsies means death. The boy learns to kill in self-defense, is brutalized into killing strangers to avenge being punished for having black eyes and hair. Kosinski calls the book "trauma personified." But with strange irony, he adds that it is

Reprinted from *Riding the Yellow Trolley Car,* by William Kennedy, with permission of Viking Penguin, a division of Penguin Books USA Inc.

the story of a happy childhood, for the boy survives the war, as millions of children did not.

In *Steps,* the boy grows older. He now relies on no morality, no group, only himself. He quests to understand that self, finds it cunning, murderous, perverse, animalistically erotic, detached from emotion. Kosinski sees his protagonist as the sum total of Western culture, "trauma perceived as a normal condition." "This," he adds, "is how we come to terms with what oppresses us. We assume it's normal." And thus does The Con work on the self: man manipulating his own mind to preserve sanity.

Now, in his new novel, *Being There* (Harcourt Brace Jovanovich), Kosinski moves outside himself and into satire. A man named Chance, perhaps a millionaire's illegitimate grandson, is raised in solitude in the millionaire's garden, fed by a servant, aware of the world only from TV. He grows up, a handsome shell, unable to read or write or think beyond the idiot level. Thrust abruptly into the real world, he is hit by the car of a financier's young wife. Driven to the financier's home, he speaks his truth. His idiocies are taken for pithiness, his talk of the garden, assumed to be metaphoric. The financier marvels at his wisdom, the wife is aroused. Chance, feeling nothing, turns on the TV for sustenance, as the plants in his garden drew sustenance from the sun. What follows is a ridiculous odyssey into fame, culminating not only in survival but perhaps in a Senate seat for this garden-variety idiot whom the world chooses to see as magnificent. Kosinski calls Chance "the Candide of the TV period" and likens his rise to Martha Mitchell being suddenly a household word and Spiro Agnew a part of American history, through TV exposure.

The Kosinski Con is still operative here. Despite his idiocy, Chance intuits a survival truth from TV: "When one was addressed and viewed by others, one was safe. Whatever one did would then be interpreted by the others in the same way that one interpreted what they did. They could never know more about one than one knew about them." Further, Kosinski's aim is still subversion. Mussolini, Hitler and Franco were like Chance, he says; the wishful thinking of the masses was ascribed to them.

Kosinski is thirty-seven, a thin, witty and vital man with thick, dark hair and dark eyes, the man grown from the boy in the cover painting of the *Painted Bird* paperback. We talked at his Manhattan apartment, its walls strikingly abstract with photos he took as a professional photographer in Poland, and with grotesque and erotic sketches by artists for whom *Steps* and *Bird* were the inspirations. Because he has kept himself aloof, this was Kosinski's first literary interview for a mass audience, and yet he is a world figure. *Being There* will be published in twenty countries. Perhaps three million copies of *Bird* are in print in thirty-two languages, and about two million of *Steps* (which won the 1969 National Book Award here) in twenty-seven languages.

After listening to Kosinski for fifteen minutes, you know he would be the last man to suffocate in the bomb shelter. He would know where the extra air was kept. His life seems in unusually tight control, as far as he can control it. He manages his own literary affairs and did so well once, the publisher insisted on secrecy about the terms. He left one publishing house after its lawyers altered his text. He left another that wanted to sell paperback rights before publication to protect the hardcover investment. Kosinski resented this absence of risk, found another publisher in three hours.

He came to the United States in 1957 after conning Poland out of a passport on the pretext that he had a Chase Manhattan Bank Foundation Scholarship. There is no such foundation. He knew Polish, Russian, French and Latin when he came, but no English. He attacked Shakespeare and Byron, saw four movies a day, read mountains of dictionaries (sixty in his apartment, more back at Yale, where he teaches unconventional drama prose and a seminar on death and the American imagination). With English in hand, he wrote two books of anticollective nonfiction in the early sixties, but switched to fiction out of a natural inclination for the abstract. "Nonfiction," he adds, "is outdated by reality. Fiction amplifies reality."

His literary antecedents: Camus, De Maupassant, Kuprin, Sartre, the Malraux of *Man's Fate,* but not Kafka, with whom he is often lumped. "I hate Kafka," he exasperatedly told one European reporter. He sees himself as the opposite of the linguistic exploders like Joyce and Nabokov. "You don't need an explosion to get at the oil. A small drill will do." His prose seems the purest possible, life abstracted to the skeletal stage, then its meaning fleshed out by the reader's imagination. "Reduction" is the key word. *Steps,* after twenty-seven reductive drafts, is a marvel of concision, as well as an imaginative powerhouse. *Being There* is Kosinski's first comic thrust, less intense than *Steps,* slight almost, but just as finely wrought and just as insidious with its afterburn. This time out, Kosinski has chosen to write a subtle polemic rather than a work of the spirit. He has now performed the remarkable feat of writing three extraordinary novels in a hostile language and in no way repeating himself. He is a masterful artist. From the exotic weeds in the garden of his own life, he fashions unique arrangements. And by his art he carries the reader well beyond mere literary experience, to ask of himself: How does *my* garden grow?

1971

Postscript: This story on the late Jerzy Kosinski was written for *Look* magazine when *Being There* was published, and was the consequence of my enthusiasm for his first two novels, *The Painted Bird* and *Steps.* There has been revisionism at work on the career of Kosinski in recent years following an exposé by a New York weekly newspaper that accused him of using collaborators to create his novels. Kosinski admitted having people work for him on the books but claimed he was the final arbiter of every line. Later writers have claimed to discredit the exposé, and I am not at all clear on what is true or what isn't on how the books were written. I was less than enthusiastic about most of his later work, and I have cooled a bit on *Being There* (though it did make a great movie, directed by Hal Ashby). But I do know that those first two books still stand as highly original works of literature; and since their importance to me as a writer has not diminished, I see no reason not to reprint my original enthusiasm for them and their author. Regarding these two books the revisionists can go pack salt.

The Fabrication of a Culture Hero

JOHN W. ALDRIDGE

In 1957, at the age of twenty-four, Jerry Kosinski arrived in this country from his native Poland and shortly began to write in English, a fine, pure English, some of the most original fiction of the postwar period. His first and still his best-known novel, *The Painted Bird* (1966), was an extraordinary work of combined fantasy and realism, a fairy-tale horror story about the experience of a gypsy or Jewish refugee child wandering in a nameless wartime landscape, threatened on the one hand by the German occupying army but tortured and persecuted on the other by the simple, sadistic peasants with whom, in his passage from nightmare to nightmare, he is forced to seek shelter. *Steps* (1968) was an essentially cinematic novel in the New Wave fashion, a book composed of fragments of experience or splinters of consciousness, having to do with a young man's odyssey through yet another Grand Guignol world in which, all standards being dead, violence and perversity register on the mind as unjudgeable increments of the given, mere data in the mechanical procedure of being. Both these novels won Kosinski large critical acclaim and important literary prizes (*Steps* a National Book Award in 1969), and they obviously did so because they represented brilliant attempts to create not merely new but exceedingly bold effects in a form in which the possibilities for adventure have for many years seemed reduced, and recent experimental efforts have so often resulted in a purely technical cleverness or the haphazard production of mere grotesquerie.

Kosinski has of course highly gifted contemporaries in the field of the experimental novel, and his work cannot finally be understood in isolation from theirs. In this country there are John Hawkes, Donald Barthelme, and John Barth, in France the so-called antinovelists such as Sarraute and Robbe-Grillet, in England William Golding, and in Germany Günter Grass. Kosinski has clearly been energized by the post-avant-garde iconoclasm which these writers represent, and there are elements in his work that undoubtedly would not be present if it were not for the influence of the Black Humor and French New Novel schools of writing. Yet he differs from both in the impor-

Originally published in *Saturday Review,* 24 April 1971, 25–27, and reprinted as "Jerzy Kosinski's American Dream," in John W. Aldridge, *The Devil in the Fire* (New York: Harper's Magazine Press, 1977), 267–73. Reprinted with permission of the author.

tant respect that his vision is primarily philosophical. He is interested not in making a satirical indictment of modern society—although satire is an abrasive secondary feature of his point of view—nor in attempting to explore in the French manner the various possible ways of dramatizing individual consciousness. He is concerned rather with understanding the nature and meaning of the human condition, the relation quite simply of human values to the terms of existence in an essentially amoral and surely anarchistic universe.

This may suggest that to the extent that Kosinski can be placed in any line of literary derivation or influence, he belongs in the tradition of classic European modernism. He may have learned something of value from those of his contemporaries who are working experimentally with the novel form, but his greatest teachers have evidently been Kafka, Camus, Sartre, and perhaps Dostoyevsky, men who have possessed not only unusual creative power but the ability to deal directly with concepts of being—in the largest sense, with ideas—and to use ideas in their fiction as concrete moods of dramatic action. This has always been the central strength of the later European novel: that in it ideas are both as important as physical sensations and may even be experienced with all the force and acuteness of physical sensations. And this also is a quality which the American novel has almost completely lacked, if only because it is part of our frontier mythology to believe that ideas belong to one sphere of perception and sensations to another—ideas to pallid and passive thought, sensations to the life of real men in the real world of robust action.

Ever since Hawthorne and Melville our novel has typically taken the form of an inflated documentary celebration of the discovery and incessant rediscovery of what it *feels* like to experience America, and this experience almost never extends above the level of raw physical sensation, is seldom redeemed by a single idea. It may be that we have been suspicious of all forms of abstract conceptualization because of the nature of our national beginnings, because of some ancestral memory that still haunts us of that sterile, life-hating Puritan obsessiveness about sin and a vengeful God and the peril of emotion, and that this is what ideas, what thinking, came to symbolize for us—so that when we began the migration westward, we were not only seeking new country but were in frantic flight from such terrible, killing intellection, swearing to ourselves that once we hit the trail we would never, never think again but only *be* and *feel* in a glorious, mindless revel out there in all those great empty wide-open spaces—Huck Finns, every one of us, endlessly lighting out for the territory ahead where there would be no Aunt Sally to "sivilize" us. It is scarcely any wonder that this pattern has had a profound effect upon our attitude toward ideas, that we conceive of them, whether in life or literature, as antithetical to creativity and honest feeling and, therefore, as unmanly, perhaps even as undemocratic. For in the ethos of the frontier the manly American was the man anxious to move on, inspirited by the lust for adventure, an unthinking love of country, while the contemplative man was, by definition, unadventurous, skeptical, aloof, slick-talking, a shifty and shiftless fellow, very probably a cheater at cards, of dubious origins, almost certainly a foreigner.

As a European Kosinski is fortunately free of this kind of grass-roots anti-intellectualism. Not only does he deal very explicitly with ideas in his fiction but he is fully conscious of the extent to which they determine the cast and content of his creative vision. In two short monographs, *Notes of the Author* (1965) and *The Art of the Self* (1968), first published as companion pieces, respectively, to *The Painted Bird* and *Steps,* he has offered, somewhat in the manner of Camus, important critical-philosophical statements which explain his technical intentions in the novels at the same time that they illuminate the ideological structures on which each was conceived. In them, Kosinski reminds us of a truth which most American novelists, just because of their abiding distrust of ideas, would much prefer us to forget: that in the most accomplished literary artist vigor of execution is finally inseparable from vigor of conception. The quality of the work can be determined only by the extent to which the work provides a powerful imaginative rendering of a powerful idea.

It is not surprising, therefore, that Kosinski's new novel, *Being There,* should take the form that is most natural for the novelist of ideas, the form of parable, the metaphorical and analogical statement of an idea—in this case, one that happens not only to be powerful in itself but to have the widest conceivable relevance to the condition of society at the present time. Once again, as in *The Painted Bird,* he is concerned with the innocent and helpless victim—there a lost child, here a man with the mind of a child—who is destined to become the object of what Henry James saw as the worst human atrocity: the usurpation by others of the privacy and integrity of the individual self. But where *The Painted Bird* was primarily a parable of demonic totalitarianism, of that form of Nazi bestiality which is not a politics but a violence of the soul and blood, *Being There* has to do with a totalitarianism of a much subtler and even more fearful kind, the kind that arises when the higher sensibilities of a people have become not so much brutalized as benumbed, when they have lost both skepticism and all hold on the real, and so fall victim to those agencies of propaganda which manipulate their thinking to accept whatever the state finds it expedient for them to accept. This Fascistic enslavement of the will, the corruption by others of the power of individual choice, is implied in Sartre's famous remark that "Hell is other people," and is explicitly characterized by Kosinski in *The Art of the Self* when he speaks of "the inability to escape from others who prove and prove again to you that you are as they see you"—or that *they* are as they wish you to see them. The hell depicted in *Being There* is clearly contemporary America but raised to the ultimate power of electronic derangement and populated with creatures who perceive life wholly in terms of the image offered them on the television screen, and who, therefore, create the personages they see on the screen in the image of their hopes for themselves, their wishful projections of transcendent glamour, wisdom, and financial success. Hence, they are vulnerable to seduction by whatever powers happen at any moment to be in control of the mass media. Since their experience of a public figure is confined to the projected media image of that figure, they have no choice but to accept that image as the reliable index of his true identity. A person is what he appears to be, and he can be made to appear to be almost anything his sponsors or the viewing public wish him to be. He can also be created quite literally out of nothing. He need have no actual history or identity, no record of failure or accomplishment, and the result will be the same. For the fatal power of the media is to confer instant celebrity upon anyone, anyone at all, simply through exposure to all those millions of people. And once such celebrity is attained, the ability to influence, to control, the thoughts and actions of those millions follows automatically. It is entirely conceivable, given these premises, that an imbecile or a madman can with luck and the proper handling be presented as a sufficiently charismatic personality to be mistaken for a man of wisdom, a potential leader, a culture god.

It is just this diabolical possibility that creates the dramatic situation of *Being There.* Like Orwell in *1984,* Kosinski has imagined what might result if existing social conditions were developed to their logical conclusions, and he has chosen for a protagonist exactly the sort of man who would exemplify those conclusions in their full absurdity and horror. There is a deadly appropriateness in the fact that this man, who is initially called simply Chance, actually *is* a mental defective, a man totally without history and public identity who, as the story proceeds, is literally created as a person and personage because of qualities attributed to him by others.

Since he is incompetent to make his way in the world, Chance has been confined from birth—in his case, an event of the purest chance—in the mansion of his guardian known to him as the Old Man. Hence, there exists no documentary evidence of any kind to prove that he has ever been alive. He has no birth certificate, driver's license, checkbook, or medical insurance card. He has never been arrested, paid taxes, been to a doctor, or once ventured outside the walls of the Old Man's garden which he spends his days tending. His view of experience has been formed exclusively on his contact with his plants and flowers and what he has been able to learn through incessantly watching television. In fact, the process of watching is his primary mode of engaging reality, and reality exists for him only so long as the images remain before his eyes on the screen. When the set is turned off, the images die, and with them the people, places, and events which they represent.

Chance lives in this way for many years and eventually grows into a tall, handsome man who speaks well but simply and who makes a most attractive appearance when dressed in the Old Man's expensive clothes. But then the Old Man dies; Chance is expelled into the world; and what follows is a series of events as accidental as his birth. He is befriended by the beautiful wife of Benjamin Rand, one of the most powerful financiers in the country. Because she misunderstands when he says he is Chance the gardener, she assumes that his name is Chauncey Gardiner and that, judging by his appearance, he must be a successful businessman. Her husband is also impressed by Chance because, in addition to looking prosperous, he seems to possess remarkable self-confidence and a rare quality of inner serenity. Then when in response to a question about his background Chance speaks in the only language he knows, the imagery of the growth and decay of plant life, Rand assumes he is speaking metaphorically and credits him with great wisdom. Shortly thereafter, the President of the United States visits Rand in his home and invites Chance to give his opinion on the state of the national economy. Again his words are taken to be oracular:

> "In a garden," he said, "growth has its season. There are spring and summer, but there are also fall and winter. And then spring and summer again. As long as the roots are not severed, all is well and all will be well." . . .
>
> "I must admit, Mr. Gardiner," the President said, "that what you've just told us is one of the most refreshing and optimistic statements I've heard in a very, very long time."

The President quotes Chance's remarks in a widely publicized speech, and at once Chance is identified from coast to coast as an extremely influential economic adviser. He is invited to appear on television and is an instant success. Viewers are charmed by his good looks, his voice, and what they assume to be the prophetic nature of his banalities. At the end, after having achieved international reputation, Chance is seriously proposed as the running mate of a presidential candidate just because he has no history and therefore no record of good or bad accomplishment that might affect the purity of his public image. His sole qualifications—and they are more than sufficient—are that " 'He's personable, well-spoken, and he comes across well on TV.' "

It is to Kosinski's great credit that in treating material of this kind he avoided the temptation, which might have been overwhelming, to fall into the stereotypical anti-utopian stance made fashionable by Huxley and Orwell. He never provides a direct view of the sociological horror that is so clearly his true subject. Instead, he allows the tragicomic story of Chance to create, through its power of metaphorical suggestiveness, the effect of that spiritually anesthetized world in which such absurd events might well become commonplace. And Chance's story is so straightforwardly told, so barren of adornment, that these very qualities preserve it from the charge of implausibility. One reads it as one might read a fairy tale, knowing that it is not a realistic description of life, but sensing also that it is a frighteningly real symbolic abstraction of life. For *Being There* exists simultaneously on the levels of fiction and fact, fantasy and contemporary history. It is a novel ingeniously conceived and endowed with some of the magical significance of myth.

The Devil Tree

Pulp-Fiction Style, Pop-Psychology Jargon, and a Genuinely Sadistic Imagination

ROBERT ALTER

When Jerzy Kosinski's "The Painted Bird" first appeared in 1965, one could not easily judge whether it was, in the language of the blurbs, a searing indictment of humanity, or whether the real horrors of Nazi-occupied Europe had somehow served as the occasion for the excesses of a peculiarly sadistic imagination. The evidence of Kosinski's two subsequent novels was not reassuring. "Steps" is scarcely a novel at all but rather a series of discontinuous erotic jottings, sometimes brutal, generally deficient in feeling, and finally repetitious. "Being There" is the sketchy design of a fantasy that even with denser novelistic realization would strain credulity beyond limit—the four-day metamorphosis of an illiterate mental defective into one of the most powerful and admired men in America.

Kosinski's latest novel unfortunately demonstrates even more clearly the thinness and abstraction with which he conceives both humanity in general and fictional characters; his imagination here slips again and again into unpleasant self-indulgence or sheer slackness. Like "Being There," this book is built on a fantasy of power. Jonathan James Whalen, the protagonist, is sole heir to one of the largest fortunes in America. In a very brief span, he manages to flunk out of Yale, run through several mistresses on three continents with a few memorable whores in between, pick up and painfully kick an opium habit in Rangoon, then return to take over his father's vast conglomerate.

At home, he tears around in a Ford with a 12-cylinder Italian engine lurking under the hood, and he seems to take special delight in allowing himself, incognito in compromising circumstances, to be seized by brutal cops—people with power are invariably, obscenely brutal in Kosinski—whom he

Reprinted from *New York Times Book Review,* 11 February 1973, 2–3.

then dismays by flashing evidence of his enormous wealth and influence. At the end, he reconciles himself to becoming a captain of industry like his unlamented dad, ingeniously murders the people who are the second largest shareholders in his corporation, hires a team of experts to make him a world-champion skier and, in the fragmentary conclusion (a partial reversion to the mode of "Steps") contracts a mysterious and, no doubt, symbolic illness.

Now, fairytale fantasy versions of contemporary life may be perfectly engaging if, as in Mailer's "An American Dream," they are imagined with verve. "The Devil Tree," however, is a dismal disappointment because from beginning to end it is a loose web of stylistic and cultural clichés. Kosinski's prose, with its series of short sentences occasionally embellished by an elaborate simile, runs readily to the characteristic vice of "simple" styles, which is to fall into the hackneyed formulas of mass journalism and pulp fiction.

A distraught young woman is described, perhaps for the ten-thousandth time, with "her face . . . very flushed and wet with tears." From a moving car at night one sees "swaying elms which arched high above the road" while in front of the driver "the highway and alley of trees seemed to disappear into darkness." A subway train entering a station "roared to a stop," and since such clichés often come in pairs, "the doors hissed open." A wobbly character must be said to have "stumbled exhausted into the bedroom." At times, the use of a pulp formula even produces an inadvertently comic effect, as when the narrator, confusing an account of loose bowels with a bad report of a boxing match, writes, "Diarrhea kept me pinned to the toilet."

Far more pervasive and deadly are the clichés drawn from the popular culture of psychotherapy. Jonathan Whalen is embarked, as the dustjacket lyricist puts it, on a "quest for self," and one of the means through which he attempts this is a confused hybrid of encounter group and group therapy. His vocabulary, perhaps infected by this involvement, instead of bringing us closer to the particular feel of his individual experience, is a cloud of vapid clichés from the new American world of the psychologically oriented. Whalen tells us quite baldly, and uninterestingly, "I still suffer from my father's rejection and my mother's indifference." He actually describes his relationship to his first girlfriend in terms like these: "The barriers that exist between Karen and me derive from her resistance to commitment."

He constantly mouths the most worn therapeutic formulas about acceptance, insecurity, sense of unworthiness, exposing the real self, reaching someone "on that level," destroying defenses, being "aware of my reaction"; and he is not above the most barbaric therapoid jargon, as when he talks about "not structuring my feelings to gain another's approval." In all this, moreover, there is no sign that the author himself has imagined the psychological and spiritual predicament of his character in any terms other than these clichés.

Kosinski has been hailed by some enthusiasts as an heir to Kafka and Céline, but the modernism of "The Devil Tree" is of the most derivative kind imaginable. In essence, it is a rehashing in pop-psychological vocabulary, occasionally spiced by sadistic violence, of many familiar notes from underground long since articulated far more profoundly by the masters of modern literature. Like Dostoevsky's anti-hero, but with none of his psychological dynamism, Whalen is "pushing {him} self to extremes in order to discover {his} many selves," pursuing an illusory dream of absolute freedom, desiring a connection with people but despising anyone imperceptive enough to like him.

He scarcely exists as a realized character, and the human figures among whom he moves are no more than crude cartoons, yet he can say, "My most private, real self is violently antisocial—like a lunatic chained in a basement, grunting and pounding the floor while the rest of his family, the respectable ones, sit upstairs ignoring the tumult." This flat assertion of the secret anarchic self, after Nietzsche and Freud, after Dostoyevsky, Conrad, Kafka, Mann and so many others, is hardly news, while even the symbolic image of the lunatic locked up in a room of the respectable house was long ago imagined much better by a novelist named Charlotte Brontë.

Last Brave Wish to Try Everything

GEOFFREY WOLFF

The title's tree is a topsy-turvy thing. Cursed, its branches are buried in the ground and its roots wave stupidly at the sun and sky. So, as this tight parable shows, might perfect freedom turn inside-out, raising, in its insistence upon perfection, its own limits, its own prison walls. The power to break through to utter liberty in this instance comes from money, that most American of fuels. Kosinski's primary actor is Jonathan Whalen, young heir to a grand steel fortune. His means are limitless: before he comes into his estate he receives (and fails to make do on) $300,000 a year.

It's not enough. It's never enough. Jonathan roams the earth, inflicting himself on his victims, suffering this and that unscratchable itch, complaining. His father was indifferent to him. So he flunks out of Yale, does drugs, plays at cruelty and revenge, buys things, manipulates. It's not enough. He tries an encounter group: "No one understands anybody else. We are wandering around in dark caves, holding our little private candles, hoping for some great illumination."

The illumination is petty, a lighting up of limits, everywhere boundaries. Not even that ultimate, most totalitarian act, murder itself, can legislate Jonathan Whalen's freedom to do what he will, be what he will. He has a girl friend and sometime lover, sometime lesbian, sometime Doppelgänger named Karen: "She said she would like to go abroad and wear silk pajamas and wander the earth, sleeping with everyone she desires, making love in threesomes and foursomes, trying everything."

In common with the generality of Kosinski's constructions, the bite of this passage is worse than its bark. Notice the terrifying wish to wander, the way the ordonnance of wishes wanders, the bleak futility of the last brave wish to *try everything*. In accordance with the laws of Kosinski's demonology there is a passive character to her desires. She says she would manipulate, but the music of her declaration sounds soft and sad, as though she is being manipulated, which of course she is, and not only by her author.

Jonathan Whalen might be her twin. On the nod much of the time, a man of such silences as Kosinski's striking blank spaces might imply, "he was

Reprinted from *Washington Post Book World,* 25 March 1973, 3, 10.

his own event," an event unmarked by all save those he injures. "I remember how, as a boy, I used to collect the cork tips of my father's cigarettes and stick them in my stamp albums. I believed they contained his unspoken words, which one day would explain everything." Such passages have given a few of the critics of this novel liberty to misconstrue Kosinski's intention, to misread, willfully, *The Devil Tree* as a soap opera about a poor little rich boy.

Fact is, Kosinski barely contains his contempt for Jonathan and Karen. He does contain it, in part because his manner is so calculated, so empty of bombast, so stingy. He writes his novels as though they cost a thousand dollars a word, and a misplaced or misused locution would cost him his life. The grand thing about his prose is its shocking coolness. The ghastly thing about his characters is their shocking coolness.

If Kosinski's settings are often unspecified, out of time and place, out of fully realized circumstances, he trusts us to hang flesh on his skeletons. His first novel, *The Painted Bird,* is an allegory of brutality assembled from the wreckage of Kosinski's wartime childhood in Eastern Poland. It passes in the pitch dark of perfect inhumanity, among peasant people beyond the reach of the terrible consolations of civilization (among which must be counted the systemized murder committed in the name of human engineering by the totalitarian state). The reader is meant to manure the novel's barren soil with the experience of Western culture, and then to watch the deadly nightshade grow.

His next fiction, *Steps,* is his cruelest, and most perfectly wrought. It aims to speculate on the nature of evil itself. At its best it refuses the help of such props as historical or psychological environments. A man is set loose (prefiguring *The Devil Tree*) to make his way in the world, and to make his own world. And his example shows that if the primitive society of *The Painted Bird* is merciless, if the technological society of the totalitarian state is perverse, man uprooted, at large, is a monster without equal.

Being There, Kosinski's third novel, is gentler, more reflective, an almost comic experience of a character named Chance who tends a garden and watches television, whose platitudes finally elevate him to the vice-presidency of our particular country, who cannot read or write. He is like the plants he tends: "it cannot help growing, and its growth has no meaning, since a plant cannot reason or dream."

Which returns us to Jonathan Whalen. His wealth, emblem of his freedom, is just such an idle vegetable thing, just such a monster, just such a perverted, upside-down growth. It feeds upon itself, asserts itself, holds its own territory, absurdly flails its roots. These are legends and emblems at the heart of our matter. Americans have confused the accumulation of wealth with Election. Americans have confused liberty with license to manipulate. American society, so this novel seems to show, is indeed a poor little rich boy, upside-down.

New Tree, Old Roots [Review of Revised and Expanded *The Devil Tree*]

BARBARA TEPA LUPACK

Jerzy Kosinski, one of the most significant writers in America today, recently published a "new" novel, the revised and expanded version of his fourth novel, *The Devil Tree.* Since the revision contains most of the original characters and situations, it naturally invites comparison with the earlier version, published in 1973. Yet such comparison reveals that the new *Devil Tree* is a different and distinctly better fiction that deserves separate critical treatment as well.

Both versions of *The Devil Tree* are, like Kosinski's third novel and screenplay, *Being There,* a contemporary American fable of power. The central character is Jonathan Whalen, a poor little rich boy whose money can buy him everything except happiness. Whalen is, in many senses, the incarnation of the American dream: the heir to one of the largest industrial empires in America, he exists on a huge monthly trust allowance. His adventures in the course of the novels find him flunking out of Yale, running through whores and mistresses on several continents, becoming an opium addict, and getting involved in other incidental nefarious activities, like participating in group therapy and murdering a middle-aged couple who are the second largest shareholders of his corporation.

Yet for all his money and freedom, Jonathan is unsatisfied. Hopelessly entangled in his search for self, he symbolically becomes the baobab or "devil tree," whose branches are its roots and whose roots are its branches. It is tempting, as Phillip Corwin suggests, to extend the novel's image of rootlessness into other dimensions as a metaphor for American society, America itself having been characterized by more than one historian as a nation without true roots, a country with an inadequate sense of historical tradition.[1] It is even more tempting—and perhaps accurate as well—to apply the symbolism to the situation of modern man, who—alienated from the present and unable

Reprinted from *The Polish Review* 29, nos. 1–2 (1984): 147–53. Reprinted by permission of the journal.

to come to terms with the past—lacks the existential capacity for affirmation in an absurd world.

In reviewing the original *Devil Tree,* some critics argued that, while "Kosinski has tried to transplant whole the terrifying consciousness of Nazi-occupied Europe between 1939 and 1945 to the United States during the 1960's,"[2] the novel failed to create the horror that was central to earlier and more successful novels, like *The Painted Bird* and *Steps.* Kosinski himself stated in an interview that "I see no essential difference between World War II and any other traumatic reality. For example, I know many people whose childhood in the United States was in its own way just as traumatic as that of millions of Central Europeans."[3] Part of Jonathan's "traumatic reality" surely involves his childhood, especially his tenuous relationship with his father, the novel's Whalen Senior, whose image hangs heavily over the entirety of the narrative and who overshadows all of Jonathan's actions. Unable to find himself or to accept the real world, Jonathan attempts to create new worlds for himself. "In defense I learned to retreat to a world of fantasies in which I was always the victor. . . . I was continually drifting in and out of situations, trying to escape from myself and my family," he states. The fantasizing takes several forms—drugs, easy sex, travel—all of them providing some temporary escape. Jonathan's erratic dabblings in the drug culture, reminiscent of Burroughs' *Naked Lunch,* for a time dispel his inhibitions; the use of drugs "gives me something to blame things on later." Yet this too ultimately proves unsuccessful. Withdrawing from his addiction, Jonathan realizes that "once more [he was] creating an artificial system of guilt from which there was no escape." Sex provides another escape; through sex, Jonathan feels he can assert power and thus assume a new role. "It's all right if I don't love you," he claims, "but I can't stand your not loving me, because I don't have any power over you." The sex-power theory also fails; he cannot control his girlfriend, Karen, and ends up in the company of prostitutes, who ironically wield power over him by charging for their services. Like the Henry Miller hero of the fifties, Jonathan literally makes his way through several continents yet never succeeds in satisfying himself psychologically.

Thus, for the duration of the narrative, Jonathan blames his parents for their rejection and indifference, Karen for her resistance to commitment, the encounter group for fostering alienation, and the world at large for its hostility and tendency to instill paranoia. In its treatment of Jonathan's rationalizations, the early *Devil Tree* is a weak novel, which often dissolves into the psychobabble of analysis and the esoterica of popular Freudian psychology without ever having produced any motivation for Jonathan's decadent behavior or solution to his rootless deviltry.[4] As Robert Alter wrote: "*The Devil Tree* is a dismal disappointment because from beginning to end it is a loose web of stylistic and cultural clichés. Kosinski's prose falls into the hackneyed formulas of mass journalism and pulp fiction. Far more pervasive and deadly are the clichés drawn from the popular culture of psychotherapy. Jonathan's vocabulary, perhaps infected by this involvement [encounter group and group therapy], instead of bringing us closer to the particular feel of his individual experiences, is a cloud of vapid clichés from the new American world of the psychologically oriented. He constantly mouths the most worn therapeutic formulas about acceptance, insecurity, sense of unworthiness, exposing the real self, being 'aware of my reaction'; he is not above the most barbaric therapoid jargon, as when he talks about 'not structuring my feelings to gain another's approval.' "[5]

Although, like Kosinski's other protagonists, Whalen is an outsider—the typical, alienated anti-hero in search of inner peace—he disintegrates somewhat as a character in the original version of the novel. As Ivan Sanders observed, "Compared to the experience of the boy in *The Painted Bird* or the narrator of *Steps,* his vicissitudes seem like a series of meaningless charades. He is trapped in his own, utterly decadent sensibility."[6] His own flatness as a character, compounded by his narcissism, senseless brutality, and sterile materialism,[7] hardly makes his problems seem compelling. Furthermore, his flatness, combined with the static characters—almost caricatures—around him, results in the reader's inability to achieve or maintain a suspension of disbelief,[8] which is necessary for this fairy tale of the superrich.

There is, however, a considerable stylistic and psychological distance between the original novel and the revised one. As Kosinski himself comments in the "Author's Note":

> When I wrote this novel initially, I felt restricted by the proximity of its story to the environment and events of my recent past decade. This might account for the cryptic tone of the novel's first version.
>
> Now, years later, in this revised and expanded edition, I have felt free to reinstate all the additional links that bound Jonathan James Whalen to those whom he loved.

In the revised edition, Jonathan has more motivation for his behavior and therefore, in context, becomes more plausible as a character. His search for self emerges as the novel's significant central motif and unifies the seemingly diverse fragments of Jonathan's experience into a whole—though a rather precarious whole. Like Abraham Joshua Heschel, quoted in the book's epigraph and again on the concluding page, Jonathan grows conscious of "the most important ingredient of self-reflection, the preciousness of [his] own existence," and he struggles to gain control of the seemingly uncontrollable environment. His adventures—diverse as they may initially seem—no longer appear merely random and discontinuous as they did in the original but instead become deliberate and progressive attempts to impose an order on existence. (He therefore is reminiscent of other Kosinski heroes: the young protagonist of *The Painted Bird,* who learns to control in order to survive; the narrator of *Steps,* an outsider who is an exile in his own land; the passive media messiah of *Being There,* who unknowingly becomes the agent for order in a weak and chaotic society; Tarden of *Cockpit,* for whom surveillance provides superiority; Levanter of *Blind Date,* who sees himself fated to act as an avenger of society's wrongs; Fabian of *Passion Play,* whose quest is for order amidst the confusion of modern morality.)

Jonathan's quest is for awareness and an understanding of the chance elements that surround him and sometimes threaten to engulf him. When Jonathan wants to learn how to ski, it is because the sport will allow him to confront the elements of nature on a "one-to-one" level, which he admits has never been his forte. On the slopes, no expensive equipment will compensate for the requisite skills; so he must be able to act immediately and instinctively. When he considers taping Karen's conversations while they are apart, he is attempting to impose a mechanical order on her nature—an order that her frenetic lifestyle and their relationship in general defy. And when he lets the Howmets' dinghy float away, part of an elaborate "accident" that he has carefully planned, he is trying to exact a sinister but righteous revenge for his godparents' destructive and malicious behavior.

Yet, in some ways, the very nature of Jonathan's quest prohibits his success. For if Jonathan's life—and modern life in general—is like the devil tree, with its confusion of roots and branches, pasts and futures, there can be no realization of actions, no linear progressions. Only circles exist, like the circular prophecy of Abraham Joshua Heschel or the many mirror images of the novel that "split, enlarge, and multiply images"—and reflect and regress ad infinitum. Thus, the consequence of Jonathan's action is forever the antithesis of his intention. For all of his talk of "man against himself and nature," he can never become a master skier naturally but only through the most mechanical of means: crash programs of "specially constructed devices to *protect* you"; a battery-powered gyroscope that would have to "be *ordered* right away"; and two assistants, two video cameramen, and professional downhillers available "*for hire*" immediately. He never tapes Karen or otherwise controls her; rather, he gives her a diary written during his drug days and thus ironically allows her one more way to wield control over him.

> Now that I have given Karen all the notes I scribbled during my travels abroad, I always wonder whether an incident from my past could one day alter what she has come to think of me. Since I have no idea exactly what that incident could be, perhaps I should have left out of my reminiscences anything that might sound nauseating or foul—or anything dull or banal.

And his revenge on the Howmets is provoked by their earlier manipulation of his mother, of his corporation, and even of himself. To avenge those whom his godparents victimized, he makes his godparents victims. Yet almost immediately after their demise, he mysteriously becomes victim to some disease. The circle continues.

And Jonathan's wish to control and to order remains as impossible as permanence with the unpredictable Karen (to whom he is attracted because she resists commitment, refuses his wealth, and is "in control"); as elusive as the misty lights of Lake Geneva in the novel's ending; as contradictory as his own state of mind:

> I have steadily progressed from experiencing the sensations of being alive to expressing my thoughts about such sensations, as if pure expression were now the only original experience that I'm still capable of. But because language belongs to everyone, I suspect that whatever I capture in crowds becomes a fictional account—of me, as well as of someone else. There must be a place beyond words—a place of pure experience—to which I wish I could return.

Nowhere, however, is the circularity of events more evident or the symbol of the baobab more brilliantly realized than in the slow recognition that Jonathan, in escaping the ghosts of his family, becomes more like them. Like his mother, who dulls herself to the pain of reality with her arsenal of drugs, Jonathan escapes his father's legacy for a time and turns to narcotics. Yet, as he comes of age, he returns—a stranger in a familiar land—to command his father's commanding fortune. Repeatedly, he notes the differences between the elder Whalen and himself:

> My father worked himself to death. At the peak of his career, his heart, unable to keep up with his unlimited drive to compete, stopped. Because my drive is limited, I could not even bring myself to go to war—the epitome of competition—since that would have unreasonably increased the chances of my death. My father's death seemed like destiny's corporate refusal to extend the loan of time he still needed to accomplish his task; my own would probably appear as an outright refusal to take out such a loan. Quite appropriately, Horace Sumner Whalen had been mourned by all who were in his debt. But if I, Jonathan James Whalen, were to die right now . . . no one would mourn the loss.

What he fails to note, however, are the remarkable similarities. Two particularly powerful scenes in the revised novel illustrate parallels between the two men.

> My fear of violence began when as a boy I lay in bed and listened to my father rage. I couldn't bear it, and I think everyone, including my mother, my governess, even Anthony, felt the same way. Those few times I dared to disagree with my father, he struck me even if others were around. One night in our summer house, I wakened to the howling of Mesabi, my little dog. I put on my bathrobe and went outside. In the garden I found Mesabi with its legs tied together, and towering above it was my father, kicking the animal again and again. Seeing me, he explained the dog had to be punished for disobedience and that pain would break its future will to resist its master. I watched in silence, torn by pity for the dog, anger at my father, and hatred for my own weakness.
>
> •

> Anthony was once my father's valet. I recently asked him to lunch. During the meal Anthony revealed to me why my father had fired him. One of Anthony's duties was to prepare my father's shaving cream every morning and, once a week, to insert a new blade in his razor. To prove his faith in the quality of products made of American steel, my father always insisted on shaving for seven straight days with the same American-made steel blade. Then one day Anthony overheard my mother complaining to my father that for the last three days he had not seemed smoothly shaved. From then on, without telling my father, Anthony put a new blade in the razor every other day.
>
> One morning my father turned to him and said, "Yesterday I shaved with a blade that had a slight defect at one end. Still, it was a perfectly good blade, and it should serve me until the end of the week. What happened to it?"
>
> "I changed the blade, Mr. Whalen," replied Anthony.
>
> "What for?" asked my father.
>
> "I thought you might need a fresh one," said Anthony.
>
> "I do not," my father replied. "Bring back the old blade."
>
> Under the scrutinizing gaze of my father, Anthony admitted that he had thrown the blade away and that he had been changing the blades every other day for some time. When he finished speaking, my father turned to him and said calmly, "If that's what you think of our steel, Anthony, you needn't work for me anymore. My secretary will prepare your paycheck, and after you've packed, the car will take you to the station." Then, without another word to the man who for years had served him like a faithful dog, my father returned to his shaving.
>
> . . . "Have you decided what you're going to do with yourself, Jonathan?" Anthony asked me. "Are you going into business? You're still young, and it would be a real pity to waste yourself doing nothing—or doing the wrong thing." . . . When he said how much I resembled my father, I became angry. I wanted to tell him that was a lie, as he of all people—a black man, the archetypical American servant—should know. But I checked myself. I started instead to talk about some of the women I had had, asking him pointed questions about his own sex life and telling him increasingly realistic stories. He laughed at first, but as the episodes became more lewd and violent, he began to grow uncomfortable, and exhausted by the thought of even the possibility of such adventures, he slumped in his chair. I don't know why, but perversely I continued until I was sure he realized that my life was beyond his experience.

As the many Calvinist references, several of which were added to the novel's second version, suggest, Jonathan is predestined to inherit his parents' sins along with their wealth. Despite his attempts at total depravity, he is nevertheless elect to the American dream of success and money, twisted though it may be—like the devil tree—and unable to provide him with the spiritual satisfaction he craves. Paradoxically, as Jonathan says, he is an exile from that same dream. Yet this seems to be precisely Kosinski's point: that such paradox is inherent in the American dream itself and implicit in American society.

By Kosinski's own acknowledgment, most of his fiction is based on personal experience. *The Devil Tree* was no doubt inspired, at least in part, by Kosinski's arrival in the United States from Eastern Europe, his coming of age among America's jet set, and his subsequent sense of physical isolation and spiritual exile. "The random succession of pain and joy, wealth and poverty, persecution and approbation [in] his own life, often as eventful as those of his fictional creations,"[9] are similar to the paradoxes Jonathan must come to terms with. There are additional biographical links and personal experiences in the new novel: in addition to mentioning his late wife by name, Kosinski plays with the reader by working into the text of the novel the titles of some of his other fictions and essays—Whalen Senior is called "the lone wolf" of American business; Jonathan dines at the fashionable disco, Cockpit; a friend of Jonathan's meets his wife on a game show called Blind Date; and a former lover of Karen's friend, a midwestern professor, writes his dissertation on passion plays. Many of the more familiar of Kosinski's literary preoccupations appear in the novel as well—concern about the precision of language; anxiety over and interest in eavesdropping and electronic surveillance; references to photography, skiing, excessive television viewing by the American public; even the motif of the suffering child/suffering animal.

The structure of the new *Devil Tree* ignores the conventional narrative in favor of a montage effect of images and impressions, through which Kosinski creates a kind of verbal photography. Each literary passage is like a still frame, intense and unique, yet simultaneously a fragment of a larger cinematographic sequence. In this way, Kosinski is able to convey the sometimes disjointed but intricately interconnected movements of Jonathan's mind as he seeks to define his sense of being.

The new *Devil Tree,* vastly superior to the original, is an interesting story, a good novel, and an important link in the cycle of Kosinski's fiction.

Notes

1. Phillip Corwin, "Evil Without Roots," *Nation* 216 (30 April 1973), 568.
2. *Ibid.*
3. George A. Plimpton and Rocco Landesman, *Paris Review* 54 (Summer 1972), 90.
4. Corwin, 567.
5. Robert Alter, "Pulp-Fiction Style, Pop-Psychology Jargon, and a Genuinely Sadistic Imagination," *New York Times Book Review,* 11 Feb. 1973, 3.
6. Ivan Sanders, "The Gifts of Strangeness: Alienation and Creation in Jerzy Kosinski's Fiction," *The Polish Review* 19.3–4 (Autumn–Winter 1974), 181.
7. J. B. Kiley, Rev. of *The Devil Tree, Critic* 31 (May–June 1973), 80.
8. Alter writes: "He scarcely exists as a realized character, and the human figures among whom he moves are no more than crude cartoons" (2).
9. From "On Kosinski," in *The Devil Tree: Revised and Expanded* (New York: Bantam, 1981), 207.

Cockpit

Jerzy Kosinski Working Out Past Imperfections

JONATHAN BAUMBACH

Jerzy Kosinski's first novel, "The Painted Bird" (1965), was internationally admired and generally misread as a harrowing social document, so that when the vastly more difficult and abstract "Steps" appeared in 1968 reviewers, looking in the wrong direction, were hard pressed to make sense of it. If "Steps" was an enigma, "Being There" (1970) and "The Devil Tree" (1973), disguised variations on the same themes, must have added to the mystification. The fact is that all of Kosinski's novels are extremely similar in method and impulse and extend into one another as if they were one long, fantastic, autobiographical nightmare, manipulations in slightly varied forms of the same obsessive materials.

"Cockpit" is a return to the seemingly random, picaresque mode of "Steps" and is in many ways a more audacious and elaborate version of it. Kosinski's novels are always more or less episodic, but "Cockpit" is a dazzling succession of bizarre, mostly sado-masochistic, erotic anecdotes, without the resting place of chapter breaks. It is composed of pieces of the narrator's life and is, in a sense, his debriefing and confession, his exorcism of waking nightmares. The pseudonymous Tarden is a former agent of the Service, a C.I.A.-like organization; he moves through the void of a self-created world, changing roles as the seasons of vengeance or survival demand. Tarden's experiences, rather than furthering the plot or developing characters as in more conventional fiction, furnish the empty spaces of this novel.

Tarden tells his story, or his succession of stories, in no apparent order: one incident seemingly recalls another ("I did not want to tell you about my past, I wanted you to re-live it"). Incidents accumulate into experience, evoking a dimly recognizable world (always the same underworld no matter what the ostensible locale), in which reward and punishment, eros and violence, survival and doom are interdependent realities. The power of Kosinski's vision comes from a relentless disorientation, the world held together by an overwhelming comprehension of its anarchy.

Tarden has become wealthy by accumulating valuable perfume and snuff boxes while an operative in the Service and is now free to indulge himself—a secret agent in his own service—in adventures and revenges. He amuses himself by entering into the lives of strangers, helping some, destroying others, a self-made godhead. To avoid being tracked down and killed—he is the only man to have defected from the Service and survived—he maintains similarly furnished apartments in various major cities, each rented under a different assumed name. With seemingly limitless wealth, without specific identity, Tarden has the power to take on whatever role he chooses, vulnerable only to chance and his own mortality.

In the opening episode, Tarden observes a woman he had been living with make love to another man in his apartment—he has set her up by pretending to go on a trip and then presents her with the photographic evidence of her infidelity. It is a mild if nasty vengeance, a display of power almost for it own sake. The woman, humiliated, steps out of his life. Toward the close of "Cockpit," Tarden murders a woman in the cruelest possible way, through exposure to excessive radiation, for violating an agreement she has made with him. Although the episode at the end takes place in chronological time not much later than the one at the start, it marks the extraordinary psychic distance we have traveled through this novel. Although "Cockpit" seems to speed inconsequentially from anecdote to anecdote, the stakes increase radically without our immediate awareness of the change in scale.

With its mix of poetic justice and whimsical viciousness, "Cockpit" undermines us, strips us of our distance. We share the pleasure of Tarden's vengeance, and so are implicated in his malign and unpredictable violences. He is a man of shifting moral coloration, like all of us (though more so). His unemotionality forces on us the burden of feeling he refuses.

In the context of Kosinski's body of work, "The Painted Bird" now seems different from the book that reviewers invented for us when it appeared 10 years ago. Much of that novel's spectacular success came from its real or imagined political implications; we tend to confuse literary seriousness with journalistic statement, are more interested in the final score than the process of the game. Compared in one place to "The Diary of Anne Frank," though it is difficult to imagine two works with less in common, "The Painted Bird" was perceived as an anatomy of Nazi cruelty. Horrific details are piled on one another—evil pervades the world as in a medieval play—while the child protagonist flees from one awful peasant village to another. The boy is a cipher through much of the novel (like the narrators of "Steps" and "Cockpit"), which comes to resemble a tour guide to a variety of evil experiences. In the end, however, he becomes something of a real character through a resolution of the plot that satisfies certain conventional novelistic expectations—he's reunited with his parents and regains his lost speech—and that seems a compromise, perhaps a necessary one, with the more complex impulse behind the work. The doomsday vision that informs most of "The Painted Bird" is the same vision that informs "Steps," "The Devil Tree" and "Cockpit," none of which deals, either explicitly or by implication, with the Nazi horror. Like the others, "The Painted Bird" is essentially surrealistic, an initiatory experience grounded in an imagined world, and is no less powerful and affecting for being what it is.

The episodic form of "The Painted Bird" is continued in Kosinski's later books, each to some extent recapitulating the structure of its predecessor. "Steps," a more spare and original work, is a replay of the same hellish obsessions, the further adventures (in a sense, certainly) of the same narrator, though with his identity erased and his world flattened into terrifying abstraction.

The third and least of Kosinski's novels, "Being There," seems an attempt to move outside the airlessness of the first two into demonstrably new terrain. A satiric parable, "Being There" lacks the weight and texture of Kosinski's earlier work. Told in the third person in a voice that never quite achieves the right pitch, the novel is an ironic success story, detailing the transformation of Chance, a gardener, whose view of the world has been wholly determined by television, into Chauncey Gardiner, wisdom speaker and Presidential adviser. His imposture is inadvertent, but Chance becomes what others perceive him to be. Identity in Kosinski's world exists solely in the eye of the beholder. To have your real self known is to be ultimately vulnerable. To have no self, no verifiable past, is the key to power and advancement.

Each new novel from Kosinski seems to be a perfecting or working out of something unrealized in an earlier work. "The Devil Tree," his fourth, picks up in ironic voice where "Being There" leaves off, though it transforms itself as it goes, looking forward at the close to the considerably darker landscape of "Cockpit." "The Devil Tree" is about one Jonathan Whalen, heir to one of America's fortunes; it alternates between satire and personal history, each mode undermining the authority of the other. An uneven, admirably ambitious book, full of misleading clues to itself, "The Devil Tree" is at once the most apparently personal and opaque of Kosinski's work.

"There is a place beyond words where experience first occurs to which I always want to return," confides Jonathan Whalen. "Cockpit" attempts a return to that place. In this book we are back with the role-shifting, vaguely sinister narrator of "Steps," a revenger and savior, manipulator of the forms of power. The voice again is matter-of-fact, in direct counterpoint to the events it describes. The man in the cockpit, the man in the driver's seat, keeps it up as best he can, though he is not always, for all his exertions, at the controls. Tarden, the only name we get, is a false identity, another disguise to keep the hero unknown to his enemies. Disguise is both literal and figurative in this book (as in the others), a means of survival and a metaphor for identity. Almost all behavior in Kosinski's world is theater, a cover, a role to protect some anonymous deeply buried self. Like Melville's confidence man, Tarden is a different person in each of his disguises. Only his flat, denatured voice remains constant and gives the novel its fragile unity.

Tarden is a gifted mimic, an expert at role playing even as a child. When he is 12 years old his family is relocated by the State and forced to sign away the rights to their home. (Like the narrator of "Steps," like Kosinski himself, Tarden grows up in a Communist country and later flees to the United States.) Angry at his father and those like him who permit themselves to be pushed around, the boy picks names at random from the phone book and, imitating the voice of the official that called his home, orders people to travel to the capital to invented government offices to sign away the rights to their property. The episode is exemplary. Tarden parodies arbitrary authority by internalizing it, by becoming in himself the vile, accountable universe.

Tarden's god-like role, Kosinski makes us aware, is like a novelist's, like Kosinski's in creating this novel. Readers and characters are similarly manipulated, initiated at their own expense into the anarchy of experience. An abrasive and risky book, "Cockpit" defines itself (as Kosinski does his hero) by the suicidal chances it takes, carrying throughout (as does Tarden) the lethal pellet of its own destruction, brilliantly defying the limitations of its form.

[Review of] *Cockpit*

IVAN SANDERS

Jerzy Kosinski frightens a lot of people. They sense impenetrable evil and an equivocal authorial attitude behind his invitingly simple fictions. Unwilling to ponder the ambiguities, they charge the author with complicity instead. Actually, Kosinski is a fictionist of the first order whose stunning verbal snapshots of violence and terror bespeak restraint, modesty even. The author knows full well that the towering evils of twentieth-century history put the most fervid imagination to shame, so instead of trying to deal with such things as totalitarian terror, racial madness, technological dehumanization in a comprehensive, realist manner, he dwells on minor atrocities, casual cruelties, private aberrations, but in a way that always hints at the historical novels inspiring them. His first novel, *The Painted Bird,* was a series of fanciful variations on the basic themes of Nazi inhumanity. In *Steps* we witness an individual's responses first to a harshly repressive, then to a chaotically permissive society. And Chance the gardener in the satiric *Being There* is at once the victim and hero of the electronic age. Kosinski's matter-of-fact articulation of the unspeakable, as well as his singular appreciation of the more elegant forms of physical and mental tortures, suggest to many an obviously antihumanist sensibility. Yet, his heroes are above all rugged individualists who cope with hostile reality by trying to understand, control, possess experience—verbally, visually, if not always physically.

In this sense, the hero of Kosinski's latest novel, *Cockpit,* is a composite of all of his previous characters. Like the protagonist of *Steps,* he is a rootless foreigner who recalls a youth spent in an oppressive Eastern European environment. Some of his more outrageous childhood memories bring to mind episodes from *The Painted Bird,* while his interest in photography, his endless fascination with recorded realities, reveal an affinity with the TV-worshipping hero of *Being There*. But most importantly, Tarden, like Kosinski's other characters, aims for total self-control. In a revealing reminiscence he tells us how shocked he was to discover as a child that wounds healed by themselves, independent of his will. "I hated the sense of an autonomous force in my body, determining what would happen to me." By forever testing the outer limits

Reprinted from *Commonweal,* 29 August 1975, 373–74.

of his (and others') endurance, he learns to manipulate not only his actions and thoughts, but his reflexes, his very instincts as well. "Since I cannot survive unless I can order every aspect of my existence," he says, "my mind exploits my body."

A former operative of the "Service," Tarden continues to live the elusive, self-sufficient life of an undercover agent, shuttling between continents and electronically fortified apartments, and devising frightful stunts with which to punish his enemies and reaffirm his own omnipotence. Insisting on absolute freedom for himself, the ex-spy nevertheless needs people if only to validate his freedom. He is thrilled to be able to manipulate others without their knowing it, but his much-cherished sense of inviolability rules out total enjoyment. Kosinski's hero is hungry for all forms of stimulation, but his fear of excessive involvement turns him invariably into a voyeur. Even when he is a full-fledged participant in a physical relationship, he derives greater pleasure from knowing he is in control than from yielding to his sexual impulses. He recalls how he frightened a girlfriend in high school by making her believe he was a sexual cripple. Actually, he had the unique ability to retract his organ and keep it hidden with the aid of a plastic-tipped metal clamp. He urged the girl to excite him just the same and tried himself to avoid having an erection which might snap the clamp. "As long as the clamp remained in place, I felt a bit of pain, but the sense of harnessed power made orgasm crude by comparison." Tarden's unremitting self-control makes him, necessarily, a cold and brutal man, though unexpectedly tender responses reestablish his humanity. Towards the end of the book he relates the bizarre escapades of a pathetic lecher, and then dwells lovingly on the old man's fantasies about living in a clean, serene Swiss village.

It might be naive to treat Tarden as a conventional, realistically conceived character. As in *Steps,* questions of motivation and credibility are beside the point; it's the episodes themselves that are important, the preternaturally sharp images, which intimate darker secrets than they reveal. Ultimately we are made to contemplate not the perversity of a single individual but a world in which systematic intimidation and subversion can be accomplished neatly, tracelessly. When Tarden, as a child, sends scores of people on a wild-goose chase with phony telephone messages; when he terrifies supermarket-shoppers by injecting a chemical into cartons of food; when he has three derelicts gang up on a disloyal girlfriend, it becomes almost irrelevant that he *is* driven by a distorted sense of justice. Our attention is focused on the incidents: the graphic, disturbingly credible details, the mounting suspense, the devastating final revelation.

Of course these episodes could also be viewed as outlandish daydreams, wish-fulfillments, paranoid visions—lucky safety-valves for a perverted imagination. After reading some of the grosser passages, one has the awful feeling he is losing his capacity to be shocked, and then realizes with some annoyance that he has put up with shameless self-indulgence, the kind Philip Roth talks about in his recent collection of essays. In such writing the author glories in all that is "excessive, frivolous, or exhibitionistic." Kosinski is unique in being disciplined about his excesses; his prose is as precise and controlled as his hero. And he does fall back on simple expedients, on man's "natural weapons": his eyes, his memory, though ironically, in his new novel he also suggests the futility of unrelenting vigilance. His hero may remain in the driver's seat, the cockpit (Kosinski no doubt appreciates the varied connotations of the term), but his precautions and elaborate strategies become, after a while, pointless exertions. Tarden's final recollection is of an old disabled tank whose "corroded gun defiantly trains on trenches and machine-gun nests, long buried in the sands of a deserted beach."

Blind Date

Love and Death in New Jerzy

ARNOST LUSTIG

At the end of *Blind Date,* Jerzy Kosinski presents George Levanter, his hero, and a friend of his wife in conversation: " 'You are a survivor, George. The war. The Ruskies. Parking cars. You've survived it all. And look at you now.' He paused, as if to let the implication sink in. 'Married to Mary-Jane, the nicest girl there is, who also happens to be one of the richest widows in America, with the most powerful friends around.' 'Mary-Jane and I met on a blind date,' said Levanter. 'Sure you did, George,' he agreed quickly. 'But have all your survivals begun on blind dates?' "

George Levanter is a Russian emigré to America, where he builds his new home. He is never able to forget his roots, but he plays with life, takes risks, tries to be just in an unjust world; he tries to understand the ununderstandable, takes and gives; sets traps and escapes from those set for him by others. From adventure to adventure he tries to survive with meaning and grace, never completely sure that he has managed. Levanter is a storyteller; the novel is made up of his stories—some are beautiful, or shocking and beautiful.

In Kosinski's stories, just as in Dostoevski, whores are the only ones who are able to scorn all the money in a world where gold means so much. They sell themselves, if it comes down to that, but as acts of free will. As in Kosinski's other books, there is a lot of sex in the stories of George Levanter (and Kosinski plays an old writer's game with hints and bridges between the hero and the author). Sex is for Kosinski not only a mysterious, never fully discovered part of our lives, but also motive, action, and impact at the same time. For him sex operates as a fully or partly opened door to human nature, to human character. Through sex man reveals the truth of life to himself: who he is, what his life is about, and, at the same time, that with every other man or woman he is a different being. So, as in an old Greek legend that originally men and women were one and that only later they were separated, Kosinski

Reprinted from *Washington Post Book World,* 27 November 1977, E3.

feels that only together men and women can re-create a lost unity, never the same, ever various. For Kosinski, people discover in sex their courage as well as their fears, their "normalities" and "abnormalities," because—perhaps long before the beginning—in every male is an embryo of a female, and the other way around. Sex is the most reliable open door to the human soul, says Kosinski; through sex a person can most reliably reveal his image to himself, as well as to others.

In his new book, Kosinski proves that he is a skillful, full-blooded, fascinating storyteller. You can object that he is a nihilist, fatalist, biologist, existentialist, and God knows what else; you can compare him to Malaparte, Kafka, Goya, and who knows to whom, but he is definitely an original, authentic, unique voice. Deep below his stories there is an important meaning and a sincere message about the frightful world we are living in. His questions are the old, but never satisfactorily answered questions: What is man? What is our life really about? What to do in this world where one must be indifferent to avoid one shock after the other? In stressing these questions of human consciousness (as Adolf Hitler put it, "a Jewish invention, which cripples the human being just as well as circumcision cripples his body"), Kosinski is a very Jewish writer reminding us in almost every story in *Blind Date* that human invention is in jeopardy.

Since *The Painted Bird,* about a lost child in the cruelest parts and times of our world, Kosinski has been like a volcano erupting for 11 years. What if a catastrophe like the sinking of Atlantis would occur and these six books were the only testimony for future people, the only documents of our times? In *Blind Date* we can trace in many stories the author's quest for justice in the face of the blind irony which takes the best people to the prisons, to torture, to the loss of their lives. "Ideas don't perish in prison cells," Levanter says. "People do."

Levanter includes in his adventures his private, never publicly confessed war with injustice which is ever-present because the world got accustomed to it. Levanter never forgets what was unjust in his life, what he has witnessed; and neither does the author. He reminds us painfully and disturbingly of the need for justice.

Learning from the best writing of every era, Kosinski develops his own style and technique, trying to avoid the classical plot and trying not to get lost in a limitless and chaotic jungle without beginning, middle and end. His style is in harmony with his need to express new things about our life and the world we do live in, to express the inexpressible. Sometimes his way of writing and the structure of his book reminds one of a steam engine where energy grows to the point where it either explodes or moves forward. Accumulating stories of different, sometimes ambiguous meaning, giving to himself as well as to the reader the same chance for interpretation, he traces the truth in the deepest corners of our outdoor and indoor lives, of our outer appearance and our inner reality.

Many of the stories in *Blind Date* have three parts, as there are three dimensions of time: the present, the past and the future. Or, let us say, all dimensions of literary time, so that for every story in the present, we have another story about what preceded, which reveals the motives of the first, and then the story of the future, or what happened after—what was the result of the original motives and of the present. It works perfectly and beautifully.

Each new book by Kosinski raises a question: Where is he going to go from here? Every writer is dead with his latest book, because he gave all his blood, all his life into it, and he must be born again. Kosinski solves these literary problems in his own way, as far as we can judge from *Blind Date.* He moves the borderline of writing to more remote, still invisible and untouchable poles, in cold and in darkness. Doing so he enlarges the borders of the bearable.

As readers we have several reasons to be grateful to him. As writers we have from him many things to learn.

[Review of] *Blind Date*

DANIEL J. CAHILL

With such books as *Passages* and *Dress for Success,* the publishing marketplace is experiencing an unprecedented surge of books which purport to answer the ancient ethical question: "How Shall I Conduct My Life?" *Blind Date* is a fateful answer to that question—an answer which may be only dimly perceived, or if perceived, rejected because it demands a massive re-orientation and the ultimate admission of the randomness of human existence: destiny is written concurrently with each event in life. *Blind Date* is a guard against this powerful feeling of an "objective destiny."

The term, "blind date," is uniquely American in origin (in its European editions, Kosinski's novel will be titled *The Unknown Person*). *Blind Date* represents an encounter, filled with strangeness and multiple possibilities. Imaginative literature dramatizes life, but above all, it dramatizes man's ability to perceive his own condition for what it is: a drama, and he is the main protagonist—but only of the moment. That moment is his *Blind Date.*

Blind Date is the story of the adventures of George Levanter: the novel opens with a deceptive innocence: "When I was a school boy. . . ." Unlike the *Bildungsroman,* the reader is not marshalled through a series of developing events from which the hero emerges in independence and wholeness. Following a fictional technique which Kosinski has perfected in several of his previous novels (notably *Steps* and *Cockpit*), *Blind Date* moves in an erratic play of episodes, circular and spiral as Levanter's own memory. Its plot has the chance selectivity of our own memory, our randomness and inability to answer why we remember certain events and not others—and our reluctance to look for the principle of such ranking.

Levanter is an adventurer in life's events. He moves across international lines and inevitably seems to be situated at a place of maximum intensity. The early portion of the novel traces Levanter—in the tragic tense of dead event—as a young man, parting from his dying Mother with whom he has shared an incestuous relation to several periods when he was a young student attending Youth Movement Camp. His teenage friend, Oscar, instructs him in the art of rape. With an elaborate new sex vocabulary, Oscar "breaks the

Reprinted from *New Republic,* 11 March 1978, 34–35. Reprinted by permission.

eye" of his blind dates. Intrigued by the sensuous violence, Levanter becomes an able student of this new art of the twist, assaulting from behind a girl who remains nameless.

In a sudden shift of the remembered past, Levanter has accepted a post at Princeton where he meets Svetlana Alliluyeva, his next-door neighbor. "It can't be," he whispered. "The daughter of Stalin an American. It can't be." Transported to his new home in America, Levanter has many blind dates—encounters with the unique, the strange, the trivial. He meets the great Nobel-prize scientist Jacques Monod and the most tragic American, Charles Lindbergh. Interlarded with these encounters are episodes of an enormously trivial nature. The unwary reader is taken on a series of blind dates which underscore the essential fragmentation of human events—the discontinuousness of moments in the drama. Kosinski is absorbing the multitude of event/episode/encounter/person and imaginatively transmuting this flow of experience into the content of fiction. This sweep of blind dates has a powerful effect upon the reader because they seem to deny the process of selectivity in art—the very notion of art as shape, pattern, form, which will reveal a significant content. As the detached and disinterested author, Kosinski remains above and beyond the remembered world of George Levanter and it's through the heavily-laden memory of Levanter that the novel takes its shape, like a painting filled with shadows, each casting a peculiar tone of light and darkness in the final composition, creating its own reality. As always, Kosinski places a heavy burden upon the reader's imagination. "The episode—in its extension, the plot—is the objective correlative of the work, the way meaning is conveyed to the reader."

A small investor, an idea-man, Levanter moves through an extraordinary scenario in travels which take him across cultures and continents. Each episode is framed in a chilling and controlled prose, designed more to evoke and dramatize feeling than to portray human action. A master storyteller, Kosinski creates a fearful evocation of the unpredictable essence of life. Like the adventures of Lemuel Gulliver, Levanter is swept into a Swiftian world in which ethics and values are beyond man's reach. In a land of slaves and scavengers, Levanter relies solely on his personal code of ethics to spell out his own destiny.

Frequently his intent is to deceive in order to wreak vengeance on people who stand outside any system of justice, as in the episode in which he kills a hotel clerk who has been responsible for assigning innocent European visitors to special rooms which he knows are bugged by their governments. Because of this covert intelligence, a number of these visitors are tried and condemned to death once they return home. The hotel clerk has been a knowing accomplice in these many deaths, but what court of justice will condemn him? "Both the authorities and the media would demand a direct connection between the crime committed and the reason for it. They would keep looking for a plot, but it was an act like an old Polaroid snapshot: 'No negative, photographer unknown, camera thrown away.' "

Blind Date is a defiance against this eternal search for a plot, a cause, an objective destiny. Plot is not cosmically true, it is not personally true. This is the fundamental vision which *Blind Date* dramatizes. If man accepts this message—accepts all it contains—then he must wake out of his millenary dream; and in so doing, wake to his fundamental isolation.

Both a fictional character within the novel and a pervading spirit behind *Blind Date* is the great French scientist Jacques Monod. Awarded the Nobel Prize in 1965 for elucidating the coordinating of all the molecular manufacturing activities that are the essence of metabolism and thus of life itself, Monod is best known for his book-length essay, *Chance and Necessity,* published in 1970. In it he postulated his chilling conviction that all existence is because of chance. "Pure chance, only chance, absolute but blind liberty is at the root of the prodigious edifice that is evolution. . . ." Destiny is written concurrently with the event, not prior to it. Levanter thus embraces Monod's scientific postulate that forces man to accept his isolation and to utilize each moment of his life as it passes rather than to dismiss it as a minor incident in a larger "passage" or zone of time. Derived and based on modern science, this philosophy presupposed an ethic which bases moral responsibility upon the very freedom of each choice an individual is free to make in each instance of his life, an instance dictated entirely by chance. Man's destiny is nowhere spelled out, nor is his duty.

Levanter meets his final blind date on the deserted Aval skiing run—the closing day of the season. "A descent was like life: to love it was to love each moment, to rejoice in the skill and speed of every moment." Overtaken by fog and chill, Levanter seems to lose all sense of direction. In a drifting memory, he recalls a scene from the warm beach. Levanter had been telling a story to a young boy but the boy is called away by his mother. The final image of *Bind Date* is that of the boy facing the lapping waves of the surf as they move in a rising rhythm past his legs. Perhaps his parents do not wish him to hear such stories as Levanter might tell.

Passion Play

The Aging Kosinski Knight, Questing on the Polo Field

JEROME KLINKOWITZ

Every one of Jerzy Kosinski's seven novels is about Jerzy Kosinski. Or, rather, Kosinski himself has been living his life as a novel. The identity between his life and his books runs far deeper than simple biographical links, or even Hemingway's advice to "write about what you know best."

Ever since he shocked the world with "The Painted Bird," Kosinski has argued for a uniquely vital sense of life. Live each moment, his books say, as an independent event, formally detached from what may follow. Otherwise you are never free. Remembering one thing and anticipating another cheats us of the present moment, which is all that ever really exists.

To live this way in the ever-present is to shape a life of fiction, and Kosinski's novels—like Emerson's essays and Walt Whitman's "Leaves of Grass"—are diaries of its process.

"Passion Play," written nearly a quarter century after its author abandoned his promising career as a sociologist in Eastern Europe to write fiction in America, recalls the style of Kosinski's earlier works but introduces many new subjects appropriate to the slowly advancing age of its protagonist and its author.

In just a few years Kosinski will be 50, and so it's not right to look for stories of brutalized orphans, ambitious young men, or dashingly romantic intelligence agents. Nor can we expect Kosinski's heroes to roam the world—they've circled it many times in his last three novels, and to repack our bags for Europe and Asia so soon will be pointless.

So "Passion Play" chooses a somewhat older character, a man nearing the end of his prime who must for the first time worry about his aching joints and faltering nerves. And his action is within carefully circumscribed limits:

Reprinted from the *Chicago Sun-Times,* 2 September 1979, sec. 3, 9. Reprinted by permission of the author.

the strict dimensions of the polo field, where the chaos of nature stands outside to watch man do his best in a self-created artificial world.

Fabian, the professional polo player who travels the country in his self-contained "VanHome," is a living laboratory for Kosinski's ethic, now tested in a climate of financial vulnerability, emotional hunger, and approaching old age. In such diminished circumstances Fabian's acts wear a bit more shabbily than they did when clothed in the fashions of international intrigue.

For one, he's unconscionably sexist. Women are always "claimed," "taken," "yielding," "surrendering," and—in the triumph of Fabian's manipulative art—being "imprinted" with desire for their master. But Fabian is a reductive hero, having trimmed his behavior to the essentials of sex and sleep, the aggressive and passive yin-and-yang of existence.

Yet Kosinski will not blame Fabian for these shortcomings. Like Kurt Vonnegut, he has yet to create a true villain, faulting instead the conditions of life we endure. And so as Fabian rides on toward old age and death, Kosinski makes him a combination Captain Ahab and Don Quixote, hopelessly striking through the world's mask but all the time trusting in the imagination's power to make existence something worthy of life.

In this sense, "Passion Play" is the perfect vehicle for Kosinski's new lesson. For the first time he's found a subject for his icy-keen style which will not shock or alienate readers: sports reporting, where the natural action finds its mirror in Kosinski's superb narrative description.

One drawback is Kosinski's growing penchant, ever since "Cockpit," for the superficially glamorous. Women have names like "Alexandra" and "Vanessa" and tower above us in Valkyrie-like stature enhanced by gold lamé sandals. Men are no longer just men, but Argentine playboys, Caribbean dictators, or multimillionaires. The Rolls-Royces are outnumbered only by private jets and helicopters whisking in with weekend houseguests.

Fabian, of course, is the only worker in the bunch, and it all serves to underscore his vulnerability. But the strategy fails, for against his noble Ahab and Quixote is played the old Hugh Hefner image from the "Playboy's Penthouse" days, making Fabian's quest a rather tawdry affair.

This anti-democratic fascination with the very rich is the book's single unfortunate element. No such people worked as characters in "The Painted Bird" or "Steps." There the coin of the realm was stark, elemental power.

But ever since "Being There," Kosinski's first thoroughly American novel (which he helped film while completing "Passion Play"), he has been struggling with this country's fraudulent currency: the superficial glamor of money and influence. Such a fine writer and insightful student of humanity should recognize how these false values jeopardize his own vitalistic ethic.

Kosinski's Hero Rides On

WILLIAM KENNEDY

Jerzy Kosinski takes on some new subject matter—polo, horsemanship and public sex—in his seventh novel, *Passion Play,* yet these things are not really his new territory. What he presents are the further psychological adventures of the Kosinski hero, who is now as recognizable as the Hemingway hero used to be. But what is genuinely new in *Passion Play* is that Kosinski's hero grows older; and we are treated to the continuing struggles of the boy from *The Painted Bird* who became the man from *Steps,* as he jousts quixotically with (as usual) women and death, loses some of his hair, and enters into a crisis of middle age and lost youth.

There is no nostalgia in this. That's not in Kosinski's emotional kitbag. But in the book's final pages, and particularly in its final image, which I will not reveal here, there is an earned poignancy whose like I have not encountered in Kosinski's work since *The Painted Bird.*

This book does not really resemble that first novel, which made its author's reputation; it is more in line with his last three books, *The Devil Tree, Cockpit* and *Blind Date. Passion Play* is still episodic, though even here Kosinski seems to be charting new stylistic territory—he has become willfully lyrical, and he is much plottier than usual, though his plot creaks and squeaks badly at times.

It creaks for it seems he has turned to the connective tissue of plot only because he's been chided too often for being fragmented and disjointed. And it seems a half-hearted turn. He still is far more interested in discrete incidents than he is in continuity. As he explained in an interview last year, an "incident is simply a moment of life's drama of which we are aware as it takes place," whereas a plot is an "artificially imposed notion of preordained 'destiny' that usually dismisses the importance of life's each moment. Yet, that moment carries the essence of our life."

Passion Play has a man named Fabian as its hero, an outlaw polo player (outlaw because he's too good, too violent for the formal play of the game and its effete practitioners), who is trying to survive at free-lance polo and riding instruction. He travels around the country, encountering mostly the rich at

Reprinted from *Washington Post Book World,* 16 September 1979, 1, 11.

their games, and he is challenged often, professionally and personally, by women as well as men. That Fabian is almost always more than the equal of his challengers is the norm of the Kosinski hero.

At certain moments Fabian so resembles the real Kosinski, as have all his other heroes, that one is tempted to consider this yet another quasi-autobiographical work. But it is more than that, to be sure. *Passion Play* is a work of both invention and astute observation: the polo matches that Fabian plays, for instance; or the spectacle he observes and joins in New York's Ansonia-type baths where orgiastic sex on a large scale may be had for the price of admission—a lurid and comic portrait at the outer limits of this pornographic age, pornographically told.

Here again the Hemingway-Kosinski analogy works because of the high-level journalistic element in the book. The specifics of a one-on-one polo match, or Fabian's dramatic entry into a jumping competition in the National Horse Show at Madison Square Garden, seem as fully understood, as lovingly savored, and as meticulously recorded as were the trout and marlin expeditions, the bullfighting and duckshooting that so enthralled Hemingway. I've neither played polo nor shot a duck, but I am persuaded that these two writers have told me how it is when it is exquisitely done.

Kosinski has often argued that success is really only an interlude between failures. And yet his heroes succeed with great consistency at the task before them, not always through playing by the rules. If they do call the shots in their lives, he once said, "It is because most of them are desperate to find out who they are. And if this requires freeing oneself from an outer oppression, then some of them have trained themselves to fend off the threat of society using complex bureaucratic means as well as camouflage, disguises, escapes and so forth."

In *Passion Play* Fabian has trained himself to be a superb horseman, a seducer on the order of Don Juan, but with decidedly kinky tendencies (check out his ménage with the beautiful latent lesbian, and the gorgeous hermaphroditic transsexual). His horsemanship is real and Kosinski of late has himself become a horseman, but in the novel it is also allegorical: a man astride life, astride his totem, along with his knowledge and his skills, tilting against the world.

The image is as romantic as it is solipsistic and the two notions fuse once again in Kosinski's romance of the self-as-survivor. It is romantic because he makes the world too frequently manipulable. His heroes are warriors who survive (maybe with scars) every battle, however bloody. It is solipsistic because the hero is not capable of love as giving, love as selflessness.

Fabian is a taker, like his predecessors. Women exist only to be seduced, or to serve as his reflecting pool. Even that latent lesbian never utters a word to explain herself and what is done to her, to let us know what she thinks of what must surely be the greatest sexual surprise of her life. While that rare ménage is in process, Kosinski devotes full attention to Fabian and Fabian's analysis of all the sexual goings-on. But he does not give any real life to either of Fabian's sexual partners. They exist merely as props in a passing show.

Fabian does live by a rigid personal code of righteousness, but rarely does this transcend self-interest. Even his compassion for the sick and dying seems chiefly a memory aide to his own mortality. At book's end during his affair with the teenaged Vanessa he does perform an act that he perceives to be selfless. But then he sees the act has been a mistake, and he changes radically.

It is here, when Fabian discovers that his selfless act was really a devastating miscalculation about himself, that he engages us as fully human, as something other than the manipulative satyr Kosinski has made him out to be. And it is in building to this humanity that Kosinski's plot succeeds; for it counters all that his hero ostensibly professes, that Kosinski himself has always professed. And it is this insight into Fabian that seems to indicate a new direction for this most solipsistic American author.

What I sense from this work that I did not find in his other fiction is a softening of the Kosinski line, which perhaps both the lyricism and the plotting also represent. It all seems like an effort to convey something beyond the stark Spartan warrior mentality, an admission of failure not against greater odds, but through emotional vulnerability.

What seems new is Kosinski's interest in unmanipulable life, life in which the protagonist is neither victim nor hero but a spiritual substance subject to forces that can neither be challenged directly nor can be more than barely understood. Kosinski has always believed in chance as an overwhelming element in human conduct, but his heroes have either resisted it, outmaneuvered it, or taken revenge against its messengers. It is the placement of the hero in a condition where the enemy is vaporous, indefinable, that gives Kosinski a new direction.

The Kosinski hero is unique in literature, and he has lived a fearful and unsettling life until now. The author can surely continue diagramming his survival tactics in the solitary cat-and-mouse games he has always played, but this risks eventual self-parody and a literary hemophilia that no transfusion of new subject matter such as polo or horsemanship could counterbalance.

The new direction, if it is more than an aberrational moment in the hero's career, holds far more promise. It anticipates profound involvement not against but with others, and it demands the definition of those others in a way that would be new for both Kosinski and his hero. If Kosinski is ready, so are we.

When Going Is the Goal

STEFAN KANFER

Jerzy Kosinski's heroes have become dependable literary fixtures, as recognizable as Kafka's K. or Beckett's tramps. Rootless, quixotic, warped by an antichildhood in Holocaust Europe, they traverse the American landscape like knights-errant on a futile search for purpose.

In *Passion Play,* Kosinski's seventh novel, the man's name is Fabian. But in essence he is the bloodless Levanter of *Blind Date* (1977), the vengeful wanderer Tarden of *Cockpit* (1975) and the haunted boy in Kosinski's first and best fiction, *The Painted Bird.* Fabian differs from his predecessors chiefly in occupation: he is a competitive horseman. The aging jockey plays a strange sort of polo—a one-on-one contest in which animal and rider become a single figure jousting on a timeless range. Like many equestrians, Kosinski's rider is graceful on horseback; dismounted from his horse, Big Lick, he becomes one more high-plains drifter out for an evening's gratification.

It is not hard to find. In the Midwest or the desert, in banana republics or along the Florida gold coast, Fabian's mobile VanHome is seldom without its lady for the evening. Adolescents, sophisticates, even transsexuals are all given equal time. Yet the warning sign on Fabian's van says more about its owner than about the alarm system: SELF-REACTOR: AUTHORIZED PERSONNEL ONLY. In this picaresque, passion is reserved for the playing field. Despite his experiments with sex and drugs, Fabian truly gets high on Fabian. With characteristic insouciance, the author describes his hero's liaisons: "He found himself selecting, isolating, soliciting partners as transient and avid as himself, as ready to initiate, as willing to discard."

This centerfold prose disfigures the novel and makes a few paragraphs indistinguishable from Harold Robbins at the gallop: "When she arrived, the flare of her seductive allure would be in full glow, the meld of her sexuality fired by the challenge of another woman." Fortunately, Kosinski's kinks are a minor portion of *Passion Play.* The reader who can get past horse-and-lady scenes that bear no relation to *International Velvet* will be rewarded with passages of great force.

The author has been around the track in every sense; he knows the sound and aroma of mornings when the woods seem to renew themselves as

Reprinted from *Time,* 17 September 1979, 105. ©1979 Time Inc. Reprinted by permission.

the rider watches; his descriptions of equestrian combat belong on the same shelf with Hemingway and Tolstoy. His accounts of a South American republic where the main sources of power are the ox and the jet are masterpieces of irony and pure narrative. He tirelessly examines what he terms "the regency of pain." Like Dostoyevsky's, Kosinski's characters explore their own souls, always reaching for limits. Fabian even visits hospitals where he knows no patient, forcing himself to meet the incurable, to witness the most vulnerable lives. The results are never less than compelling, but they are never more than set pieces.

The fault, like the virtue, is the author's. He writes powerful interludes, only to vandalize them by reducing his characters to prototypes. By mid-novel, Fabian is shown to be, in his creator's phrase, "a portable man," at home everywhere and nowhere. Like other Kosinski men, he is unable to love without domination or lose without humiliation. His fears are for himself, not for the human condition; his vaunted independence is merely a lack of compassion. His wanderings are like those of the brain-damaged who range farther away from an object when they try to approach it.

Kosinski is 46, and readers have a right to wonder whether his unparalleled ear for language and his eye for social nuance are to be used solely for elaborations of the same theme. For the past several books, Kosinski has been as aimless as his characters who believe that the going is the goal. That is not true for polo. It is even less so for novelists, even gifted ones.

Pinball

Grand Guignol with Music

BENJAMIN DEMOTT

Goddard, hero of Jerzy Kosinski's eighth novel, is a reclusive rock superstar who records his work in his own state-of-the-art studio on a desert ranch in Southern California, tops the charts every year, banks his millions in Switzerland and allows nobody to penetrate the mystery of his identity. (Among the reasons for the reclusiveness are Goddard's fear of wounding his father, who is in the classical music business and despises rock, and his own hyperconsciousness of the numberless rock stars before him whose failure to seal themselves off from the mob destroyed them.) The action of the book centers on a scheme contrived by a post-Stockhausen-style composer named Patrick Domostroy, whose career is in disarray, and his sexually kinky girlfriend to locate Goddard and penetrate his secrets. The theme, as in many of Mr. Kosinski's books, is the universality, throughout the human community, of rage and bestiality; the denouement, predictably, is violent.

Several worlds figure in "Pinball." Domostroy lives in a giant disused South Bronx ballroom and banquet center and works as an occasional accompanist and sideman in a seedy Bronx bar-restaurant. The pursuit of the rock star leads from far-out Manhattan discos to the CBS "presidential suite" and various music conglomerate headquarters, from Carnegie Hall studios packed with fame-hungry pianists dreaming of international competitions to the terraces of Tijuana hotels where, billed as "Paganini Electronico," Goddard sometimes performs incognito.

Among the more carefully evoked settings is Dead Heat, a SoHo bar, notable for "a dozen catacomb-like rooms," that is filled on weekends after midnight with "people who came there to use its stark, savage spaces for their stark and savage rituals. It was a gathering place for people who dressed in leather or rubber; for women who wore heavy makeup and high stiletto heels and were accompanied by anemic-looking lovers in sweatshirts and shorts; for men in tank tops and shorts who liked to show off their muscular bodies, as well as the frail beauty of their scantily clad, if clad at all, female or male lovers; for people seeking partners who were as wild and momentary as the love they craved and whose only real stimulus to intimacy was to be found among a steady stream of strangers. At Dead Heat the beautiful mingled with the deformed, the old with the young, the naked with the clothed."

"The Painted Bird" and "Steps," Mr. Kosinski's first two novels, were memorable partly because the grotesque, brilliantly lit scenes of fury and coupling in their pages seemed rooted in an objective time and place—a primitive world with laws of its own, grim, necessitous, somewhat independent of the author's individual sensibility. But in his more recent work, blood-cruelty and beating have had the character of personal choices—items selected from the great bazaar of Possibility merely because his taste so directs. And the result in "Pinball" is a descent into self-indulgent laxness—depressingly flat ("the old with the young"), ridden with pulpish Grand Guignol ("stark and savage") and exceptionally high in cliché density ("scantily clad," "heavy makeup," "steady stream," etc.).

Some of the music talk in the book, both about electronic keyboard technology and about the use of the soft pedal by Chopinists, is well informed and earnest. The author's effort to find an intellectual focus on the world of rock music intermittently achieves critical force. (There are telling contrasts of vapid rock lyrics with fully realized passages from Yeats and Auden, and Mr. Kosinski quotes a memorable denunciation of the music by Ralph Ellison.) A few meant-to-be-intense moments—a near gang rape at the Dead Heat, for example—come close to horror.

Not close enough, though. One tries dutifully to attend to events and characters—sex partners screaming, thrashing, arising from bed to photograph each other's anguish. But in truth, taking in the action is difficult. What's most visible on any given page isn't a scene at all but the spectacle of self-imprisonment—of a writer locked by choice in a cage through which no glimpse of the living common world can be caught. It's a pitiable sight, and a sadly unrewarding book.

Trebles

STEFAN KANFER

Of all hazardous materials handled by Jerzy Kosinski, none has been as volatile as the metaphor. Properly used, it illumined a century; in *The Painted Bird* (1965) the speechless child became a great symbol of the inadequacy of language confronted by atrocity. In *Being There* (1971) the hero, Chance, acutely parodied the modern condition: he was a blank; the cyclopean screen was full of ideas.

But in recent works, Kosinski's metaphors have proved unstable. Life was presented, with mixed results, as a cockpit, a series of blind dates, a skirmish on a polo field. In his latest novel, existence is viewed as a pinball machine complete with odd caroms and freighted signs: BEGIN GAME. ONE TO FOUR CAN PLAY. The device obscures an intriguing notion: What if America's greatest rock star was unseen by the public, known only by his voice? The man who lived at the top of the charts would be as disembodied as a ghost and as influential as a President.

His name is Goddard and he becomes the elusive quarry of *Pinball,* pursued by Domostroy, a burned-out composer whose trebles are all behind him. Like almost all Kosinski heroes, Domostroy is an adrenal wanderer, ready for any existential errand. His employer is the beautiful groupie Andrea Gwynplaine, who mails Goddard hard-core snapshots and waits for him to emerge, panting, from his lair. With Domostroy's collaboration, she manages to run her quarry to earth. But Andrea's success is her undoing: her purpose is not worship but murder, and Goddard's is not obscurity but survival.

On the trail, exclamations detonate with the force of comic-strip balloons: "You have such light eyes and fair skin!" "I know who you are!" "Yes I do!" Yet, despite these excesses, *Pinball* has its payoffs. Throughout his prolific career, Kosinski has been a novelist of ideas, and his observations of the American way of lifestyle have kept their salinity. He deftly lampoons contemporary lyrics, his scenes of the South Bronx seem torn from a Bosch triptych, and his discussions of classical music are informed with the insights of a connoisseur.

Reprinted from *Time,* 22 March 1982, 84, 87.

This has been a peculiar period for Kosinski. He is one of the best actors in *Reds,* and he supported and later repudiated the parole of convicted murderer Jack Henry Abbott. These excursions on nonliterary turf may have contributed to the inconsistencies of a work that, in the end, can only prompt admirers to respond: "What a premise!" "What talent!" "What a waste!"

The Hermit of 69th Street

The Annotated "Roman à Tease"

JOHN CALVIN BATCHELOR

"Good poison is hard to find," sighs Norbert Kosky, the unhappy middle-aged hero of Jerzy Kosinski's clever new satirical novel, "The Hermit of 69th Street." Norbert Kosky is said to be a *most* famous and brilliant Polish émigré novelist, author of some eight startling fictions that not only have made him wealthy, distinguished, celebrated and endlessly serviceable by statuesque, orgiastic women, but also have created in him a need to write one more amazing book that will illustrate his "inner terror"—his soulful pilgrimage from a childhood in the Holocaust to a well-appointed hermitage on New York's West 69th Street.

Unfortunately for Norbert Kosky, his victories with the pen suddenly poison his life ruinously when a local journal accuses him of being a plagiarist, creep, whoremonger—and just about every other way the yellow press can say impotent liar. The charge: Norbert Kosky did not write his own books; he jobbed out his work; he is a "floater" not a "swimmer" in the ocean of literature—he is not Norbert Kosky.

This may remind you of the squall some years back when two literary journalists at The Village Voice published a piece suggesting that Jerzy Kosinski had not written all of his own books, that he had employed assistants who contributed significant ideas, scenes, energy. The allegation was rebutted in The New York Times and the waters calmed, though apparently not for Mr. Kosinski. Norbert Kosky is less a stand-alone character than a stand-in for the impugned author. Jerzy Kosinski has worked up an elaborate scheme to revenge himself against what he calls "docu-slander." He also seeks to demonstrate that no one ever wrote a book without the hands of others living and dead, and to exhibit the mystical notion that if Kosky/Kosinski is not what he says he is—a gifted, hard-working Polish émigré novelist—what writer is what he says he is? What writer is not an impotent liar?

Accordingly the book is built as "autofiction," which Kosky/Kosinski defines as neither truth nor fiction. It purports to be the unfinished manuscript left behind by Norbert Kosky when he is lost at sea, and the author Jerzy Kosinski has annotated it with eccentric, intriguing footnotes and bibliographical citations that make the text resemble biblical exegesis. The text is layered with boldface quotations from every imaginable learned source: famous writers (Maugham, Conrad, Dostoyevsky, Kafka, Bruno Schulz, Jerzy Kosinski); famous books (the Talmud, the Tantras, Genesis); famous promoters (Lenin, Diane Arbus, Samuel Goldwyn, Nietzsche, Kinsey); famous villains (Pilate, Goebbels, Stalin, Chaim Rumkowski of the Lodz ghetto); famous religionists (Abraham Heschel, Henry Ward Beecher); and the simply famous (Garbo). The hoped-for effect of all this, according to Norbert Kosky when he is asked at one point what he is working on ("*roman à tease,*" he jokes), is to render the subtext worth the price of admission.

Nevertheless Kosky is a winning *luftmensch* whose personality is consistent with the charming, fumbling characters Jerzy Kosinski has favored in such earlier books as "Being There," "The Devil Tree" and "Pinball." Kosky is simultaneously obsessed by numerology and the sex act, and he has worked up a none-too-mature way of looking at the world based on the number 69. He also translates this smuttiness into the totemic letters SS, so that everything from Sesame Street to the Soviet missiles designated SS-N to the infamous German SS are co-conspirators.

Norbert Kosky also likes books, the Alps, polo and being famous, and he pursues such a pleasant life of telephoning and entertaining editors, accountants and Hollywood flacks with unflagging sweetness. He is not the nasty fellow he would like to be, nor is he crude enough to be believed when he promotes himself as lecherous. He does have this "inner terror" like 10 extra pounds around the middle, and it is carefully revealed in flashbacks and footnotes that Norbert Kosky, like his literary executor Jerzy Kosinski, survived the German and Russian vivisection of Poland to escape eventually to America. Worst of all, he does not know why.

The ambition of this novel is not to answer such an incomprehensible question, but rather to commit a poison-pen letter that will serve as an antidote to an overexamined life. Jerzy Kosinski writes fluidly and wittily, explores his privileged world like a Conradian adventurer, soldiers worldwide for literature and makes a first-rate prosecutor of the 20th century's true criminals. It is also possible that he is not the best mockingbird for himself. Cynthia Ozick's short story "The Mercenary" remains the high-performance aircraft of Kosinski-pricking. For now, Kosky/Kosinski has yet to reach such a height, weighed down as he is by being the pilot and ordnance of his Stealth bomber of a soul.

Kosinski's Mask behind the Mask

LARRY MCCAFFERY

The appearance of this, Jerzy Kosinski's ninth novel and his first since a sensationalized *Village Voice* article six years ago alleged that he had misrepresented his writing methods and his life, indicates what we should have known all along: Kosinski, a spiritual child of the Final Solution, is a survivor. Indeed, he has emerged from the Great Kosinski Furor (which resulted from a scrupulously researched, but misguided distillation of rumor and innuendo that Kosinski himself had helped to perpetuate) with a vengeance, creating a defiant, highly personalized literary response to the charges leveled against him. *The Hermit of 69th Street* is a peculiar blend of intimate revelations and abstract musings on the nature of the self and the sources of artistic creativity. It is Kosinski's most ambitious, experimental and nakedly confessional work to date.

The basic aim of this massive, unclassifiable text (Kosinski has dubbed it an "autofiction") is to allow readers a myriad of entryways into the mysteries of his own personal writing habits and the alchemic processes of all literary creation. *The Hermit* is designed to be a vast labyrinth of words, a dizzying series of textual passageways that must be negotiated individually and which ultimately all lead to a final destination: Kosinski's inner self, his soul. It is the confused welter of fears, memories, fantasies, factual knowledge and personal experience that comprise his identity and are the source of his creativity.

The most fascinating aspect of *The Hermit* is watching Kosinski develop an utterly original form to express this "self" without reducing it to the formulaic simplicities implicit with both autobiography and realism. Finally abandoning the masks, disguises, false beards and wigs he and his characters have favored until now, he invents a novelistic alter ego (the Norbert Kosky of the book's title) whose life and works are blatant extensions of Kosinski's own; he then provides for the reader dozens of accesses and perspectives involved in the creation of Kosky and the fictional world he inhabits. These "accesses" take the form of a profusion of footnotes (worth the price of admission alone), quotations from hundreds of literary and nonliterary sources (often inserted into the narrative as a Burroughs' cut-up), notes to editors and

Reprinted from *Washington Post Book World*, 10 July 1988, 1, 9.

proofreaders, authorial asides—all of which comment upon and otherwise interact with the main narrative, whose existence we are literally seeing being formed before our eyes.

Naturally many features of Kosky's existence bear a striking resemblance to what we know about the outlandish realm that Jerzy Kosinski appears to have lived in these past 55 years. But Kosky's world is also a realm of words governed by esthetic structures, so clearly it is different as well, which is at once the most obvious and most profound point of this autofiction.

Norbert Kosky is a 54-year-old survivor of the Holocaust who emigrated to America from Ruthenia, an Eastern European realm that Kosinski uses to explore his deeply ambivalent, painful links with his native Poland and his Jewishness. Propelled into the status of literary superstar after writing a number of controversial but widely respected novels, Kosky for a while hobnobs with the elite, plays polo and skis with the international jet-set crowd, is cast in the movie-role of Bukharin (whose farcical trial and subsequent murder by Stalin produce eerie reverberations) and engages in a series of peculiar sexual encounters. He also enjoys immersing himself in water and then levitating in public—an ability that becomes a central metaphor for the artist's need to "float" above the currents that make up his existence, to at once be a part of but always the master of his elements lest he drown.

Gradually we begin to see how Kosky has transformed the elements of his "real life"—which includes his private obsessions, fantasies, personal problems, traumatic memories, metaphysical musings and reading, as well as the actual events he experiences—into the controversial autobiographically based novels that have established his reputation. These novels are, of course, notable for the same sort of things Kosinski's works are: their cool depiction of shockingly violent and erotic scenes, their focus on the needs of individuals to take refuge within a shifting series of disguises in order to survive the massive brutality and dehumanization of modern life, their fascination with the way the media are able to infiltrate and influence even the most private reaches of our sense of identity and value systems. Exploring Kosky's obsessive, haunted, yet playful literary sensibility therefore allows Kosinski to expose the inner theater of his own mysterious identity more openly than he has ever dared to in the past.

Kosinski also makes us privy to Kosky's actual writing processes—hence, presumably, his own—in exhaustive but revealing detail. Partly because he is obsessed by the need to control and partly because English is not his first language, Kosky's manuscripts are subjected at each stage of their composition to a rigorous series of proofreadings and technical examinations by editorial assistants (often young women who quickly find themselves engaged in providing more personal services). This background—especially when coupled with hundreds of telling references to authors like Balzac, Thomas Wolfe, Goethe and (most notably) Joseph Conrad, whose writing methods are linked to those found here—allows us to empathize with Kosky's bewilderment and rage when he is accused by two journalists of (you guessed it) being an inveterate liar about his past and being only the nominal "author" of his books. Kosky's response to these accusations makes up the remainder of the storyline.

Any such plot summary greatly distorts the actual experience of reading *The Hermit*. At every turn, Kosinski impedes our progress through the work by his constant textual interventions. The result is a vast, convoluted book whose different planes of existence interact with one another to embody the mysterious processes that somehow combine to produce a novel. It also functions as an elaborate vindication of Kosinski by relentlessly laying siege to the concept of authorial originality, by exposing the provisional, intertextual nature of all "meanings" and by pointing out the dangers implicit within any society where the "ownership" of language is rigidly defined and the free play of creativity and collaboration are unable to function.

Georges Bataille once made the useful distinction between the avant-garde novel whose experiments seem to be made for the sake of experiments versus the novel whose peculiar features seem born out of necessity. *The Hermit of 69th Street* is a work so excessive and self-involved, so obviously written by Kosinski for himself, that it seems born out of precisely that sense of necessity and compulsiveness. It is a sense that is rare among writers but common among survivors.

INTERVIEW

◆

The Psychological Novelist as Portable Man

GAIL SHEEHY

The spidery figure in the driveway is a weekend guest at a relaxed country house on eastern Long Island. He is in no danger. He is among friends. Yet once or twice a day he slips out to the driveway and half-buries himself in the trunk of his convertible. Pulling out a variety of items, he examines and rearranges them, handling each one with such reverence that one imagines the contents to be rare minerals or perhaps high explosives.

Upon closer scrutiny, the observer will note that the items are quite pedestrian: canned foods, a drop-legged bed, nonalcoholic beverages, notebooks to write in and novels to read, cash, weapons (or what the owner refers to as "relative protection systems," the "strength of character" being the only absolute one), and an odd-looking, charred, one-quart can with holes punched in its sides and a wire loop for a handle. This, the owner will explain, is an item essential to survival without human help: a comet.

Few Americans would be in a position to know that a comet, a simple can, when packed with moss, bark, and damp leaves, and lighted, will serve as a stove to roast birds' eggs plucked from the nest, will repel insects and snakes, and—when swung in a broad arc so as to spew menacing sparks like a comet—it can even drive away savage guard dogs and undependable human beings. The owner spent a great deal of time with comets on his childhood odyssey during World War II through the backwoods villages of Eastern Europe.

All this and more travels with our protagonist on even the most innocuous of outings. One never knows from second to second when the need might arise to escape.

Jerzy Kosinski is his own law and his own survival. Dedicated to outwitting society in its every attempt to impinge on the individual, Kosinski works at being the utterly portable man. The trunk of his car is one of his many exits. They are always ready.

Plunging into the back seat of Kosinski's mind, we are in for a swift and startling ride. The driver is one of the foremost psychological novelists in the

Reprinted from *Psychology Today,* December 1977, 52, 55–56, 126, 128, 130. Reprinted by permission of the author.

world (as well as the author of two books on collective behavior). The route he chooses, the hopes and perils he sees on his sightseeing trip through the human landscape, are as instructive as more traditional teachers.

Kosinski was born of Russian parents in Poland in 1933 and raised in both Russian and Polish. He came to the United States in 1957 at the age of 24, speaking almost no English, and rapidly became fluent in his adopted language.

Today, with millions of his novels in print, Kosinski is primarily known as the author of *The Painted Bird, Steps, Being There, The Devil Tree,* and *Cockpit. The Painted Bird* earned him status as an underground cult hero in the 60s; official recognition followed: the National Book Award (for *Steps*), the Award in Literature of the National Institute of Arts and Letters. His most recent novel, *Blind Date,* will be published by Houghton Mifflin this month. In the following conversation, Kosinski talks about the underlying psychology of his work.

Gail Sheehy: I think there is something in your protagonists that we fear to see in ourselves. What do you think that might be?

Jerzy Kosinski: They represent the essentially tragic condition of life: the condition in which our own conduct is often a spectacular mystery to ourselves, as well as to others. The mechanics of society are equally unpredictable, and its mass-managed consciousness is hostile to man's real aspirations, fears, and joys.

In *The Painted Bird,* a war-torn society turns against a boy. In *Cockpit,* Tarden, a middle-aged, supertrained ex-intelligence agent, wages irreversible war against a mindless state and some of its institutions. *Steps* centers on sexual and moral entanglements; *Being There,* on the emergence of Chauncey Gardiner, a retarded character, via media-induced charisma. *The Devil Tree* portrays the inability of Jonathan Whalen, a young American heir to a large industrial fortune, to sustain his totality in a world of fragmenting values.

And now *Blind Date,* the story of George Levanter, a small investor who leads his life eminently aware of the overwhelming role of chance in each of his life's encounters. I realize that these are not readily digestible situations, but I would consider myself a fraud if I were to give my characters any other philosophy of life.

And yet I feel that putting an individual on a constant moral and emotional alert has a positive effect in that it heightens the sense of life, the appreciation of its every moment, the sheer miracle of existence in a basically hostile environment.

Sheehy: Do you have to experience threatening situations, as you did as a child, in Eastern Europe, to have that sense of "moral alert"?

Kosinski: I refuse to perceive myself and my life as threatened. Rather, I tend to see my life as being challenged by the forces which are implicit in the process of being alive.

Sheehy: But you intensify those challenges.
Kosinski: I intensify only my awareness of them. As a human being, I answer not only to reality but also to plausibility—to the plight of my imagination. Nothing bars me from perceiving my life as a series of emotionally charged incidents, all strung out by my memory—all dictated by chance, nature's true fantasy.
Sheehy: Why incidents?
Kosinski: An incident is simply a moment of life's drama of which we are aware as it takes place. This awareness and the intensity of it decides, in my view, whether our life is nothing but a barely perceived existence, or meaningful living. To intensify life, one must not only recognize each moment as an incident full of drama, but, above all, oneself as its chief protagonist. To bypass that moment, to dilute it in the gray everydayness, is to waste the most precious ingredient of living: the awareness of being alive.

That's why in my fiction I stress an incident, as opposed, let's say, to a popular culture, which stresses a plot. Plot is an artificially imposed notion of preordained "destiny" that usually dismisses the importance of life's each moment. Yet, that moment carried the essence of our life.
Sheehy: You've spoken about your six novels as part of a cycle exploring the relation of the individual to society. It would seem that if you were to create your own world, you would want to give the individual the greatest amount of power of will and of freedom and reduce the power of the state, the restraints of collectivity. Yet, many people want the various protections that society offers; so they often submit to restraints and relinquish many freedoms in exchange for such a collective protection.
Kosinski: This collective protection does not remove the threat of chance. With or without it, we are on a blind date with society, and the society promises a mutually rewarding encounter. To me, such a promise is a lie. The institutions of society are objectively there, no doubt, but in terms of our private drama, they are nothing but a backdrop. We play our drama by ourselves, and when we finally exit, our play has come to an end.
Sheehy: Still, society is an immensely powerful illusion.
Kosinski: It certainly is. Most of us, by the time of adolescence, carry in our head a veritable totalitarian state of illusions and most of them suppress us. Take the sexual arena: our inner censor is far more powerful than all the combined real-life censors of the Western world. The two lovers on the solitary lover's lane more often talk and answer to their inner censors than to each other.
Sheehy: Your protagonists seem to call all the shots in their own lives.
Kosinski: If they do, it is because most of them are desperate to find out who they are. And if this requires freeing oneself from an outer oppression, then some of them have trained themselves to fend off the threat of society using complex bureaucratic means as well as camouflage, disguises, escapes, and so forth.

Sheehy: Those are all methods you yourself use.
Kosinski: Why not? I need the examples of my protagonists as much as they seem to have needed mine. Yet, my protagonists do not isolate themselves. They are adventurers but also self-appointed reformers of an unjust world: they interfere on behalf of the weak and the fallen and the disfigured. I see this as an important part of the philosophy of the self: you cannot be faithful to your own sense of drama in your life if you disregard the drama in the life of others—those right next to you.
Sheehy: Your novels ingeniously catch us in the trap of our knee-jerk attitudes to those born deformed, and the new novel is no exception.
Kosinski: George Levanter, the protagonist of *Blind Date,* is about to fall in love with a woman who, after surviving an early-childhood illness, had a normal-sized head, but whatever little was left of her body was shrunken to the size of a baby and disfigured. Well, I knew such a woman once (she is dead now), and I found her, her vision of the world, her entire experience, fascinating. She was one of the most wholesome, most alive, beings I've met. Because of her joy of life, she was able to acquire and to convey a range of feelings, fantasies, and observations few of us have and all could benefit by. But, in the eyes of popular culture, this woman and her experience would be, at best, outlandish and rudimentary.
Sheehy: You spoke once of the necessity of embracing your fears. Can you give me an example?
Kosinski: I think you start by imagining yourself in the very situation which frightens you. Hence, the enormous importance of imagination, our ability to project oneself into the "unknown"—the very "blind dates" of our existence. For instance, you are in the midst of playing tennis and suddenly you see yourself as not being able to play it ever again—a victim of a car accident, a crippling disease, old age . . . all possible, after all. In the moment of such a projection, you are at peace with both your own current condition and with a change this condition implies. You're true to yourself, and by implication, to all of those who have failed—and who will never play tennis. You intensify your joy of the moment—your game of tennis—and you ready yourself for whatever might be, for the innumerable contingencies you might have to face in your life.
Sheehy: What do you think is the primary influence in your life that has caused you to feel a special compassion for those who fail?
Kosinski: Possibly growing up in Poland and the USSR, societies so ravaged by the war that during its five years, Poland, for instance, had lost one-fifth of its entire population. And if one out of five people died, bombed, murdered, exterminated, think of the remaining four—how many of them survived maimed for life, wounded, traumatized? All of Eastern Europe and Soviet Russia was, during and after the war, a battlefield populated almost entirely by incredibly damaged human beings. Throughout my school years, most of my fellow students were one way or another crippled by the war and its after-

math. Most of them suffered from serious physical and mental problems. I was no exception: from the age of nine, I was mute for several years.
Sheehy: No other functions were impaired?
Kosinski: I like to think they were developed to make up for the imposed silence. But when I look back at the years of that imposed silence, I have no complaints. They might have reinforced in me my belief that I should write: fiction is a silent process. Confronted as an adolescent by human misery of such staggering proportions, I found myself feeling privileged to be alive, to feel, to think, to be among people, to seek friends. I am 44 now, and I don't recall one single moment in my life when I saw myself as a victim chosen by fate, even though I remember being beaten, molested, ridiculed, punished, pushed around. I remember bleeding and vomiting and crying and suffering a lot of pain and looking for God to help me out, but what I remember above all is that in the midst of my misery, I kept seeing myself as merely one of a majority of people who suffered and were not happy—my oppressors included. Happy men don't waste their time beating and punishing others, I thought, and I kept imagining how unhappy those who caused my pain would be the day they realized how uselessly they lived the only life they had.
Sheehy: I wouldn't be the first to observe that next to the protagonists of your novels, you are probably your most interesting character. First of all, I wonder what you would have faced if you had not left Eastern Europe for America in 1957 when you were 24?
Kosinski: As a social scientist I would have continued to aim at preserving the sense of self in a totalitarian society which objects to such preservation. I would have tried to maintain an active inner life by becoming an artist, a photographer. I remember I used to call myself an inner *émigré.* I would have remained such an inner *émigré* all my life. For artistic expression, I would most likely have continued actively with the work I was doing as a photographer—never as a novelist.
Sheehy: Could you tell me why you chose photography?
Kosinski: It offered a temporary escape from politically infested social sciences—and a darkroom I could lock myself in. Also, as art, photography was less ambiguous than fiction and more open to general scrutiny.
Sheehy: When after you came to America and began writing in English, did you feel less, or more, articulate?
Kosinski: It was a great surprise to me, one of many surprises of my life, that when I began speaking English, I felt freer to express myself, not just my views but my personal history, my quite private drives, all the thoughts that I would have found difficult to reveal in my mother tongue. It seemed that the languages of my childhood and adolescence—Polish and Russian—carried a sort of mental suppression. By the time I was 25, in America, my infancy in English had ended and I discovered that English, my stepmother tongue, offered me a sense of revelation, of fulfillment, of abandonment—everything contrary to the anxiety my mother tongue evoked. Come to think of it, there

is something ominous even in the phrase "mother tongue" and I utilized some of this linguistic experience in *Blind Date.*
Sheehy: "Mother tongue" appears to carry all the prohibitions and directions of one's infancy. . . . Have you ever heard of anyone else who has exchanged languages in a similar way?
Kosinski: I have. I have talked with some of my compatriots, writers, filmmakers, and other artists who in midlife emigrated from Eastern Europe and have been forced to embrace English, French, or German as their second language. Like me, most of them profess to be creatively freer in the adopted language.

I have taught at Princeton, Wesleyan, and Yale, and I advised some of my students that to free themselves from that inner oppression they felt in English, they should consider settling in a foreign country and start to write in another language.
Sheehy: What is the purpose of fiction?
Kosinski: To engage the reader in a drama that is much more condensed and crystallized than the drama of our daily existence, yet made of the same ingredients: human beings in a state of interaction, of conflict. I believe that through this process, the reader's awareness of his or her life—as a drama—is increased. As we tend to perceive our life in a "diluted" way, fiction—good fiction, anyhow—counteracts that by "dramatizing" it. It insinuates that we, like the fictional characters, can also have a position of relative importance, of certain mastery vis-à-vis our life.
Sheehy: Suppose the reader rejects your vision of life as drama?
Kosinski: The purpose of fiction—of any art—is above all to evoke a concrete dramatic response: to accept the artist's vision *or* to reject it. My fiction aims at acceptance very democratically; it does not place itself *above* the reader by insinuating the novel's "moral" and providing the judgment. As in ordinary life, it is the reader who, in the act of reading, judges the fictional events and the characters as they come by. The moral is, of course, implicit in any encounter—whether with a fictional protagonist or with real heroes or villains.

Fiction doesn't propagandize or advertise—it merely evokes; thus, to generate a moral judgment in a reader is yet another didactic purpose of literature.
Sheehy: Isn't your fiction, then, rather demanding on the reader?
Kosinski: If it is, so is life. After all, life is not only demanding but, like a novel, also ends. To me, the formidable purpose of life is to perceive it as drama plotted not by design, but by chance concurrently with each event of life (not prior to it), and oneself as its central protagonist. That's why the importance of strong fiction that mobilizes imagination, calls forth motion. The popular culture renders us passive; most of our novels, television, and films tend to distract rather than to confront us by being true to our emotional and physical environment. And how often these days does anybody

shake us up? I think literature is the last surviving awakener, the last form of art which still requires a profound effort from within.

Sheehy: Do you think of yourself as having a spiritual life, having a belief?

Kosinski: I guess I simply worship feeling alive.

Sheehy: But you would not feel uncomfortable calling it a force given by God?

Kosinski: I'm not preoccupied by the giver; I am preoccupied with the gift. And I'm immensely grateful to the previous owners, my parents, both of whom are, sadly, dead.

Sheehy: In the last few years can you evoke a time, a moment, when you felt most intensely alive?

Kosinski: I have such moments during most days of my life. I think the advantage of the imaginative life is that when reality slackens, at any time you can summon up some of these strong images—memories, fantasies, stories by other writers—that can speed it up.

Sheehy: You can be lying on the beach and you can summon up these images?

Kosinski: Certainly. Today, for instance, on the beach, I tried to recall all the beaches I lay on in the past. I wondered why is it that three of my six novels end with an image of a large body of water. . . .

Sheehy: Water is not a comfortable element for you.

Kosinski: I guess the world has not been created as my water bed. I wondered about it today: I was traumatized by water many times. Once, as a child, I was pushed under ice and barely survived. I recalled a lot of other moments of panic and terror when suddenly submerged. In the moment of recalling these moments, I was petrified again—and promptly reassured that I was on the sand, quite safe, and among friends, all very good swimmers, none of whom would want to drown me. I guess that's what I meant by summoning dramatic images, a fusion of memory, fantasy, and emotion, without which that might have been a dull hour in the sun next to a terrifying ocean.

Sheehy: Some people say that the protagonists of your novels are so preoccupied with death, terror, and violence that they must be paranoid.

Kosinski: If paranoia is a delusion, a broken bridge to objective realities, then to me the culture that systematically refuses to be realistically concerned with the place of terror and violence in our proper life is paranoid, not a character who chooses to acknowledge its dimension in our life.

The leading causes of death in America today are heart disease, motor-vehicle accidents, cirrhosis of the liver, and suicides. Yet, do you know of any major film, TV series, or a fictional potboiler that would address itself to those subjects? Is heart condition so much less dramatic than *The Deep*? A motor car, America's most potent killer, less frightening than *Jaws*? Isn't alcohol our real-life *Omen*? Cigarette smoking the *Towering Inferno*? No wonder only 24 percent of the total U.S. population knows what hypertension actually means! Of people with hypertension, only 33 percent knew what it was. And is it a wonder that over 22 percent of Americans believe in astrology? That one-half of all hospital beds in the United States are devoted to psychiatric patients! And that, in some of our mental hospitals, the ratio of patients to psychiatrists is over 200 to one!

As it goes along, popular culture develops its own audience. People who enjoy certain shows are going to enjoy these very shows in an even cruder form when they grow older: the stuff of imagination diminishes faster than all other natural resources and is progressively so diminished that to satisfy it, even cruder and cruder entertainment is needed. If you look at the content of most of the television shows and popular films as opposed to the films of the American 30s and 40s, you will find a staggering reduction of true concern for what makes life human.

Sheehy: You have looked at the world from both ends of its ideologies: Soviet totalitarianism and American capitalism. Also from both ends of its class ladder. When you first arrived in this country, with no English, you were scraping ships, cleaning bars, parking cars, chauffeuring in Harlem. You were a truck driver and lived in the YMCA. By 1962, in four short years, you became a known author, you met and married a woman who was one of the largest taxpayers in the United States. Then, until her death 10 years ago, you lived in the environment that this tax bracket provided. At which end of your experience of fear or freedom, rich or poor, did you find the greatest sense of being alive?

Kosinski: At both ends—and in between. As I have no habits that require maintaining—I don't even have a favorite menu—the only way for me to live was always to be as close to other people as life allowed. Not much else stimulates me. I have no other passions, no other joys, no other obsessions. The only moment when I feel truly alive is when, in a relationship with other people, I discover how much in common we all share with each other. Money and possessions—I care little for the first, hardly for the second—were never necessary to experience life as I live it. As greatly as my wife, her wealth, and our marriage contributed to my knowledge of myself, of America, and of the world, they contributed just as much—no more, no less—as all other moments have contributed to my curiosity about myself, others, society, art—and to my sense of being alive.

Of course I've always known moments of loneliness when I felt abandoned, rejected, unhappy—but, in such moments, I also felt alive enough to ponder my own state of mind, my own life, always aware that any moment this precious gift of awareness of the self might be taken away from me. That state of awareness has always been, to me, less a possession than a mortgage, easily terminable.

Perhaps that's why, in the 60s, in the midst of the affluent existence my marriage had provided, so much removed from the misery I'd once known, living in secluded villas, flying in private planes, floating on custom-built boats that turned the world into one's playground, I sat down to write *The Painted Bird,* a novel of an abandoned boy in the war-ravaged, small pocket of rural Europe, which I remember so intimately.

Sheehy: Perhaps the picture you had of the world inside and outside at the age of 12 continues to supply your picture of yourself as an adult.
Kosinski: The war was my kindergarten, my introduction to modern society and its capacity for a senseless destruction and terror. What I witnessed and lived through as a child and then as an adolescent in a Stalinist society might have been responsible for the respect I have for the individual—total state's first victim. All my novels, really, are about conscious or unconscious victimization—our mental traits, our customs and mores—by the institution of society and the individuals who fall prey to them.
Sheehy: Do you think that Americans are used by corporations, by educational systems, and by our governmental institutions in ways they don't recognize? Or that we submit to being so used because the rewards are so plentiful?
Kosinski: Not the way they would be used in a totalitarian state but, to a degree, yes: we are all used. One recent poll established that about 70 percent of American businessmen admit they have been expected, on occasion, to compromise personal principles in order to conform to corporate standards. Almost 30 percent said that increased strain and business tension have hurt their health. Some of these businessmen are undoubtedly victims of a popular culture that for years has insisted that one's career is one's only "given" plot, a sure way to counter and even to avoid unpredictability in life, the dangers of old age, and so forth. In dismissing the possibility of many choices which these businessmen could and should make from day to day, by discouraging change, by playing up fears and insecurities of growing old, the popular culture has helped to dehumanize their predicament even faster.
Sheehy: How can we start cleaning up our own psychic cupboard from the unholy influence of the popular culture?
Kosinski: A very difficult task. Whenever an authentic quest for life's meaning spontaneously emerges on the margin of American life, the popular culture—whether political, social, psychological, or literary—in pursuit of an easy box-office success or best-sellerdom or high ratings, packages and sells it. The quest becomes yet another entertainment commodity, as dispensable and replaceable as merchandise, and in time is replaced by another effortless cultural fad. Many Americans seem by now no less indoctrinated by the Pollyanna values of their popular culture than are, let's say, their Russian counterparts by the decades of dehumanizing ideology of omnipotence of the Party.
Sheehy: As a result of entering your 40s, have you noticed certain changes in your perspective?
Kosinski: I certainly have, thanks to practicing sports—skiing and, more recently, horseback riding. I constantly notice my body's inability or refusal to carry out certain sustained or more elaborate efforts, even though my brain seems to be quite capable of projecting and demanding them in great detail.
Sheehy: Do you find you are becoming less dispassionate as you grow older?
Kosinski: More compassionate, more attentive to the voice of life and more forgiving of its various failures, in myself as well as in others, but also more

critical of a society so cruel to the old, sick, infirm. And I begin to perceive certain periods of my past, like certain skiing tricks I used to perform, as not available to be reproduced by me anymore. From now on, they will reside in me only as memory—and as a play of my imagination. Nostalgia and sentimentality—this is new.

Sheehy: Sentimentality?

Kosinski: Yes. Once, I considered it merely a mood undefined. To be sentimental was not to be clear about oneself or others. Now I feel it as a minor but necessary shade, a mixture of regret and of desire.

Sheehy: In *The Painted Bird,* you presented a wandering boy whose demeanor caused others to believe that he possessed magical powers, that he was able to cast evil spells on others. In your own life, you sometimes take on this persona and like to convince others that you are casting spells on dogs you don't like, children who invade your privacy, or adults who betrayed your trust.

Kosinski: Art is about casting spells. Every artist should believe in his or her power to spellbind us long enough for the work of art to slip new awareness into our commonplace existence. If there is magic to art, there must be—shouldn't there be?—a mystery to the artist. I am very possessive about my powers to cast spells and if indeed I cast them, I do it seldom—at a misbehaving horse, a playful friend, or an unsuspecting but willing reader.

ESSAYS AND ARTICLES

◆

Jerzy Kosinski: Retreat from Violence

DANIEL J. CAHILL

In the decades since the close of World War II, both contemporary fiction and drama have recorded the devastating effects of that global conflict on man's moral consciousness. Historians too have unearthed masses of data to consign the guilt, the horror of it all. More recently, the fiction of Jerzy Kosinski, the American writer of Polish origin, has tracked the impact of that brutal worldwide event, of the power of incessant violence to sear the mind, to distort—perhaps forever—man's power and capacity to recapture any moral balance. Kosinski's brilliant fiction, like the works of Nietzsche, stands as a vivid warning to mankind, a warning to be heeded lest we too, like Dionysus Zagreus, suffer the fate of being torn apart. The moral descent of Kosinski's protagonists portrays the failure of both community and communication.

Unlike the plaintive hero of Shelley's poem "Alastor," Kosinski's figures do not seek to evade the gross and "unseeing" multitude; they do not yearn for communion or "intellectual intercourse" with kindred spirits. The powerful quest of the rejected and alienated romantic soul is not at stake in his fiction; nor is the Faustian desire for unbounded knowledge a striking motive. The world of the Kosinskian hero has a closer parallel to the dark irrational universe of Kafka—man trapped in a world of dissolving meaning, in which there are few fragments to shore up against his ruin. Without Kafka's power for symbolic absurdity or a similar rich vein of rational irrationality, Kosinski's imaginative writings proceed out of a varied and dense past of vivid and personal nightmare.

Himself a temporary war-orphan at age of six, he trudged alone and friendless through the Eastern European countryside during the oppressive German occupation of that part of the Continent. At the age of eleven, the author was reunited with his parents at the close of the war in 1944. These nomadic experiences of the young boy later became the substance of his first novel, *The Painted Bird.*[1] Before turning directly to that fictionalized drama, let me sketch, however briefly, several points of Kosinski's biography and his career as a writer. His personal past is clouded. If one can trust the inferences

Reprinted from *Twentieth Century Literature* 18, no. 2 (April 1972): 121–32, with the permission of the journal.

from *The Painted Bird,* there is a close parallel of dates and ages between the author and the boy of the story. Again, Kosinski has stated that all of the events of the novel—however bizarre and unreal they may seem to the reader—have a basis in corporate fact and human reality. From 1944 to 1957, Kosinski lived in various European capitals, and he also studied extensively in Russia during this period. Since his Americanization in 1957 and under the pen name of Joseph Novak, he has published two diary-like studies of Russian life: *The Future Is Ours, Comrade* (1960) and *No Third Path* (1962). Kosinski was awarded both the 1969 National Book Award and the 1970 Award in Literature by the National Institute of Art and Letters for his novel *Steps,* which was published in 1968.

In the earlier Russian studies, which precede his fiction, the author acted as the "recording" center for the experiences of others. In one sense, *The Future Is Ours, Comrade* and *No Third Path* are political case histories. As observer, Kosinski sought a position of detachment and neutrality as he attempted to describe objectively the dailiness and human routines of Russian life. This neutrality was the pose of a social scientist whose cumulative facts eventually explode in a devastating account of Russian life. Both the "recording" point of view and the intense distrust of Russian motives provide an underlying approach to Kosinski's fiction, and ultimately to his vision of man's spiritual desperation.

As a writer, Kosinski's movement from the "recordings" of a social historian to imaginative fiction was a natural one. Like the young Dickens as court reporter, Kosinski had trained his mind to look acutely and to mirror faithfully that which is unique, peculiar, marked by a fine excess—indeed the "*inscape*" of life's varied experience. Because of his own personal history, he possessed within himself an abundantly full range of human adventure. Personal memory served him well, as did his practiced talent for recounting the vivid detail of event.

Kosinski's first novel, *The Painted Bird* (1965), is the story of a young boy, separated from his parents in the war-torn days of the German invasion of Poland. The sequence of unique adventures which constitute the substance of the novel is told from the point of view of the boy as he relives each episode—distanced by time and place, and filtered through the vivid memory of a mind now more composed, more reflective. The episodes achieve the status of journal entries—a sense of the more or less prolonged interval between the actual experience and its final crystallization into language. The journal of the child is composed of detached entries, each existing by itself and separated by a gap from those around it. The continuity of memory and basic symbol of the painted bird serve as principles which sustain a pattern of meaning working out from individualized encounters. The range of episodes in which the boy is treated with suspicion and abuse, derision and hatred, is fantastic. His dark hair and eyes, the olive tone of his complexion, his raggedness, all serve to mark him as a stranger—one who does not belong.

This motif of estrangement is reinforced by the central symbol of the painted bird. In a previous book, Kosinski had recorded a childhood memory of a young Russian girl. She had recounted "how once a group of us kids caught a sparrow in a trap. He struggled with all his might—tiny heart thumping desperately—but I held on tight. We then painted him purple and I must admit he actually looked much better—more proud and unusual. After the paint had dried we let him go to rejoin his flock. We thought he would be admired for his beautiful and unusual coloring—become a model to all the gray sparrows in the vicinity, and they would make him their king. He rose high and was quickly surrounded by his companions. For a few moments their chirping grew louder and then . . . a small object began plummeting earthward. We ran to the place where it fell. In a mud puddle lay our purple sparrow—dead; his blood mingling with the paint . . . the water was rapidly turning brownish-red." (*No Third Path,* p. 107.) The image of the multi-colored sparrow and his pitiless death expanded for Kosinski as an expressive symbol, drawing unto itself man's paradoxical and conflicting aspirations for a unique identity and his instinctive psychological need for acceptance and love. Like the heroes of Camus and Robbe-Grillet, the boy in *The Painted Bird* is a stranger, fiercely proud of his independence, but seeking—shyly and cautiously—comfort in the hearts of those who will accept him—who will love him.

The order of the episodes in which the boy plays out his cruel adventure with life is itself miscellaneous, event following event, threaded only by chance. To those whom he meets, the boy has only the value of an object—to be bartered or sold into slavery. With the memory of his parents and home still strong in his mind, he longs for the day when they will be reunited—when he will cease to be a stranger and be restored in love. Such a desire sustains him through his earliest encounters. But these encounters are themselves emblematic of what awaits the child in the dark journey ahead. The quality of these early adventures establishes for the boy the quality of life itself.

In the first episode, he is living with Marta, an old peasant lady. Their languages are different and while no spoken words pass between them, a feeling of protection for each other binds them together. The boy passes his time playing in the yard, watching the few domestic animals cavort and scratch for food in the earth-bordered farmyard. One day a black hawk attacks the fat hen who could not scramble for shelter; one day a group of village boys set a squirrel aflame: "with a squeal that stopped my breath, the squirrel leapt up as if to escape from the fire. The flames covered it; only the bushy tail still wagged for a second. The small smoking body rolled on the ground and was soon still." (p. 7.) One day Marta's hut burned to the ground. "I stood by the door, ready to run, still waiting for Marta to move. But she sat stiffly, as though unaware of anything. The flames started to lick her dangling hands as might an affectionate dog. They now left purple marks on her hands and climbed higher towards her matted hair." (p. 12.) The boy trembled and vomited. Frightened by the sounds of approaching villagers, he fled into the forest.

Later, the boy is living with a miller nicknamed Jealous. A young plowboy, suspected by the miller of lustful desires for his wife, is invited to dinner. Filled with drink, the miller cannily observes the plowboy and the wife cast desirous glances upon each other. While this scene of human sexuality transpires, in the background a screeching tomcat mauls a female in heat. Enflamed in jealous rage, the miller gouges out the eyes of the plowboy with a soup spoon. "The cats timidly moved out into the middle of the room and began to play with the eyes as if they were balls of thread . . . the cats rolled the eyes around, sniffed them, licked them, and passed them to one another gently with their padded paws." (p. 43.) The boy fled the house in the quiet of the drunken slumber which had come upon all.

In the next encounter, the death of Stupid Ludmila assaults the mind. A wild and homeless forager of the woods, Stupid Ludmila is set upon by the enraged women of the village. Without the power to prevent the tragedy, the boy watches murder. "Stupid Ludmila lay bleeding. Blue bruises appeared on her tormented body. She groaned loudly, arched her back, trembled, trying vainly to free herself. One of the women now approached, holding a corked bottle of brownish-black manure. To the accompaniment of raucous laughter, and loud encouragements from the others, she kneeled between Ludmila's legs and rammed the entire bottle inside her abused, assaulted slit, while she began to howl and moan like a beast. The other women looked on calmly. Suddenly, with all of her strength one of them kicked the bottom of the bottle sticking out of Stupid Ludmila's groin. There was a muffled noise of glass shattering inside. Now all the women began to kick Ludmila. When the last woman had finished kicking, Ludmila was dead." (p. 62.)

Here three events—the fiery death of Marta, the maiming of the plowboy, and the horrific slaying of Ludmila—are compounded with many equally revolting encounters of man's bestial powers to wreak evil upon his own kind. The violence which the boy witnesses is an unrelieved, tormentingly constant human experience. His only recourse against the turbulence and evil of life is to protect himself by deceit and cunning. Because he is an eternal stranger to the world, he makes a merit of that position. He is not tied to a place or to people, and like a stranger, he can desert a situation without regret. Perpetual flight becomes his only means to avoid the corrosive human contact. Like the purple sparrow, he sought to join his kind, to find a place amid his fellowmen. They, like the angry flock of sparrows seeing a stranger in their midst, attacked him. Through a whole labyrinth of encounters, the implacable evil of mankind is affirmed. With the intuitive sense of a child, the boy recognizes that "joining the flock" is damnation, a willing complicity with evil itself. To be a painted bird, lonely but free, is perhaps best. Trapped within the unyielding meshes of violent life, the young boy realized, paradoxically, that he had been free within the forests and villages; that within the limits of his own determination and skill he could escape whenever the turbulence of mankind threatened to draw him into its own drowning evil.

The dominating quality of Kosinski's fictional vision in *The Painted Bird* is his vivid rendition of violence. He portrays the power behind this violence as a manifestation of instinctual depravity in man. As Hannah Arendt points out in her brilliant essay "On Violence," the climax of terror is reached when mankind begins to devour its own children, when yesterday's executioner becomes today's victim.[2] Continued violence cannot derive its opposite—strength and peace must flow from the roots of the individual. With a wisdom that is preconscious, the boy identifies with the painted bird, with the symbol of individualism.[3] That is his consolation, his stay, in a world which offers no opportunity for hope. Nothing in human life is secured in its origin unless it is verified in the intimate meeting of concrete experience. In *The Painted Bird,* no basis for faith and hope is nourished by the violent quality of life. The unfolding human cycle is not marked by love.

In Kosinski's second novel, the landscape of violence is retained. In *Steps,* there is an extraordinary increase in the author's stylistic power, and the dramatic evocations of his prose make a comparison with Joseph Conrad's "The Heart of Darkness" almost inevitable. Like the Conradian prose of that tale, Kosinski's words are weighted with a brooding portent. Differing from his previous books, *Steps* is marked by a cold lucidity and a finely disciplined poetic atmosphere. Like the work of Franz Kafka and Samuel Beckett, *Steps* is a uniquely modern document, a genuine "sign of the times." Its import as an artistic vehicle may, indeed, have a serious effect on the future of the novel as a literary form.

One's initial impulse in reading *Steps* is a futile search for analogues of form. Its dark and surreal Kafkan mode is impressive. The novel is clearly anti-conventional, but here even the loosely critical term "anti-conventional" offers little insight into the nature of the problem. The word "novel" appears on the title page, but one's expectations of character delineation and plot structure are quickly destroyed. In a series of notes[4] made by Kosinski during the writing of *Steps,* he states that his novel has "no plot in the Aristotelian sense, for in Aristotelian terms, in the revelation of the action, the end establishes the beginning, and the middle serves as a means to evolve towards the end." His novel, Kosinski further insists, precludes an ordering in time. "It is," he writes, "between the past and the present of the multitude of incidents of *Steps* that the projected contest takes place. Given this distortion of time, the novel gains its effect from no predetermined emotional group response. The reader must draw from his own sources of experience and fantasy, automatically filling in his own formulated response." The "projected contest" possesses its own reality in the imagination's power to seize the elusive threads of the past and the future, in the capacity for recollection and expectation. Through this seizure of the present, the "experiment" of *Steps* does not have an apt parallel in Joyce or Woolf or Beckett, nor do Kosinski's puzzling notes accompany the novel proper. The reader is thereby left undirected and must fashion for himself a unity of time, a center around which to apprehend significances. The "experiment" of *Steps* is clearly a part of the continuing problem of fashioning a vehicle adequate to the artist's special vision. The absolute nature of that vision is not without paradox and ambiguity, and certainly Kosinski's literary intentions cannot be divined solely with the book itself.

Kosinski's first novel, *The Painted Bird,* casts a partial illumination on the moral implication of *Steps.* In the previous novel, the scenes of sexual perversity and individual brutality are overbearing to the point of revulsion. In the end, the boy is molded by the brutishness of man, and he joins the ranks of hatred and animalism. The bond of hatred becomes the common inheritance of mankind.

In *Steps,* Kosinski is working with an extension of the same theme. While *The Painted Bird* offers neither grace nor hope to mitigate the pains of our brutishness, Kosinski's second novel exposes the psyche of his central figure to the same process whereby life is drained of any meaningful content. This agony of man's arrival at "the broken center" is identified by Nathan A. Scott as a version of modern tragic vision. "Life is experienced as having broken down: that congruence between the highest aspirations of the human spirit and its world environment, apart from which existence seems utterly futile, is no longer discernible, and the protagonist finds himself adrift in a rudderless bark whose passage is through deeps unchartered and unconsoling."[5] According to Scott, modern man has arrived at "the broken center," and mere anarchy is loosed upon the world. The distance between man and environment is immeasurably lengthened, and the laws of participation and reciprocity have been abandoned in the face of a silent and unyielding world. The human landscape is now marked by fluidity, rootlessness, anonymity, and moral indifference.

Kosinski's *Steps* charts this tragic and inchoate world. His story moves like a set of bad dreams over many nights of fitful sleep.

Steps is a very brief novel, less than 150 pages. There are no chapters in the accepted sense. The book consists of some thirty-five individual episodes of extraordinarily diverse action. Interspersed throughout these vignettes are elliptical moments of conversation between a man and a woman. Their conversations are italicized and in present voice. The subject of these dialogues is always a variation of some sexual activity or impulse. The other episodes or vignettes are always written in time past, and the narrator who holds them together is never identified beyond I, the presiding voice and memory. These episodes are frequently moments of recollection or fantasy, and the differences between the recording of a fact or the yearning of a desire or wish are never made apparent. There is no logic or rationale for the sequence of events, although a few episodes hinge upon a common experience; that is, when the narrator was a student, or in the army, or in New York. But even this clue of position or place does not essentially determine the content of the episode itself.

The episodes depict a range of brutal and bizarre experiences. In the opening episode, the narrator is penniless and alone on a sparsely populated island: he wins some food by succumbing to the sexual advances of two extremely fat and sweaty matrons. He travels to unspecified places, meeting people without names. He is the victim of a homosexual whore, sees a "show" in a small town where a young girl copulates with an unspecified animal; he later meets a circus acrobat who can brush his mouth with her womb and face simultaneously. As a young student, he recounts a gang rape of his girl friend and how he seized the psychological advantage of this event to make her the object of his own sexual defilement. In two events, he poses beautifully the senseless and wanton destruction of butterflies by little children and an equally senseless murder of a night-watchman; both episodes are motivated by the narrator's desire to clinically observe the death agony of the victim.

After the novels of Herbert Selby and William Burroughs and the late works of Gore Vidal, this range of horror strikes the reader as the all too familiar stuff of perverse modernist imagination, "a derangement of the senses." In the Kosinski novel, however, the horror is rigidly controlled in the sharpness and verve of each episode. The coldness of Kafkan lucidity informs the prose, while the words themselves spin out the abominable; and the echo of Kurtz's "The horror! The horror!" sounds in the distance. What takes place before the reader's sight is not gratuitous or hallucinatory as the nightmarish events of *Naked Lunch* or *The Soft Machine.* In both of the Burroughs novels, the reader is not threatened by a sense of complicity because the fictive events are filtered through a nightmare reality. In Kosinski's novel, the aesthetic distance is closed and the reader does not have the safety and comfort of a mere spectator at unspeakable events. The horror in *Steps* is committed in places without names by persons unspecified. The personalities involved are faceless actors in a social order of destructive force. Their brute acts are the final result of the interplay between a world of distrust and hate and the pliant but feeble impulse of hope and grace, the battened instinct that raises man above the brute. The image of *Steps* is a moral descendance, a spiral downward—a recoil into disgust.

Kosinski's power to create a special seizure of reality, to make vivid as "felt experience" the painful stripping of man's internal and external worlds, is more compelling than he himself allows. Referring once again to his own notes for the novel, Kosinski states, "Each incident in *Steps* is morally ambiguous. The reader is guided to an area of experience by himself. His gain is the product of his own sifting through and refining much of the author's imagery. The reader should do this unconsciously, leaving each episode with a tingle of recognition, an intimation, no more." Through such a stratagem, the author effaces himself; and he offers to the reader the entire burden of coherent response. That burden of recognition, the intimation, is inescapable. The tragic devitalization is everywhere present in the individual frames or episodes of the novel.

The major artistic and moral effects of the novel are achieved—as Kosinski himself indicates—in the imagery and in his refusal to follow an Aristotelian "revelation in action." Of the two, the central image of "steps" is the most elusive because it has no internal reference in the book. Whatever pattern the image conjures up—whether that pattern be a staircase, a spiral, or simply a footfall, pace following pace—one can find no explicit correspondence for it in the text. Initially, the reader may be reminded of the process of death as it overtook Tolstoy's suffering protagonist, Ivan Ilych. How it happened, it is impossible to say, because death came about "step by step," unnoticed. For Ivan Ilych, the advent of death was obscured by his own blindness to the glory of life. In some measure, the sequence of events in Kosinski's novel suggest a similar death-like process—moving "step by step," unnoticed. But the sequence provides no direct line to the image. With its own strange imprecision, the image hovers over the narrative journey, elliptically guiding the reader through an uncharted corridor. The journey exists out of datable time, but with its peculiar presence grounded in the time of memory. The immediate actuality of the novel exists in what Kosinski himself calls "the divide between past and present" which emerges out of the mind's capacity for recollection and expectation, "in the imagination's fusion of its memory of the past and its anticipation of the future." This profound awareness of time, of the singular presence of modern man, exhibits him stripped of defenses . . . a deprived and abandoned self.

In opposition to this notion of man as a lonely and isolated self, the revolution in psychoanalytic thinking, fostered in the writings of Erik Erikson, has provided modern man with a bulwark against the desperation of estrangement from the earth and his fellowman. At the center of Erikson's thought is the question: "Is life a series of steps, each with one before it and after, and each person's set of steps very much beside and connected to those that belong to others?"[6] The great power of Erikson's influence has been precisely in his capacity to see the hidden threads of human interrelation and man's psychic history woven into the nature of his individual and cultural history. *Steps* is a portrait of man devolving in a hostile cultural history.

If one accepts the novel as the sole document for interpretation, the moral evolution of man is an unrelieved blackness. It is the point of despair from which no writer can rise for further artistic development: he is destined to continue repeating the agony of the steps downward and to the repetitious dramatization of "the death of man." But here one needs to separate the faceless, nameless narrator from the author. The narrator has felt the pulse of the world, so seemingly bereft of grace, and he has descended into tragic devitalization. The author, still possessed of moral passion and visionary hope, retreats from the violence, from the devaluation of the human spirit. Convinced that Jerzy Kosinski is both a serious and a profound writer, one searches the novels for signs of this affirmative spirit, the belief that man can retreat from a violent devitalization.

It is only when one turns to the epigraph of *Steps* that one can discern a glimmer of the author's intent. Taken from the sacred book, *The Bhagavad Gita,* this epigraph reads:

> For the uncontrolled there is no wisdom, nor for the uncontrolled is there the power of concentration; and for him without concentration, there is no peace. And for the unpeaceful, how can there be happiness?

The moral equipoise which Kosinski seeks is the ascendant step, a direction opposite from that which he fictionalizes, a new world in which the control, peace, and happiness of the *Bhagavad Gita* is restored to the life of man. For Kosinski and for his reader, the moral imperative is clear, but the journey back to life remains uncharted.

In interpreting Kosinski's fictional vision, in attributing to him an affirmative passion for a retreat from violence, the implications of a single epigraph are a fragile base. One is forced to search for a more substantive statement of commitment, and in this process, Kosinski's discursive political writings must play their part. In contemplating the total canon of Kosinski's writing, a critic runs headlong into the question—why the delay in novelistic expression of the compelling reality of violence witnessed in his childhood? The novels took their imaginative shape after the studies of Russian life in 1960 and 1962. Prior to the publication of the novels, Kosinski's primary energies, as a thinker and writer, were directed toward attacking a dehumanizing political philosophy with which he had a personal and intimate knowledge. He fled Communist dominated Poland in 1957, as did the narrator in the closing scenes of *Steps.* Brilliant and detailed, *The Future Is Ours, Comrade* and *No Third Path* both record the devitalization and suppression of individualism and human personality in Russia. The political concepts of freedom and responsibility could not, for Kosinski, survive on so alien a soil as Soviet Russia. Although both of his studies of Russian life are directly concerned with the power of an oppressive political system, his primary objective was to observe and record the debilitating impact of a communal and collective society upon the individual. Within this political framework, the value of the individual is always subordinated to the collective goals. The weight of harm and destruction to the individual is made appallingly clear. But more ominous than the loss of any one individual is the concerted and sustained effort to erase any vestige of the individual human right. As this political pattern exerts itself from generation to generation, it ultimately produces a psychic tyranny whose power is unshakable, because it has destroyed the history of man's political evolution toward individual dignity. Constrained by a frightening political system, Kosinski fled his native land, and he recorded his fears for mankind in the Russian studies. Those immediate political fears had a priority in his career as a writer.

Only later, when he turned to fiction was he able to make vivid and concrete that vision of fear. The process of dehumanization in each novel is portrayed against a political and moral atmosphere, a portentous presence which conspires to brutalize man by sustaining him in dark ignorance. The young boy's conversion in *The Painted Bird* to a world of hatred and distrust may, from one point of view, be conceived as a psychic success for the forces of dark ignorance. The protagonist of *Steps* is propelled to his "journey's end" by an equally destructive element—an internal and external stripping away of human personality.

To an understanding of this process of human destruction, the incisive writings of Erik Erikson lend themselves significantly because they illuminate both the spiritual power of the *Bhagavad Gita* and the "dark journey" in Kosinski's novels. When one returns to the epigraph of *Steps,* one recognizes that Kosinski has selected the appropriate epigraph with uncommon skill. The emphasis on "control" and "concentration" as virtues as special centers of human strength from which flow peace and happiness is at the spiritual core of the *Bhagavad Gita.* These values of soul and mind are, from the perspective of Erik Erikson's psychoanalytic writing, the same structures upon which humanity must depend or sink into the derangement of individual and social chaos.

As Erikson clearly establishes, the pathology of uprootedness in our time has destroyed for many the "control" and "concentration" which breeds peace. The individual torn away—as Kosinski's protagonists are—from the multiple sources of strength of a society in moral balance, becomes a transmigrant—a stranger in the world. Kosinski and Erikson both raise similar questions in regard to the cosmic stranger. What motivates and moves the transmigrant; how has he been excluded or has excluded himself from his previous home? By what process, by what evolution of "inherent strength" can man traverse the distance between home and his destination? Erikson tries to come to grips with this question by establishing a cycle of individual human virtues which are themselves a part of the fabric and cycle of generations of man. It is, for him, the interdependence and mutuality of "human strength" that provides the key to the balance of meaningful life. The rudiments of virtue developed in childhood—the strength for hope, will, and purpose—are the foundation for the mature virtues of adulthood—love, care and wisdom. "Any span of the cycle lived without vigorous meaning, at the beginning, in the middle, or at the end, endangers the sense of life and the meaning of death in all whose life stages are intertwined." The "concentration" and "control"—the collective wisdom of an age—Erikson declares, maintain and convey the integrity of human experience. Only if vigor of the mind combines with the gift of responsible renunciation can life be preserved. In his fiction, Kosinski imaginatively intuits the truth that each cycle of man must transmit its collective inherent strength to the oncoming generation. On the same truth, Erik Erikson writes: "Only such integrity can balance the despair of the knowledge that life is coming to a conscious conclusion, only such wholeness can transcend the petty disgust of feeling finished and passed by, and the despair of facing the period of relative helplessness which marks the end as it marked the beginning."[7]

The power of Erikson's wisdom is the product of decades of study in psychoanalysis. His model of evolving "virtue" or "inherent strength" suggests from a purely humanist point of view, the same power Kosinski is trying to call back into existence in his epigraph—the restored capacity for control and concentration, for a vigor of mind combined with the gift for responsible renunciation. Both Kosinski's Russian studies and his novels reaffirm the final necessity of turning from violence and turbulence if mankind is to be restored to a vigorous life. While Kosinski's present canon of fiction may be too slight, too elusive a basis for a crystallized direction, he is among that slim band of modernist writers whose acute cultural and spiritual dramatizations are reflective of hope—without which life ceases to be.

Notes

1. In this essay, the following texts have been used as citation sources: 1. *The Painted Bird* (Boston: Houghton Mifflin Company, 1965); 2. *Steps* (New York: Random House, 1968). Kosinski has also written two nonfiction books under the pen name Joseph Novak: 1. *The Future Is Ours, Comrade* (New York: Doubleday and Company, Inc., 1960) and 2. *No Third Path: A Study of Soviet Behavior* (Garden City, 1962). References to these volumes are cited by page number in parentheses after each quotation.

2. Hannah Arendt, *On Violence* (New York, 1970), p. 46.

3. The concept of self or individualism is a primary notion in Kosinski's mind. In a brief essay (The *New York Times,* October 13, 1970), he explores the contemporary college student as a "dead soul"—"isolated by a collective medium which permits each of them to escape direct contact with the others. Deafening sound effectively rules out every interchange. No one ever questions the intruding voice, for unlike an individual character, the collective identity requires no explanation or justification: it is and that is enough."

4. Kosinski's essays (*Notes of an Author,* 1965; and *The Art of the Self,* 1968) were originally written as correspondence between the author and some of his foreign-language publishers (Germany, Spain, Portugal, Italy, and Holland). Since this correspondence was conducted in English, and since some of these publishers wanted to publish the essays in translation as an appendix to Kosinski's novels, the author had no choice but to comply with the United States Copyright Law, and he agreed to have this correspondence first published in the United States. Otherwise, the essays would become public domain. The citation for these essays is as follows: 1) *Notes of the Author on the Painted Bird.* New York: Scientia-Factum, Inc., Gregory House, New York, 1965. 2) *The Art of the Self.* New York: Scientia-Factum, Inc., Gregory House, New York, 1968.

5. Nathan A. Scott, Jr., *The Broken Center: Studies in the Theological Horizon of Modern Literature* (New Haven, 1966), p. 122.

6. Robert Coles, *Erik H. Erikson: The Growth of His Mind* (Boston, 1970), p. 161.

7. Erik Erikson, *Insight and Responsibility: Lectures on the Ethical Implications of Psychoanalytic Insight* (New York, 1970), p. 187.

Jerzy Kosinski: The Painted Bird and Other Disguises

GERALD WEALES

I

In *No Third Path* (1962), in "The Price of Being Different," the chapter on the *stilyagi* and other manifestations of controlled nonconformism in the Soviet Union, Joseph Novak meets Varia, a literary specialist whose career was wrecked when she tried, at the wrong time, to revive interest in Alexander Grin. She describes an incident, presumably from her own childhood, when she and some other kids caught a sparrow and painted it purple. When they released the bird, it flew up to join the others of its own kind. For a moment, there was a flash of color among the drabness and then free-falling purple. The bird fell, conveniently, in a puddle of water, so that the children could gather around it and Varia could remember, "The water was rapidly turning a brownish-red. He had been killed by the other sparrows, by their hate for color and their instinct of belonging to a gray flock." When Novak, in one of his changes of feathers, put on his other and real name, Jerzy Kosinski, and turned novelist, he reworked Varia's story, finding in it the central image for *The Painted Bird* (1965). The political implications of Varia's version, obvious in phrases like "their hate for color" and "gray flock," still exist in the last chapters of the novel, but Kosinski's Painted Bird, much more generalized than Novak's, becomes the outsider, a label that encompasses everything from the village outcast to the Jew on the way to Auschwitz. Kosinski-Novak, whether he was writing fiction or socio-political reportage, from *The Future Is Ours, Comrade* (1960) to *Being There* (1971), has been preoccupied—argumentatively or dramatically—with the individual bird and the flock, with the danger and attraction of the painted feather, with the methods the flock uses (flockways?) to punish or repaint the bird or to alter its own group vision.

At the end of *The Painted Bird,* in an epilogue of sorts, Kosinski returns to the expository third person with which the book opens (the novel is told in the first) and takes his protagonist into the present, putting him aboard a

Reprinted from *Hollins Critic* 9, no. 3 (October 1972): 1–12, with the permission of the journal.

transoceanic plane. Although Kosinski has dismissed the autobiographical overtones of that novel (in an interview in *Publisher's Weekly,* April 26, 1971), this presumably is one of the admitted "resemblances" between the author and his character. The flight, then, would be the one that brought Kosinski from Poland to the United States in 1957, and there is irony in the last line of the novel: "In this flight the Painted Bird again became himself." What he became, literarily at least, was the mysterious Joseph Novak, the author of *The Future Is Ours, Comrade.* As one reads that book, it is never very clear just who the narrator is, what he is doing in Russia, why everyone seems willing to talk to him, even when the visit takes place. He appears variously as a student, as a scientist (in the wider Soviet usage that takes in the "humanistic sciences"), as "a minor bureaucrat from one of the satellite countries"; at one point, he differentiates between "my country" and Poland. All this might seem to be an obvious and understandable attempt not to identify himself for personal and political reasons, to protect family and friends in Poland, perhaps, or Russian connections (there are several pages in *No Third Path* on the unhappy consequences to the inhabitants of *A Room in Moscow* after Sally Belfrage's book appeared), but by 1965 and the publication of *Bird,* the identity of Novak was no longer a secret; besides, Kosinski was a graduate student when he wrote the Novak books and, as he told *PW,* "My former experience had taught me that when you are a student you are not supposed to write books, you are supposed to read them." That is, look to your feathers. I have gone on at this length about the slippery identity of the author largely because Kosinski, as Novak, and his narrator, who has almost no existence except as a recording ear, seem to me illustrations, in a larger context, of the main theme of the book.

II

In *No Third Path,* Kosinski defines his "sociological investigation," of which *The Future Is Ours, Comrade* is the first American manifestation, as a study of "the relations existing between the individual and the small group in socialist cooperative systems." Despite the hint of "scientific" objectivity in that phrase, both books become illustrations of the disappearance of the individual in Soviet society. Whatever the ostensible subject of any of the chapters in *Future*—education, say, or medicine—we get a picture of the person living communally, likely to be called on by his Party unit, his Komsomol group, his union, his whateveritis (and often several at once) to account for any nonconforming action. "After all, man errs," says Fedor, the young scientist in *No Third Path* who is reprimanded for being absorbed in himself, "and the collective can notice and brand this in time." *Future* is, finally, a portrait of "the New Man," who willy-nilly (and usually more willy than nilly) allows himself to be shaped to fit the presumed need of the community (that is, he has his painted feathers clipped). The implications of this national character become politically significant and a little frightening in the final sections of the book in which a long discussion of war and peace posits the inevitability of a war with the United States and gives point to the title of the book. *Future,* then, is a late-blooming Cold War flower. What begins as an examination of the people at work, at play, at home, becomes an exposé of "the New Man" as victim of "the government which surrounds him, shapes his imagination, limits his horizons, and cripples his character."

The content of *The Future Is Ours, Comrade* is now less interesting than its method, for one reads it in 1972 not for Joseph Novak, Russian specialist, but for Jerzy Kosinski, incipient novelist. The structure of the book suggests the later novels, the gathering of parts that never quite become a whole. In *Future,* Kosinski introduces a number of exemplary characters, each of whom contributes to the immediate subject of the chapter and the overall theme of Soviet conformism. There is, however, no attempt to bridge between figures. One conversation simply stops and the next begins. In form, then, if not in material, there is a suggestion of the self-contained tales in *The Painted Bird* and the fragments that make up *Steps* (1968).

Each person in *Future* is presented through what we are supposed to take as his own words, although, later, in *No Third Path,* Kosinski admits that he uses "condensed and composite" interviews and that "the subjectivity of the quoted comments" is filtered through "the subjectivity of the author." This implies that the reported speeches are artificial concoctions which, even if one accepts the substantive truth of the interviews, are designed for a particular effect. Certainly, Kosinski manipulates his material in other, more obvious ways, uses journalistic tricks which are also novelistic devices. The two most in evidence, both ironic, are juxtaposition and the too-neat tagline closing off an anecdote. The first can be seen most obviously in the foreword to the book, in which the narrator sits on a train, chatting and dining with an embassy official. A small boy, one of the "gray, colorless people" they have seen standing on station platforms, presses his face to the window and stares longingly at the fruit on their table. A few paragraphs later, the official, coming on like an old *New Masses* capitalist, peels "the golden skin of a banana" in a way that calls attention to "a large, heavy signet ring with a red star engraved on a gold background." For pat final lines, consider the convenient rain with which Kosinski ends his discussion of the social pressure to fulfill excessive production quotas: "It ran down the inside of the glass distorting the faces of the shock workers and washing away the big-bellied figures representing norms exceeded." As these two examples indicate—and I have chosen them for their representative quality, not for their clumsiness—Kosinski at this point is still an amateur, going for easy effects. Although he learned to use them with a great deal more skill in the service of much more complicated emotional and artistic responses, these devices remain the staple of the later novels. Even in these, he too often slips into a kind of facile cleverness. *Steps* is full of examples, but let me take one from *The Painted Bird* which I think cheapens one of the best and most horrifying chapters in the novel. At the end of the tale that gives the book its title, the account of Lekh and the destruction of Ludmila, Kosinski adds a last, unnecessary, almost smug line: "Above us wheeled a flock of birds, chirping and calling from all directions."

In language, too, the early books offer hints of what is to come. For the most part, the novels avoid the heavyweight, poli-sci profundities that fill the interstices between interviews in the early books (not completely: when Gavrila turns up in *The Painted Bird,* we are in for heavy weather) because the novels tend toward the anecdotal, the dramatic, the pictorial. The language usage that I have in mind is the choice of the *mot injuste.* For instance, in the chapter on the family in *The Future Is Ours, Comrade,* Kosinski records with "objective" distaste the way the old are separated from their children and grandchildren and closeted in homes for the aged. "Their weak, pale eyes stared at me as I listened to their tragic complaints, whispered through toothless mouths." One might pass over the "weak, pale eyes," forgetting the hawk-eyed old men one knows, even accept reluctantly the "tragic complaints" as an example of the kind of banal American usage that fascinates Kosinski (see the *PW* interview), but those "toothless mouths" are hard to take. Surely, even in the Soviet Union, there are occasionally men and women among the discarded old who have their own or false teeth. What Kosinski is attempting in that sentence is not necessarily dishonorable. After all, one of the primary uses of language for the artist is to channel the reader's emotional and intellectual response by a dexterous choice of words. Perhaps, knowing that Americans also junk their elders, Kosinski went for sentiment because he could not trust the material to make its own point. The resulting sentence, however, is heart-tuggingly overwritten and the effect is a falsifying of the situation by rhetorical inflation.

I am probably on dangerous ground when I suggest that this kind of verbal manipulation—much more skillfully employed—is too evident in the novels. Despite his predilection for rather ornate simile ("Her lids were like furrows in deeply plowed soil"), Kosinski has been celebrated for the simplicity of his language, and critical opinion has, for the most part, agreed with Irving Howe, who wrote in *Harper's* (March 1969), "Simply as a stylist, Kosinski has few equals among American novelists." Stylistic simplicity in Kosinski is likely to take the form of understatement (ending a sentence which appears to be leading the reader along a descending line of importance with "and shot one or two peasants to set an example"), and it works best when the horror of the situation—the blinding of the plowboy in *Bird,* for instance—is much more intense than the words that describe it might imply: "For a moment the eye rested on the boy's cheek as if uncertain what to do next; then it finally tumbled down his shirt onto the floor." In contrast, the description of the sexual encounter between Labina and one of her men ("the man howling like a dog, the woman grunting like a pig") appears to have a great deal more to do with a recurrent Kosinski attitude toward sex as demeaning violence than it does toward the scene itself, even when we accept that it is being watched by the boy, crouching on the dirt floor "covered with cat feces and the remains of birds they had dragged in." It seems designed to make us accept a label ("So that's what love was: savage as a bull prodded with a spike; brutal, smelly, sweaty") rather than experience the truth of either the coupling peasants or the unwilling voyeur. Considering the evocative power of so many of Kosinski's dramatic images, particularly in *The Painted Bird,* it is somewhat unfortunate that he feels the need to keep his readers at a constant level of shock and must fall back on artificial verbal stimulus to pump up the scenes that do not make it on their own. Unfortunate, but not surprising after *The Future Is Ours, Comrade.*

In the paragraphs above I have used *Future* and *No Third Path* interchangeably. That is somewhat misleading. Although the devices under discussion do appear, somewhat infrequently, in Kosinski's second book, *Future* is the real source for them. *No Third Path*—although it gave Kosinski *The Painted Bird*—is little more than a rather dull echo of *Future.* The first book was something of a success—excerpted in *The Saturday Evening Post,* abridged in *Reader's Digest*—and *No Third Path* reads like an attempt to cash in on its predecessor. It is put together from leftover notes from Kosinski's research in Russia, fattened out with extensive quotations from Soviet publications and occasional post-emigration chats with Soviet or East European types. The difference between the two books can perhaps be seen most easily in the two introductions; Irving R. Levine's slightly skeptical admiration of *Future* gives way to Joseph G. Harrison's Cold War testimony to *Path* as an "eye opener" in the best *Future* tradition. *No Third Path* turns out to be interesting neither for its predictable political point (the same as *Future*'s) nor its accidental prophecies of what is to come literarily, but for the few things it says about the author. In this book, the Russian visit becomes clearly an attempt to fit into the Soviet system, one that fails and sends Kosinski to the United States; since Gavrila figures in the book as an officer rather high in the military hierarchy, presumably the "influential official" who sponsors Kosinski's visit, his rejection of the Soviet option prefigures Gavrila's failure to keep the boy in *The Painted Bird.* Then, too, Kosinski quotes or invents words for Zina, a girl toward whom he is attracted but who rejects him as insufficiently committed to the system: "And yet you are a little egoist, wrapped up in yourself! Your own nose, which you consider too long, your naturalistic remembrances of childhood and the war, your hatred of village life and primitive conditions, your 'exercise of intimacy.' " In *No Third Path,* Kosinski is plainly on the way to *The Painted Bird.* He said as much when he told *Publisher's Weekly* that his nonfiction "was an attempt to turn a major aspect of my growing up into a literary experience and therefore the natural progression was towards the novel."

III

Although it is easy now, looking backward, to find the seeds of Kosinski's novels in his nonfiction, it would have been impossible for a reader of *The Future Is Ours, Comrade* and *No Third Path* to predict the power, the inventiveness, the sophistication of *The Painted Bird.* Kosinski's narrator/hero is a small boy sent "to the shelter of a distant village" at the beginning of World War II; when his foster mother dies, he begins to wander from village to village, occasionally finding refuge, but generally suffering violence and humiliation because he is dark-haired, dark-skinned and to the blond, blue-eyed peasants of Eastern Poland a "Jew," a "gypsy," one of the official outcasts of the German invaders. The result is a series of disconnected stories—horror stories for the ugliest kind of realism. The narrator is an actor in some of them, but in others he is no more than an observer. The cumulative force of these chapters, as cruelty piles on cruelty, superstition on superstition, outrage on outrage, creates a world in which casual violence, ugly sex, deforming greed are the standards and in which the outsider bears the brunt of the daily horror. Although the boy, the Painted Bird, carries the main burden of this theme, it is reflected in many other ways: at length, in the stories of Ludmila, so brutally punished by the women of her village, and of Handsome Laba, who is driven to suicide; briefly, in the scene early in the book where the boys torture and burn a squirrel or in the passages in which Lekh, in sorrow at losing his love, kills his birds by painting them bright colors and turning them loose to be destroyed by their own kind. Since all this takes place in the context of World War II and the Jewish holocaust—trains on the way to the camps pass through the book and the boy at once identifies and separates himself from the faces he sees—the hideousness of flock behavior, almost understandable in the subsistence world of the villages, is raised to encompass genocide.

The difficulty with the book lies in the final sections, after the boy is rescued and adopted by the Russian troops. For one thing, the book ceases to be dramatic, turns ideological. The last few pages of the chapter in which Gavrila appears read like a précis of the early nonfiction books. Aside from the abrupt shift in tone, this section of the book is suspect thematically. The narrator makes a specific analogy between his gypsy wanderings and the "life of these Soviet grownups" in the maze of professional and political paths. Yet the "Soviet grownups" in question are clearly part of the Soviet flock and the real analogy lies with the author (the narrator grown up) and his inability (and unwillingness) to conform. Kosinski saves the book thematically and dramatically by rescuing the boy from his rescuers, showing him in the orphanage and among the night people of the city where he can be seen with his nonconforming plumage on display. This prepares for the "message" note on which the book ends, although such preparation is not necessarily artistic justification.

Kosinski is not interested in conventional narrative technique. Early in the book, he either carries the narrator from one scene to another by highly artificial means (for instance, having finished with one village, he lets the boy float away on an inflated fish bladder) or else he begins a chapter in a new location with new characters and makes no attempt to show how the boy got there. (It may have been this sense of separate anecdotes that lets him forget and allow the boy to howl after he has been struck dumb.) Even so, the novel develops a narrative interest, if not an old-fashioned story line. We become involved with the fact of the boy's survival and his growing sense that he will come through. Elie Wiesel (*New York Times,* October 31, 1965) explains that the boy manages to stay alive by learning to hate and to use his hate, but the development is more complicated than that. He goes through a number of philosophical-theological stages, each of them related to a need to find a flock identity, before he comes finally to depend on himself. He accepts the ghosts and ghoulies, the superstitions of Marta and Olga, at the beginning of the work, and takes uneasy shelter in their mixture of witchcraft and folk belief. Later he allies himself with God, uses prayer to build up a pile of indulgences that he assumes will protect him. When that leads to immersion in a pit of human excrement, he embraces the Evil One with no better results. At last, Gavrila teaches him to put everything metaphysical behind him and put his dependence in man alone, but the lessons of Mitka's revenge ("Man carries in himself his own private war, which he has to wage, win or lose, himself—his own justice, which is his alone to administer") and of Gavrila's failure to save him from the parents he no longer knows, lead him to turn Gavrila's man-centered philosophy to his own uses, to reject the Marxist mythology with the religious ones and to choose to be a Painted Bird rather than to have the paint thrust upon him: "Every one of us stood alone, and the sooner a man realized that all Gavrilas, Mitkas, and Silent Ones were expendable, the better for him."

The philosophical wanderings that thread in and out of the narrator's physical wanderings are fascinating as long as Kosinski keeps them within the boy's range of perception, allows him to conceive the spiritual world in concrete terms, and as long as the consequences of his misconceptions are presented dramatically. But there are long sections of theological games-playing, rather too sophisticated for the narrator, and these, I am afraid, are an offshoot of Kosinski's greatest weakness as a novelist, his desire to explain things—his symbols, the significance of his scenes, the political and philosophical implications of the action. One corner of his mind seems never to have got on that plane that let him escape from a society in which ritual self-examination is the norm. "I think a novel should speak with its own voice," he told *Publisher's Weekly,* "and therefore I never talk about a book." That is nonsense, of course. The final italics section of *The Painted Bird* is more a comment on the novel than an integral part of it. What is more, the front matter of *Being There* lists among the "Books by Jerzy Kosinski," two things labeled

"Essays"—*Notes of the Author* and *The Art of the Self.* These are not easily identifiable, but I assume that they are authorial comments on *The Painted Bird* and *Steps.* At least *Notes* sounds as though it might be *The Author on The Painted Bird,* the essay Kosinski wrote as an Appendix to the German edition of *Bird,* which the Library of Congress Union Catalogue lists as a separate pamphlet, published in 1965, but with no publisher given. And *Art* was added to the list of Kosinski's works after *Steps* came out.

All disavowals aside, Kosinski is a highly conscious philosophical novelist, as I suggested in my opening paragraph. Yet, for me, he is most successful when he creates a scene which has a frightening artistic reality and which keeps its extra-dramatic implications carefully unspoken. The image in *The Painted Bird* which sticks most vividly in my mind—some days I wish it would fade away—is that of the stunned rabbit which comes to as the boy is midway in the process of skinning it and runs about, its skin flapping crazily around it. That scene, like so many in the early section of the book, is hypnotically compelling and, for that reason, *The Painted Bird* remains, so far as I am concerned, the most impressive of the Kosinski novels.

IV

By comparison to *The Painted Bird, Steps* is a marvelously allusive novel, one which leaves the reader to find his own structure, hence presumably his own meaning—or so Kosinski says in a statement that Irving Howe quotes in his *Harper's* review. For that reason—given my doubts about *Bird*—I should find *Steps* particularly attractive. Instead, I found myself at first intrigued, then annoyed, finally bored by it, a progression that I had to make in less than 200 pages. The book consists of a number of fragments—sketches, anecdotes, bits of conversation—some of which are set in the villages of *The Painted Bird,* some in the collective society of the nonfiction books, some in the country to which the escaping narrator comes. Each of them makes a point, either discursively or dramatically, more often in terms of the kind of balanced image and ironic fillip that Kosinski used, with so much less control, in *The Future Is Ours, Comrade.* Some of them are extremely good. I like particularly the relatively long story in which the narrator discovers a woman caged in a barn, a lunatic kept to service the men of the village; after having engineered the woman's release, the narrator returns to the village—months later—to accuse the priest of having known what was going on. The priest admits as much, but denounces the narrator for failing to understand the village. It is the final image that gives the story its power. Sitting in the church, the narrator sees the priest's "bony hand" issue from the confessional box to be kissed and we can see (and happily are not told) the way the priest, like the woman in the cage, is used by the village. This story is an exception, however. For the most part, the fragments have the coldness of exercises and a few of them strike me as a little simple-minded. Take, for instance, a reworking of a character from *No Third Path.* There, Kosinski describes a bookkeeper, a man who chooses not to distinguish himself, opts for smallness as self-protection. The only thing singular about him is his love for men's rooms, which he sees as temples of a sort in which he can find the refuge of being alone, safe behind a locked stall door. Comfort stations in a benedictory sense, although Kosinski never phrases it that way. When the bookkeeper reemerges as the philosopher in *Steps,* he is boxed into a neat little anecdote which ends—oh, irony!—with his suicide in a lavatory stall.

Irving Howe, unwilling to buy the novel as a do-it-yourself experimental package, solves it structurally by working from "steps" to a journey: "The narrator's journey comes to seem a gradual stripping or destruction of social personality as it is enforced by the pressure of social experience." Not to me, I'm afraid, although certainly such a theme is very close to the continuing concerns of Kosinski, as man and writer. As I read *Steps,* I am aware of repeated ideas (love as an instrument of manipulation), a compulsive preoccupation with certain kinds of material (violent and perverted sex), a cumulative sense of mannerism, an addiction to grotesquerie for its own sake, but if there is one theme on which all this is threaded, it seems to be the inevitability of isolation, forced or chosen (*cf.,* the "stood alone" quotation from *Bird* above). Yet, I remained so distracted by the fragments that I never felt the force of the novel as a whole—and not distracted in the positive sense, as was the case with *The Painted Bird.* I found myself sighing: ho, hum, here comes another gang shag, here comes another beheading. My favorite image in the book comes in the last scene, in which the girl goes swimming and looks up at the leaf floating on the water. It seems to me particularly appropriate to *Steps* itself in the face of the critical attention it received—its having won the National Book Award, for instance. If you are under water, a little leaf throws a large shadow.

V

In his most recent novel, Kosinski has moved away from the material of the early books (except for the inevitable kinky sex), if not from the themes. *Being There* is a parable about how a society, with the help of its media, provides the colored glasses that alter the image if not the fact of a bird's plumage. It is the story of Chance, a slightly retarded young man who has spent his life within the walls of a garden which he tends, or of his room, where his television set is his only contact with the world outside. Chance—wouldn't you know it?—throws him out of the garden and into the world where, thanks to a happy accident, he becomes, in rapid succession, the friend and confidant of a leading industrialist, a presidential advisor, a successful television personality, a figure to reckon with in international politics and, finally, a probable vice-presidential candidate. The joke is that, since his behavior is correct (he models himself on the television images he knows), the people he meets take him as one of them and hear what they want to hear. Since he is not very bright, he can only speak literally ("Our chairs are almost touching," he tells the Soviet diplomat who has been suggesting that they are "not so far from each other") and, if there is no question to call up a direct answer, he falls back on the only thing he knows and discusses gardens. Taken metaphorically, he becomes a sage. In a parallel plot, he apparently satisfies both a homosexual he meets and the financier's wife; they accept his sexual inadequacy (he is impotent, but would not know what to do in any case since sexual behavior cannot be learned from television) as sophistication and use him, as voyeur, as a masturbatory object.

Although the United States in *Being There* has no tactile reality, it is possible to read the novel as an indictment of American society and values. Yet "indictment" suggests a core of social concern which Kosinski rejects in the *Publisher's Weekly* interview. "If the progress of mankind is toward making the human being . . . a composite of external forces, rather than a bastion of human resources," he says, ". . . then this movement would be only natural. I am not going to cry over it." A philosophical tale, then, although such a designation gives *Being There* more dignity than it requires. What it is, really, is a simple, mildly satirical parable, devoid of character and obvious in its message (and in its detail since, as usual, Kosinski cannot refrain from explaining: "His name was Chance because he had been born by chance"; "Whatever one did would then be interpreted by the others in the same way that one interpreted what they did").

In his foolishly chatty column in *Saturday Review* (April 17, 1971), Cleveland Amory tells how he got Kosinski to demonstrate that he could, in fact, make himself disappear in his tiny New York apartment. This game of hide-and-seek might well stand for Kosinski's ability (and need perhaps) to separate himself from other men. That facility, that habit of mind, explains much about his writing, and I suspect, indicates its limitations. Howe, who called his review of *Steps* "From the Other Side of the Moon," worried about the relation between the narrator and author and found "something unnerving about the detachment . . . that rules this book." And not *Steps* alone. Although Kosinski's manipulative hand is clear in all the books, directing the reader's eye to a particular object, his mind to a particular reading of it, he (or his narrator) has little substance. Except for the boy in *The Painted Bird,* presumably the father to all the grownup narrators, none of them exists as a character, and the boy is simply an observer a good part of the time. There is nothing wrong with the writer as observer, but the separating device in Kosinski tends to reduce the thing observed to an example. There are no people in any of his books, not even his nonfiction ones; his characters are either folktale caricatures, the stick-figures of parable, or voices from a sociologist's tape recorder. The flock, Kosinski tells us, fails to recognize the Painted Bird and kills it, but I suspect, after having gone through all his work, that the author as Painted Bird, consciously different, apart, watching, may not be able to see the flock very clearly either. Kosinski's scariest image may be Kosinski himself. In *The Future Is Ours, Comrade,* he describes his romance with Agniya, a girl he met in one of the provincial towns. As a result of his friendship, she changes her hair style and begins to wear make-up until her Komsomol group reprimands her and rescues her from his Western influence. Despite reprimand, despite reversion, she slips down to the station to say goodbye to him as he moves on to his next town, his next interview. "It was hard to remain unemotional," he says, but he manages it pretty well, for the chapter ends, "The train picked up speed. I drew the curtains closed across the compartment window and began to complete my notes."

Horatio Algers of the Nightmare

ELIZABETH STONE

To read Jerzy Kosinski's novels is to invite pain—not the surface pain of a punch, but the pith pain of an assault on one's nerves. Kosinski's characters are casualties: stray threads in a tattered social fabric. They belong nowhere, and wherever they are, they are liars, manipulators, rapists, murderers, poseurs, spies, self-appointed instruments of epicurean retribution—members not of the derelict class (which would give us motivation for them), but often loners of the moneyed upper strata.

Novelists usually write about our private lives. Kosinski's characters have no private lives—they are separated from their cankered intimate pasts by time, space, or language, and have no intimate enduring ties in the present either. In *Devil Tree* (1973), for instance, Jonathan Whalen is left enormously wealthy by a remote and distant father. He recalls the time that, after the death of his mother, a collector sold him several letters his father had written to his mother. They're in an illegible scrawl; he can't decipher them. Even the relationship between lovers fails to provide: in Kosinski's just-published novel, *Blind Date* (1977), George Levanter, a private investor, has a "relationship" with a woman for several years—he doesn't know her last name or where she lives; he doesn't know the work she does or when he'll next see her.

And yet, though we resist the recognition, the sharp chill from this alien world is familiar. In the lives of Kosinski's characters, there is something of ourselves, our time and our condition. If Eden, for the sake of argument, was one life in one place with one set of well-known others, we are all long beyond Eden. One has one's familiars, of course, but in our daily, upwardly mobile lives, how long have we known the person we've known longest, and how much of the rest of our world does he or she share? And even if our answers to these questions are reassuring, how much of our lives do we pass in our cushioned contexts?

The nerve pain comes, though, because Kosinski's novels pierce the social skin and go deeper. They are all accounts of the self in extreme psychological peril, and they make sense the way dreams make sense. Whatever they say to the rational mind—about police states, political prisoners, and social evil—to the anarchic primitive troubled sleeper in all of us, the novels

Originally published in *Psychology Today,* December 1977, 59–60, 63–64.

recreate the aura of nightmare paranoia, rouse fears of psychic petrification, depersonalization, engulfment. These are not simply modern fears, but the founding terrors of infancy rehearsed in myth and fable. Kosinski's characters know the quality of jeopardy felt by Perseus facing the Gorgon; by Odysseus stranded with Circe; by Hansel caged by the witch; by Jonah entombed in the whale. His characters chronicle not only what, at its worst, the world is like but also what, at *our* worst, it feels like. His thematic preoccupations are the dangerous deceitfulness of appearances; isolation, loneliness, anxiety, and violence in a Hobbesian world. In this, Kosinski is a member of the same esthetic coven as Kafka or Dostoyevsky, Bosch or Munch. He exemplifies the preoccupations of thinkers like R. D. Laing or Bruno Bettelheim.

The appeal of his novels is not simply our fascination with the abomination. Kosinski's characters do not die, retreat into permanent catatonia or autism, or dissolve in romantic *Angst.* Rather, they are all Horatio Algers of the nightmare, the first and last frontier. As such, they are relentless, industrious, and inventive survivors. And what each novel probes is: given an infinitude of dangers—many of them the dangers of our own perceptions—by what strategies can we survive relatively intact? In a world that gives nothing, how can we provide for continuity and sustenance?

The answers are as varied and ingenious as the complex psyches of his characters. For Kosinski, as well as for most psychotherapists, language is a primary tool of psychic survival. In fact, in Kosinski's world, the inability to talk is a sure index of one's brutalization. In *The Painted Bird* (1965), Kosinski's first novel, a young Jewish boy is, for five years of his childhood, an on-the-road fugitive from the Nazis, though it is the peasants meant to protect him who harm him the most. Midway in his wanderings, he succumbs to muteness, after repeated brutalization. Garbos, for instance, beats him and hangs him by his hands from hooks in the ceiling for hours at a time while his savage dog snaps at the boy's heels. The peasants drag him from church and toss him into a pit of human excrement.

But at the end, in an April scene, he reclaims language and is "enraptured by the sounds that were heavy with meaning, as wet snow is heavy with water." Yet, not too much meaning. The novel, presumably told from some point after the fact, is a catalogue of horrors rendered in a flat, descriptive monotone. It is not a victory of language over experience, but a way of using language to keep the experience at a safe emotional distance. As such, it embodies the essence of a self-protection that Robert Jay Lifton, in *The Life of the Self,* calls "psychic numbing . . . various degrees of inability to feel . . . gaps between knowledge and feeling."

The boy is the surviving child in all of us, as well as a contemporary Everyman. Lifton believes that those who, by work or happenstance, are in the thick of blood or turmoil mute the horror with such nerve-end retraction, but the price is carting around dead experience, becoming a partially dead self.

Jonathan Whalen, of *Devil Tree,* speaks in the same listless monotone as the boy in *Painted Bird,* though, unlike the young boy, he adds self-analysis to his anecdotes. He is aware, however, that the flat repetition is but a palliative rather than a cure. He seeks out therapy, though with great terror—it will be like having a bone broken *twice,* he feels, and he is haunted by images of bloody violence. But, ultimately, Whalen cannot afford the risk of replicating his feelings, even in order to exorcise or transcend them. "Here we are," he thinks one night during therapy, "a bunch of grown-up kids locked in an empty room playing naive games with each other. No one understands anybody else. We are wandering around in dark caves, holding our little private candles hoping for some great illumination." Close to the novel's end, he suffers a complete nervous breakdown, the proof that reason unaccompanied by feeling will not get us very far, though in the final scenes, his recovery has begun.

The most salutary and adroit use of language is achieved by George Levanter, Kosinski's latest protagonist. "In Russian, the language of his [own] childhood and adolescence, he regressed . . . to early emotions of shame, fear and guilt. Only in English could he name the nature of his desires; his new language was the idiom of his manhood." "Russian" and "English" need not be taken at all literally; however devastating an experience, one has the power to argue its impact, to counter it, through a figurative or metaphoric refashioning of it. Levanter's method of transformation is precisely the one that Lifton suggests best assures psychic survival. "The human being," he writes, "is a perpetual survivor . . . of birth, and of the holocausts large and small, personal and collective . . . a survivor capable of growth and change, especially when able to confront and transcend these 'holocausts' or their imprints."

Giving voice to one's experience, then, is one of the tools Kosinski's characters use to abet their own psychic survival. A secondary strategy is using one's wound as one's weapon—in the case of Kosinski's characters (as well as Ralph Ellison's), a primary wound is the feeling of invisibility. In one of the episodes in *Steps* (1968), a disembodied voice is attracted to a woman coworker who rebuffs him. He subsequently arranges for a male friend, a businessman, to meet the woman, who falls in love with him. As proof of her love, she consents to be blindfolded and to have intercourse with the man of the friend's choice. "She never knew I was her lover," reports the voice.

Well acquainted with invisibility, Kosinski's characters cultivate it, turn it to their advantage, and survive by it, meting out invisible retribution to those who have treated them invisibly. Levanter of *Blind Date* rapes (from behind) a girl he is attracted to; she has not acknowledged his existence. Tarden of *Cockpit* (1975), disappointed in a woman's failure to be available, as she had promised, contrives to get her exposed to a lethal dose of radar emissions. Dying, she will know neither who did it nor how. The rest of Kosinski's protagonists follow this invisible suit: they are not only rapists and faceless murderers, but they are snipers and apartment-buggers. Occasionally, they resort to the telephones, in false voices.

Invisibility need not only mean being faceless. A third strategy for survival, akin to facelessness, involves the false face, a theatrical play-acting that permits a "real" experience, but suggests—to others who are the danger—that it is happening to someone else. The real threat is not physical but psychic assault, so what must be shielded is not so much the body as the intangible self one believes is one's own.

The protagonist in *Steps* is fond of playing a deaf-mute in various social encounters. He doesn't examine his motivation, but the choice reveals the wish for perfect psychological caulking—nothing can come in by the ears or go out by the mouth. Equally versatile is Tarden, aptly a former secret agent. He insists that the conditions under which he left the service force him to continue with his disguises, but in fact he prefers false appearances. He decides to have a uniform specially designed for himself, and enjoys the authority that comes with the costume. He has not fooled others, he argues; they have fooled themselves. On other occasions, he wears his own clothes but adopts new identities—he pretends to be a janitor in a publishing company, or he creates the circumstances that will lead others to believe he is a murderer. His most extreme self-protection has to do more with his *concept* of sexual identity than with his body. "When I was in high school," he recalls, "I discovered that, by squeezing my member, I could force it back into my body. I practiced keeping it retracted, and later discovered that [during sexual encounters] I could keep it hidden with a plastic-edged metal clamp which made it look as if I were recovering from an amputation."

In the most extreme situations, Kosinski's characters remain experientially absent from their own experiences, with or without the masks. At one point in *Steps,* the nameless protagonist decides to participate in another country's revolution. When he is ordered to execute enemies, he reports that "I had to believe that I was not myself any more and that whatever happened would be imaginary. I saw myself as someone else who felt nothing." A double protection, this, since even what Laing would call the "false self" is depersonalized.

What we have so far, then, is that the invisibility (in any of its varieties) that guarantees the characters their psychological safety furthers the feeling of insubstantiality for which they exacted vengeance in the first place. Feeling invisible, the characters have virtually no witness to their "real" actions, no corroborations, and no externally provided sense of continuity.

Especially acute is their need to anchor and literally to substantiate themselves with their own internal experience. In his lightest novel, *Being There* (1971), Kosinski presents his bleakest warnings about what the lack of inner weight can lead to. The book is about a man who isn't there; though he has physical substance, he has no experiences, or doesn't know he has had the experiences he *has* had, which amounts to the same thing. The protagonist of

Kosinski's fantasy/parable is Chance, who has passed his entire life in the Old Man's house and garden, with no regular company except for television. Early in the novel, he contrasts people with the plants in his garden: "No plant is able to think about itself or able to know itself; there is no mirror in which the plant can recognize its face; no plant can do anything intentionally: it cannot help growing, and its growth has no meaning." Kosinski's characters frequently deceive or withhold from the reader (why should we get special treatment?), but Chance isn't lying; he is simply wrong about his own condition. When the Old Man dies, Chance is dispatched to "the other side of the wall" and within a week, through accidents of fate and plot complication, Chance (now known as Chauncey Gardiner) is nationally heralded as a financial wizard and economic adviser to the President, all because his simple, literal statements about his garden are misconstrued by others, who then create him as they will. The real horror of this success story lies in our fearful fantasy that the self without the traction or weight of internal experience really can be transformed by a glance or a word (and, of course, a police state) and will have no resources with which to resist or counter. That Chance's fate is benign is Kosinski's irony.

Specifically, then, the fourth strategy for psychic survival is the careful cultivation of one's own memory. Never mind Wordsworth's "emotion recollected in tranquility." Kosinski's characters have no tranquility, and what they recall is neither the glory nor the dream. But memory does serve; it is the hub for the sundry spokes of random roles and costumes and locales and languages. It is the act of remembering that might integrate disparities, and possibly provide the thread, albeit fragile, of self-continuity. Memory will verify not just that *someone* existed through time, but that it was a particular someone whose psychic fingerprint may be the very pattern of his recollections. "I remember how, as a boy," says Whalen in *Devil Tree,* "I used to collect the cork tips of my father's cigarettes and stick them in my stamp albums. I believed they contained his unspoken words, which one day would explain everything.

"I have not changed. Now I explore my memories, trying to discover the substructure hidden beneath my past actions, searching for the link to connect them all."

Memory is also the strategy for survival the young boy in *Painted Bird* discovers first. After an episode in which a plowboy's eyes have been plucked out, the boy begins to be terrified that he too will lose his eyeballs, and he walks and climbs fences carefully, remembering to hold his head up. "I made a promise to remember everything I saw; if someone should pluck out my eyes, then I would retain the memory of all that I had seen for as long as I lived." As such, memory is one way out of divided selfhood. One dare not in the present moment *have* one's own experiences, or feel them as they occur, but in the privacy of one's mind, candor and the hue of emotion are at least possible. "I" is the one who remembers. I remember, therefore I am. It is not much, but it is something, although the price is that the past moment forever seems more "real" than the present moment.

But as nothing in Kosinski's world is wholeheartedly trustworthy, memory cannot be either. In *Steps,* as the protagonist leaves his own Eastern European country forever, en route to what seems to be the United States—as Kosinski himself did—he realizes he is seeing familiar sights for the last time. "Scattered somewhere around those buildings, suspended between those monuments like wisps, were 24 years of my life. The knowledge brought me no emotion. My memory broken and uneven, was like an old cobblestone road." Without memory, one's very self seems to exist *outside* of oneself, diffuse and insubstantial.

If we are what we remember, then if our memory fails us, we risk annihilation—but what if we remember everything? Then there is no selective principle at work, no self defining itself by the essence of its memories. To remember everything is to forswear significance, to become—light-years away from Proust—a witless recording machine. "Since my childhood," says Tarden of *Cockpit,* "I have learned to guard my memory from becoming overloaded with unnecessary data. When I don't use the method and, for instance, allow myself to look at people on a subway, I instinctively memorize every detail of their features, coloring, and expression, the clothes they wear and what they are carrying."

Memory may be the way of taking the world in, of providing continuity in the absence of others, but, paradoxically and regrettably, it is also the faculty that further isolates; for the fuller one is of one's own memory, the more one is separated from others, or so the young boy in *The Painted Bird* believes. "Every one of us stood alone, and the sooner a man realized that . . . the better for him. . . . His emotions, memory, and senses divided him from others as effectively as thick reeds screen the mainstream from the muddy bank."

Jonathan Whalen of *Devil Tree* feels the same isolation, but his double bind has a different twist. "I am always afraid," he says, "that some incident from my past will destroy other people's affection for me. Since I have no idea what that incident will be, I have learned to be defensive. I have become a master of the art of concealment, of tailoring my reminiscences to the person I'm talking to." The self that emerges from Whalen's "tailoring" is or feels like yet another disguise.

Since memory is at once so crucial and so wispy, Kosinski's people find ways to help it; they are relentless data-gatherers—photographers, buggers, and gadgeteers. Not having real experience in the world, they appear to steal it, and so, paradoxically, some of the memories they have do not even "belong" to them. This is particularly true of Whalen in *Devil Tree.* He carries a minute tape recorder in his pocket that he can turn on inconspicuously. Scattered throughout the novel are samples of his aural theft. The nameless protagonist in *Steps* perversely connects himself to those nameless others in his apartment complex by bugging them.

Kosinski's characters rarely talk about themselves in the present to others, but in their more or less benign moments, they reveal their memories. The revelation is rarely prompted by a simple desire to make and sustain contact in the present, however. Tarden of *Cockpit,* who generally insists that despite his isolation he is contented enough, tells a woman he knows, "I did not want to just tell you about my past. I wanted you to relive it." And, then, "It wasn't the thought of dying that disturbed me, but that I might die without leaving a trace." In part, he wants to deposit his valuable memories in her just as he deposits his important papers in his bank vault.

George Levanter of *Blind Date* is Kosinski's most optimistic portrayal up to now. He does want to make contact (and is the first Kosinski protagonist to risk marriage), but he does so in an enormously complicated and oblique way. At a ski resort, he meets a woman to whom he tells an anecdote from the past—not about himself, but about a circumstance that *might* be a gloss on himself. He does so not with their present in mind at all, but with the idea that should they happen to meet in the future, she will remember the story and perhaps remember him.

"How do you want to be remembered?" she asks when he seeks her out—on impulse—200 pages later.

"As a memory with feeling," he says.

The rest of the passage bears repeating because late in Kosinski's most recent novel, it is the first and only time a character not only admits to, but consents to, his own longing, a spokesman for the others as well.

> "I'm afraid of losing you," he said. The sound of his words brought him a faint memory, so faint that he dismissed it.
>
> "Why?" she asked again.
>
> "I want you to fall in love with me," he said, "to want me as I am now. Somehow, I think you're my last chance."
>
> She disengaged herself from his embrace and stepped back.
>
> "Your last chance? For what?"
>
> "To be wanted, rather than remembered. To have a fresh emotion, a sensation that isn't just ricocheted memory. To be part of that spontaneous magic."

What follows is a scene of sexual consummation that in its recourse to bondage will strike some as perverse, but is delicate in Levanter's recognition of the woman's sexual individuality. Perhaps not surprisingly, the remaining pages of *Blind Date* race away from Levanter's epiphany; there is no further mention of the woman or the experience.

Is this, then, simply Jerzy Kosinski's latest chronicle of the nightmare life of the psyche in our time? Probably not. Of all the protagonists to date, Levanter is the least numb, the most emotionally articulate, and the least invisible. He is the least hampered by elaborate rituals, and since he is engaged with the world economically, politically, and sometimes personally, his memory need not be merely his haven or the only legitimate proof of his existence. From the first line of *Painted Bird,* the single sensibility that informs all of Kosinski's novels has been working its way through to the moment of affirmation and longing Levanter voices with the woman. And so it is enough for now. As a peripheral character in *Blind Date* comments, "I'm myself—it's the ultimate risk." But also the ultimate aspiration.

The Romance of Terror and Jerzy Kosinski: *Cockpit*

JACK HICKS

"*Who will understand the true reasons for the confession?*" ask the closing words of *Cockpit* (249). Kosinski quotes Dostoyevski's *The Possessed* and points to the use of still another classic genre, the confession, as the ordering shape of his fifth novel. The confession dates back to the fifth century and St. Augustine's concern for his humble soul, but Kosinski's modern version forms around the agent Tarden and his unburdening of a godlike past. *Cockpit* is a debriefing that is much more an assertion of strength and liberation than an admission of man's weakness or a self-indictment. Confession requires a confessor; the reader serves that function here, as the author stretches the fictive skin to make literal the "you" ordinarily implied in first-person narration. "You probably do not recall," Tarden begins on the first page, continuing in an easy lover's voice, but he remembers more deviously than we can imagine and by his final memories he has possessed us. Recollection is not a passive act; memory is a weapon. By the novel's close, he has invaded our consciousness, emerging fresh from the wreckage of a past in which we are trapped.

Tarden is an undercover agent, retired from the American "Service." He has been a character of great appeal to the literary imagination since World War II, particularly since the cold war and the rise of the CIA. He appears in serious fiction—in raincoat in Graham Greene's "entertainments," in cassock in Anthony Burgess's eschatological spy novel, *The Tremor of Intent,* and as the sinister Hollingsworth in Norman Mailer's *The Barbary Shore.* He has been extraordinarily popular in paperback because of Ian Fleming's James Bond fantasies and John Le Carré's accomplished thrillers, and imitators have rushed with him to the bank, supported by a mass taste for intrigue and escape. Sex, violence, elaborate plots involving empires, gorgeous women, the power brokers of the planet, and foreign intrigue are the substances of mass fiction, and Kosinski has been accused of seeking the sensational. His intent, however, is not to exploit but to reclaim certain territory and experience as the rightful terrain for serious fiction concerned with mortality in contemporary life. He uses the spy novel, like Anthony Burgess, as a means of reflection on spiritual matters, on the vagaries of personal morality and social responsibility, on the conflicting obligations to a pure self and a corrupt modern world.

Kosinski is a mature flier and accepts the full conditions of his existence, as the epigraph from Saint Exupéry opening the novel suggests. He is in control of his flight and alert to its turnings. In retrospect he sees his pattern as "*a child* [who] is not frightened at the thought of being patiently turned into an old man" (i). The surname Tarden echoes that of an earlier unseen hero, the Norden who invented the precision bombsight that reversed the second air war to Allied favor. Historical and fictive, they are both visionary bombers, but, in place of a mechanism calibrated by a uniformed officer, Tarden catches his victims in the crosshairs of memory and imagination. "*I too play my games,*" he continues from the cockpit, echoing Saint Exupéry: "*I count the dials, the levers, the buttons, the knobs of my kingdom*" (i). Older and retired, the aging warrior summons forth his most intense memories. He affirms life, instead of being passively resigned to it, and embraces the dialectics of body and soul, fate and free will, blind chance and imaginative action, death and life, that torment his younger alter egos in *Steps* and *The Devil Tree.*

Tarden's confession is a seamless expanse of anecdotal memory that is divided arbitrarily into seventeen unnumbered sections, broken only by a capital at the head of each section. The breaks are random, sometimes opening or closing a story but more often serving as brief interruptions or pauses for breath in a continuing tale. Beneath this deceptive drift of mind is a broad pattern, for Tarden's memory is cyclic and contains the oppositions reconciled in his life. As a child he believed that "the wheel was animated by a powerful spirit," and this image continues as the dominant figure in *Cockpit.* But one may be constantly freed within its turnings, not broken endlessly like Ixion or Whalen. As a creative agent, Tarden renews the dead languages of political and military science: circles of power, spheres of influence, rounds of negotiations, global security. An early, warming memory is that of playing with a hoop, and it rolls into his adult life. "Now I have devised a new kind of wheel game. . . . Confronted with hundreds of anonymous faces, hundreds of human wheels, I choose one and let it take me where it will. Each person is a wheel to follow, and at any moment, my manner, my language, my being, like the stick I used as a boy, will drive the wheel where I urge it" (148).

His own freedom is purified in movement through expanding circles of personal power. A precocious child and a credit to the communist State, he outwits family and cell and comes to the United States and the Service. He has passed beyond that time in his life and is now retired, an agent employed by that most generous and demanding of agencies, the self. His duties have led him around the world through city and country, wealthy and poor, conventional and bizarre, but he attends now to the "urban remains, deserted glass and steel structures," the corpse of modern society. Landscape is character, and Tarden redeems the droning world by invading "real estate firms, insurance or employment agencies, collection services, marketing research firms, publishing houses or magazine offices" (152). Character is landscape, and he sees the detritus of modern life in the millions of "flaccid bodies" in the city around him, noting how "soon they will grope toward narrow doors and shuffle into the dirty streets" (236).

The novel wheels from Tarden's childhood toward death, and his carefully edited past suggests that the child is father to the man. His strong character is defined from birth, and the lessons of the active self learned in child's play are refined in later life. His earliest memory establishes familiar terms. At age two, he is a sleepwalker, climbing nightly from a tall crib to the warmth of his nanny's bed. He is "cured"; wet towels soon drape the sides of his crib and "their chilly dampness would send me back to the warmth of my own blankets" (110). The sketch would be innocuous elsewhere, an interlude in every child's life, but it contains the first hint of an oblivious desire by the unformed self to thwart its own growth, to return to the impossible womb of the past.

The motif of entrapment painstakingly established in *The Painted Bird* is more deftly sketched in *Cockpit.* Young Tarden is born aware of the forces of human mortality, of death. His flesh is the first prison and he is provoked by his juvenile body. His own fluids circulate independent of his control, and even weeping cuts pose a challenge: "Although I often tried to keep a wound open and bleeding, it always sealed itself overnight, challenging my power over myself. I hated the sense of an autonomous force in my body, determining what would happen to me" (13). To live in the flesh is to be sealed in; sexuality, the second cell, is a blind turning downward toward the animal world and death. A local skier, the Flying Gnome, becomes a national hero. He is a cretinous boy, stuttering and gross-featured, but brilliant and graceful in flights from the snowy skin of the earth. Envious, Tarden finds the secret of his success and the cause of his death. The Gnome was trained and seduced by a German temptress, the Red Whore, a Stupid Ludmilla in furs. Though her sexual attentions coax great performance from the potter's son, he is finally conquered by her flesh and his desire. He soils himself aloft, crashing to an awful end, "his body appearing to have given up, refusing to complete the jump at all." The Red Whore also lures Tarden, but he is repelled by her explanation of the Gnome's death: "The jumper had grown up surrounded by snow and ice, she said, and he could love only when his bones and his body were frozen like stored meat. He saw rot in everything hot and wet and would touch her warmth only when he was drunk. And there she had been, hot and wet, inviting his touch all the time. She said he felt soiled by her love" (126).

The small circle of his child consciousness defines the first meaning of cockpit, a fatal ring for the fights of animals. He and his mountain friends celebrate the last November season of the Ruh, "the wet wind from the warm lakes . . . keeping the snow and the skiers away." It is a watery dead world. Tarden is hydrophobic, recalling how they rush to a swampy pond to appease the spirit of the Ruh and to summon the complementary wind, the dry, cold, life-giving Thule. "Each child brought a canvas bag or a box containing a live animal—a rat, a dog, a cat, a duck, a goose or a muskrat. . . . Attaching stones or iron bars to each animal's underbelly to slow it down in the water, we released the creatures, throwing them into the pond." The animals were blinded and pushed from the shore by the child handlers and their long poles. This is a grotesque cockfight, slogged out in water by dying spirits that fight against the deadening force that drives the blood downward. A cold front sweeps in and the Thule turns the pond "to a platter of thin ice, its glaze broken only by the trapped animals." The wind is overbearing, and they are caught in the cycle of life as it pitches over: life to death, water to ice, blood slowing, thickening, and freezing. The winning animal is the last to die, but they all succumb, "their heads cocked to one side as though listening, their eyes frozen open" (119).

Although the motif of this scene resembles that of *The Painted Bird,* where life in the body is linked with the cages of lower consciousness, social man, sexuality, and the great entropy slide toward death, Tarden's experience has a very different timbre than the painted bird's. Though this young flier is disturbed by the inertia of the blood, we should note that in his world these powers are regenerative and healing. The watery Ruh evokes the Thule, bringer of the cauterizing ice and the flight of the skiing spirit. His young consciousness is seasonal and he soon finds that the apparent enemies of life are joined with, even create, the freedom he desires. Thus the wheel turns or is turned by an active hand to all things in their own time: the Ruh brings the Thule, death yields life, a pained memory of animals trapped like people in a crowd triggers the liberating acts of the individual.

Tarden's first weapons are his most enduring: his memory and a complementing ability to manipulate life in the present. At age ten, his mnemonic genius is confirmed by tests and from that point he enjoys his talent immensely. He is not oppressed by his personal history and takes pleasure in circling back through images of the past. Memory and action, fantasy and desire, they exist in an exponential relationship: each acknowledges and expands the other. Like the process of healing, the autonomy of remembering disturbs the young man: "If I evoke a single memory picture, others will spring up automatically to join it and soon the montage of a past self will emerge" (13). Later, however, the free dynamic of recollection excites the mature man. Our young gunner is uneasy in the presence of the accidental, but the older Tarden has an appetite for those instants in which existence is permuted again, instants when the spontaneous is released and his own potential is made kinetic in the world.

Tarden is the shape-shifter in *Cockpit,* a master of active disguise who delights in cosmetic changes of voice, face, costume, and bearing. In these adjustments, he transforms the boundaries of flesh and is paradoxically released by them. He delights in the free movement of the actor behind a painted face.

A self is a mask and there are endless Tardens. As a ten-year-old, he finds in disguise an exhilarating power. The State telephones. A steely voice instructs that the family will move at once to a distant relocation settlement. A choice deceit revels in truth; the boy's miming voice creates havoc by telephone, cleverly reaching into other lives, multiplying himself in an army of victims the State did not create, does not wish, cannot assimilate. As a mature agent, Tarden is born each time he metamorphoses himself with each new job, new victim, or new lover. But in maturity, as in childhood, he is a morally ambiguous agent. Though he wars on fraudulent and repressive forces, he is not necessarily an operator on behalf of familiar personal or social ethics, because the moralities of the purging self and the dozing Other—individual or collective—do not rest easily together. He can be a monstrous hero, even as a young boy. At three, resting in a nanny's lap, he stabs her deeply with a pair of scissors. A year later, incensed at a young friend, the precocious agent tosses a flower pot at him from a high building.

Tarden grows older and moves from the family to the State into a second circle of power. "The State was a vicious enemy," he recalls, and his memory evokes an incident in which he almost dies from anaphylactic shock brought on by a simple dental anesthetic. His mind binds together the strangulation of collective life, the numbness of the drug, and the death of the self, but it also acknowledges again the ironic creative powers therein. He is physically and psychically revived: "Like the elusive substance that had once healed my wound, now the State has saved me without consent" (15). Thus if the State tries to devour him, it also creates an appetite in him—what Hegel calls Desire, the will to know, to master, and to assimilate the world that characterizes self-consciousness and gives rise to the Master self.

We see young Tarden's Desire first as a photographer for the labyrinthine State Academy of Science. His job is to document "an endless bureaucratic jungle," to produce images of a fixed and certified political reality. Photography for the State is scarcely an act of consciousness; it is a deadly interaction, and Tarden in communist Europe is a collector of dead souls. But he uses his talents to create an elaborate hoax, "to turn that confusion back on itself." In the most autobiographical segment of *Cockpit,* Tarden creates a brilliant, liberating fiction from the holds of the octopoid State and flees to the United States. Thus he masters the State and transforms his own image in the process. Tarden continues as a photographer, first as an operator for the Service and then for the self. He uses every sort of camera to seize people, to create deception and expose the next layers of human behavior. He peels lives like onions. Photography becomes an extension of memory that makes visible the electricity of the brain and freezes the moment in a scar of chemicals on microfilm and studio paper. Furthermore, the metaphor is a mode of being in Kosinski's work; like Novak's sitting, metaphor is at once active and passive. The lens of the camera is a voyeur's eye that reaches into a scene, a life, a brutal or tender moment, but it also preserves and creates a record. For Tarden, photographs make it possible to relive the excitement of the moment at a later time, when he pricks his imagination by holding those prints in hand and mind. As photographic accountant for the State, he becomes a dealer in lives. Picture taking is transformed into a complex act of desire: an unfelt touch, a slap, a lover's caress.

His special Desire is to photograph the women in his life. Here we note the second graphic significance of the title *Cockpit,* for Tarden is above all a cocksman. His sexual impotence is a willed extension of the strong and conscious self but also, paradoxically, a blind pulse of the blood that courses beyond the mind's grasp. He is excited by women, first by their psychic and physical attractions, then by the process of imagining them and photographing them—clandestine and exposed—as if the lens were a phallus or a needle mounting a biologic specimen. He is even further moved by the reactions of his women when they confront their images in the double mirror of his skill and their photographs: their curiosity, their outrage, their desperate need to enter the chemical fantasies he creates, their compulsion to release the worm of daily life to the lepid beauty he traps in paper and stain.

Tarden is not only an occupier of other selves—note again the shared language of love and war—but also a liberator, for his attentions evoke spontaneous actions, hidden aspects of personality, and the Desire of the Other. His special taste is for unformed souls, particularly young women and children. Their armor is readily pierced, their substance released more suddenly, because the shell of the self has not yet hardened. His own protean being is released by the presence of youth. He delights in ventriloquism and storytelling, drawing children into fictions that are serious play. The lover's lingering touch is a tale told to a child, an open self whose response is unpredictable and often passionate. He "seduces" a young skiing student with his stories, fantasizing the time when they will see the world together: "She hung on every word as I described the strange animals we would see in jungles and the parties we would attend on the roof-top terraces of skyscrapers" (49). She lives in these stories and, when he leaves at season's end, she leaps from a roof like an abandoned lover. Later Tomek, a Ruthenian boy, annoys Tarden on an airplane. He wraps the boy in a devious threat, terrifying the child and provoking him to rail uncontrollably at his parents.

But Desire is mainly sexual, and Tarden is a relentless priapic lover. "Some must break / Upon the wheel of love," Stanley Kunitz writes, "But not the strange, / The secret lords, whom only death can change."[1] The wheel is a literal sign in some scenes from *The Painted Bird* and *Steps,* where peasant men sprawl, spokelike, an old woman circulating from one to the next, relieving them like animals. But here the wheel is unstated, turning through Tarden's life from sexual maturity toward death. He is indeed "a secret lord," unbroken but tested endlessly on that great round. His memory turns, sealing one lover's experience to that of another, and in the process, we can see, radiant in his life, a complex meditation on the dialectic of modern life. The dualities that spring from the paradox of the spirit in the flesh are illuminated by sexual life, which is experienced, acknowledged, and recorded as a rich shuttle that creates life and ebbs for a time in a single death.

His being—the current and potential self—is defined and refined by sexual performance. What starts as juvenile fear and repulsion for sex in the Red Whore's story, becomes a necessary aspect of a full existence. Sex is a threat, a stream of blood that seeks another in a second body. Although the young Tarden first senses sex at a distance as forbidden, dangerous, and repressed, the adolescent knows it as an ecstatic revelation, a liberating action. The mature Tarden embraces the full realm of sex as both totem and taboo. He takes up the psychic knots of moral restraint, social taboo, psychological repression, and orgasmic denial; he finds delight in manipulating these strands, himself, and his partners to release a transforming flow of psychic and sexual energy. Thus the political spy is a sexual agent; his disguises are the protean self made substantial, and his own freedom emerges from that deceiving process. The male self is also an impulse held in check, and Tarden sustains and creates sexual energy, in fantasy and action, by manipulating what were once the hardened spasms of moral and social convention.

His memory weaves together many sexual experiences: the Swiss child seduced by his stories (he recalls her leaping from a building as he parts); his lover Theodora, first weaver of the cloth of master and slave (her body collapses from cancer as he leaves the hospital); a psychiatrist's wife taken ruthlessly and anonymously, in which time both partners discover buried selves (she fades as a memory, sleeping in her husband's arms); an elegant French woman with whom he is a rare victim—a slave to his failing body, his image of her, and her power (a time he would like to forget); a village of Italian whores, all offering to satisfy him, "but not inside," saving their aging virginity for marriage (a vivid scene, exciting as yesterday). He is many men: a skier, translator, an agent posing as anthropologist and industrial representative, a tourist, always a lover.

Kosinski has been severely criticized for the sexual morality of his protagonists. The common assumption is that novelist and central character are identical, especially in the destructive creators of *Steps, Cockpit, Blind Date.* The author's vision shuttles us constantly between the lover's bed and the field of battle, and he uses that dual metaphor as a means of exploring an essentially profane modern life. What starts as a military patrol reveals that the righteous and the enemy are one. An ambush breaks the self open, revealing dark and terrible potentials, surprising actions, hidden fears, and false strengths. Sade, Mishima, Genet, Kosinski: they share the common view of a band of warriors, inverted heroes whose antisocial, immoral, illegal, and often murderous gestures are the last purging and cauterizing hope of waking the body of modern life. The struggle on a killing ground may become a lover's shared embrace, a violent rape, the choking of a victim, or a slave's mutilating revenge. Genet's "miracle of the rose" breaks forth in a prison pit—there are many such transformations in the works of these authors, but underlying them all is an unwillingness to accept human sexuality as a predictable exercise. Kosinski denies both the repressions of the past, sex deadened by social code and religious cant, and the false liberation of the present, the consummate act made banal by "immediacy," "honesty," "openness." His agents, like Sade's priests, Genet's thieves and murderers, and Mishima's samurai, refuse sex as a genuflection or a handshake but instead explore it as a ceremony (often incompatible with social norm), a mysterious, deadly, life-giving ritual in which the antinomies of contemporary existence are illuminated, shared, and temporarily reconciled.

Tarden escapes, and the third and fourth circles of power, the Service and the self, fan out imperceptibly and inseparably. One can only say that his investigations gradually abandon explicit political purpose. They are of two kinds: (1) actions taken against domestic and foreign agencies and groups that hold individuals hostage; (2) invasions of single lives by which the Other is created, consumed, reborn, and devoured again in an endless cycle, all under Tarden's gaze. His work is unified, however, by a profound moral intention, as the author notes. Speaking of Tarden and Levanter, impatient with a popular culture that he despises and with increasingly hostile critics who see his work as sensational, Kosinski concludes angrily that "my characters are all agents in the service of counteracting the emotional suppression."[2]

If the State finally offers him freedom and makes him its highest agent (an unclassified "hummingbird" and a wealthy man), it also destroys him as a social being. He survives by his wits beyond the usual early death of operators and is released to face the world, a conspiracy of enemies. Freer than ever, he is also more alone, for "as a result of the circumstances under which I left the Service, I cannot join any professional, social or political group." He travels from secret apartment to apartment, anonymous in the major cities of the earth. It is a mixed life, sweet and tart: "Yet to live alone, depending on no one, and to keep up no lasting associations, is like living in a cell; and I have never lost my desire to be free as I was as a child, almost flying, drawn on by my wheel" (148).

But the mature Tarden does not despair. Many of the anxieties and obsessions of childhood and young manhood are finally dissolved. He is no longer plagued by accident or blind fate; indeed, he invites chance and is animated by coincidence, the breaking of pattern. He achieves new perspectives on past absorptions, photography for instance, and is almost amused to discover, once again, the primacy of the memory over literal images: "When I think about the energy expended during the past decades in picking up these women, and in taking, developing and enlarging these photographs, I am overcome by its pointlessness." The voyeur's clearest eye is in memory, and he becomes aware of the strength and impermanence of his own human consciousness: "When I die and my memories die with me, all that will remain will be thousands of yellowing photographs and 35 mm. negatives locked in my filing cabinets" (180).

But one should not be deceived by the wistful tone. For all his sense of living within a harmonious cycle, for all his acceptance of failure, illness, accident, disaster, and even death as part of the human condition, Tarden remains a profoundly unsettling figure. He is pleased with his life in large cities and goes for long walks at night "like a solitary visitor in a vast, private museum." But he has no use for his fellow citizens, noting disdainfully that at four a.m., "one can easily imagine that mankind is nearly extinct" (236). He is a negating hero, as Hegel would have it, because the proper function of consciousness is negation rather than pure destruction, and his hand is always on that wheel.

The third significance of the title *Cockpit* is made clear in one of Tarden's final efforts for the Service, the most disturbing scene in the novel. He meets Veronika, a woman of flawed beauty and marred past, and offers to stake her to a new life on the condition that she be available for his pleasure.

They strike a Mephistophelian bargain, and her life blossoms in the soil of a new identity. She becomes wealthy and desired; she moves in the company of an international elite. She tries to avoid Tarden, but he brings her to heel several times, once by a grotesque "blind date" during which she is drugged and sexually tortured by four derelicts. Still she grows anew, beyond his needs, each time. He begs a final meeting at an Air Force open house, pleading for a last set of sentimental photographs. She poses before the newest jet fighter, alluring and impatient, tossing her black hair in the sunlight as he shoots from ground zero:

> I sat back, and tripped the switch. Instantly, the hazard light began flashing. The silvery radar display indicator brightened and the luminescent dots at the center of the screen began to coalesce into a blurred shape, like rapidly multiplying cells. I glanced at Veronika through the jet's open canopy. Posed against the peaceful green field veined with runways, she had no idea that invisible missiles were assaulting her body and brain. I turned to the pilot. His face was flushed. He stared at the screen's dim glow as though it reflected something horrible. I switched the radar off, and the screen darkened, then went black. (235–36)

Thus Tarden punishes an act of bad faith with murder. She is cool and indifferent as they part; he basks in his pleasure behind a sad face: "I could bear the thought of never seeing her again only because I knew a part of me would always be with her. Nothing would please me more, I said, than to know there would be days and nights when, unable to sleep, she would recall our arrangement and how it had ended" (236).

The agent's last memories speak of the element of disaster that lurks unknown in every future. While photographing one of his women, he leaves on a quick trip for fresh film and is suddenly trapped in a malfunctioning elevator. He runs through his entire emotional life in several minutes, panicked in fear of a plot, but settles stoically to await his fate. After eight hours, he is rescued and goes home exhausted, his girl friend having grown bored and departed. Looking out his window, he watches ice skaters in a city park, "moving smoothly in their circle of light." His tired mind transforms that placid scene. First the skaters become an afterimage of the childhood animals frozen in the Thule pond, standing "like frozen sculptures growing out of ice." Then, in the last picture, they are transmuted into a "great old army tank, hit decades ago by an enemy shell, sunken in a shallow lagoon." In the pale light of morning memory, he imagines it "washed over by the waves; its corroded gun defiantly trains on trenches and machine-gun nests, long buried in the sands of a deserted beach" (248).

Thus the mind turns from memories in the distant past to the present, exhausted and accepting, weary and godlike. From frozen animals, rusting tanks, and gliding skaters, all lost in dormant pools, the mind wheels to the present of the confessor's debriefing. This triad suggests and reconciles many old oppositions, but the final martial image of the tank held forever in battle is the truest one. Tarden's last victory as agent is precisely in the terms of his confession, for the "true reasons" are not so much to surrender, to ease his soul and share his burden, but to take another victim, to imprint his experience on yet another consciousness. As he warns us, his lover and confessor, very early, "I did not want to just tell you about my past. I wanted you to relive it" (2).

Notes

1. Stanley Kunitz, "Lovers Relentlessly," in *Selected Poems 1928–1958* (Boston: Little, Brown, 1958), p. 20.

2. Ron Nowicki, "An Interview with Jerzy Kosinski," *San Francisco Review of Books,* 3 (March 1978): 13.

Blind Date: The Resurgence of Relationships

Paul Bruss

Despite all the incident packed into *Steps* and *Cockpit,* Kosinski's novels remain a fiction without content. The narrator of *Steps* may have devoted himself to the processes of demystification and neutralization, and Tarden in *Cockpit* may have pursued as many wheel games as his imagination can contain, but in the end what the reader is left with, in both novels, is merely a sense of human—and, more specifically, imaginative—processes that Kosinski associates with maturity. In a certain sense, to be sure, these processes can be regarded as a "content," particularly if Kosinski is urging (as he seems to be) that his readers identify and then invest in these processes in their own lives. That qualification notwithstanding, Kosinski avoids layering his fiction with specific values, and to the extent that his text is free of such value and thus challenges the reader merely to become aware of the processes of perception and of language in his own experience, the text—even with its emphasis upon demystification or upon perceptual expansion—matches up rather well with what Robert Morris and other minimal sculptors have attempted in their art of the 1960s.[1] By retreating from specific contents, Kosinski essentially forces his reader to establish a new and much more active relationship to the text. It is the reader who, in the absence of the traditional signals of theme, metaphor, structure, etc., must make the associations and relationships that give the text some coherence and significance. Ultimately, in fact, if the reader becomes comfortable with such responsibility rather than being outraged by the shocking grossness of the *apparent* content, he will assimilate for himself some of the fundamental configuration of Kosinski's own imagination. Such assimilation surely lies, as with the minimal artists, at the very heart of Kosinski's intention throughout his fiction.

What distinguishes *Blind Date* from the earlier novels is Kosinski's increasing interest in the protagonist's relationships with other "survivors" who have themselves discovered the necessity of understanding and exploring the limits of perception and of language that finally give shape to their experience.[2] Whereas the protagonists of previous novels, particularly the narrator of *Steps* and to some extent Tarden, have in part regarded themselves as "educators," as the privileged whose insights into the nature of man's essential dilemma require dissemination among the uninitiated, George Levanter of *Blind Date* finds his role (especially beyond the first chapter) shifting from that of educator to that of mere participant in, for want of a better term, life's wheel games.[3] Like Tarden, Levanter explores as fully as he can the nature of the transactions he initiates or becomes involved in. Unlike Tarden, however, who was determined to dominate the other party in all his transactions, Levanter also manages to ally himself with others of like mind and attitude without trying, at least in a determined fashion, to turn such relationships to his advantage. Not surprisingly, therefore, *Blind Date* as a novel reveals a mellowing of tone or, more likely, an even greater narrative restraint than that of the preceding novels. It is almost as if, having fully explored the problems of perception and language in *Steps* and *Cockpit,* Kosinski can now explore the more subtle features of his fictive world.

The most subtle feature of this novel, as I have already indicated, is the matter of human relationships. That this matter is so subtle is, of course, a result of Levanter's sophisticated understanding of the processes of language in his life. Early in the novel, for example, when Levanter encounters in New York City a lovely actress who had starred in two Soviet films he remembers from his student days, he becomes conscious of a struggle within himself between at least two different languages. He wants to establish a sexual relationship with the former actress, but when he tries to express his passion in "the language of Turgenev and Pasternak," he comes up hard against what is suddenly an insurmountable obstacle: "In Russian, the language of his childhood and adolescence, he regressed to memories of parents and schoolteachers, to early emotions of shame, fear, and guilt" (*BD,* 58).[4] For Levanter, clearly enough, Russian is the language of constricting boundaries. It is the language that he, as a child, had to learn in order to approach the adult mysteries. Having learned that language, however, he is now dominated not only by its association with the painful memories of childhood but also by its inescapable relationship to the prevailing social attitudes of that time. For him, Russian was—and still is—the language that bound him up with a specific social milieu. It is only upon leaving Russia and his other tongue, in fact, that Levanter enjoys his first significant opportunity to develop a new relationship with language. For at that point, learning English as an adult, he becomes conscious of his new tongue as a language within which he himself chooses to contain whatever desires (or personal mysteries) emerge in his experience: "Only in English could he name the nature of his desires; his new language was the idiom of his manhood" (*BD,* 58). If Russian were the language of his childhood,[5] then English is the language of his maturity.[6] More than that, English as a language represents, for Levanter, an opened field where the possibilities for exploring the many configurations of experience are almost limitless.[7] It is for this reason that English becomes the language in which Levanter, the victim of Russian, establishes himself as the agent for shaping the nature and the quality of his life. Late in the novel Jolene will remark that it is only newcomers like Levanter who know "how to change their lives overnight, how to develop new interests, take up different professions, generate fresh emotions" (*BD,* 110). It is a shrewd comment. Because he is acutely conscious of the range and the limits of the language that he assimilates in his new territory, the newcomer does enjoy a greater opportunity for becoming the agent of his own fate.

It is not merely the learning of English, however, that provides Levanter with his sophisticated perspective. Even before he has left Russia, he has deliberately trained himself (in preparation for his day of departure) in photography because of the supposedly universal character of its "language." In the course of his studies, to be sure, he has discovered that despite its apparent universality or neutrality photography as a medium actually "depended on imitating reality in an imaginative, subjective way" (*BD,* 54). For him, consequently, the language of photography turns out to be as unstable as any spoken word.[8] Such a discovery parallels what Tarden, too, has learned as a result of taking photographs of an accident in which a taxi hits a woman. After enlarging some of the photographs of the accident, Tarden selects shots for the cab driver that tend to prove the driver's innocence: "the woman had crossed the street in the middle of the block and tripped because of her high heels" (*C,* 188).[9] Then he selects shots for the woman's relatives that suggest a careless driver is at fault: "she had waited on her side of the dividing line for the cab to pass, and had fallen only after its fender had knocked her off balance" (*C,* 188). Clearly, despite its appearance of neutrality, photography never captures or stabilizes reality. Once Levanter recognizes that fact, of course, he has good reason, at least if he intends to be an artist in the medium, to scurry after a technique that is his alone. In that search he is very shrewd, for recognizing that he can easily duplicate the technical styles of most photographers, he deliberately commits himself to the development of techniques and a peculiar style that other photographers could not readily copy. He succeeds, but what is even more important in his careful search for a language (or art) that is all his own is his increased sophistication about the problems of language in general. At the very least he is conscious of the necessity of becoming the agent, not merely the respondent, in the complicated matter of shaping the texture of his experience.

An interesting verbal parallel to Levanter's experience in photography appears midway through the novel when he encounters Jolene. Jolene, much like Levanter, finds herself separated from her childhood context (she has fallen from Impton's favor), and when she recites for Levanter a version of her autobiography, it is in a style and method that matches up rather well with a snapshot camera technique:

> Snapshots from Jolene's album. Womanhood begins in grade school, age twelve. Jolene loses her virginity to a high school varsity basketball player, who

> also loses his. More dates. Click. Jolene discovers the orgasm. Click. High school. Meets Greg, law student. Local rich boy. Click. Going steady and bedding steady with Greg. Click. No orgasms with Greg. Click. Orgasms alone. Click. (*BD,* 104)

After continuing with snapshots of her marriage, of an active social life in a split-level house, and of her marriage failing, Jolene concludes her recitation of this snapshot album with the suggestion that her life was "a perfect subject for any lens to fondle" (*BD,* 104). The suggestion is surely ironic, for in the end what is so striking about the recitation of the album is that Jolene is not at all interested in justifying herself. Much in the manner of Kosinski himself, who does not provide his texts with the qualifications and the transitions that tend to contain and thus shape the content of a traditional novel, Jolene presents the episodes stripped of all subtle modifiers. Instead of trying to fix the interpretation of specific snapshots, she allows the pictures to remain in the open field—subject to Levanter's inferences. It is as if, separated from the language and thus the justifications of her childhood, she recognizes that she possesses no means for developing convincing transitions or a web of coherence for her life. Because she views herself as existing within the open field, her snapshots must remain there too.

As a result of her bewildering relationship with Greg, whose experience has remained completely within the constraints of childhood expectations, the imaginative Jolene has increasingly found herself outside the pale. Levanter may at one point remark that the people of Impton seem to notice her activities, but she herself knows that such interest is predicated only on their determination to bring her back within the pale, and thus for her the only possible response to Levanter's remark is, "What do I care what they think?" (*BD,* 105). Once she has separated herself from Greg's influence, in fact, the Jolene who has become aware of the problem of "contents" actually interests herself in techniques and styles that she can not only regard as her own but also use as a means of maintaining her distance from the townspeople. She is the woman, for example, who wears a grope suit into her husband's office—where the imaginative challenge becomes that of whether she can control the expression on her face so that no one will discover what is happening inside her as the conversation moves forward. She is the woman, furthermore, who, recognizing how most runaway housewives merely renew their old habits in changed surroundings, develops "a system for running away while remaining at home" (*BD,* 110). Unquestionably Jolene is one of the "survivors," an imaginative being who has found it necessary to establish her own textures of experience, but in the process of forsaking social content in favor of her own style and technique she has also pushed herself so far out into the open field that she has lost genuine contact with other human beings. When Levanter comes to town, of course, she may enjoy at least a momentary reprieve from her isolation, for despite feeling some apprehension because she knows so little about him, she recognizes that in his presence she has no reason to feel cautious: "I am not afraid to say or do anything that might displease you, as I have been with other men. I'm myself—it's the ultimate risk" (*BD,* 110). For her the experience with Levanter is a refreshing change, but given the snapshot character of her life, the reader must yet question whether she shall ever manage to sustain herself during her long periods of isolation. The people of Impton eventually cut her dealings with Levanter short, and at that point there must be some doubt whether style and techniques are enough. In theory a life of snapshots is intriguing; in practice, however, as shall be even more clear later, such a life is exhausting and, perhaps, impossible.

In addition to the effects that the learning of English and the working out of a new photographic style have had upon him, Levanter as a young man has experienced the disorientation of a sexual relationship with his mother. The narrator, to be sure, after recounting in some detail the character of the first encounter between mother and son, backs off presenting a full discussion of this sexual relationship, but finally the narrator's silence tends only to match up with the silence that develops between mother and son—a silence that surely bespeaks their awareness of having stepped beyond the trammels of social language, and a silence that now cannot be broken without thrusting them back into that very language and its condemnation of their act. The mother and son obviously cannot escape the language of social traditions altogether, but in an effort to free themselves of the constriction within conventional boundaries the two of them have established a game or ritual for their encounters that amounts, perhaps, to a liberation of language itself: "They were together only in the morning. By sleeping in the nude and making love with him only when she had just awakened, his mother never undressed especially for him. She never allowed him to kiss her on the mouth and . . . always insisted that he caress nothing but her breasts" (*BD,* 9–10). Whether such a ritual constitutes an easy modification of their old language or an attempt to build a radically new language is probably yet debatable. There is little doubt, however, that the demystification and the neutralization that underlie the language manipulation within the ritual prepare the way for Levanter's later interest in sophisticated relationships—such as with Jolene. While the mother and the son never talk extensively about their encounters, their ritualized activity does speak eloquently of their sensitive awareness of each other, of their mutual recognition that they have crossed an important boundary, and thus of their willing acceptance of responsibility for what they have done. Even more than his learning of English or his success in developing a new photographic technique, therefore, Levanter's relationship with his mother may function as the crucial foundation for his adult maturity. The relationship with his mother has repeatedly exposed him to a risk of monumental proportions: at any moment, losing courage, his mother or even he himself might have reduced the relationship to a "transgression" defined in conventional language. He survives the risk, however, and thereafter possesses a sophistication far beyond the reach of most men.

Considering the level of Levanter's sophistication, then, the reader of *Blind Date* may have good reason to expect that Levanter will avoid the trap of domination that prevents Tarden from having, say, an enduring give-and-take relationship with Veronika. Levanter has discovered how to suspend himself in a relationship as a result of the experience with his mother, and if his attraction to the imaginative Jolene is any indication of his future preferences for women, it seems likely that he will manage to make the adjustment to the other person's perspective that will allow for the continuation of a vital relationship. Circumstances (his flight from Russia and then the interference of the Impton police chief) may have prevented the prolonging of his relationships with his mother and with Jolene, but with both of them it is clear that, instead of dominating them in the manner of Tarden, Levanter has sensitively responded to their needs. The question, therefore, is how Levanter responds when he in more propitious circumstances meets up with other women who, like Jolene, are his equals as "survivors" and thus good possibilities for sustained relationships. In the Foxy Lady and in Serena, both of whom inhabit an imaginative world outside the boundaries of socially acceptable language and ritual, Levanter encounters at least two such women. What happens in his dealings with them, particularly in light of his presumed contrast with Tarden, is, however, jolting—and finally also instructive.

The Foxy Lady is, of course, the man who has had his "tumor" surgically removed and who then, aware of the Menopause Room as "her" ultimate doom, relies on hormones to create from nothing a fragile world that was not given to her at birth to inhabit. As Levanter himself observes, her sexuality following the operation always appears somewhat ambiguous, but from the beginning of her new sexual stature, even when she cannot yet submit to a man's insertion of himself, she plays out her new role with genuine verve and enthusiasm. Upon meeting up with Levanter shortly after her operation, for example, she takes great care to be inventive and is even determined to compensate "for the part of her body that still had to remain dormant" (*BD,* 140). She is so resourceful in her frank response to Levanter's needs, in fact, that despite the pain of her healing she continues to unleash all his deepest feelings and longings and then monitors "every detail of his release, anxious to know the duration and intensity of each spasm" (*BD,* 142). The source of the Foxy Lady's artistry is obviously her precise knowledge of male sexuality. It is as if, now a woman, she possessed the "language" of male sexuality that is normally beyond the province of the woman. She may never possess for herself the full language of female sexuality—witness her sexual ambiguity—but in terms of responding to men she will always enjoy an advantage over those who were women from birth. Given her artistry and enthusiasm as well as Levanter's appreciation for the achievements of the imagination that have involved genuine risks, therefore, the reader might expect a thriving relationship between the two of them. In the logic of Kosinski's fiction they are kindred spirits. What is striking about Levanter's relationship with the Foxy Lady, however, is the fact that he immediately retreats from her once he discovers that she is a transsexual.

Before that discovery Levanter has actually accommodated himself to the necessity of sharing her with other men. At that point, in fact, he seems to have made the decision that he will allow no barrier to separate the two of them. Once the facts of her surgery are out, nevertheless, he immediately isolates himself from further involvement. Such a response, at least in light of Levanter's previous relationship with his mother, must be taken as a failure of imagination on his part, for while the Foxy Lady develops her "act" against impossible odds (the Menopause Room), Levanter simply withdraws on the lame grounds that he had been intrigued by the mystery of the Foxy Lady and now the mystery has been "solved" (*BD,* 146). Apparently, as long as Levanter feels a certain ambiguousness that generates for him a sense of risk, the relationship with the Foxy Lady fully engages his imagination. With the introduction of specific content (the Foxy Lady as transsexual), however, his relationship with her withers. What that withering tends to imply is that Levanter, no matter how sophisticated his awareness of the problems of perception and language is, remains the victim of certain deep-seated attitudes that prevent him from continuing the relationship. The mystery surrounding the Foxy Lady has for a time intrigued him, and to the extent that he has accommodated himself to her "strangeness," he has demonstrated the rich character of his own imagination. Such character notwithstanding, in the end a latent but inflexible attitude—strict heterosexuality—prevents him from surrendering any further to her world. Like Tarden's, Levanter's imagination does have its limits.

These limits again surface in Levanter's relationship with Serena. Much like the Foxy Lady, Serena is a high-class call girl who not only is resourceful in her handling of men but also is rather contemptuous of the predictability inherent in orgasm, particularly when the orgasm is triggered too soon: "To her, an orgasm was a failure, the death of need. What touching was to the body, desire was to the mind: all she wanted was to sustain the passion, to make desire flow incessantly" (*BD,* 188). Serena's sophistication, nevertheless, seems to be of a slightly different order, for while the Foxy Lady has "murdered" the character of her own former existence, Serena has murdered a lawyer who had fallen in love with her and who had hired detectives to pursue her once she tried to escape from him. Whereas the Foxy Lady remains somewhat ambiguous and even hesitant, therefore, Serena appears to have become one of those Kosinskian characters who, once cut off from prevailing social patterns, must seek the challenge of the risky and the unusual—that edge where the conventions of language blur and thus where the survivor can most fully come into contact with his deep self. As a prostitute, Serena enjoys easy access to wheel games in which she might not only profoundly affect the fortunes of others but also explore the texture of that deep self. In the end, however, despite her initial appearance as the ideal Kosinskian character, one who might match up well in temperament, say, with Tarden, she tends to ignore other people and imaginative engagement with them because she encounters so few people of like mind and attitude. Much in the fashion of Jolene, in fact, she informs Levanter fairly early in their relationship that with old friends she tries to be "what they want me to be" and consequently, that only with strangers like Levanter is she able to be "what I really feel myself to be" (*BD,* 187). There is no question that Serena is one of the survivors, but because she does not determinedly suspend herself in ventures that repeatedly expose her to risk, she is even less involved in the play of the imagination than is the Foxy Lady—who every day must muster all her available energies for the delivery of her "act." Serena likes strangers such as Levanter, whose stories and games provide an invigorating alternative to her everyday experience, and yet, always ready to listen to Levanter rather than to develop actively her own stories, there is a profound sense in which she is constantly retreating from the resources of her own imagination. There are, to be sure, moments when she does achieve some intensity. Immediately after Levanter has disposed of the body of the man who seemed to be kidnapping them, for example, Serena initiates a sexual encounter with Levanter in which the dead man's blood figures so prominently that the two of them must feel introduced to new heights of freedom and abandon. Such moments for her, nevertheless, are very rare.

Despite the fact that Serena does not enjoy all the resources of the Foxy Lady, she represents an opportunity for Levanter to develop a sustained relationship rooted in imaginative satisfaction. As long as Levanter, in fact, is unable to connect his desire for Serena to a specific attitude or longing—in other words, as long as he feels suspended in a relationship he does not fully comprehend—such satisfaction seems accessible for both of them. Serena comes and goes unpredictably. At the same time Levanter's response to her fluctuates because he cannot decide whether it is her body that he desires or "her way of perceiving him, of giving him a sexual reality that he had lacked before" (*BD,* 188). Serena's style is important to Levanter, and with her sudden comings and goings she provides "the only real break in his life's routine" (*BD,* 200). Again the presence of mystery in the relationship appears to account for almost everything vital in its character. Once Serena has identified herself as a prostitute, therefore, it is not surprising that Levanter—much in the fashion of his final response to the Foxy Lady—withdraws from the relationship. At that point practical considerations, such as the possibility of undetected venereal disease, intrude into the relationship and completely defeat its character. As a parting gesture Levanter may express his desire to open a trust fund for Serena's support, on the condition that she spend at least six months each year with him, but Serena—again revealing her status as a survivor—flatly rejects such an arrangement on the grounds that she can earn all the money she wants, with no conditions attached. Once more, with the introduction of a specific content (Serena as prostitute), a vital relationship disintegrates because Levanter comes up hard against a limit in his imagination. Despite his sophistication, he in two separate instances finds himself wanting. In a certain sense, perhaps, both the Foxy Lady and Serena are his superiors.

Having failed with the Foxy Lady and with Serena, Levanter seems to enjoy one more opportunity in the novel to realize a sustained relationship—this time with Mary-Jane Kirkland. When Mary-Jane first meets Levanter, she appears to be another of the survivors because of the adroitness with which she conducts the charade of being Mrs. Kirkland's secretary. In addition, she invites Levanter to her private quarters in a fashion that parodies his own earlier invitation (to the effect that she join him in his apartment), and thus she seems to possess a rich measure of that imaginative vitality which belongs to Kosinski's privileged characters. Mary-Jane, nevertheless, as a result of her long relationship to a dominant husband such as Mr. Kirkland (whom she herself describes as "master of his family, not its guardian"), does not have a history of experience—particularly of the imaginative variety—that she can regard as peculiarly hers. Unlike Jolene, the Foxy Lady, and Serena, therefore, she cannot challenge Levanter with the character of a hard-won experience that is the equal of his own. But for her money and the privileges it entails, in fact, she probably would never have gained the attention of this man who has accumulated such strange contacts. What is shocking in this situation is the fact that Levanter marries her anyway. Not only is he the first Kosinskian protagonist to enter such a conventional arrangement, but he also marries one of the women least likely to stimulate him. Marriage as an act, to be sure, terrifies him, and thus there is a chance that it is the act more than the woman that engages his interest. At the very least he perceives in such a definitive act the risk that chance will turn terrorist and punish the two of them for "trying to control their own lives, trying to create a life plot" (*BD,* 220).[10] The possibility that Levanter responds more to the act of marriage than to the woman also seems to underlie his deliberate retention of his old apartment. He may regard the keeping of that apartment as merely "a gesture to chance" (*BD,* 225), but finally such retention also implies that he has entered the marriage as if it were an experiment that may not have much duration.

What this discussion of Levanter's relationship with Mary-Jane lacks, however, and what all the previous discussions of his relationships with other women finally lead up to, is an awareness of the fact that in terms of energy and enthusiasm for the unusual Levanter has experienced a significant falling off during the novel. Levanter, it must be remembered, is the man who in the first chapter alone has established the possibility of spying through the mails, has deliberately slowed down the cross-country ski race in order not to appear inept himself, has forced three men to assist a woman down a ski slope, and finally has blown up the gondola carrying the Deputy Minister who had created "the notorious PERSAUD" (*BD,* 33). Like the Tarden who dominates his environment, Levanter is at the beginning energetic, courageous, and imaginative. By the end, however, he is a man much diminished—at least in terms of Tarden's spirit. He may at the end, to be sure, remain that shrewd representative of Investors International who "always did everything as well as he could" and who, when he did not live up to his own expectations, worked diligently "to improve himself" (*BD,* 234). Certainly his attitudes continue to reflect a claim his own father had once made—to the effect that civilization at any given moment in its history is the product of "sheer chance plus a thousand or two exceptional men and women of ideas and action" (*BD,* 87–88). Like his father, Levanter continues to regard those exceptional people as the "small investors," the people who risk their own energy and personal fortune in order to gain "certain unpredictable ends" (*BD,* 88), and in his own mind he himself belongs to that elite. At the end of the novel, however, regardless of his earlier Tarden-like stature as an investor, Levanter has lost much of the intensity that had characterized his earlier activities. There is a good reason for this loss.

In *Blind Date,* finally, the skill of the survivor-investor is not enough. While Levanter is surely a good match for the narrator of *Steps* or for Tarden, he does not possess as strong a faith in his control over the circumstances of his existence as do other Kosinskian protagonists. Like them, he is conscious of the "languages" with which he has learned to play in his life, but at the same time he is much more aware than they of the extent to which chance influences all the affairs of the universe.[11] As a boy he had heard his father emphasize the importance of "sheer chance" in the development of civilization, and then when he listens to Jacques Monod, the French biologist and philosopher who has argued that "blind chance and nothing else is responsible for each random event" (*BD,* 86) of the universe, he receives an important confirmation of his father's views. As a friend of Monod, Levanter realizes that, regardless of how careful he is with his "investments," chance will dominate all his words and deeds. In a world where Stalin's daughter, Svetlana Alliluyeva, moves halfway around the world and becomes his "ordinary next-door neighbor" (*BD,* 79), Levanter—whose friend Romarkin has been imprisoned for challenging Stalin's authority—must conclude that "anything can happen." Or in a world where physical decline finally dominates mental acumen, Levanter eventually has no choice but to back off from his earlier emphasis upon rational control: "While his mind retained its ability to consider circumstances and issue commands, his body, which had once reacted automatically, was now frequently unable to respond as expected" (*BD,* 21–22). Like such protagonists as the narrator of *Steps* and Tarden, Levanter previously had allied himself with the view that the heart merely acted "in uncomplicated, clockwork response to the sovereign brain" (*BD,* 30), but with time, especially after a succession of failed relationships, he has had to face up to the realization that he had allowed himself to fall into the trap of the French—who "confused logic with facts of human existence and emotion" (*BD,* 171). In the sense, therefore, that the relationship to Mary-Jane Kirkland represents an opportunity for Levanter to explore the "whims" of the heart, rather than the logic of the mind, that relationship may serve as the beginning of Levanter's even more sophisticated dialogue with experience. In these terms, obviously enough, the marriage represents, not a failure, but Levanter's accommodation to the fact that his determination to dominate his experience by way of the acts of the mind is not sufficient. If so, it finally makes little difference whether or not Mary-Jane is his imaginative equal. What counts is only the attitude of their hearts—and Levanter's new willingness to let that attitude achieve its own fullness, with no interference on his part.

The marriage to Mary-Jane Kirkland, then, is even more jolting than I first suggested. As a test of Levanter's ability to separate himself from an orientation toward the mind and its acts, which he now knows are insufficient, the marriage allows Levanter to come into contact with and to explore a dimension of experience—the world of the heart—that he has hitherto neglected. Levanter does in the end love Mary-Jane very much, and while he may not be able to comment on the character of that love (because the acts of the mind, i.e., language, cannot effectively contain such experience), he surely reveals the extent of his feeling in his grief over her death from brain cancer.[12] It is with Mary-Jane that Levanter finally manages to sustain a relationship, and even though her death abruptly terminates the time that they have enjoyed together, Levanter is left in its aftermath with a profound realization—that his success with Mary-Jane was the result of his having avoided his previous tendency to dominate the mystery of a relationship with an act of the mind that could only reduce that relationship, as in the cases of the Foxy Lady and Serena, to a category that no longer interested him. For Levanter, therefore, especially given the earlier configuration of his experience, the marriage to Mary-Jane constitutes his supreme act of courage (it may also represent the supreme act of courage for all of Kosinski's protagonists). What happens to Levanter following Mary-Jane's death confirms this interpretation.

At the end of the novel Levanter gets involved with one more woman—the Pauline whom in the first chapter he had taken into an underground grotto. Like Levanter, Pauline is an investor, in her case an accomplished pianist, and as she continues in an almost relentless fashion to add to the grand total of performances that she has given during her career, she has finally understood the artist's essential dilemma—the fact that, regardless of the care, the intensity, and the enthusiasm that she expends upon each of her performances, her playing never achieves the enduring sufficiency, the absolute character of genius, for which she has always striven. As she says of her concert the night that Levanter visits her, "All that's left is the recording, a memory" (*BD,* 226). It is a comment fraught with meaning, particularly for a Levanter who has recently lost Mary-Jane. Pauline herself, as an artist who has over the years invested so much energy in an effort to raise the performance level of her art, has recognized that what matters most in her art is not the pursuit of genius but the attitude, the feeling, that sustains her playing. Unlike Levanter, who through much of his life has tried to contain his experience within the acts of mind and of will, Pauline has for some time realized that such acts neither account for nor sustain whatever genius does emerge in an artist's achievement. Because her stature as a pianist, like Levanter's stature as Mary-Jane's lover, depends upon an expression of heart, she serves as a good match for Levanter following his loss of Mary-Jane.

When Pauline remarks that her concert has merely become a memory, Levanter immediately reveals his recently acquired sensitivity and consoles her with the fact that at least it is a "memory with feeling." At the same time, when Pauline asks him how he wants to be remembered, he responds without hesitation, "As a memory with feeling" (*BD*, 227). Clearly for Levanter, as for Pauline, feeling now counts very heavily. Having lost Mary-Jane, Levanter may at first seem only in search of an intensity comparable to what he had enjoyed with her. When he broaches his invitation to Pauline that she join him in his apartment for the night, however, she knows that it is not so much the need for another Mary-Jane as it is a need for genuine feeling that brings Levanter to her arms. In response to her query about why he wants her, she hears what amounts, at least for a Kosinskian protagonist, to an incredible declaration:

> I'm afraid of losing you. . . . I want you to fall in love with me. . . . Somehow, I think you're my last chance . . . to be wanted, rather than remembered. To have a fresh emotion, a sensation that isn't just a ricocheted memory. To be part of that spontaneous magic. (*BD,* 227–28)

If the extremity, here, of Levanter's emotion strikes for the reader a bit of a false note, the reader must remember that Levanter has only recently made what is, perhaps, the most significant adjustment in the whole of Kosinski's fiction. Lacking yet the confidence of responding to the feelings of his heart rather than to the logic of his mind, he probably has good justification for pursuing Pauline with such determination. Pauline, on the other hand, having recognized in him some of the intensity of her own being, opens herself to him in a similarly unprecedented fashion. Given the fact that she has never before experienced sexual orgasm, the reader can probably conclude that her contact with investors such as Levanter has been very rare. Whatever her past associations with men have been, the experienced Levanter subjects her to a variety of oral and manual play (he eventually inserts his hand up to his wrist), and finally she achieves what had never before been hers. For both of them, therefore, there is suddenly a rich measure of "spontaneous magic," and even if they should (as apparently they do) go their separate ways, their moment of "magic" is at least a sign of their present vitality and their genuine suspension in that life of feeling which now seems so important to Kosinski himself.

Blind Date, then, represents a significant revision of the novels that have preceded it. To be sure, because the novel tends to avoid any explicit moral comment—about all that can be said is that the heart must count at least as heavily as the mind—the reader of the novel may still have great difficulty establishing the nuances of Kosinski's vision. As I suggested at the beginning of this chapter, Kosinski's novels have always tended to exist as a fiction without content—a fiction in which Kosinski and his narrators have attempted to examine the processes of perception, of language, and finally even of feeling, but also a fiction in which the nature and the quality of the processes, not their contents, count for everything. Even at the end, *Blind Date* must exist as selected blocks of human experience, each of which is stripped of the attitudinal associations that in a traditional novel would have converged in some formulation of vision. As blocks of human experience, nevertheless, the novel does serve to examine the various processes whereby Levanter himself makes some connection with the world about him, especially with the people about him, and thus it can become, if not a statement of value, an opportunity for the reader himself to become more sensitive to the same processes within his own life.

Notes

1. For further discussion of this point, see Allen Leepa, "Minimal Art and Primary Meanings," in *Minimal Art,* ed. Gregory Battock (New York: E. P. Dutton, 1968), pp. 200–208.

2. While their number is small, the "survivors" in Kosinski's fiction have faced up to the decline apparent in Western traditions and have, accordingly, assumed the direction of their lives for themselves.

3. The term *wheel games* derives, of course, from *Cockpit.*

4. All page references in parentheses refer to *Blind Date* (Boston: Houghton Mifflin Co., 1977).

5. In the interview for *Paris Review* 54 (1972): 194, Kosinski does speak about the decision not to write in Polish: "I would never have written in Polish. I never saw myself as a man expressing opinions in a totalitarian state. Make no mistake about it: all my generation was . . . aware of the dimensions of our existence. To be a spokesman in a field which used language would require one to be a spokesman for a particular political situation. My generation considered this a trap. . . . So what happened was that I slowly moved towards visual expression, and I became a photographer."

6. Again in the *Paris Review* interview, pp. 193–94, Kosinski comments about the importance of learning English: "English helped me sever myself from my childhood, from my adolescence. In English I don't make involuntary associations with my childhood. I think it is childhood that is often traumatic, not this or that war."

7. In the interview, "Authors and Editors—Jerzy Kosinski," *Publishers Weekly* 199 (April 26, 1971): 15, Kosinski talks about the liberating influence of an adopted language: "Once you begin to write in another language, you discover how much freer you are, because the new language disconnects you and requires from you—because you do not know all the clichés yet—some of your own."

8. In a certain sense this passage contradicts Kosinski's assessment of photography in the Klinkowitz interview, in *The New Fiction,* p. 148: "As a photographer I knew that the basic purpose of the photographic process was to reproduce reality and that photography would actually accomplish it. If there was a tree in the field and I photographed and developed it in my darkroom, I actually could do this so it would match exactly the imaginary photograph in my mind. Well, I found this profoundly distressing. If my imagination was able to conceive of the images which could be so easily reproduced in the Soviet darkroom—in any darkroom—then clearly there was not much to my imagination. I found it very humiliating that in a photograph I actually could produce what I thought. . . . With writing I can only approximate the vision I have." Here it is fiction, rather than photography, which is the unstable medium.

9. The page references prefaced with *C* in the parentheses refer to *Cockpit* (Boston: Houghton Mifflin Co., 1975).

10. Here the dangers of creating a tight, well-defined fiction become apparent. In Kosinski, fiction-making at its best is an open-field gesture.

11. Kosinski has acknowledged a major influence in Jacques Monod's *Le Hasard et la Nécessité* (Paris: Le Seuil, 1970).

12. Brain cancer may serve in this novel as a metaphor for the death of the mind. Clearly this novel stresses the vitality of the heart.

Vision and Violence in the Fiction of Jerzy Kosinski

PAUL R. LILLY JR.

Reviewers of each of Jerzy Kosinski's seven novels—from *The Painted Bird* (1965) to *Passion Play* (1979)—have been quick to point out this writer's fascination with violence. A random sampling of his books will involve the reader in scenes as grisly and varied as a Manson-like multiple killing in a Beverly Hills estate, a man eaten alive by rats, a trussed-up Russian spy dispatched with a dueling saber, a decapitation by a slammed car door, a rape of a school girl at a summer camp. Add to the list scenes of seemingly gratuitous cruelty: a child fed bread balls filled with fish hooks, an injured horse strangled by its owner, birds painted grotesque colors to ensure that they will be torn to pieces by other birds. Finally, some of Kosinski's own comments draw further attention to the place of violence in his books. In an interview with Joe David Bellamy in 1974, Kosinski theorized about the aggressive nature of fiction itself. "Fiction assaults the reader directly, as if saying: It is about you. You are actually creating this situation when you are reading about it; in a way you are staging it in your own life."[1] What Kosinski says about his manipulation of the reader is not surprising; all reading involves conscious deception on the part of both writer and reader. But his candor about arranging words so as to assault the reader's imagination completes the picture of the writer as aggressor, the reader as victim, the word as a weapon.

Understandably, Kosinski feels such a picture is distorted and untrue to the nature of his vision. In an interview with Daniel Cahill shortly after the publication of *Blind Date* (1976), he reflects on what he thinks is unfair criticism: "A serious novelist's effort to confront reality that is anything but rosy is quickly labeled 'morbidity,' 'pornographic imagination,' 'lonely rituals.' My novels and I get our share of such labeling. In most cases, though, such reviewers are not really critics; they are, rather, 'cultural Kapos.' They don't bother to examine the novels' (and the author's) point-of-view, they simply reprimand, they denounce, and all they seem to miss is an opportunity to kill his vision and put the writer in jail."[2]

Reprinted from *Literary Review* 25, no. 3 (1982): 389–400. Reprinted by permission of the author.

The issue of violence in Kosinski's work, then, is a complex one, and one which he knows touches the center of his achievement as a writer. Whatever that achievement is, his books are not so much a preoccupation with violence as they are complex studies in the shifting identity of victim and oppressor. Power, not violence, is what fascinates Kosinski. All of his main characters—the boy in *The Painted Bird,* Tarden in *Cockpit,* Levanter in *Blind Date,* Fabian in *Passion Play,* indeed Kosinski himself—have known powerlessness and victimization. Their natural impulse (and here is where Kosinski is most compelling as a writer) is to transform themselves from victim to oppressor. When Tarden, for instance, designs a hybrid military uniform for the purpose of deception, he asks the tailor to create an image of "power, but restrained power."[3] In the world of Kosinski, there are no other options open to the victim: he must seize power through deception or remain powerless. Divesting one's self of the identity of victim means assuming the identity of the oppressor. Or, as Mitka the Cuckoo explains to the boy in *The Painted Bird,* "Man carries in himself his own justice, which is his alone to administer."[4] Since each person is intensely alone, everything that is outside the individual self—political structures, nation states, business institutions, friends, lovers—represents a potential enemy, and must be constantly deceived or destroyed before it transforms that person into victim.

For Kosinski, violence is neither an abstraction nor an isolated event without a meaning. It is instead a relationship between two role-playing agents—the victim and the oppressor. The act of violence is the end result of a dynamic flow of power between these two agents. Kosinski is interested less in the outcome of this flow, that is, the act of violence itself (Mitka the Cuckoo's sniper attack on the peasants, for instance) than he is in the special dynamics of power that define the identity of victim and oppressor. Neither role is a static one; each may become the other, and it is this unpredictable transformation of victim into oppressor or back into victim that characterizes his best novels. Identity is all. The identifying marks of the victim are sometimes easily determined (the Jew in German-occupied Poland), sometimes not (the wealthy guests in a Beverly Hills estate). Violence is sometimes planned (Jews carried in box cars to their deaths according to railroad timetables), sometimes random (the killers turning up at that particular Beverly Hills estate). But the violence occurs only after the roles of victim and oppressor are sorted out and the power of will begins to flow. In a sense, the novels are a compendium of cautionary fables, warnings, admonitions: the self must establish the role of oppressor simply to avoid the only alternative, victimization. Kosinski himself, discussing his intention in writing *Blind Date,* sees the book as a "warning." "It is a warning that, given the staggering proportion of violence in our society, life is, at best, uncertain—we might not live through the very next moment, our next blind date, so to speak."[5]

Although violence in Kosinski's fiction appears in a variety of guises—political, racial, and sexual—each scene tells us something of his vision. But it is his use of violence between writer and reader, or, as Kosinski puts it, the "assault" on the reader's imagination, that is perhaps the most unsettling.

For Kosinski, every political system works against the integrity of the individual, forcing that individual to assert himself in an act of self-preservation. Whatever violence is committed is justifiable retribution for the initial violence done against the self. Here, for example, is what the boy in *The Painted Bird* learns from Gavrila, his Soviet Army tutor: "In the Soviet world a man was rated according to others' opinion of him, not according to his own. Only the group, which they call 'the collective,' was qualified to determine a man's worth and importance" (*TPB,* 204). But this determination of the worth of the individual by the collective does violence to the self. The boy wonders about the implication of Gavrila's teaching, and asks himself the question, What if the collective decides he is best suited for deep-water diving? "Would it matter that I was terrified of water because every plunge reminded me of my near-drowning under the ice?" (*TPB,* 204). Already the boy senses that the collective's decision—whatever its high-sounding intentions—represents a physical threat, a forced venture into an area that the self, were it free, would not go. The boy's sense of the implicit threat of the collective (the image of being pushed into deep water) prepares him for the violence he must do to preserve himself. In *Steps* (1968), another narrator, also unnamed, recalls his first defiance of the state. Assuming the voice of the commander of a university unit in the national guard, he orders the current officer, a fellow student and personal enemy, to attack the city arsenal. The attack takes place and the student officer is arrested for treason.[6] Later, the same narrator is cited by his student branch of the "Party" for the crime of "lack of involvement." Sensing he cannot victimize the state indefinitely, he plots his revenge on the state, escape. In *Cockpit,* Tarden, the narrator, asserts that the state is a "vicious enemy." Most people, Tarden continues, surrender their lives "to the State's omnipresence. I could not deny its existence, but I could abstract myself from its power" (*C,* 15). Tarden then forges letters of recommendation from fictional university professors, receives a visa to leave the country, and heads for the airport with the incriminating false documents on his person. "Even though I realized that the documents could destroy me at airport control, I decided to take them with me: they had been my dueling weapons" (*C,* 35). The metaphor is significant: Tarden sees the state as an enemy locked in a duel to the death. In *Blind Date,* Levanter takes the dueling image literally. He discovers working in a New York hotel a Soviet agent who has been responsible for destroying Levanter's friend, a Russian fencing master. Luring the agent to a public bath house cubicle, Levanter kills him with a thrust of a dueling saber. The oppressor has become victim, and Levanter is avenged. The violence Levanter commits against the agent is retribution for the violence done to one of the state's victims. Few readers would object to the appropriateness of Levanter's grim eye-for-an-eye retribution, although some might wince at the particular mode of vengeance.

What we call the Free World is for Kosinski no less an enemy than the Communist collective. Rampant consumerism is the counterpart of the Marxist state and it presents simply another collective assault on the self. Here is how Kosinski defines the nature of consumerism's unique brand of violence:

> In the parlance of popular culture, "totality of Experience" is simply another label for a sort of popular religion, which is to people who feel lost in the midst of the so-called free economy what a Soviet version of Marxism is to the masses hopelessly locked behind the Iron Curtain. The popular religion's elements are all there: one's destiny is somehow "predictable"; just as one's life can be predicted, or, at least, not escaped. For me, this trend represents a further repression of the development of an awareness of life as it happens in each of its moments, and that man must treat each of those moments as unique.[7]

Consumerism's deadly weapon is what Kosinski calls the "Master Charge attitude to life," and thrives on a society of "parrot trained consumerists" who take their models from the mass media, especially television. Kosinski's *Being There* (1970) satirizes what he sees as the popular religion of consumerism supported by a steady diet of televised blandness. Chance, the main character, is the victim of TV. All he knows of life comes from the garden he tends and the language of television he learns to mime. But Chance is also the unwitting deceiver of the consumer society that looks to television for meaning: news center commentators, newspaper editors, the FBI, the KGB, the President—all are gulled into thinking that Chance is what they want him to be. Because there is no physical violence in *Being There,* it is perhaps the only one of his books that could survive a translation from words to screen images, and the recent film version permits Peter Sellers to exploit the comic role of Chance to the hilt. But the tension between the oppressor and the victim still holds: consumerism is a political system that victimizes the individual. And because the individual is frequently unaware of his role as victim, such as Chance in *Being There,* the power of this system is perhaps even deadlier than the more overt power of the Communist state.

Kosinski's experience as a child in war-time Poland provides *The Painted Bird* with some of the most graphic scenes in which victimization is established by racial identity. Because the boy in *The Painted Bird* is "olive-skinned, dark-haired, and black-eyed" he resembles a "Gypsy or Jewish stray" and must play victim first to the local peasants ("fair-skinned with blonde hair and blue or gray eyes") and then to the German soldiers, including an SS officer with "smooth, polished skin" and "bright golden hair" (*TPB,* 119). Then, as the Soviet Army closes in on the German occupiers, the Kalmuks appear suddenly on horseback to reinforce the boy's—and the other villagers'—role of victim. Their skin, the boy says, is "even darker than mine"; but their arrival transforms the role of the villagers, whose blondness and blue eyes have now become the identifying marks of the victim. Finally the Soviet soldiers arrive and hang all the Kalmuks, whose dark skin is easily distinguished from the peasants. Throughout all these transformations of oppressors and victims the boy learns that the only escape from victimization is to adopt the disguise of the oppressors, now the Soviet soldiers. At the conclusion of the book the boy has managed to establish this new role with *élan*. Wearing the uniform of a Soviet soldier, he tests his new power on a four-year-old child adopted by his own parents. He grabs the child's arm and squeezes it until "something cracked and the boy screamed madly" (*TPB,* 243). Because he is a victim of his racial identity, he does violence to that identity in order to escape from it. In *Passion Play,* Kosinski's latest book, a young girl by the name of Stella passes herself as white and enjoys the life of a Southern horsewoman, whose racial hallmarks she had adopted. When the main character, Fabian, discovers her secret, she becomes his victim. Only minutes before Stella had been commanding a black servant working in a riding stable. But with Fabian's sudden knowledge, Stella is transformed from oppressor into victim.

The racial violence that Kosinski records in *The Painted Bird*—Poles, Germans, Kalmuks, Russians all killing one another according to shifting patterns of racial identity, while boxcars crammed with Jews ride through the countryside—does not surpass in credulity the documented knowledge of the mass killings of the Holocaust and of the occupation of Poland. Although certain scenes, such as the one in which a peasant named Rainbow rapes a Jewish girl whose arm is broken, are described in painful detail, no reader could object that the violence Kosinski portrays in this book exceeds what we know of this place and era.

It is Kosinski's treatment of sexual violence that troubles most readers. Racial and political violence seem forces that loom large in life, and if they provoke the individual into acts of vengeance, such provocation is understandable. But sexual violence stems more from a personal whim, a conscious pose. Irving Howe, commenting on *Steps,* objects to "the immorality of the spectator whose detachment is from the other side of the moon."[8] Not only in *Steps* but in the rest of Kosinski's novels we find main characters and narrators all too willing to detach themselves within a sexual relationship, to take part in, as Fabian states it in *Passion Play,* "a spectacle of which he was both protagonist and solitary witness."[9] But even with this said, sexual violence nevertheless has its own relentless logic, stemming from Kosinski's belief that the individual is alone. To avoid being victim, each person must strive to become the oppressor in the relationship. Thus every sexual partner in his fiction (and there are many combinations: man-woman, woman-woman, man-man, a number of *ménage à trois* variations, woman-goat, man-rabbit, and so on) is involved in a war of wills: who shall be the oppressor, who the victim?

Deception is the single constant in all these relationships. One lover poses as victim, for example, then, at the right moment, transforms himself into the oppressor. Sexual activity for a typical Kosinski character resembles not so much a passion play, to borrow one of his titles, but a power play. Here is Tarden again, this time boasting of one of his sexual triumphs. He recalls how as a youth he taught himself to retract his "member," hiding it by means of a "plastic-edged clamp, which made it look as if I were recovering from an amputation" (*C,* 129). He invites a girl to his house and, after assuring her that he is incapable of penetrating her, they begin to make love. "As long as the clamp remained in place, I felt a bit of pain, but the sense of harnessed power made orgasm crude by comparison. Later, when the girl was too aroused to be aware of what I was doing, I surreptitiously removed the clamp and shot into her without warning" (*C,* 129). Tarden poses as victim of sexual mutilation, lures his partner into a state of vulnerability, then attacks, his missing member appearing suddenly as a weapon of vengeance. In *Steps,* the narrator arranges a complicated tryst in which his friend's lover agrees to submit herself, while blindfolded, to a total stranger. When the narrator enters her room at the arranged signal and sees her blindfolded on the floor, he is torn between passion and detachment, the conflicting roles of victim and oppressor. "I was aware that to her I was no more than a whim of the man she loved, a mere extension of his body, his touch, his love, his contempt. I felt my craving grow as I stood over her, but the consciousness of my role prevailed over my desire to possess her" (*S,* 101). In *Blind Date,* Levanter himself is transformed into a victim. He meets an attractive young woman who calls herself Foxy Lady. But after a seemingly satisfying sexual relationship for some months, Levanter discovers that Foxy is no lady, but rather a transsexual. In *Passion Play* Fabian is attracted to Manuela, a transsexual who has not permitted herself the final transformation, surgical removal of the male organs. But Manuela is ostensibly female in every other way. Together Fabian and Manuela lure a woman into Fabian's luxury mobile van, and the two cavort with the woman who thinks, alas, she is making love to a man *and* a woman. With all this power flowing back and forth between sexual partners, the result is often violence, and these scenes represent the most disturbing side of Kosinski. The narrator in *Steps,* for example, walking with his girl friend at night in a park, is assaulted by a group of men. They beat him into submission and then rape her. Although he is dazed, he witnesses her in the role of victim, and dwelling on what he feels is her degraded state, he finds he can afterwards only respond to her as an oppressor. Although they resume the relationship after she recovers, the balance of power has shifted. He can only make love to her as a rapist, a vicarious participator in the rape he saw. "Afterward she asked me why I had been so violent [when they made love]. I told her the truth. Our relationship had changed" (*S,* 56). In *Cockpit,* Tarden, involved in a liaison with Veronika, decides that he has been victimized by her. After he had arranged for her to marry a wealthy suitor, she wishes to break with Tarden. Determined to direct the flow of power back to himself, he brings her to his apartment, ties her to a chair, and goes out into the night to hire three derelicts to rape her. While the men perform Tarden's vengeance on Veronika, Tarden records it all with his camera.

One of the most sustained and graphic scenes of this kind occurs in *Blind Date.* At a youth camp in East Europe, a 15-year-old Levanter listens avidly to his friend Oscar, who is an accomplished rapist, formulate a new grammar of sexual violence. Oscar calls rape "breaking the eye," and applies his personal vocabulary to every part of the female body he intends to violate. "Along with these bits of terminology, Oscar had developed a whole sex vocabulary. A female's head was a melon, her mouth a lock, hands were grabbers, the back a sun deck, breasts points, nipples contacts, and her belly a plate; her legs were sticks, the groin the cut, and her buttocks pillows, divided by the narrows."[10] Armed with this new vocabulary, Levanter decides to experience "breaking the eye" himself. He sees a girl at the camp who attracts him, and he secretly calls her "Nameless." Levanter not only figuratively rapes her of her personal identity by such a naming, he later succeeds in literally raping Nameless in the woods. His power play, learned from Oscar, is so effective that her scream of terror and pain seems to articulate victimization at its most extreme: "There was something unnatural about the sound. He imagined an inner spring had snapped inside her" (*BD,* 77). The young Levanter shows no remorse at snapping this inner spring, and when, a year or so later, he meets Nameless (who never saw her attacker) he begins to date her. But a certain gesture gives him away, and she suddenly knows Levanter is the person who raped her. Levanter is chagrined not at what he had done, but at being discovered. His knowledge of her is no longer superior to her knowledge of him, the flow of power begins to reverse itself, and so Levanter breaks away.

This whole scene might well stand for the sexual violence that has received so much comment by Kosinski's critics. Irving Howe's word, "detachment," is at the heart of the problem. When Kosinski claims that his fiction is "about you," the reader, and that the reader is a co-creator ("you're creating this situation when you are reading about it"), he is positing much more freedom to his readers than the actual reading experience can justify. The "you" cannot create a situation outside the sequence of words that Kosinski has arranged with such craft. In fact, the reader is more an observer than a creator, and his evaluation of what he is observing is generally at variance with that of the narrator. Take, for instance, the scene in *Cockpit* in which Tarden ushers into his apartment the three derelicts he has chosen to rape Veronika. As Tarden coolly photographs the scene, his detachment is a model of Kosinski's detachment as he creates the voice of Tarden. The voyeurlike nature of this special reader-writer relationship is perhaps what one critic, Raymond Sokolov, referred to in his review of *Blind Date:* "This collusion between writer and reader is obscene, but that is its point."[11]

Kosinski's reply to all these objections is that his novels are neither amoral nor immoral, but that they explore the possibility of an entirely new morality, one based on the scientific discoveries of Jacques Monod, whose work, especially as summarized in the book *Chance and Necessity* (1970), demonstrates that nature has no plan, no scheme for the future, no destiny.

"Destiny," Kosinski claims, "is written concurrently with each event in life, not prior to it, and that to guard against this powerful feeling of destiny should be the source of our new morality. . . . Thus Levanter embraces Monod's scientific postulate that forces man to acknowledge his isolation, to utilize each moment of his life as it passes rather than to dismiss it as a minor incident in a larger passage or zone of time."[12] Kosinski insists on the moral nature of Levanter. He speaks of Levanter's "development of soul" and his deep concern for "moral issues." He dismisses the rape of Nameless by pointing out that Levanter "was willing to suffer the legal consequences for the rape, but that the authorities refused to believe he was the rapist."[13] But surely his willingness to suffer the legal consequences is not the point: the reader's experience of Levanter's rape of Nameless is disturbing because Levanter experiences no feeling, no emotion, neither remorse nor elation. He remains detached, clinical, and his willingness to admit publicly to rape might well be a sign of perverse pride—Oscar's pride, say, in being a rapist.

Kosinski's personal vision, his insistence that we should develop "an awareness of life as it happens in each of its moments, and that man must treat each of those moments as unique," is consistently and convincingly portrayed in his novels. But if the vision is new, it is not a moral one. A code of behavior that treats each moment as unique but excludes an evaluation of the meaning of that moment, especially the moment's possible ramifications of pain and suffering for others, can not also be a moral code. Granted, the moment is unique, unrepeatable; the question, and one which Kosinski begs continually in his fiction, is what to *do* with the moment. Rape Nameless? Help a refugee from a police state? Photograph Veronika being raped? Arrange to have an imprisoned writer released? The problem with the vision, and with the code of behavior derived from the vision, is that it is too simple: life is reduced to a series of unique moments that elude evaluation. Human relationships are reduced to power plays between victim and oppressor. But a moral vision implies awareness of complexity, the presence of doubt, ambiguity, involvement, despair, joy. Kosinski offers sequences of moments, each unique and powerfully narrated, but with all the complexity of life simply abstracted (Tarden's words came back: "I could abstract myself from its power") until the moment is nearly a hollow shell.

Notes

1. Joe David Bellamy, ed. *The New Fiction: Interviews with Innovative American Writers* (Urbana: University of Illinois Press, 1974), p. 145.

2. Daniel Cahill, "An Interview with Jerzy Kosinski on *Blind Date*," *Contemporary Literature,* XIX (1978), p. 139.

3. Jerzy Kosinski, *Cockpit* (Boston: Houghton Mifflin Co., 1975), p. 131. Further references will be cited in the text using the abbreviation *C.*

4. Jerzy Kosinski, *The Painted Bird* (Boston: Houghton Mifflin Co., 1965, 1976), p. 217. Further references will be cited in the text using the abbreviation *TPB.*

5. Daniel Cahill, p. 138.

6. Jerzy Kosinski, *Steps* (New York: Random House, 1968), p. 65. Further references will be cited in the text using the abbreviation *S.*

7. Daniel Cahill, p. 138.

8. Daniel Cahill, "Kosinski and His Critics," *North American Review* (Spring, 1980), pp. 66–67. Cahill quotes Irving Howe as an example of the "waywardness of critical praise and blame" he finds in a number of Kosinski's critics.

9. Jerzy Kosinski, *Passion Play* (New York: St. Martin's Press, 1979), p. 112.

10. Jerzy Kosinski, *Blind Date* (Boston: Houghton Mifflin Co., 1977), p. 69.

11. Raymond Sokolov, "Jerzy Kosinski's *Blind Date,*" *Newsweek* (November 21, 1977), p. 122. John Leonard saw something similar in *Passion Play:* "A kind of rationalism is suggested that metastasizes into fascism." *The New York Times* (September 13, 1979), p. C 21. Anatole Broyard also commented on the sense of detachment Kosinski relies on for his fiction: "In *Blind Date,* Levanter's cool detachment, all too reminiscent of Clint Eastwood, tends to congeal not only the passion of the author's vision, but his high seriousness as well, so that incidents meant to evoke horror often come across as merely lurid." *The New York Times Book Review* (November 6, 1977), p. 14.

12. Daniel Cahill, "An Interview with Jerzy Kosinski on *Blind Date,*" p. 135.

13. Daniel Cahill, p. 137.

Betrayed by Jerzy Kosinski

JEROME KLINKOWITZ

[*Note to the reader:* You are reading what is known as a *samizdat*—an informal essay prepared for circulation among friends and editors in circumstances where formal publication would seem impractical (the term originates with Soviet dissidents who were denied easy access to the established media.) I first wrote it in February 1981, drawing on partial drafts dating back to October 1979 when I returned from a brief visit to Poland where I had lectured on contemporary American fiction for the Ministry of Higher Education. Its purpose was, and still is, to set the record straight on the two Kosinski pieces that I'd done much earlier for the academic press: "Jerzy Kosinski: An Interview" (conducted in November 1971, first printed in the premier issue of Joe David Bellamy's *fiction international* [Fall 1973], and then reprinted in Bellamy's anthology *The New Fiction: Interviews with Innovative American Writers* [1974]) and the chapter on Kosinski in my study *Literary Disruptions: The Making of a Post-Contemporary American Fiction* (1975). Even before going to Poland, I'd begun to note inconsistencies among the autobiographical stories that Kosinski had told me, and by the summer of 1979—when I'd read galleys of his forthcoming novel, *Passion Play,* and heard conflicting reports bouncing around New York—I came to regret having endorsed his unverifiable material as scholarly fact. Kosinski's autobiography seemed to have been reinvented for a transient market at each turn of events.

At the same time, I began to dislike his newer fiction, which disappointed me with its self-indulgence and gratuitous cruelty—two familiar charges which his earlier novels had successfully withstood. Therefore, when the Chicago *Sun-Times* asked me to review *Passion Play,* I submitted a notice praising some of its good elements but deploring its "anti-democratic fascination with the very rich." When the review appeared on September 2, I sent a copy to Kosinski, adding that I felt badly about this new direction in his work. "Even 'Stupid Ludmilla,' " I told him, referring to a tormented character in *The Painted Bird,* "was loved," whereas *Passion Play* was disproportionately hateful and overwrought. A few weeks later, Kosinski phoned, wishing me a good trip to Poland and saying that he didn't mind the review, even though it had "followed him around the country"—apparently the Field News Service had put it on their wire and local papers covering Kosinski's promotional tour had reprinted the piece nearly everywhere he appeared. Abroad, I heard even more conflicting stories about Kosinski—not rumors but points of fact, such as those concerning the political circumstances in the Soviet Union and in Poland at the time that he had left. Because of the conflicting stories that Jerzy himself had been telling me, I felt obliged to sort out my own experiences with the man and his writing.

Happily, I can report that, for good reasons, his texts survive intact. For the very same reason, however, his autobiography does not. Since I first drafted and circulated my *samizdat,* there have been a great number of essays published in its wake, most notably Barbara Gelb's "Being Jerzy Kosinski" in the *New York Times Magazine* (21 February 1982), Geoffrey Stokes and Eliot Fremont-Smith's "Jerzy Kosinski's Tainted Words" in the *Village Voice* (22 June 1982), and John Corry's "A Case History: 17 Years of Ideological Attack on a Cultural Target" in the *New York Times* "Arts & Leisure" section (7 November 1982). All were front-page stories.

I still consider myself a critical advocate of Kosinski's literary work, and I admire his skill and charm as a self-publicist (talents to which I myself succumbed). The "betrayed" in my title is an allusion to Manuel Puig's novel, *Betrayed by Rita Hayworth,* in which the act of betrayal is gently seductive and pleasurable even in retrospect—yet a betrayal just the same.]

It was Jerzy Kosinski on the phone—an instrument which he uses like a whip—and his shrill voice was snapping out instructions with an intensity which gave everything he said an aura of truth and authority.

Everything. Before, it had been such matters as his traumatic childhood in war-torn Poland (context for *The Painted Bird*), the pranks that he'd enjoyed playing on Soviet and Polish officialdom before his surreptitious flight to the U.S. (*Steps*), his claims against the collectivizing force of the American news and entertainment media, especially TV (*Being There*), and a whole series of adventures, object lessons, and caustic lectures about life in the modern world (which are pretty much the topics of *The Devil Tree, Cockpit,* and *Blind Date,* the other novels which he'd published up to then; a few years later, I'd be able to recognize his own climb to national and world celebrityhood in *Passion Play* and *Pinball*). As they would appear, Kosinski would embellish the stuff of these novels with frantic conversations about his own life, whether on television talk shows, in formal interviews for magazines, popular and academic alike, or in the sudden and disturbing phone calls that one was liable to receive virtually anytime, day or night.

The drama, it now seems, was a product of method acting. One had the sense—and maybe Kosinski believed it himself—that he was calling from a bus station phone booth, rushing you the most crucial important news as his bus was starting to pull away.

And here was Kosinski again, creating a verbal structure within which I was to read the galleys of his new novel, *Passion Play,* which, he said, he'd mailed to me that morning.

"It's about a *polo player?*" I asked with some surprise. His last two books had favored characters closer to Kosinski's ideal of himself—Tarden the master secret agent, Levanter the speculative investor—each of them disposed to travel the world giving demonstrations on how to live securely and how to practice sweet revenge. So why this suddenly new interest in polo?

"Don't you know?" Kosinski, now in a more subtle mood, invited me to ponder. "I have been a semi-professional polo player for the past seven years. In fact, I've just come back from a tournament in Dallas. Next month we'll be playing in Oak Brook, near Chicago—that's close to you, so why don't you come see?"

I didn't make it to Chicago, nor did I have to. *People* magazine later showed me and a million other Americans a six-page photospread of Kosinski at his hobby: dressing like a polo champ, in action on the field, and taking shots from a sawhorse installed on his Manhattan apartment balcony. Seven years of polo playing! How could I have missed all this?

Passion Play itself, filled with information about the sport and packed with allusions to his own work as well, read with typical Kosinski authority. Fabian, the polo-pro protagonist, was a writer, too, and his books on horsemanship stood in perfect parallel with the titles and contexts of Kosinski's own novels: from *The Runaway* (trauma from early accidents), through *Obstacles* (a warning to unseasoned riders), and up to Fabian's latest, a *Blind Date* look-alike called *Prone to Fall. Obstacles,* Fabian's equivalent to the National Book Award novel *Steps,* had even won the "National Horse Lovers Award." Like Kosinski at Yale, Fabian occasionally taught a university seminar, here called "Riding Through Life." The parallels were endless, and topping them all was Kosinski's proficiency in polo, the point at which his and Fabian's lives touched most intimately. Seven years of polo playing! I'd obviously overlooked a substantial chapter of his widely publicized in-progress autobiography.

The novel was still several weeks from publication when I visited New York to interview another writer. We finished our work, and in the small talk which took us to the door, the subject of Kosinski's work came up.

"Are you seeing anybody else while you're in town?" my friend asked. He knew that an afternoon of shuttling up and down the 7th Avenue local would take me to the doorsteps of several other writers that I'd been working on, from Donald Barthelme in the West Village to Jerzy Kosinski up on 57th Street.

"No," I replied. "Barthelme's down in Houston, and Kosinski is off somewhere playing in a polo tournament."

"Polo?" he laughed.

"Of course," I proudly announced. "Kosinski has been a semi-pro polo player for over seven years!"

Now my host was really chortling. "Why, I taught Jerzy how to ride last summer in Central Park!" he announced.

Inventing his own life of fiction is Jerzy Kosinski's most natural act. His novels record this process, and virtually everything he does reinforces his writing and further secures his own existence. The process becomes involuted, the fabrication of circles within circles: who was Jerzy fooling, the critic who was led to believe that there had been a seven-year career in polo or the writer who supposed that he was teaching him to ride? In Kosinski's world, each act is equally suspect. Like a secret, the real Jerzy Kosinski remains unknowable, inviolable, secure.

He has made this a program for his fiction, and he is fond of quoting Proust: what our memory recalls is just as arbitrary, just as creative, as any act of the imagination. Our memories are neither more nor less authentic than dreams. Fair enough. But when your childhood is filled with horrors from the war and with memories of unspeakable atrocities practiced on a very personal level—atrocities which you survived simply by your own cunning—the imagination's role becomes creative indeed.

As a six-year-old child, Kosinski was stripped of all the structures and buffers of civilization and quite literally tossed to the wolves of superstition, hatred, and despair. *The Painted Bird* is the fictional event distilled from this past, from memories themselves at least partly fictional. The Boy in this novel is a survivor, as they say, because he too can create—and in not very pretty ways. As Kosinski admits in his comments on the novel:

> Maybe hate is a way of self-fulfillment? For hate takes on a mystical aura; to possess hate is to possess great power, and the wielder of that power has control of magnificent gifts. Like Prospero he rules his kingdom, and justice is meted out according to his will. Things are as he sees them to be; if not, they soon submit to his vision of the world. He can shape his world as he wills: Prospero's wand becomes revenge. (*Notes of the Author,* p. 27)

Masters of revenge are indeed the protagonists of each Kosinski novel from *Pinball* back to *The Painted Bird.* Creative revenge, not destruction—that's what makes these books readable, even enjoyable and, most of all, instructive.

The problem is that Jerzy Kosinski's life of fiction goes on night and day, on and off the page, influencing lives other than his own. Stories about him rebound as reactions to the sometimes cock-and-bull narratives that he's created about himself or perhaps to rumors whose seeds he has planted to spice up the plot. Does he work for the CIA? This is a common rumor, sparked by his continual jet-set travels. Does he, as he once told me, donate all of his novel royalties to a charity account for orphans like himself? Does he really believe that the figures and even the print runs of his books "cannot be revealed" because "the Arabs" would use it for publicity against his cause? He has no visible means of support, but a reasonable supposition is that he might simply have invested the earnings from his two pseudonymous books on collective behavior, *The Future Is Ours, Comrade* (1960) and *No Third Path* (1962): each was published by a major commercial house—Doubleday—and one was both serialized in the *Saturday Evening Post* and condensed by *Reader's Digest.*

Questions about Kosinski's life, lately front-page matter for the *Village Voice* and the *New York Times* "Arts & Leisure" section, have been knocking around for years. There was talk of a young woman who was introducing herself around Manhattan (and being so believed) as the ghost-writer of Kosinski's novels; on widely separate occasions, Mike Krasny and Ron Sukenick told me about her without revealing her name. His written English was atrocious, the woman was apparently claiming; he merely sketched out the plots and she wrote them up. The truth of this accusation and others may never be settled, but Kosinski does play interminable games with his assistants, editors, and publishers: as his manuscripts go through copy-editing, he will, for example, purposely introduce silly little errors to keep in-house readers on their toes and to monitor for careless proofing. Like F. Scott Fitzgerald, he seems to regard typeset galleys and even page proofs simply as succeeding drafts, and he rewrites heavily at each stage. My own interview with him typed up as nearly one hundred pages, and after three exchanges of the manuscript, hardly one word remained the same. Jerzy has been known to take a paragraph out onto the street and quiz passers-by for their sense of its rhetoric—he did this for a passage in my *Literary Disruptions* which he didn't like. His apartment is lined with dictionaries, and few visitors can pass an hour in his presence without being plumbed for their sense of words. He's curious as to how native speakers of other languages might differently express a common event (having been raised in Polish and Russian, he worries about being linguistically conditioned by Slavic structure when writing in those tongues). In a deconstructive age which has exposed the prison house of language, Kosinski is a liberator par excellence.

As a matter of fact, his novels have tempted others to experiment and pull practical jokes of their own. A few years ago, California writer Chuck Ross typed several clean copies of Kosinski's National Book Award winner *Steps* and submitted them to major U.S. publishers—including Kosinski's—as original work. Predictably, it was not recognized; indeed, it was unanimously rejected as unpublishable.

It's the *real* stories, however, that are more troublesome: the ones which Kosinski tells about himself and which, while they have great pertinence in both form and substance for his fiction, are later contradicted by undeniable fact—often by a subsequent story that Kosinski himself tells a reliable journalist or academic scholar.

Sometimes, of course, Kosinski's flair for publicity is amusing and harmless. My first contact with him, for example, was back in the fall of 1971; he was one of many contemporary writers that I was just beginning to read and enjoy while teaching Hawthorne, Melville, & Company at Northern Illinois University. I sent routine requests for interviews; most authors would answer by letter, and some didn't answer at all. Only from Kosinski did I get the whole public relations treatment, as if I had written a tourist bureau for a bit of information and called down an avalanche of booklets and brochures on every conceivable attraction. I received *Notes of the Author* (New York: Scientia-Factum, 1963) and *The Art of the Self* (New York: Scientia-Factum, 1968), his self-published pamphlets on *The Painted Bird* and *Steps* (actually an English version of an afterword that he'd written for the German-language Swiss edition of the former and some self-advertisements for the latter which were published in the *New York Times Book Review*); there was even a copy of *Tijd van leven—tijd van kunst* ("the time of life, the time of art"), a Dutch version (Amsterdam: Uitgeverij de Bezige Bij, 1970) of the same two booklets with, as my colleague Gus Van Cromphout pointed out to me, extensive additions to the text packed with further clues to Kosinski's method of writing. Plus any number of photocopied interviews, essays, and remarks. If I'd been writing a doctoral thesis on the man, my research would have been half-done.

A meeting was arranged for several weeks later at Yale, where Kosinski was now teaching. Meanwhile, I worked up the material for my interview questions: the three novels to date plus his studies of life under Soviet collectivism and also the details of his personal experiences which had been appearing in print—his years as an abandoned child in wartime Poland; the odd jobs, some with underworld associations, that he'd worked during his first years in the States; and, most interesting (to me), his friendship and close artistic affinity with the film director Roman Polanski, whom he'd known since college days in Lodz. In the most famous story then circulating, Kosinski was described as being on his way to a party at the Polanski–Sharon Tate residence and missing it only because his luggage was misplaced en route. As everyone now knows, that was the night that Charles Manson's crowd showed up instead. So when our campus film series announced a Halloween-night screening of Polanski's *Repulsion,* I put aside my aversion for horror films and, since Kosinski's critical autobiography was obviously involved, made plans to attend.

Which was my first mistake. *Repulsion* is more than a horror film: it is a brilliant, if at times sadistic, exercise in the conditioning of an audience, to the point that even a subtle shift in light or break in the music sends unsophisticated viewers into shudders and screams (this was DeKalb, Illinois, after all). The mayhem and violence, and even the murders, are the least of it, for Polanski's worst threats (on which he delivers) are the ones that he makes to the irrational fears and unimaginable horrors that he himself cultivates within the audience's own emotions. Were there tonal similarities to *The Painted Bird,* published the same year? That was one good question that I wanted to explore. But here I was, screaming my head off through a damn fool movie! And I was to meet this director's long-time friend and artistic soul-brother in just a few weeks—what was I getting into? I should have stuck with Hawthorne and the nineteenth century, I told myself; those ghosts are safely buried.

There's no easy sleep after such a film, and at daybreak I was still tossing fitfully when my bedside phone rang—and then the whip, the shriek, the breathless voice rushing through all sorts of details faster than my mind could register them.

"Professor Klinkowitz," sang an eerily high-pitched and inflected voice that I'd never heard before, speaking in a heavy Polish accent that my drowsiness was turning into Transylvanian *à la* Bela Lugosi. "This is Jerzy Kosinski in New Haven; will you please come and see me *tonight!*"

"NO!" I gasped in reply, pure terror making the same judgment that cool reason would.

"I may have to leave the country very suddenly," the voice protested, even more rushed now, "with no advance notice at all. Perhaps I might never return, who knows? I could be dead tomorrow, as the saying goes. So please, we should do the interview very soon while we still have the chance!"

Quite unhappily I agreed, and with books and notecards and emotions all in disarray, I changed my reservations and flew to New York, where my friends Lynn and Mel Bendett drove me up to New Haven. By the time I'd dropped my bags at the Sheraton, it was almost 9:00 P.M.—a dark and windy night, cold for early November, the streets deserted, Davenport College (where Kosinski lived) frightening and menacing in its Gothic gimcrackery. Past an iron gate, up the narrow winding stairs to the fourth-floor top: at any moment I expected arms to come reaching out of the walls and blood to start pouring from the ceiling—two tricks which Polanski's film had played on me and which I'd never forget.

But the Jerzy Kosinski who answered the door was from another world: warmly gracious, anxious for my comfort, and, with practiced calm, ready to offer a cozy chair, a few imported beers, and answers to my silliest questions. All I had to do, he explained, was sign over the copyright to anything he said on tape. The request came as a surprise, but as a novice interviewer I presumed it to be kosher and—after coming this far—gladly signed on the dotted line. He glanced at my signature and said, "Klinkowitz—that's *Klinkiewicz,* Polish, right?" I said yes, my great-grandfather had changed it to avoid Bismarck's infamous draft (or so my relatives would always claim).

So we sat back and talked for an hour, my tape recorder and his backup system (as he called it) getting every word: his muteness as a child; the escape from Poland, accomplished by forging documents, creating references, and finally conducting a mock bureaucratic war over his exit visa, all to make it look good; his first days as an expatriate in New York, hard work at menial jobs, and so forth. Kosinski at his desk. Myself in the easy chair—sumptuous leather, fireplace at one elbow, leaded windows at the other, with Davenport's stupid gargoyles peering in. All the horror was safely locked outside.

Then at 10:30 P.M., the phone rang. Kosinski snapped off both his tape recorder and mine and, after his first "hello" in English, spoke on the phone in rudimentary French for a few moments before rushing on in Polish. After a minute, he covered the mouthpiece and spoke to me, ever the courteous host worried about the comfort of his guest. "You must excuse me," he begged, "but the conversation I am about to have will be in a language other than that in which we have been speaking."

Then back to the phone and into Polish, a language that I could not understand, even to catch occasional cognates and guess at what was being discussed. But neither did Kosinski leave me in the dark. After nearly twenty minutes of talk, his companion Kiki brought us more beer; Jerzy paused, excused himself to the caller, and told us who it was.

"It's my brother in Warsaw," he announced.

Kiki looked worried.

"You see," Kosinski said, turning to me, "my mother in Poland is very ill. I was told just recently that she had three, perhaps six, months to live. That's why I expect to leave suddenly: I wish to see my mother and she wishes to see me, but I cannot return to Poland, for obvious reasons." With this he gestured to the tape on which he'd documented his story of illegal exit. "So it has been arranged," he continued, "that we will each fly to Amsterdam, a free city. That's where we'll meet," he said, turning back to Kiki, "Tuesday."

"Is that what your brother says?" she asked.

"More," Kosinski added. He was now staring straight ahead, speaking more to himself than to either of us. "I was told to look into the matter of disposing a body in Amsterdam."

Kiki gasped.

"The flight, the doctors say, will kill Mama."

Any further pedestrian questions that I may have planned for that Sunday night deserted me. Kosinski quickly concluded his call and reached forward, tripping the record button on each machine, and answered the question that I had asked him nearly half an hour before.

Our interview continued, stretching three more hours into the early morning, and concluded with a second session the next day, when I was supposed to be having lunch with Tom Stats, a kid from my old block in Milwaukee who was presently a drama student at Yale; I saw Tom later that day, packed my notes together, and trained back to my friends' home in New York with a briefcase full of tasty Kosinski stories that I was eager to show and tell. After three painstaking revisions and a foolish submission to *The Atlantic* (where Michael Curtis rejected it as press agentry), the piece appeared as scheduled in Joe David Bellamy's *fiction international* and was published again in his university press collection, *The New Fiction: Interviews with Innovative American Writers.* It was, I can say without vanity, one of the meatier discussions in the book, since everything took on a more serious tone after that scary, traumatizing phone call. My questions lost their silliness and gained some depth: my first impressions so rudely shocked, I had gone beyond feelings of fear and beery camaraderie and stood suddenly in perfect awe of the man.

I left New Haven thinking that I'd had a private audience with the likes of Henry Kissinger or the Pope—or, better yet, with a combination of the two. My grandchildren would hear the story, as would theirs, for by then Jerzy Kosinski would surely be enshrined as one of the greatest writers of all time. The phone call in the midst of my nightmares, the hurried flight east, the comfortable study into which flashed that transatlantic message from the Polish night—I had been privileged to witness the making of a myth! What testimony to give: Kosinski was larger than life.

The myth began to crack a bit when I tested it out on Kosinski's friends. Zjizslav Njader, a Polish Conrad scholar who visited my university that year, said that he'd known Kosinski since his first months as an émigré in New York and scoffed at the notion of Jerzy's inability to return home. Under such circumstances as a mother's impending death, Njader claimed, there would be no problem at all.

"Those Polish bureaucrats don't care that Kosinski left so many years ago," he chided me. "Kosinski must certainly know the type: they're a bunch of old sentimentalists. He'd say his mother was dying and they'd cry their eyes out as they let him in and let him out again."

But this, I told myself, was just politics. Njader, as a Pole living in a friendlier Eastern Europe and enjoying free and frequent travel back and forth between the two blocs, no doubt had too rosy a view of things. The myth demanded the image of Kosinski at the border, pulled one way by trench-coated government agents and the other by freedom fighters—a scenario favored by American audiences since the Hungarian uprisings of 1956. I myself had been witness to part of the Kosinski legend, which reminded me of heroic Father Goulet, an escapee from Budapest who had joined our parish in the Milwaukee suburbs sometime late in '56 after God knows what tortures, and that was how I wanted to see the legend.

And see it that way I did, until it turned against me. Within a few years, I'd expanded the phone call story into a full-fledged after-dinner entertainment and was putting it through the paces for friends of Professor Ihab Hassan in Milwaukee—a divertissement before the coffee, cognac, and cigars. This was, after all, the perfect audience, for Ihab and Sally Hassan had been colleagues of a younger Kosinski at Wesleyan years before. Surely, they too were partakers of the myth, and so I told my story, expecting gasps, wonder, and confirmation of my awe. Instead, I got knowing looks and a few disconcerting chuckles.

"How remarkable," Sally said after a few moments, imitating my own concluding rapture. "To think of that little room in New Haven, and from across the dark Atlantic that startling telephone call from Poland, a glimpse of the horror beyond all horrors!"

She smiled at Ihab, who continued in the same gently mocking tone. "How even more remarkable," he said, "and perhaps more likely, to think of that phone call coming from across the Yale campus, from Jerzy's graduate assistant who'd been instructed, 'Ring me up at 10:30 tonight and let me talk Polish to you for half an hour so we can scare the pants off Klinkowitz'!"

So which was the truth? Jerzy Kosinski, champion of life, survivor of the holocaust and later calamities, caught in the most maddening and pathetic of international circumstances as he flies his mother out of Poland to almost certain death? Or Jerzy Kosinski, manipulating an interviewer, as he must manipulate them all, into just the awe-struck mood that he wanted for this talk? As with the polo story, you can take your choice. Kosinski has insured that, at the bottom line of truth, where he lives secure, where *he* reveals the secrets, you and I will never know.

Circles within circles: the mother's-death story eventually made its way into *Blind Date,* published six years after the experience that he'd put me through. Other stories, both public and private, popped up in this book: fellow novelist Jim Sloan's tale, for example, told at the MLA, about Kosinski learning English mainly because his various Slavic languages lacked the proper vocabulary for gentle sexual seduction; Kosinski's own talk-show routine describing a friend speaking "Esquimaux" in a Parisian cafe and being assaulted by two burly Soviets who assumed that they'd been targeted for insult by the scatological Russian which had in fact been spoken; the trick Kosinski told me about using a garden hose to squirt horse cabs along 6th Avenue from his eighteenth-floor balcony while the doormen below transformed the inexplicable event into meteorological myth; his ploys for cutting through bureaucratic indolence and for speeding letters through the lethargic mails, plus news stories of his involvement with such celebrity authors as Reza Baraheni, Jacques Monod, and Leopold Sedar Senghor. All nice little narratives. But now they were confusing because they'd first been reported as facts involving Kosinski and were now being presented as fiction.

Another *Blind Date* tale that was apparently drawn from life was the experience of being kidnapped by a maniacal taxi driver. For me the effect was double, as the event happened to Kosinski at the Los Angeles International Airport on the day after his speech at the University of Northern Iowa (where I was now teaching)—or so he claimed in a phone call to my colleague Dan Cahill the following afternoon. He then told the same story on "The Johnny Carson Show" that night.

Climaxing the book was a lengthy dramatization, blow by sickening blow, of the Sharon Tate murders. Here the names were changed, but the fictional personalities were clear transparencies for six of Kosinski's closest friends. Unlike the novel's other scenes from life, Jerzy himself had not been there, and so, like Nick Carraway recounting Gatsby's death, he had to work entirely from imagination. And as in *Gatsby,* the results were stunning, resulting in some of Kosinski's best prose on record.

Why did he use these stories in his novel? Or, better yet, why had he told them as truth if they were later to appear as fiction? "To try them out on an audience," he advised. But that seemed too simple: in the fictional versions, most of these tales took on added dimensions and played more games still. For example, *Blind Date*'s taxi cab story develops just as it did in Kosinski's televised autobiography, right up to one crucial and climactic point, just as does the mother's-death tale. One can only guess that Kosinski is inviting the knowledgeable reader to play along, implying that the parallels between his life and his hero's are harmless and even amusing. Those charming anecdotes end on little upbeats, in quaint moral lessons, or simply laughs. Senghor mistaking Kosinski for a bellboy: cute. Baraheni freed from a Savak prison by Kosinski's intervention: an impressive happy ending.

But as in Polanski's *Repulsion,* we are being conditioned. For right at the end of *Blind Date*'s taxi story—which to this point has been matching Kosinski's "Johnny Carson Show" account step by step—comes the unthinkable: the cabbie is outmaneuvered by his intended victim and is most brutally and sadistically murdered. Nor does the fictional story of the protagonist's mother end with her death: instead, we return to the earlier days of her life spent in blissfully incestuous union with her son. Are these concluding touches autobiographical as well? That's what Kosinski knows we're too shocked to ask, although he's tricked us into wondering.

This is, after all, how *The Painted Bird* works. We read along, perhaps beyond our depth, because the uninviting topics of psychotic mayhem have been safely contained in perfectly acceptable prose. If we can read this far, we think, everything must be okay. At which point Kosinski springs his trap, shocking us with previously unimaginable horror that less skillful writing would have let degenerate into titillation or farce.

The stories that Kosinski tells in life, whether true or false, serve the same purpose. Their author reveals them so that they will be talked about in all their contradictions, and those contradictions are the key part of the tale. Catching Kosinski in an occasional slip-up only makes the genius of his behavior easier to admire: like the action of his novels, his life story may be unverifiable, but it is never boring, and his rewriting of the past reveals his absolute commitment to the present as our only firm reality. As I met more people who'd known Kosinski earlier in life, these inconsistencies became more frequent and more strikingly transparent. Zjizslav Njader had told me that Kosinski's claim to have mastered photography simply as a way of facilitating escape to the West was a fiction. "He desperately wanted to be a photographer all the time," Njader claimed.

"But Kosinski says he threw away his cameras when he landed at Idlewild in 1957," I protested.

"Listen," came the reply. "I remember a whole week back then driving Kosinski all over New York City and Long Island, from Eastman Kodak to every other photo outfit in the book, as he sought work in photography or photographic chemistry."

Was he indeed an associate professor at the Polish Academy of Sciences in Warsaw? That was how he translated the rank of *aspirant,* his formal title.

"Nonsense," Njader replied. "*Aspirant* means 'graduate assistant.' "

On my visit to Poland in fall of 1979, I was further deluged with curious stories about Kosinski: how *The Painted Bird* was allegedly plagiarized from Polish sociological books and journals; how *Being There* was supposedly cribbed from a prewar novel by Tadeusz Dolega-Mostowicz called *The Career of Nikodemia Dyzmy,* a book so popular in Poland that it became a successful film and has in recent years been the basis for a TV serial. More pointedly, several critics not at all hostile to his work assured me that Kosinski's tale of forged documents and surreptitious flight sounded like a needless fabrication. "He left late in 1957," they said. "That was during a six-month thaw in relations with the West: you can look up the announcements from the Party Congresses here and in Moscow. Visas were very easy to get; going West was encouraged. Kosinski would have had nothing to worry about—a cyanide capsule under his tongue, indeed!"

Admittedly, this took some of the drama out of Kosinski's emigration. Looking back, one sees that *The Future Is Ours, Comrade, No Third Path,* and even *The Painted Bird* were published with right wing endorsements; perhaps the marketing of these books, like Kosinski's great escape story, pandered to Cold War sentiments. In any event, Kosinski had fashioned his own American myth out of his daring flight to freedom—a flight in the style that Americans admired in countless other escapes from Hungary, East Germany, and other Warsaw Pact states. Without real danger, his story would lack mythic proportion.

Which may be a clue to understanding Kosinski's fabulative existence. The novels, he may feel, need a myth surrounding them, and he's been careful, furthermore, to keep that mythology consistent with the changes in American political sensibility, from Cold War hostility through detente and back again to rambunctious anti-Communism. Hence, the excited phone calls which accompany each new book. On matters of lesser substance, I've caught him in embarrassing contradictions, in midstream changes in the hype with which he accompanies each successive work. For years, he'd cultivated a rather flamboyant pose in not allowing his novels to be filmed. Cinema was a manipulative medium, Kosinski would claim, a product of the American collective that he so despised. His books demanded the activation of the reader's imagination, while movies imposed the director's design. His books were internal affairs, encodings of language, while film was of course external and visual. These were familiar principles in his essays and interviews, and therefore when he phoned me with the news that *Being There* was going Hollywood I cited his principles for him.

"I *must* film this book," he said with some impatience, "because I feel America needs to know its message," and then he went on to describe a very intricate approach to filming which would keep his earlier principles intact. "All the minor characters, all the supporting roles," he reported with great relish, "will be played by well-known actors—so well-known that they themselves are institutions, just like the ones that *Being There* employs." Okay. "The role of Chance, however, will be played by a complete unknown, a new actor to whom the audience can have no predictable response." About this he went on in great detail: a "nationwide talent search" for the Great Unknown Actor, "filming in secret" so that the fan magazines could create no public expectations which would interfere with Kosinski's perfect blank of a cinematic protagonist. And so forth.

When the filming did get underway, Kosinski himself was the center of a well-orchestrated publicity campaign in the Washington, D.C., papers, where the movie's location scenes were shot. Moreover, magazines everywhere quoted Kosinski as saying that Peter Sellers—who'd been cast as Chance—had nailed down the role eight years before. Sellers, of course, was a great mimic; critics loved to say how his own personality could never be known, so thoroughly did he assume the parodic roles he played. So this part of Kosinski's myth was intact. But for the first time, I'd been privileged to be standing not in awe but somewhere behind the scenes, witnessing a few last-minute set and cast changes before the curtain rose on The Great Kosinski, new and improved for the 1980s—just as his stridently right wing image had been jettisoned for the later 1960s.

Any day now, I expect the phone to ring and to be danced upon his puppet-master's string once more. Will I ask about these latest contradictions—contradictions with which the *Times* and the *Voice* are still struggling? No: you don't quibble with Henry Kissinger, the Pope, or Jerzy Kosinski. Here at the University of Northern Iowa, my friend Dan Cahill can point out odd textual inconsistencies which contradict certain biographical myths. My colleague Jim Martin can show me how Kosinski, contrary to the claims on which his "necessary English" was based, did in fact publish a stateside book in Polish, *Socjologia Amerykanska* (New York: Polski Instytut Naukowy w Amercye—no copyright, but listed in the firm's backlist as a 1962 publication), which anthologizes essays written in the objective style of the Columbia University Sociology Department, where Kosinski was working on a Ph.D. (and which is not at all the subjective, even lyrical style of his own collective behavior books being published under the name "Joseph Novak"). And my old Marquette officemate Jim Hiduke can show me how the rhetoric of Kosinski's public life has been a twenty-five-year struggle to take America's penchant for making fetishes out of her authors and turn it back against herself—and to Kosinski's own survivalist benefit!

But who really cares about such arcane matters of muddled autobiography—matters which, at this writing, have generated both a full-fledged press war in New York and devastating parodies published as fiction by *The New Yorker* and satire by *The Nation.* As far as novelists and literary critics should be concerned, these are circles within circles, and the real Kosinski story will never be known—a fact which this master fictionist has been teaching me ever since that spooky night at Yale eleven years ago.

Thinking back to Kosinski's interview of me that evening, I recall that my great-grandfather changed Klinkiewicz to Klinkowitz in 1870; maybe he thought Bismarck would like it better. He was a pretender, like the grandfather of my friend and colleague Jim Bittner. Jim's grandfather changed the family name from Bitnar and also claimed that he was dodging the Prussian army—and not in fact the Czech police, all of which would make for a much lesser myth. Which am I, Klinkiewicz or Klinkowitz? Who is Jim, Bittner or Bitnar? Who is Kosinski? Does it matter? Yes, because it gives us all something to write about, to tell stories about. To tell stories is to generate secrets, and that is the central point of Kosinski's life and art.

Chance Encounters: Bringing *Being There* to the Screen

BARBARA TEPA LUPACK

Few novels lend themselves more naturally to analysis of their adaptation to film than does Jerzy Kosinski's *Being There*. That is, in large part, because few novels have as their subject the effects of a medium so closely related to film—a medium, moreover, powerful enough to render individuals incapable of intelligent and free choice and thus to create a force as collectively supreme as the Combine in *One Flew Over the Cuckoo's Nest* and as totalitarian as the military machine in *Catch-22*.

Being There (1971), Kosinski's third novel, is on one level a simple story of chance. On another level, it is the story of simple Chance, an innocent Gulliver possessed of a Lilliputian intellect, a contemporary Candide who wants only to cultivate his own garden. His knowledge of the world is restricted to the television set that he watches in his room and the yard that he tends at the home of his benefactor, known only as the Old Man. Chance's origins, although never specified, are somewhat suspicious: there is the suggestion that he is the Old Man's son by one of the domestics. Once the Old Man dies and his house is closed, Chance is thrust onto the street, where almost immediately he is struck by EE Rand's limousine, which pins and injures his leg. The Rands become his new benefactors, and numerous interesting adventures follow. Those adventures, usually the result of others' mistaking Chance's simplistic recitations of gardening lore for profundity, take Chance to the pinnacle of American popular-cultural superstardom. He becomes a media darling and eventually a candidate for high office (Vice-President in the novel, President in the film).

Through Chance, Kosinski decries the contemporary condition of video idiocy—Kosinski called it "videocy"—that affects young and old Americans alike, who allow the artificial world of TV to become their only reality. Such passive response, according to Kosinski, also leads easily to the usurpation by others of the privacy and integrity of the self, a concern central to all of his fiction beginning with his celebrated first novel. But, as John Aldridge noted,

Reprinted from Barbara Tepa Lupack, ed., *Take Two: Adapting the Contemporary American Novel to Film* (Bowling Green: Popular Press, 1994). Reprinted by permission of the publisher.

whereas *The Painted Bird* (1965) was a parable of demonic totalitarianism, "of that form of Nazi bestiality which is not a politics but a violence of the soul and blood, *Being There* has to do with a totalitarianism of a subtler and more fearful kind, the kind that arises when the higher sensibilities of a people have become not so much brutalized as benumbed, when they have lost both skepticism and all hold on the real, and so fall victim to those agencies of propaganda which manipulate their thinking to accept whatever the state finds it expedient for them to accept" (26).

Kosinski was personally familiar with the adverse effects of both totalitarianism and propagandism. Born in Lodz, Poland, in 1933, he survived the war by eking out a meager existence among the often primitive and sometimes brutal peasants, events that he fictionalized in *The Painted Bird* and to which he alluded in other novels. The repressive atmosphere of postwar Stalinism made him determined to escape his native land; and, after concocting an elaborate plan (premised upon a fictitious "Chase Manhattan Bank Fellowship"), he arrived in the United States in 1957, where he worked a series of low-paying jobs. After securing an actual grant, from the Ford Foundation, he wrote and published two nonfiction books, *The Future Is Ours, Comrade* (1960) and *No Third Path* (1962), based on his experiences as a college student in Russia. The books, well received in an era of cold war, generated much fan mail, including a letter from Mary Hayward Weir, the widow of American steel magnate Ernest T. Weir. Mary and Kosinski soon met (after she played a trick on him by impersonating her own secretary—a trick fictionalized and recounted in *Blind Date* [1977]) and married. Once Kosinski became a part of Mary's world of wealth and power, he discovered a life as sensational as that of fiction. "I had lived the American nightmare," he said, "now I was living the American dream" (Lavers 6). And he used many of those American-dream experiences, especially in creating the privileged world of Ben Rand, a character based loosely on Ernest Weir, just as he endowed Chance with his own perspectives as a foreigner, an outsider observing with wonderment the sociopolitical landscape of his new world.

It is not Chance, though, whom Kosinski targets for his parody and criticism; rather it is Chance's society, a people so visually oriented that they thrive on the superficial, so easily swayed by others' opinions that they become dupes of the collective forces of television and the media. Chance is assumed to be a wealthy businessman because he is attractive and well-dressed. Though his only assets are that "he's personable, well-spoken, and he comes across well on TV" (116), he is soon reputed to be a Presidential advisor whose many attributes include great intelligence, linguistic ability, impeccable manners, and social presence.

The fact that Chance never responds directly to the specific question posed to him is easily overlooked; ironically, his evasiveness is hailed as directness and lauded as a political and social virtue. He has, says his dinner companion, an "uncanny ability of reducing complex matters to the simplest of human terms" (106). Similarly, his inability to contemplate or calculate is praised as a naturalness that most public figures lack. Like the media, who make him their golden boy, the various audiences who watch Chance perform become quickly enamored of him since he is the fulfillment of their shallow expectations. Hungry for balms, they seize his literal remarks and transform them into profound metaphors; yet his purportedly insightful comments—that spring follows winter and that gardens need tending—are no more than echoes of their own hollowness and superficiality. (Kosinski documented this tendency of Americans to accept without question or challenge what others offer to them as reality. One week, in a course on Creativity and Reality that he taught at Yale University, he announced that, at the next class, teachers from a professional dance studio in New Haven would come and show the students how to tap dance; after the dance session, he would have a point to make. As Adrienne Kennedy, a student in that course, recalls: "The following week the dance teachers came and gave us lessons in basic tap steps. We practiced for more than an hour. When the lesson was over, Mr. Kosinski told us we had just had a lesson in reality. He pointed out that, as inept as the teachers had been, *because* he told us they *were* dance teachers, none of us, not one, had even questioned it. The dance teachers were, in fact, undergraduate students at Yale. It had all been staged" [A. Kennedy 29].)

An instant celebrity, Chance becomes the quintessential screen upon which others try to act out their own drama, a mirror that lacks depth itself but reflects and duplicates the images it is presented. His ability to reflect what he observes is emphasized by the many mirror images in the novel.

And Chance also serves as a mirror for the book's other characters. Although he merely mimics the actions of the lovers he sees on television, EE believes that he shows her how to evoke her "innumerable selves" (74) by unleashing both her sexuality and her individual identity. On the Gary Burns late-night talk show, "the viewers existed only as projections of his own thoughts, as images," and Chance in turn "became only an image for millions of real people" (65). He becomes Ben Rand's protégé, a reflection of his mentor's views on business and life, so completely that Chance is expected to fill the dying man's place. (In one version of the screenplay that he wrote for the film, Kosinski added an even more pointed mirror image: Ben explains, "When I was a boy, I was told that the Lord fashioned us from his own image. That's when I decided to manufacture mirrors" [Kosinski and Jones 103].) And much of Chance's conversation is nothing more than an aural reflection of what others have said to him.

The mirror images are particularly appropriate, given the mythic dimension of the protagonist. As a contemporary Narcissus, he echoes the shallow and narcissistic values of his society. While it is the other viewers who become enamored of his image, Chance is drawn to his television as Narcissus was drawn to his pool of water; he uses the TV to inform his behavior. When dining with the Rands, for example, he chooses to imitate "the TV program of a young businessman who often dined with his boss and the boss's daughter" (39).

Narcissus is not the only archetype upon which *Being There* draws; an equally important mythic dimension in the book is the biblical one. Kosinski's novel, a kind of contemporary parable, is written in seven parts and occurs over a period of seven days, which parallel the seven days of creation. The Old Man, in whose home Chance for many years resides, is portrayed as a distant but god-like figure; after he dies, Chance is expelled from his garden paradise into the fallen world, where he meets EE—whose full name is Elizabeth Eve (changed simply to "Eve" in the film)—who, like her biblical counterpart, tries to corrupt her innocent companion. And Chance himself is cast quite deliberately as Kosinski's "American Adam," to borrow R. W. B. Lewis's popular term, an archetypal man in his new world garden, fundamentally innocent in his very newness—a type of the creator, who creates language itself "by naming the elements of the scene about him" (Lewis 5).

At the same time, though, the Adamic Chance is an outsider, estranged from the society of *Being There*. His estrangement is not simply physical but also linguistic: he is incapable of true communication with anyone, from the Old Man's maid to the President of the United States. Words simply mean something different to him than they do to others. When the Old Man's lawyer asks him to sign a legal document, Chance says, "I can't sign it. . . . I just can't" (24). It is the lawyer who assumes that he refuses to withdraw his claim against the Old Man's estate; Chance means that he does not know how to write words and is therefore unable to sign anything. When EE visits Chance in his bedroom late one night and he tells her, "I like to watch" (114), he means precisely that: he enjoys watching television. It is EE who concludes that he is interested in kinky sex and who obliges him—and herself—by masturbating while he looks on. And when his Soviet dinner companion Skrapinov says to him that "We are not so far from each other," and Chance responds literally, "We are not. . . . Our chairs are almost touching" (89), his response is greeted as a fine metaphor when in fact there is no subtlety to it whatsoever. Similarly, when he is extended the recognition of an honorary doctor of laws degree, he dismisses it because "I do not need a doctor."

Although these exchanges, like so much of the novel's sharp and witty dialogue, read almost like a movie script, Kosinski insisted he did not write *Being There* to be a motion picture. He claimed repeatedly to have rejected offers to film the story since its 1971 publication. On a number of occasions he stated that he would *never* allow any of his works to be filmed. As William Kennedy observed, Kosinski's literary integrity is immense, "another way of resisting collectivization," and he tells all comers that "the books were written as novels, not scenarios" (W. Kennedy 12). At a panel in 1975 on "Making Movies Out of Books," Kosinski offered another reason for not wanting to film his novels. "I do like movies, and have known of many excellent screenplays," he explained, "but the book and the film have little in common.

Movies are a much more dynamic industry; so much is done so quickly it diminishes those who write" ("Press Panels" 49). In a subsequent interview with *The New York Times,* he elaborated on his position. Films "are basically about plot and action," he said, "and to transfer my novels to film would strip them of the very specific power they have, and that is to trigger in the reader his own psychological set-up, his own projecting. Film has the very opposite effect. It doesn't trigger anything from within. It sets things from without and you, the viewer, are there to be an observer, not a participant" (Fosburgh 13).

Kosinski nevertheless experienced a change of heart with *Being There.* Reportedly, one studio had ordered a script to be written based on Kosinski's characters. Fearing a quick, cheap version in which he would have no authorial or financial control, Kosinski began to reconsider. At the same time, Peter Sellers, who ultimately won the lead role, was escalating his own campaign.

Sellers had read Kosinski's book shortly after it had been published and decided that he was the only actor who could play Chance. He saw in the role an opportunity to bring his career to its culmination, a curious ambition for a man whose reputation and popularity rested largely on his portrayal of multi-charactered and multi-voiced roles, usually in a staggering array of makeups (Schickel 64). More importantly, though, Sellers, who had already suffered several heart attacks, felt that the novel expressed his philosophy that life was dictated by chance.

Sellers also believed that the trauma of his heart condition gave him a unique point of identification with Chance. "They later told me that I did not suffer any brain damage [as a result of the heart attacks], but I have reason to believe I did. My mind has deteriorated since then." Citing absent-mindedness and a general vagueness, he said, "I think I'm probably going a little soft in the head, which is why I have something in common with Chance" (Schickel 68).

Desperate to play the role, Sellers began sending Kosinski cryptic telegrams which read, "Available my garden or outside it. C. Gardiner" (DeSalvo 1). A telephone number—Sellers'—was always included. Sellers tried other stunts, too: he would spend long portions of his meetings with Kosinski portraying Chance, sometimes sitting for hours in front of a blank screen. Kosinski recalled: "Once we were in a hotel suite with a lot of guests, and he physically moved them to one side so he could turn on the television. Nobody ever caught on to what he was doing, just as nobody in my novel ever realized that Gardiner was a frail man behind a facade, that he had no substance" (Harmetz 19).

Even while giving interviews, Sellers would refer to Kosinski's novel. On one occasion, appearing on a TV show before he started work on *Being There,* Sellers was told, by a figure no less auspicious than Kermit the Frog of *The Muppet Show,* to "just relax and be yourself." He responded that that would be altogether impossible. "I could never be myself . . . because there is no me. I do not exist." He confided further, "There used to be a me. But I had it surgically removed" (Schickel 64). His good joke, on the one hand an expression of his profound fear (and perhaps every actor's insecurity) that the real man has no personality apart from the particular fictive self he adopts at any given time, is also an explanation of why he so coveted the role of Kosinski's protagonist, who is nothing more than the image of him that others have created. On another occasion, Sellers provided a similar insight; he said that his whole life "has been devoted to imitating others. It has been devoted to the portrayal of those who appear to be different from what they are. If I were to tell you that Chauncey Gardiner was the ultimate Peter Sellers, then I would be telling you what my whole life was about. If I don't portray him, he will ultimately portray me" (Schickel 67).

Sellers won the role he so doggedly pursued after Kosinski finally agreed to allow the film to be made and even to write the screenplay for it—a screenplay that eventually garnered awards from the Writers Guild of America and the British Academy of Film and Television Arts. Kosinski had already written a first version of the screenplay in the early 70s when he was teaching at Yale in order to illustrate the difference between a screenplay and a novel. (A novel, he explained, is an "internalizing" medium; it "describes." A screenplay, on the other hand, as an "externalizing" medium, "announces" situations that are eventually going to be described in images by someone else.) Kosinski subsequently wrote two more versions of the screenplay; the film used portions of all three (DeSalvo 2).

Although the book is set in New York City, for the final version Kosinski moved the setting to Washington, D.C. The move was appropriate, he claimed, since—in the decade between the time the book was published and the movie was made—America's real power base had shifted accordingly (Arlen 57). Indeed, he said, the Watergate scandal was another manifestation of the situation he predicted in *Being There*—that of the corrupting influence of television, which gives politicians the confidence to try anything, even the manipulation of the media. Similarly, before Carter's election, Kosinski considered Jimmy Carter the perfect media candidate, because he had no known past, no negative viewer recognition, prior to 1975 when his media persona appeared on network television. And, while Kosinski did not live to witness the ultimate Chance-like candidacy of H. Ross Perot, conducted largely via television time purchased with his own millions, he surely must have appreciated the irony of actor Ronald Reagan's two telegenic terms in office as well as understudy George Bush's subsequent lackluster performance in the White House.

When *Being There,* the movie, was released in late 1979, it was not the first film to examine the impact of television on modern life: *The China Syndrome* (1979) had already explored TV's power in current affairs, and *Network* (1976) had caricatured the people who run the broadcasting empires. But Kosinski's vision of television viewers as passive empty victims was in marked contrast to Paddy Chayefsky's "mad-as-hell" audiences who refused to take it anymore (Broeske 147); conversely, Chance's society can't seem to get enough of a bad thing. The subtlety and understatement of *Being There* were also notably different—cinematically as well as thematically—from the special effects used so widely in other films that year (including *The Invasion of the Body Snatchers; Superman: The Movie; The Black Hole; Battlestar Galactica; Buck Rogers in the 25th Century; Alien;* and *Apocalypse Now*). "I'm elated to see such a literate movie succeed," film critic Nora Sayre wrote of *Being There;* "its wit challenges the flying cutlery and sooty holes and mirthless farces of midwinter" (70).

Much of the credit for the film's success belonged to director Hal Ashby, best known for his critically and commercially successful *Coming Home* (1978) and for cult hits like *Harold and Maude* (1971) and *Shampoo* (1975). With *Being There,* though, Ashby was faced with an especially complex directorial challenge—sustaining a single, though witty, joke for almost two hours. "This is the most delicate film I've ever worked with as an editor," Ashby admitted. "The balance is just incredible. It could be ruined in a second if you let it become too broad. Peter's character is a sponge. He imitates everything he sees on television and everyone he meets. In one scene, he imitated the voice of a homosexual. It was very funny, but we couldn't allow it. It would have destroyed the balance" (Harmetz 29). Some of the outtakes seen as the credits roll at the end of the film show the exercise of a similar control.

Ashby chose to direct *Being There* with a deliberate, slow pace to amplify the dulled emotions of the deadpan Chauncey and to give the film the languid and removed quality of a dream (Broeske 147; Champlin 1), much as Mike Nichols did in portions of *Catch-22*. Kosinski initially feared that Ashby's film "would give all the answers. That would have been the death of my vision." But eventually he recognized that "Hal made the exact cinematic equivalent of my novel, a film where the observer is inside the film looking out. You take Chauncey Gardiner's place. You are there" (Harmetz 19).

Given the main character's spiritual and emotional nullity, a film so pensive and interior could have been quite soporific. But Ashby's use of the TV screen keeps it nimbly dramatic: absurd and hilarious fragments of random programs punctuate the blankness of Sellers' demeanor (Sayre 123). Whereas in the book Kosinski rarely described the shows Chance watches, for the movie film-researcher Dianne Schroeder carefully selected TV show clips to further the message. The selections were crucial. As Colin Westerbeck observed, in *Being There* the opportunity existed to use television sets as if they were telegraph keys, as a way to flash urgent signals to the audiences. But "the comments that the television insertions make to the movie are more oblique and imaginative" (118).

Ashby knew the importance of such seemingly simple visual statements. In his earlier film *Coming Home,* he used television to create especially poignant and meaningful moments: for instance, when Jane Fonda turns on a set late on the night that her husband has shipped out for Vietnam, a picture of the American flag appears on the screen; as the sound of the "Star-Spangled Banner" plays in the background, the screen suddenly goes blank. In *Being There,* there are a number of scenes in which the characters' actions are cleverly linked to or even foreshadowed by television programs. For example, when Chance goes up to see the Old Man, lying pale and dead in his bed, he has little reaction to the death. Turning his back to the corpse, he clicks on the TV and watches a commercial for Sealy Posturepedic; the unapproachable young woman on the mattress is a more attractive reality than the stiff Old Man on whose bed he is still sitting. Later, as Chance prepares to leave the Old Man's home, he tunes in a show about a widow grieving at the cemetery; "she" turns out to be Agent Maxwell Smart in disguise. The scene not only prefigures Chance's relationship with soon-to-be widow Eve Rand (played by Shirley MacLaine) but also suggests that only through television can Chance ever "Get Smart." Later still, at the Rand home, while talking to *New York Times* reporter Courtney on Mrs. Aubrey's phone, Chance gets a glimpse of an exercise program; unable to flex any mental muscles, he instead resorts to the most literal of responses and flexes his pecs. And after appearing on the Gary Burns show and delivering several powerful—though unintentional—verbal punches to the President, Chance views a martial arts demonstration on the limousine's set on the way home.

But the best use of television clips occurs when Eve stops by Chance's bedroom late one evening. Having just watched the amiable "Mr. Rogers" chatting with neighbor Mr. McFeely, Chance is now tuned in to a late-night love story. As Eve enters his room with the intention of seducing him, Chance begins to mimic the screen lovers' actions; he grabs Eve and—in a particularly comical play on the name McFeely[1]—kisses her and twirls her around the room while romantic music from the TV show plays in the background. But the TV picture dissolves in the passionate clinches and Chance cannot consummate the act. With no idea what to do next, he responds to Eve's frustration by telling her he would rather watch. Misunderstanding, she masturbates on the floor below him. Chance's attention span, though, is short; and as he loses interest in Eve, he becomes engrossed in a program of yoga exercises on the screen. As Eve climaxes, he imitates the exercise hostess by standing on his head—a fitting symbol for himself and for the inverted values of his society.

In still another scene, this one a significant departure from the novel, Chance's accident occurs as he is watching a TV screen in a department store window: looking at an image of himself being filmed by a camera in the store, he backs off the curb, only to be struck by the Rands' chauffeur-driven car. Thus, he actually observes his own accident by means of the television screen—a marvelous example of his detachment from reality and of the "screen[s] thrown between the self and awareness" (Tucker 222).

To emphasize Chance's dependence on TV, in the film Ashby has him carry a remote control, which he always keeps close by; when he is uncomfortable in a particular situation (as in the scene—original to the film—with the black youths, Lolo and Abbaz, who taunt him and accuse him of having been sent by Raphael), he clicks it and hopes to change his surroundings. Sellers' brilliant exaggeration of this remote-reflex—one of many comic touches original to the movie—affords a further comment on Americans today, who, with the touch of a button, expect to tune out any unpleasant reality. In another nice coupling of plot and television clip, Chance loses his remote as he is being driven to the Rand home after his accident; on the limo television is a commercial that urges people to protect themselves with a remote-controlled radar-tracking device called a "fuzzbuster."

Just as sights are important to the film, so are sounds. In the novel Chance realizes that people usually have two names and that Chance alone "didn't seem to be enough" (31). So he adds that he is Chance—the gardener. EE hears "Chauncey Gardiner" and assumes immediately that he must be related to her old friends, Basil and Perdita Gardiner. The assumption of this new identity is handled more elaborately and even more cleverly in the film. As he is drinking the cognac that Eve has offered him, Chance starts to introduce himself. But he has never tasted alcohol before and it stings his throat; he chokes out his name, garbling the words "Chance-Chance-the gardener."

Colin Westerbeck writes that in the film, though not in the book, there is an irony in the fact that the acceptance of Chance among all his fabulous new friends results from their having gotten his name wrong. "The film explores an irony missed by the book when Sellers endows Chance with the social grace of never making a mistake like this. Chance gets everyone's name right the first time and remembers it from then on. The way Sellers emphasizes this knack Chance has, it might be the only talent possessed by an *idiot savant,* a single way he has discovered that he can get approval from the world. Chance repeats everybody's name a bit too insistently, just as he thanks people for small amenities a bit too effusively" (119). In similar fashion, Sellers as Chance ingratiates himself to others by repeating what they have said. He parrots back the end of their sentences and other snippets of their conversations; his listeners, unaware that they are hearing only the echo of their own opinions and prejudices, are struck by the profundity of his remarks. For example, after Chance says that the lawyers have closed his house, Ben (Melvyn Douglas) assumes he means that legal complications have brought about the demise of his business. The doctor (Richard Dysart) concurs and says that lawyers will soon legislate even the medical profession out of existence. Sounding quite knowledgeable, Chance responds, "Yes. Right out of existence."

As with the naming scene discussed earlier, many of the most humorous moments in the book occur as a result of some misunderstanding. In the film, precisely because they can be seen and heard, Chance's silly gestures and remarks are even more effective than in the novel; still others, just as effective, are original to the script. For instance, before going to breakfast, Chance hears a meteorologist's prediction that there is a lot of snow in the forecast.

"What a morning!" the TV weatherman warns. At breakfast, Louise the maid (Ruth Attaway) informs Chance that the Old Man has died; "Oh Lord, What a mornin'!" she says. Chance associates her comment with the weatherman's and repeats instinctively, "Yes, Louise, it looks like it's going to snow." After watching a black slave on a TV show tip his hat to his white mistress, Chance, in an interesting racial reversal, greets Louise the same way on the following morning. When he is brought for treatment of his injury to the Rand estate, Chance is wheeled into an elevator by Wilson, one of the Rands' servants. Referring to the elevator, Chance says, "I've never been in one of these." Thinking that Chance is talking about the wheelchair, Wilson explains that "It's one of Mr. Rand's. Since he's been ill . . ." When Chance wonders if the elevator has television, Wilson—still thinking their conversation is about the wheelchair—laughs and responds, "No—but Mr. Rand does have one with an electric motor." When Chance asks, in his continuing curiosity about the elevator, "How long do we stay in here?" Wilson replies, "I don't know; see what the doctor says. . . ."

Later, when he and Wilson are again in the elevator, Chance remarks literally, "This is a very small room"; Wilson laughs and takes Chance's words as a joke. "Yes sir, I guess that's true—smallest room in the house." Wilson, in fact, is so impressed by what he presumes is Chance's wit that the next time they are on the elevator together, he breaks out laughing in anticipation of Chance's forthcoming jest.

In another scene, when the doctor tells him to stay off his leg for a while so that it has an opportunity to heal, Chance complies fully with the order. He raises his injured limb and stands, in a ludicrous stork-like posture, on his good leg. Later, when Chance is able to walk around the estate, he wanders to the entrance of the house. A servant, Lewis, asks him if he would like a car. Chance takes Lewis's question literally; he pauses a moment and replies, "Yes, I would like a car." Lewis assumes Chance wishes him to arrange a chauffeur to bring one of the Rands' vehicles around for his use. The car pulls up to the front steps; Lewis announces, "Your limousine, sir"; Chance says, "Oh, thank you," and then, without looking at Lewis or the limo, returns to the house with the doctor. Another time, Chance—ever literal—tells the President he "looks much smaller on television."

There are also numerous visual gags, as when Chance shakes hands and addresses the Chief Executive by his first name, the way Ben did, or again when Chance does a childish hopscotch step down the hall of the Rand estate. And the parallel images of Chauncey and Ben, in their wheelchairs in the billiard room or in their adjoining beds in the converted medical area of the Rand estate, suggest (as Kosinski does in the novel) that the two are metaphysical twins—both dependent upon machines for their survival[2]—and that Ben is grooming Chance to take his place.

Yet the film portrays even more vividly than did the book the limitations of Chance's knowledge of the world. Since to him the real world outside the walls of his former home is a novelty, Chance does not know how to react to it and relates according to the few behaviors that are familiar to him. And because he has never been rebuffed, it never occurs to him that he might be (Hatch 92); he has no fear of failing because he has no appreciation of achievement or any awareness of failure. Immediately after leaving the Old Man's house, for instance, he sees on the street a middle-aged black woman carrying a bag of groceries. Associating her with Louise, he approaches her and says, "I'm very hungry now. Would you please bring me my lunch?" The woman is understandably terrified by this bizarre request and ducks into the nearest doorway, that of an adult bookstore, just to escape him.

Once at the Rand home, Chance is treated for his injury by several physicians. Chance stares at Billings, the X-ray technician who is attending Ben, for a moment and then asks, "Do you know Raphael? . . . I have a message for him." He assumes that since Billings is black, he must know—or even be—Raphael. Chance is indeed like a traveller lost in space, as implied by the use of the music from *Also Sprach Zarathustra,* the familiar theme from the film *2001*.

While much of the script of *Being There* is faithful to the novel, some other changes were made in bringing the book to the screen. In addition to the shift in locale from New York to Washington, a few characters were modified—though none significantly. Chance, for example, is older (to accommodate Sellers in the role); as mentioned above, EE becomes simply "Eve" (to emphasize Chance's Adamic and biblical dimension); and a few minor characters are more fully fleshed out (the party guest who alleges on the basis of what he has heard that Chance is multi-lingual and multi-credentialed is given a suitable moniker: "Senator Slipshod"). The President, played by Jack Warden, becomes part of a running gag in the film; sensing that his renomination is in jeopardy and feeling stress and distress over his agencies' inability to turn up any information about Chauncey Gardiner, he is unable to respond sexually to his libidinous wife. Dr. Allenby, Ben's suspicious doctor, also has a dimension not explored in the novel. Carefully investigating his new patient at the Rand home, the doctor soon realizes that Chance "really is a gardener"; he is then content to keep this information to himself. No comparable character in the book is able to see Chance for what he really is. And Louise is given a small scene (not in the novel) with which she almost steals the movie. Shocked at seeing Chance elevated to superstardom on national television, she screams: "Goobledegook! All the time he talked goobledegook! . . . hell, I raised that boy since he was the size of a pissant an' I'll say right now he never learned to read an' write—no sir! Had no brains at all, was stuffed with rice puddin' between the ears! Short-changed by the Lord and dumb as a jackass." Her conclusion that "it's for sure a white man's world in America" brings hilarity as well as a certain topicality to the movie (Kosinski and Jones 72).

The greatest change, however, from novel to film is the ending. In the book, Chance leaves the blur of the ballroom to find momentary peace in the garden. Whether he will return to society or remain in the garden is unclear; like so many of Kosinski's works, *Being There* ends on a note of deliberate ambiguity. In the film, however, there is no such ambivalence. Rand dies (another departure from the novel, though in the book his death is imminent), and at his funeral Chance becomes the only heir to Ben's legacy. As Ben's coffin is about to be placed in the Rand family crypt, which is topped by an emblem that very fittingly resembles the image on a dollar bill, he leaves the service to wander around the estate grounds. Stopping to examine a sapling, he then walks towards a pond. In the closing scene, he walks into the pond and on to the water. So the viewer does not mistake the fact that Chance is performing a rather miraculous act, the film shows Gardiner checking the pond's depth by dipping his umbrella several feet down and then walking on the water without sinking or getting wet himself. What is merely implied in the novel is made clear in the film: Chance is the new social messiah.

The ending is a weak moment in an otherwise fine and sustained handling of Kosinski's fable, and it has been universally criticized by reviewers. The *Los Angeles Times* wrote that "the last image in the film, which does not exist in the book, suggests that no one so innocent and so guileless, speaking in parables and making those about him feel better, could exist without the endorsement of an even Higher Power than television. The book does not so much end as stop. The film does solve the problem of an ending, although . . . the implications are not very helpful. The choices include that it takes a heavenly patience to put up with that much television, that you have to be crazy to be nice, or that a later Gabriel will blow his SONY instead of his horn, and we had better be listening" (Champlin 1). The reviewer for *The Nation* concluded: "It must have been hard to find a way to end this fantasy, but . . . [this one] spoils the not at all innocent fun of watching Washington drink from the fountainhead of folly" (Hatch 92). And *Commonweal* observed that in the closing scene, "Hal Ashby's worst instincts" begin to get the best of him; the whole mood gets "ominously allegorical"; and only Sellers' underacting the miracle defuses "the annoying allusion to Christ" (Westerbeck 119).

Despite the criticism of the ending, Kosinski, it seems, was pleased with the finished film. Referring to the "many people [who] listen to your story on the big screen," he noted that through the medium of film "You literally open on a street corner," which he contends is "one of the original ambitions of a story teller" (Kakutani 30). Delighted with Ashby's direction and Sellers' performance as Chance, he even considered filming other of his works and began a screenplay of *Passion Play*.

And indeed Ashby's film retained much of the fun as well as the bite of Kosinski's novel. Moreover, excepting the momentary lapse at the end, it offered essentially the same warning as the book did: that as Americans continue to give precedence to the medium over the message, they invite collectivization and usurpation of their selves. They move from "being here" to "being there," and ultimately to the most passive response of all, just "seeing there." And while Kosinski's cautionary tale allows the reader to imagine that danger, the film allows the viewer—quite appropriately—to see it for himself.

Notes

1. Westerbeck (118) observes that " 'McFeely' sounds like a cutesy way to say feeling, as if emotions were, like excrement, something you have to make up euphemisms for. 'McFeelies' are what Chance has instead of feelings. He has about him that same inane sweetness that Mr. Rogers has. He offers to the world the sort of instant-on affection that Mr. Rogers offers to children. At the death of the Old Man whose garden he has tended all his life, Chance shows no grief. But when the industrialist (Melvyn Douglas) who has taken him in for a few days dies, Chance's eyes are moist. Only the 'chance' relationship, the brief acquaintance such as one might have with a character on a soap opera, can move him. The software of the emotional life is all that's available to him."

2. As Robert F. Willson, Jr., notes (in "Being There at the End," *Literature/Film Quarterly* 9.1 [1981]: 60): "Most devastating of all the film's ironic truths is that despite the apparent differences in economic, social, and intellectual standing between Chance and Rand, they are twins locked up in a world of illusion and dependent on machines for their survival."

Works Cited

Aldridge, John W. "The Fabrication of a Culture Hero." *Saturday Review* 24 April 1971: 25–27.

Arlen, Gary H. "From the TV Viewer's Perspective." *WATCH Magazine* March 1980: 54–57.

Broeske, Pat H. *"Being There," Magill's Survey of Cinema.* English Language Films. First Series. Vol 1. Ed. Frank N. Magill. Englewood Cliffs, NJ: Salem Press, 1986.

Champlin, Charles. "A Best Role for Peter Sellers." *Los Angeles Times* 28 December 1979, Sect. 4: 1.

DeSalvo, Louise. *Being There: An Introduction.* n.p., n.d.

Fosburgh, Lacey. "Why More Top Novelists Don't Go Hollywood." *The New York Times* 21 November 1976, Sect. 2: 1, 13-14.

Harmetz, Aljean. "Book by Kosinski, Film by Ashby." *The New York Times* 23 December 1979, Sect. 3: 1, 19.

Hatch, Robert. "Films," *The Nation* 26 January 1980: 91–92.

Kakutani, Michiko. "The New Hollywood Writer Vs. Hollywood." *The New York Times* 25 April 1982, Sect. 2: 30.

Kennedy, Adrienne. Letters Column. *The New York Times Magazine* 13 October 1970: 20.

Kennedy, William. "Who Here Doesn't Know How Good Kosinski Is?" *Look* 20 April 1971: 12.

Kosinski, Jerzy. *Being There.* New York: Bantam, 1972.

Kosinski, Jerzy, and Robert C. Jones. Screenplay of *Being There.* 10 January 1979.

Lavers, Norman. *Jerzy Kosinski.* Boston: Twayne, 1982.

Lewis, R. W. B. *The American Adam: Innocence, Tragedy, and Tradition in the Nineteenth Century.* Chicago: University of Chicago/Phoenix Books, 1967.

"Press Panels: Movies—and the Unexplained." *Publishers Weekly* 23 June 1975: 49–50.

Rich, Frank. "Gravity Defied." *Time* 14 January 1980: 70.

Sayre, Nora. "Films." *The Nation* 2 February 1980: 122–24.

Schickel, Richard. "Sellers Strikes Again." *Time* 3 March 1980: 64–68.

Tucker, Martin. "Being There." *Commonweal* 7 May 1971: 221–23.

Westerbeck, Colin L. "Going Nowhere: The Software of Emotional Life." *Commonweal* 29 February 1980: 117–18.

The Kosinski Conundrum

STEPHEN SCHIFF

Jerzy Kosinski can't even buy a tie without stirring up a commotion. He needs one for tonight's lecture at a Chicago synagogue, and as he gallops through the Carson Pirie Scott department store, heads swivel, and shoppers murmur behind cupped hands. Do these people recognize him? Or is it the Kosinski spectacle itself that gives them pause? "The air in here is poisonous," he informs me in his customary high-pitched shriek. "You feel it? Department stores have poisonous air. The reason is chemicals. All these products emit chemicals. Breathing chemicals means no air. No air means no oxygen to the brain." His words clatter beneath the Polish accent like popcorn.

From a distance, he's a blackened Q-Tip, a dark ball of hair blossoming from a stick. Up close, he's a bird of prey, two hard eyes atop a ferocious beak. "Breath controls everything," he announced, sweeping me through the men's-wear department. "I can quite easily change my body temperature at any time. I can make you believe I have fever. Just by breathing a certain way, I will be so hot—look, you put cold, wet sheets on my chest, *right here*"—he thumps his sternum—"and they will be completely dry in two minutes. You will see the steam." In distant aisles, people have stopped to watch him; perfume clerks are gawking. "I can change my heartbeat," he says. "It's royal yoga. I could bring my heart to two hundred, and you would not know; I could burn everything I have eaten for lunch in one minute. Look. Now it's fifty." Suddenly he grabs his own arm, thrusts it high in the air, fingers his pulse. "Look!" he chortles. "I'm dead! I'm dead!"

Actually, Jerzy Kosinski is alive and well and doing all the weird things he's always done. He still sleeps twice a day, in four-hour stretches, still consumes unlikely meals of raw onions and lemons (washed down with rum-and-Coke), still shows up at Elaine's disguised in various mustaches and hats, and, yes, still parties with the drawing-room titans of both coasts: Henry Kissinger, Abe Rosenthal, Ahmet Ertegün, Warren Beatty. In a Hollywood high-society comedy of the thirties or forties, he would be the wild man played by Mischa Auer or Oscar Levant, the jumpy, foreign-looking creature at the piano, burbling inscrutable jokes—the intellectual as court jester, imported to amuse the somnolent rich. Kosinski lives frugally—dividing his

Reprinted from *Vanity Fair,* June 1988, 114–19, 166–70. Reprinted by permission of the author.

time between a small apartment in Valais, Switzerland, and a downright tiny one on New York's West Fifty-seventh Street—but he's a frequent and pampered houseguest, heavily in demand for polo or skiing, and expert at both. And he gives good value. Wherever he goes, he spins yarns, pulls pranks, scribbles notes, tinkers with people and their lives—conscientiously playing the role he's assigned himself: Major Twentieth-Century American Novelist.

In fact, it's hard to tell at first that Jerzy Kosinski is still reeling from the most infamous literary scandal of the decade: the 1982 uproar that left much of the intellectual world convinced he was a charlatan, a con man, a fraud (as he put it then, "I must now prove that I even exist"). Six years later, the scandal is still the most intriguing chapter in the whole richly intriguing Kosinski saga. And in digging to the bottom of it, I soon discovered that one could never comprehend the truth behind the Kosinski Affair without first exploring the way the man lives—or, more to the point the way he performs.

"A novelist is the supreme spiritual entertainer," he tells me. "And this is true in every moment of his life and in every moment of his performance." In other words, writing books isn't necessarily the only thing a novelist does in order to play Novelist—and in the case of Kosinski, it may not even be the main thing. He has just finished a new book, *The Hermit of 69th Street;* it's his first since *Pinball* in 1982—and his first since the scandal. But most of his friends will never read it. The Kosinski they love talks a better novel than he composes—in fact outtalks, outthinks, and outcharms far more accomplished writers than he. Endowed with a life more outlandish than any fiction, he has long made a practice of smudging the borders between his biography and his storytelling. Which is why the tales he tries out at dinner one night may contradict the ones he spouts on TV, why the harmless jokes he plays on friends may turn up in his books sounding sordid and murderous, why the people who accept the incidents in his novels as purely autobiographical—especially those in his first and best one, *The Painted Bird* (1965)—may feel betrayed when they learn that he made many of them up. Is he some sort of flimflammer? "Look, I'm a storyteller," he replies, his peregrine eyes daring me to dissent. "I invent things. Once you ground them in only one life, the reader will feel that he is not reading about himself, but is reading about the author. That's a different literary adventure altogether."

We are sitting in one of his New York apartment's two Spartan rooms; the sound of frenetic typing in the other comes from Katherina "Kiki" von Frauenhofer, a tall, handsome, exceedingly lively woman who has been Kosinski's companion for the last twenty years—and his wife since February 1987. There's no question of their mutual devotion: Jerzy has dedicated all his books since *Being There* in 1971 to her, and she is, in Liz Smith's words, his "all in all": agent, typist, amanuensis, cheerleader, muse, nursemaid, and adoring audience—she even cuts up his food for him. To Kiki, a former advertising executive, every word Jerzy utters is a pearl. "I married her," he says, "because the name was the only thing I could give her. And also we had just been through this big project together."

The "big project" is *The Hermit of 69th Street,* which Henry Holt will finally bring out next month after years of rumor and delay—and after rejections from at least three other publishers. It is Kosinski's longest and most personal novel to date; it is also his most peculiar. Gone is the omnipotent Kosinski hero, half Robin Hood, half James Bond, whose hugger-mugger and priapic derring-do dominate so many of the other books. In his stead is one Norbert Kosky, a balding Polish-American writer very like the hairier Polish-American writer Jerzy Kosinski. Gone, too, is the terse, grim Kosinski style. *The Hermit*'s prose is rococo, prolix, clogged with the sort of clangorous puns that can sound charming when Kosinski whizzes them past you over dinner but look sodden and strained on the page. All the book's characters talk the same way (" 'So how is all this press prostatis affecting your prostrate literary prostate?' asks Cesare, sitting down next to Kosky on a sofa"). And sprinkled atop the story (such as it is) are hundreds of lengthy quotations from what looks like every book in the Barnes & Noble remainder catalogue. These in turn are supplemented by footnotes, several to a page—we get Balzac, Schlegel, Kafka, Conrad, Emerson, Baudelaire, Cabala, various Tantric oracles, Holocaust history, sundry girlie magazines and how-to guides, and more, much more. *The Hermit* is an attempt to portray what goes on inside a writer's mind as he composes a novel—his sexual fantasies, the readings he refers to, the way he associates his own predicament with his character's and with the predicaments of history. It is a book of both impressive erudition and bizarre naïveté, the product of a brilliant and ambitious mind that has long since outstripped its owner's talent. It's Kosinski's unwieldy contribution to Joycean metafiction. And as far as he's concerned, he's hit upon The Next Big Thing.

"I love it," he crows. "I think it's a profoundly imaginative work. You want to know the truth? I think it's the most imaginative novel I have written and certainly the most imaginative I have read in a very long time. By far. Because it departs. *The Hermit* says to the reader, 'You don't need any other book but this. You may not want to read any other books from now on, because this book gives you basically insight to the whole genre.' *The Hermit* may not be readable, but it was sure great fun to work on it. And anything in literature that can compete in fun with polo and skiing and sex is fine with me. This was my Nirvana."

One man's Nirvana, of course, is another's purgatorio, but those indefatigable readers who manage to plow through *The Hermit* will soon realize that the novel is largely a response to the Great Kosinski Scandal, the literary stink bomb that practically smothered his career: the June 1982 *Village Voice* article, written by Geoffrey Stokes and Eliot Fremont-Smith, that accused him of being an inveterate liar and, smellier still, something less than the writer of his own books. For Kosinski, nothing has been the same since.

"He was very badly hurt, as you would be," says his friend Abe Rosenthal, now a *New York Times* columnist but then the paper's editor. "He was stunned, angered, sorrowed, saddened. And I would say bewildered was a lot of it." According to some close friends, his health suffered. He lost weight, and his German publishers canceled a book tour for *Pinball* on the grounds that no one wanted to talk about anything but the scandal. Worldwide, over six hundred articles pondered Kosinski and his veracity, including the notorious blunderbuss the *Times* itself fired off some four months later: a 6,400-word Kosinski defense by John Corry murkily linking the *Voice*'s charges with disinformation promulgated by the Polish Communist Party. As Eliot Fremont-Smith, one of the *Voice* article's co-authors, puts it, "I remember joking that it would be terrible enough to be accused of taking our orders from Moscow. But to be accused of taking our orders from Warsaw—shit!" The fumes spread. The *Voice* accused the *Times* of Red-baiting; *Newsweek* accused Rosenthal of abusing the *Times*'s power by defending his old pal so crudely and at such ludicrous length; Rosenthal snapped back at his detractors in one interview after another. And Kosinski? He wisely spent the next year abroad, licking his wounds and working on *The Hermit.*

"This was not a scandal for me," says Kosinski, with a blitheness that seems a bit studied. "Suddenly I saw myself as being used in someone else's fiction, which is perfectly all right. It was traumatic only in the sense that I suddenly realized how vain I was." But his career is still shivering. The advance he received for *The Hermit* was $100,000—quite a comedown from the $300,000 he received for *Pinball* and from the approximately $250,000 he first demanded from his usual publisher, Bantam. "That figures," I say, in what I hope is a soothing tone. "*The Hermit* is a different sort of book." But instead of agreeing, as I expect him to, he grows pensive and stares down at his desk. "No," he says, "nothing to do with the book. The events of '82 made it hard. The publicity director at Bantam would say, 'We don't want all that stuff again. Distracts from the book.' So Bantam didn't publish it. It wasn't easy to find a publisher who would. This is a nonreversible thing."

To understand just what happened to Kosinski, and why it made such a profound impression not just on him but on the literary world at large, one first has to examine the curiously symmetrical trajectory of his life. It's a parabola that begins with one kind of disaster—the great European cataclysm of the Holocaust—and climaxes in a very different kind: peculiarly American, peculiarly personal, peculiarly a product of Western culture during the Envious Eighties.

Kosinski was born in Lodz, Poland, in 1933, to a prosperous Jewish family (his mother was a concert pianist and his father a philologist); when the Nazis invaded, he was only six. No doubt he would have died in the Lodz ghetto in 1942 had his parents not entrusted his care to an acquaintance, a peasant woman who lived in the countryside. But she soon abandoned him and Jerzy spent the next few years wandering among the destitute villages of the remote Ruthenian-Ukrainian region. Most of his friends believe that *The Painted Bird,* his first novel, is an account of those wanderings, but Kosinski has never claimed as much. In fact, he tells me, he purposely transposed certain incidents from his childhood into "an entirely different, Bosch-like universe," a universe based largely on Polish folklore and fable. "*The Painted Bird* is not necessarily about Poland," he says, "not about any specific country. It's about childhood as war, and war as a specific childhood."

What Kosinski does avow is that while serving as an altar boy in a Catholic church whose priest was hiding him from the Nazis, he became exceedingly apprehensive during a Mass and dropped a Bible. His tension at that moment apparently traumatized him; seconds later, he discovered he had lost the power of speech. (This incident is recounted in *The Painted Bird,* but it ends with the boy's being thrown into a manure pit—Kosinski now says the manure pit was an embellishment.) When his parents finally recovered him from an orphanage after the war, he was still mute (his speech would return only six years later, after a skiing accident). He had also lost some sixty of his relatives.

He made the most of his school days in Lodz after the war, and though his fervent anti-Communism often got him into trouble with school authorities, he earned two M.A.'s (one in history and one in social science), published two monographs on Russian social history, and garnered a number of photography awards. In December 1957 he arrived in America, armed only with a slew of documents attesting to his scholarship, and a scorching ambition to succeed. Kosinski has told varying yarns about his escape from Poland, and the first time I asked him what the truth was, he snapped, "I'm not going to tell you my life. No. I write fiction, I don't write biography. I'm not going to talk biography. I managed to get out because I'm a clever man, and let's leave it at that." Robert Loomis, the Random House editor who worked with him on *Steps,* says, "He told me he sent some photographs to a contest in New York and he got a prize. Then he doctored the check so that it looked as if it was for more than it was, and he went to the comrades and said, 'Gee, I got this prize, but I don't want to go.' They insisted he go, just as he knew they would, and gave him a round-trip ticket. So he went and he stayed." But the most fascinating passage in his 1975 book *Cockpit* details a more complex scenario. The hero, Tarden, painstakingly invents four academicians and, through a byzantine series of maneuvers, uses them to hoodwink the bureaucracy into issuing him a passport, a visa, and a plane ticket. When I press Kosinski about this story, he sighs and says, "Look, I came to America in such a fashion that the only way to secure the future of those who helped me was to maintain that sort of a fiction. We are talking about lives. We are talking about people who are going to be responsible for my not coming back. Do you think I am going to describe how I left Poland, and thanks to whom?"

With Kosinski, one often has to decide for oneself: either the tales he spins about his life are true or else his literary imagination is more prodigious than his detractors have suggested.

People who knew the young Kosinski when he arrived remember a man in a hurry, a man eager to make a big impression. By 1958, he had won a Ford Foundation fellowship and enrolled as a Ph.D. candidate in the Department of Sociology at Columbia. His English by then was, according to many accounts, quite good—good enough, in fact, for him to launch a small lecture tour, addressing Lions and Rotary clubs and the like and finally to publish, in 1960, *The Future Is Ours, Comrade,* a pointedly anti-collectivist study of Soviet behavior, which he brought out under the pen name Joseph Novak. Serialized in *The Saturday Evening Post* and condensed in *Reader's Digest,* the book attracted a good deal of attention; among Kosinski's most fervent fan letters was one from Mary Weir, the widow of the steel magnate Ernest Weir, and at that time one of the richest women in America. Two years later, she and Kosinski were married—she at forty and he at twenty-eight.

For Kosinski, it was a stunning coup—suddenly, like some Judith Krantz heroine, the Holocaust survivor was living the American Dream. Their yacht, for instance, had a crew of seventeen, and their private plane routinely ferried the Kosinskis between Southampton and Hobe Sound; there was a Park Avenue apartment, a villa in Florence, a suite at the Connaught in London, and a floor of the Ritz in Paris. When they traveled, Jerzy's book income covered the tips.

But three years later, Mary was diagnosed with brain cancer, and when she died, in 1968, her fortune reverted to her late husband's estate. By then, however, Kosinski had become a celebrated author. *The Painted Bird,* which he had started writing in 1962, had been published in 1965 to instant acclaim, and *Steps* was being taught on college campuses almost from the moment it was released; it went on to win the 1969 National Book Award. Jerzy had already met Kiki, a Hungarian baroness who had been born in America and raised and schooled in England; now they began seeing each other, and she followed him as he moved from one teaching job to another, first at Wesleyan, then at Princeton, then at Yale.

Meanwhile, an extraordinary incident added to his aura. On August 9, 1969, he was flying from Paris to Los Angeles when his luggage was accidentally bumped off the plane in New York, and Kosinski was forced to spend the night there. What he missed in Los Angeles that evening, at the home of his old high-school friend Roman Polanski, was the Manson murders—in fact, the coincidence was so eerie that in the immediate wake of the killings some Polanski allies accused Kosinski of having had a hand in them.

As absurd as that charge was, no one would deny that the novelist's reputation had acquired a somewhat sinister sheen. He was known for terrorizing his students, clapping a Ouija-board gaze upon them and proclaiming that he could see early death in their eyes. Denounced repeatedly in the Polish press, he would often tell friends that Polish agents were following him, would even hush them up for fear of long-range microphones. At home in New York, he and Kiki would be entertaining dinner guests when suddenly Kosinski would excuse himself, dash to a nearby closet, and lock himself in. Presently the astonished company would hear a typewriter banging away in there, and Kiki would soberly explain that Jerzy was going blind: he was training himself to write in the dark. (It's true that Kosinski has had recurring eye problems; even so, the dinner party theatrics seem more the habit of the Novelist than the novelist.)

The books, too, were getting pretty spooky. Largely mediocre after *Steps,* they were all (except for *Being There* in 1971) plotless strings of unnerving incidents, of crimes and punishments orchestrated by protagonists who had been stripped of almost every trait except raw Nietzschean will. Laced through the novels like a leitmotif was the detachment of identity from Self: Kosinski's people forged false dossiers, donned phony uniforms, posed in disguise, all to protect their inviolable Selves from having to take responsibility for their skulduggery. And the real Jerzy Kosinski seemed to be doing the same thing. "Why should I run my life differently than I run my fiction?" he says. "I have to be imaginative about both. Look, this is what drama is all about. It has to purge the reader of dangerous emotions. Every reader is willing to commit a perfect crime. I am committing it for him. Every reader is full of negative emotions. I am naming them, and relieving the reader of them. I think that's the purpose of art. In my life I plot the same actions, but the difference is that I am a very moral person. A small difference, actually."

And so it was that Jerzy Kosinski, novelist, became the activist president of the American branch of PEN, campaigning for the release of imprisoned writers throughout the world and receiving honors from the American Civil Liberties Union. Meanwhile Jerzy Kosinski, Novelist, was titillating friends with tales of his erotic escapades and his naughty after-hours sojourns. While other boulevardiers were hanging up their dinner jackets, Kosinski was nosing his 1970 Buick into the night, making for Times Square or the Hudson River piers, for sex clubs like Plato's Retreat and S&M clubs like the Hellfire. Talking now about those days, Kosinski waxes nostalgic; AIDS and the prevailing conservative mood have killed his old haunts—what he calls "community clubs"—and he misses them.

"The clubs were theater to me—Grand Guignol. At the Hellfire, you would see some man stretched out and hanging like this, and he would be winking at you. And the bartender would be there, naked with his dick out—well, this was theater, fantastic." He's talking rapidly now in that Bela Lugosi-on-speed accent of his, high on the memory of it, his tongue peeping out from between his lips the way it always does when he's reveling in his own words. "I'm truly a born voyeur—I love watching people. I love it! I get never bored. I can sit in what might appear to others to be the most uneventful place, and I am totally enchanted by what I see. It's the kind of enchantment you get from a fable. I went to all the clubs. I went to heterosexuals, homosexuals, trisexuals—my God, in the years in New York there is no aspect of American life I haven't seen. I went with friends—women—who were streetwise journalists, or I went with actresses who are also waitresses, because they could pretend and they were very streetwise. And I would be a participant only in the sense that I would observe. I would not do the strange things, I would watch the strange things—for reasons commonly known as hygiene, of which I was aware when I came from Poland, when TB was rampant. For me it was Hieronymus Bosch, it was my triptychs. These were my vision hours. I saw these people as libraries. Some as hardcover, some as paperback, some as leaflets, some as booklets, some as daily newspapers, overread. I had this whole vision of these people—is there anything in them that I could guess by their behavior? And then I would talk. I'm a very good talker, and people in sex clubs often find a high degree of sexual release by talking about it. Talk is free, and very hygienic. This was the oral tradition."

Differing cultures have differing notions of what constitutes mastery, macho, panache—cool. The American version descends from the myth of the frontiersman: it's about one clean shot, about showdowns and gunfighters, about tough guys, gangsters, hero cops. But for a Holocaust survivor, mastery may mean something very different. For Kosinski it has to do with the ability to escape or vanish, or to make people believe you are not the Jew or Gypsy they think you are. While other novelists have played at being boxers and bullfighters, Kosinski has worked at proving to his friends what his characters always prove—that in order to survive, the Self must fool the world, must distract it with false identities, or, failing that, hide in places it can never be found. All of which may explain some of the perplexing things Kosinski does.

Norman Mailer, for instance, sits down to dinner at Marylou's in Greenwich Village only to find an annoying waiter badgering him, flattering him, fawning so sedulously over him that Mailer begs him to go away. The waiter, of course, turns out to be Kosinski in disguise. During a party at Marion Javits's house, the Israeli foreign minister Abba Eban and the film director Louis Malle are sitting together on a sofa trying to pretend that the cushion behind them isn't leaping and lurching and pounding their backs—Kosinski has somehow squeezed himself under it, and he's kicking away. "One night I was shooting *Reds* and I was very tired," says Warren Beatty, who cast Kosinski as the Bolshevik thug Zinoviev. "And I came down to have dinner with Kiki and Jerzy, and I said, 'Where's Jerzy?' Kiki said, 'Well, he's a little angry with you.' And I said, 'Why?' and she said, 'Well, because you're five minutes late. But don't worry; I'm sure he'll get over it. It's nothing serious.' We began to order and we started to eat, but I was not enjoying myself. I didn't need Jerzy to be angry with me. And I'm sitting at the table, and I feel that my feet are perspiring for some reason. And I don't understand why. Was some strange anxiety state overtaking me? And suddenly I realized I was sloshing around down there. And I looked under the table and he had been there for twenty-five minutes, pouring warm tea into my shoes."

In 1979, Hal Ashby's film version of *Being There,* written by Kosinski and starring Peter Sellers, was released to widespread acclaim. By now, Jerzy could be seen on the society pages nearly every week hobnobbing with the beau monde of both coasts. He was a Johnny Carson regular. And at the same time, *Passion Play* was published—it was about the swellegant life of a wandering sex-mad polo player who was, you guessed it, very like the wandering sex-mad polo player Jerzy Kosinski. In short, our author was riding for a fall. Every time his face appeared among the party pics, a new rumor would slink through the literary world. And the main rumor was that he didn't do his own writing; everybody, it seemed, knew someone who claimed to be dragging through her days at the old publishing house because she was spending her nights composing Jerzy Kosinski's novels. When *The New York Times Magazine* published Barbara Gelb's frothy (and error-ridden) piece on what a giddy good time Jerzy was, you could hear hackles creaking to attention all over Manhattan—even those who didn't read it were stunned by the Annie Leibovitz picture of a bare-chested Jerzy in polo regalia on the magazine's cover.

Then Elizabeth Pochoda, the literary editor at *The Nation,* received a letter from Kosinski about an article she'd written, "and I realized he didn't write English. And I started hearing these rumors, and I was going around saying, 'Is it true? Is it true?' And everybody said, 'Of course it's true.' " Pochoda asked the *Village Voice* writer Geoffrey Stokes to look into the rumors and then ceded the story to the *Voice,* whose Eliot Fremont-Smith was already on the case. Stokes and Fremont-Smith combined forces, and their salient conclusion, published in a long front-page story, was that "no novelist with any claim to seriousness can hire people to do without acknowledgment the sort of *composition* that we usually call writing. To purchase another's words is to cheat the reader, to trash the tradition. For almost ten years now, Jerzy Kosinski has been treating his art as though it were just another commodity, a widget to be assembled by anonymous hired hands." The odd thing about the article was that of the three "hired hands" it quoted, only one agreed with the authors' assertion that what he was doing was more than ordinary editing. Yet in many ways the charges stuck. Stokes and Fremont-Smith had done their homework honestly, scrupulously; if their article seemed ill-supported, its conclusions nevertheless jibed with what the rumor mill had been pumping out. However, those conclusions were wrong.

The failure of the *Voice* article was not a failure of reportage so much as a failure of imagination. Stokes and Fremont-Smith's thesis emerged from the Just the Facts, Ma'am school of big-city journalism. But they were investigating something much subtler than a robbery or a homicide: they were investigating an artist's search for method. I've seen their evidence (including most of the material they were saving for a follow-up piece); I've also interviewed

Kosinski, examined pages and pages of manuscripts in various forms, interviewed eleven of the people who worked with him on his books, and talked to friends, enemies, and literary professionals who've received letters from him and with whom he has discussed his methods over the last twenty-three years. What emerges from all this is a portrait of something far more intriguing than an assembly line.

Kosinski has the difficulties of any second-language writer residing this side of that Olympus inhabited by Conrad and Nabokov. He can write perfectly in English, but not quickly. If he dashes off a letter or inserts a paragraph into a galley without going over it a couple of times, the prose in it will look pretty ragged: there may be missing articles—"a"s, "an"s, and "the"s—and some messy punctuation, and the sentence structure will jerk and buck. The same may not be true of, say, John Updike or Norman Mailer, but it's true of plenty of other American-born writers, as any professional editor will attest. Kosinski has not been gushily confessional about any of this, but then, he's not that way about anything. He likes to hide. The hiding, the disguises, the endless shaping and honing of his mystique—these are all the marks of someone who is, for want of a better phrase, a control freak. And for good reason: Kosinski comes from a world where any chink in the armor, any question about whether you were who you pretended to be, could have proved fatal. Watch him gussy up for an evening out and you already know something about his artistic method—he checks and rechecks until every hair and seam is perfect. Likewise, he has never submitted his manuscripts to publishers in the traditional fashion. His work almost always comes in "clean"; publishers purchase from him what is, more or less, a finished product. (Then, to the horror of his editors, he invariably continues to fiddle and fuss. As Bantam's Stuart Applebaum says, "If he had his way, he'd be climbing on top of the printing press to change the order of the type.")

Almost everyone in the book business will agree that being an editor in a publishing house isn't what it used to be. Editors used to edit; now they acquire books. Kosinski needs a lot of line editing, and he's always acknowledged it; his method has been to hire his own editors, often two or three to a book—either people his publishers suggest or else students or odd acquaintances: people who intrigue him. "He is the only person I know who hires his own copy editors," says Les Pockell, who was his in-house editor at St. Martin's Press. "He has got a great grasp of the English language, but sometimes he comes up with silly things. Either they're ungrammatical or they're just bad images, or whatever—like any writer." Nor does the editing always fix those silly things; the first printing of *Pinball,* for instance, makes reference to a hitherto unknown medical anomaly: a "limpid" penis.

Kosinski's editing arrangements were never clandestine; the only secrecy he asked of his hirees was that they not divulge his plots. And of the editors I talked with for this piece, only one, Richard Hayes (the same Richard Hayes whose testimony dominated the *Voice* article), felt that his work for Kosinski went beyond the normal bounds of editing—but then, the book Hayes worked on is, as we shall see, a special case. The others' responses were remarkably uniform. "When I worked on *Cockpit,*" says John Hackett, then an instructor at Wesleyan and now a political activist in San Antonio, Texas, "he had most of the manuscript ready, but it was rough. It needed a lot of work. But all I did was standard editorial work. It was the kind of thing where I might read a chapter and I would say, 'I'm not sure I like the way this shapes out vis-à-vis the previous chapter.' Or I might say, 'These two sentences right here don't quite jibe.' But the sentences he was writing were his sentences, and they were of the same quality, with lapses here and there, as the sentences in *Steps.*" Barbara MacKay, now the deputy chairman of the Denver Center of the Performing Arts, labored over more Kosinski manuscripts than any other editor: *Being There, The Devil Tree, Cockpit, Blind Date, Passion Play,* and *Pinball.* "He sometimes dictated to me," she says, "and I would take it down in longhand, and that would be typed up and we'd go through it and I would make editorial suggestions and we would edit it together. I don't even feel it was collaborative. Those books were all his, and the ideas were his, and the language is very much his." And Rocco Landesman, who worked on *Being There* and *The Devil Tree* and then went on to become a Tony-winning Broadway producer, says, "His prose was no rougher than typical first or second drafts. The editing was like anything any editor would do at a publishing house. The idea that we were writing is silly. The stuff was already all written."

But there's another curious aspect, as yet unexplored, of Kosinski's methodology. Kosinski wanted more out of the English language than a mere vehicle for his storytelling. He wanted an escape from his past, from his memories—from the plight of the Polish-Jewish outsider, the painted bird, he had always been. "I came to this country to become universal," he says. And he told one interviewer, "When I began speaking only in English, I felt freer to express myself, not just my views but my personal history, my quite private drives, all the thoughts that I would have found difficult to reveal in my mother tongue. . . . English, my stepmother tongue, offered me a sense of revelation, of fulfillment, of abandonment."

In his own terse way, Kosinski was a sixties-style literary experimenter in the tradition of Rudy Wurlitzer and Leonard Michaels and Ronald Sukenick: he was searching for an English he could commit himself to, an English the self-invented Novelist could wear. The sanitized jabber in books and movies and television wasn't roomy enough for him; he would solicit linguistic advice from telephone operators, students, passersby in the street, professional translators. "He's very interested in how people who have different mother tongues might write something in English," says Jerome Klinkowitz, a literary critic from the University of Northern Iowa who knows Kosinski well and has written extensively—and often quite skeptically—about him. "He'll have people whose native languages are Spanish or German write things out for him, because he believes they'll do it differently because of their linguistic conditioning. Very few authors take the time to do this sort of thing. The problem is people like me, literary critics, all have been too lazy; we haven't invented a word to describe what Kosinski does. It's not ghostwriting, it's linguistic experiment. He's just interested in how these people who work with him would cast a scene." And to those who accuse Kosinski of not owning up to his approach, Klinkowitz adds, "I never saw him hiding it. Back in the late sixties, he foregrounded a lot of his experimentation, talking about his use of language and talking about how his works were done. And obviously the critics didn't want to hear this. He found out it wasn't gonna fly, and so he just sort of shut up about it. But if you read his early pamphlets and interviews, he's very candid about his method."

Oddly enough, the most common criticism directed against Kosinski's books before the *Voice* article appeared was that they were all alike. And it's true: the prose, the characters, and the dialogue are numbingly consistent. With one exception: *Passion Play.* "Prior to *Passion Play,*" says the book's editor, Les Pockell, "all Jerzy's best-sellers were in paperback; his hardcovers hadn't done that well. So we decided that we were going to make *Passion Play* into a more accessible Jerzy Kosinski book." The result was the flossiest novel Kosinski had ever written; it read like Jackie Susann with a Jesuit education. It was also, in some ways, Kosinski's maddest experiment, his retreat into the basement lab, where the lightning arcs and the thunder roars and the beakers bubble and steam.

Kosinski hired Richard Hayes, a writer who had taught drama at New York University and Berkeley, and who warned Kosinski right off the bat that his own mandarin, "Latinate" style would not mix well with Kosinski's stubby prose. According to Hayes, "Kosinski said that was precisely what he wanted—a field of tension between the two." But Hayes threw himself into the job with an intensity no one else had ever exhibited; he spent five, sometimes six days a week at the Kosinski apartment, from August through December 1978 and then again for several weeks early in 1979. As Hayes says, "It was not what I think of as collaboration, but it was more than editing. And the one thing that really did bother me was that Kosinski told Stokes that all I did was proofread. You do not proofread a book of three hundred pages for seven months."

Kosinski must have been startled by his new assistant's zeal. Hayes would take Kosinski's typed copy and, in the spaces between lines, write his own, more florid version of it, often providing three or four word choices from which the author could make selections. When Kosinski wanted to set a sequence in a desert, Hayes volunteered a list of deserts and their characteristics; when Kosinski wanted to describe an outdoor cooking pit, he primed Hayes's inexhaustible pump by first drawing him a picture. No other assistant had ever, in Hayes's words, "combed, filleted, elevated, or amplified" Kosinski's prose in quite this way—it wasn't so much editing as deconstruction. And Kosinski, who was as hungry for novel linguistic experiences as he was for novel erotic ones (at the time he was busily cultivating the friendship of transsexuals—though not, he says, sleeping with them), soon abandoned himself to his helpmate's ministrations. Before he knew it, the "proofreading" had spilled over into a kind of folie à deux, and the result was his worst book ever—a two-headed monster, born babbling infelicities.

Reading *Passion Play,* one can't help wondering how anyone could have cooked up its chewiest morsels—who, for instance, conceived "the moist enigma of the mare's insides" or "his longing as translucent as the spill of a jungle cataract"? Did Jerzy Kosinski choose *Passion Play*'s words? Well, yes and no. Nobody owns words, any more than a composer owns the notes he uses. Certainly Kosinski selected and ordered and stewed over every mouthful in *Passion Play.* He did so, of course, using a menu he would never have had without Richard Hayes. As Faith Sale, who worked on *Blind Date* and is now a senior editor at Putnam's, puts it, "It's almost as if he has the ability to use a live person the way somebody else would use a dictionary or a thesaurus." But he also used real dictionaries and thesauruses, and everything he was reading at the time, and the sights and sounds at Plato's Retreat and on the polo circuit and in the august corridors of the Century club. Writing, especially the composition of literature, is not an antiseptic process; writers are by nature literary crows, scavenging among the detritus of their experience for the materials with which to build their dream houses.

That process, in fact, is the true subject of *The Hermit of 69th Street.* Kosinski briefly used an editor for *The Hermit,* but the book sounds exactly the way its author does at a party, when he's really rolling; it's transparently an attempt to tell the world, "You think I no speaka the English? Just listen to these wordplays, these glorious tropes, these waves of Nabokovian persiflage. English is mine!" *The Hermit*'s endless quotations and footnotes dare us to accuse Kosinski of purloining them—no, he didn't compose these passages, but does that make him any less the author of his book? Other writers, the novel argues, used methods that parallel Kosinski's—look at Balzac, Joyce, Orwell, and, inevitably, Thomas Wolfe. And *The Hermit* ranges through history, citing numberless misunderstood experimenters, literary, political, and religious, whose plights vibrate sympathetically with Kosinski's own. Some of them are artists condemned for dandyism or promiscuity; others are ugly or sickly or otherwise unpleasant. All of them are, in a way, painted birds, hounded from the flock because of their singularity. On the face of it, this argument sounds facile and self-serving, but as one hacks one's way through the book's unforgiving thickets, it acquires a steady moral force. What you hear in all these stories, and also in Kosinski's tone, is a note of touching bewilderment and hurt. Like so many of his historical forebears, from Cagliostro to Oscar Wilde, Kosinski had always regarded himself as a master, as someone who had taken the world's measure and triumphed over its hazards. His is the tale of an old-world storyteller, inventing himself as he went along, who ran head-on into the teeth of the new American celebrity culture—a culture that proclaims, "Forget about your art; we want to know about your life. And don't try to bullshit us about that."

In fact, *The Hermit* proves that Kosinski is no longer truly a novelist, or even a Novelist. He's become some sort of daft conceptual artist, his life a blueprint for his work, and the work incomprehensible without an in-depth knowledge of his life. *The Hermit*'s plot, for instance, follows Norbert Kosky as he is hounded by two downtown reporters hell-bent on exposing him. His terrible secret, they claim, is that he uses hidden supports when he floats. When he what? Well, after the debacle of 1982, it seems Kosinski found solace in his yoga—hence his rant about "oxygen to the brain"—and the yoga practice he took most to heart was one he learned in Thailand. He'll slip into a swimming pool, or any other body of water (he claims he once tried it in the oil slicks of the Hudson River), and without treading water or paddling or, in fact, moving in any way, he'll sit vertically in the deep and, uh, float. His head will stay above the surface, he says, because he's breathing properly, and he can tell when he's not breathing properly, because he sinks. Ever since *Life* magazine ran a big article about this stuff, it has been almost as great a source of Kosinskian pride as his sexual prowess, his highlife, even his novels. "After the events of '82, I no longer saw myself as a sexual being," he says, "and therefore I had to see myself as someone else. Sex for me has become sex in the Tantric sense, the only force responsible for concentration. Dismissal, therefore, of the pleasure sex, dismissal of the procreative sex. Concentration became the central issue. And hence the water trick, the floating. And vanity was reassured on another level, with what I could do in the swimming pool, with people standing around saying, How does he do it?—kids and all that."

He is talking quietly now, almost resignedly; something in him has softened since the 1982 brouhaha. A night out with Kosinski these days is likely to be dinner at Marylou's and a long, harmless schmooze into the wee hours. "There's another thing, too," he says. "The community clubs, Hellfire and all that, are gone now. Therefore the voyeuristic aspect has been taken away from me. So I am going on a different adventure. Now I am going among the worlds of financial people who can help me with the Foundation." He has become chairman of the board of the Polish-Jewish Heritage Foundation of America—and, as with any organization he presides over, he is a passionate activist. The Foundation has turned him back toward his roots, toward Poland and Judaism, toward the sort of questions that in his search for a distinctive all-American identity he's always shunted aside. Now he's planning a star-studded fund-raiser, and he wants advice, names, phone numbers. He begins to quiz me, the way Kosinski the novelist must have quizzed all those editors, and his voice becomes high and speedy again. His spine goes broomstick-straight, his head begins to jerk and thrust on its axis, the way a bird's does, the way Kosinski's does when he enters a tony drawing room and sets all his social dials to red alert.

What the Foundation most awakens in him is the taste of Self. Kosinski may grow weary of his circumstances, of being misunderstood and rejected and accused, but he never tires of the flavor of Self—he never tires of remembering how it feels to be Jerzy Kosinski. He will do almost anything to quicken that sensation. He loves the echo of his voice during a lecture, the shocked look on the faces of his posh friends when he pulls one of his tricks, his image transfigured on TV—anything that mirrors his uniqueness back to him. For Kosinski, Self is indomitable, sacred; it's the secret pleasure that neither the depredations of the Nazis nor of the great American rumor mill can strip from him. And as he talks I can see the way he uses the Foundation to reinflate the life raft of Self, buoying him up, keeping him afloat—oxygen to the brain. It was Gerard Manley Hopkins who wrote what Kosinski calls his "favorite definition of Self," and watching him now reminds me of it. Only it's not a definition, it's a rhapsody, a hymn to "my selfbeing, my consciousness and feeling of myself, that taste of myself, of *I* and *me* above and in all things, which is more distinctive than the taste of ale and alum, more distinctive than the smell of walnutleaf or camphor, and is incommunicable by any means to another man . . . this selfbeing of my own."

Kosinski's War

James Park Sloan

"Jerzy was a fantastic liar," said Agnieszka Osiecka, Poland's leading pop lyricist and a familiar figure in Polish intellectual circles, as she alternately sipped Coke and beer at a sidewalk café in Warsaw. "And so what?"

While she spoke, Osiecka kept putting on and taking off a wide-brimmed red hat of the kind once affected by Frank Lloyd Wright. Years ago, she and Kosinski had sat at tables just like this one. "If you told Jerzy you had a Romanian grandmother, he would come back that he had fifteen cousins all more Romanian than your grandmother"—she returned the hat to her head and gave it a half turn—"and they played in a Gypsy band!"

Osiecka was responding to a recent exposé by the Polish journalist Joanna Siedlecka, in which she argued that Jerzy Kosinski, Poland's best-known Holocaust survivor, had profoundly falsified his wartime experiences. According to Siedlecka, Kosinski spent the war years in relatively gentle, if hardly idyllic, circumstances and was never significantly mistreated. She thus contradicts the sanctioned version of his life under the German occupation, which has generally been assumed to be only thinly disguised in his classic first novel, "The Painted Bird," published in this country by Houghton Mifflin in 1965. Siedlecka's revelations have stirred up a tempest in Warsaw café circles, and Polish intellectuals have been busy staking out positions.

In stark, uninflected prose, "The Painted Bird" describes the disasters that befall a six-year-old boy who is separated from his parents and wanders through the primitive Polish-Soviet borderlands during the war. The peasants whom the boy encounters demonstrate an extraordinary predilection for incest, sodomy, and meaningless violence. A miller plucks out the eyeballs of his wife's would-be lover. A gang of toughs pushes the boy, a presumed Gypsy or Jew, below the ice of a frozen pond. A farmer forces him to hang by his hands from a rafter, just out of reach of a vicious dog. In the culminating incident of the book, the boy drops a missal while he's helping serve Mass and is flung by angry parishioners into a pit of manure. Emerging from the pit, he realizes that he has lost the power of speech. The book's title—and governing metaphor—derives from a feeble-minded character named Lekh, who amuses

Reprinted from the *New Yorker,* 10 October 1994, 46–48, 50–53.

himself by capturing wild birds, painting their feathers in brilliant colors, and releasing them to be pecked from the sky by their own kind.

"Written with deep sincerity and sensitivity, this poignant account transcends confession," Elie Wiesel wrote in the *Times Book Review.* At the time of Kosinski's suicide, in 1991, Wiesel said, "I thought it was fiction, and when he told me it was autobiography I tore up my review and wrote one a thousand times better."

Wiesel's review sanctified the work as a valid testament of the Holocaust, more horrible, more revealing—in a sense, *truer*—than the literature that came out of the camps. Other writers and critics agreed. Harry Overstreet wrote that "The Painted Bird" would "stand by the side of Anne Frank's unforgettable 'Diary' " as "a powerfully poignant human document," while Peter Prescott, also comparing it to Anne Frank's "Diary," called the book "a testament not only to the atrocities of the war, but to the failings of human nature." The novelist James Leo Herlihy saluted it as "brilliant testimony to mankind's survival power."

"Account," "confession," "testament," "document," "testimony": these were the key words in the book's critical reception. What made "The Painted Bird" such an important book was its overpowering authenticity. Perhaps it wasn't exactly a diary—six-year-olds don't keep diaries—but it was the next best thing. And in one respect it was better: Kosinski was Anne Frank as a survivor, walking among us.

"The Painted Bird" was translated into almost every major language and many obscure ones. It was a best-seller in Germany and won the Prix du Meilleur Livre Étranger in France. It became the cornerstone of reading lists in university courses on the Holocaust, where it was often treated as a historical document, and, as a result, it has been for a generation the source of what many people "know" about Poland under the German occupation. At the height of Kosinski's reputation, there were those who said that somewhere down the road Kosinski was a likely candidate for the Nobel Prize.

Kosinski himself, who emigrated to the United States in 1957, quickly crossed over into popular culture. Beaky, wiry, and intense, he became a writer whose mystique and experiences often seemed more important than his books. On TV, he was a knockout; appearing on the Johnny Carson show, he brought a suggestion of high culture along with his stiletto wit and Polish accent. Always lurking beneath the surface of his public persona was the sense that he was a man who had been through unimaginable horrors, who had been to Hell and had returned to tell about it.

The literary establishment, too, embraced Kosinski, electing him to two terms as president of the American Center of PEN, the writers' organization. The movie made from his third novel, "Being There," was a hit, and when Kosinski appeared at the celebratory parties he seemed as much a star as Peter Sellers or Shirley MacLaine. His friend Warren Beatty cast him as Zinoviev in "Reds," and the writer won praise for his screen presence. Kosinski's magnetism was undeniable. He held court at Elaine's and at the dinner table of the Oscar de la Rentas. He played polo with the Dominican playboy Porfirio Rubirosa and discussed the state of the world with Zbigniew Brzezinski and Henry Kissinger. His celebrated nightly forays to Plato's Retreat and S&M clubs by the New York piers helped make those establishments fashionable.

When a 1982 article by Geoffrey Stokes and Eliot Fremont-Smith in the *Village Voice* accused Kosinski of relying upon excessive editorial assistance in the production of his novels and giving discrepant versions of his departure from Poland, it struck the literary world like a small earthquake. The *Times* came to Kosinski's defense, and the resulting controversy broke out of the literary ghetto to become a national news story. Now, in Poland, a second quake has struck.

To say that Kosinski never claimed every incident of "The Painted Bird" to be the literal truth is a bit like saying that Jesus never claimed to be the Son of God: it may be accurate in some narrow, legalistic sense, but such an edifice came to be constructed upon the assumption that the legalistic niceties were a moot point. Kosinski's occasional hedging often took the tortuous shape of explaining that the book described a set of experiences lived in one language and "unfrozen" by its expression in another. This explanation was preserved in his otherwise baffling 1965 commentary "Notes of the Author," appended to the book's German edition.

Certainly Wiesel and the other reviewers were not alone in their belief that the book was essentially autobiographical. Friends who remember Kosinski from his first years in the United States recall his telling the stories contained in "The Painted Bird" as the literal truth of his wartime experience. In the final decade of his life, in articles published in 1981 and 1985, Kosinski reiterated the basic elements of his wartime story: that he was sent away by his parents, in the care of a man who was supposed to place him with a family but instead abandoned the six-year-old in a village in the Pripet Marshes of Polesie and kept much of the family savings.

According to Joanna Siedlecka's "Czarny Ptasior" (the book's title, a play on that of Kosinski's novel, translates as "the ugly black bird"), Kosinski's wrenching accounts of his wartime experiences were fabricated from whole cloth. On the basis of conversations with inhabitants of the Polish town of Sandomierz and the nearby village of Dabrowa Rzeczycka, both some distance from the Pripet Marshes, Siedlecka contends that Kosinski spent the war with his family—his mother, father, and, later, an adopted brother—and that they lived in relative security and comfort.

The Kosinskis survived, she suggests, in part because Jerzy Kosinski's father, whose original name was Moses Lewinkopf, saw bad times coming and acquired false papers in the common Gentile name of Kosinski; in part because they had money (acquired in the textile and leather trades) and were able to pay for protection with cash and jewelry; and in part because a network of Polish Catholics, at great risk to themselves, helped hide them.

Siedlecka portrays the elder Kosinski not just as a wily survivor but as a man without scruples. She maintains that he may have collaborated with the Germans during the war and very likely did collaborate with the N.K.V.D., after the liberation of Dabrowa by the Red Army, in sending to Siberia for minor infractions, such as hoarding, some of the very peasants who saved his family. Her real scorn, however, is reserved for the son, who turned his back on the family's saviors and vilified them, along with the entire Polish nation, in the eyes of the world. Indeed, the heart of Siedlecka's revelations is her depiction of the young Jerzy Kosinski spending the war years eating sausages and drinking cocoa—goods unavailable to the neighbors' children—in the safety of his house and yard, and hanging standoffishly, if sadly, on the fence to watch other children play.

When I arrived in Poland not long ago to conduct research for a biography of Kosinski, I found I had landed in the middle of a full-fledged literary furor. The *Gazeta Wyborcza,* one of the leading Warsaw newspapers, had a full-page article lambasting "Czarny Ptasior," and opinion among Warsaw intellectuals was running heavily against Siedlecka. I sought an explanation from Ryszard Matuszewski, a leading Polish critic, now eighty, who, with his thick white hair and rumpled trousers, looks a little like Robert Frost. "Siedlecka writes, as we say here, 'from the kitchen,' " he said as we sat in his austere apartment. "She did up Witold Gombrowicz by interviewing the household help, and it was really a very amusing book—and she did a job on Witkacy, too," he said, referring to two eminences of modern Polish literature. But doing up Kosinski was different. "Don't mistake me," he said. "It was always my opinion that 'The Painted Bird' was pure fantasy. I never much cared for it. But Siedlecka couldn't find the key."

A secondary scandal, on a much smaller scale, erupted recently when two men who had reason to be indebted to Kosinski—a museum director with whom he had worked and a priest who had been given an award, named in memory of Kosinski, for encouraging interfaith dialogue—participated in a literary evening in Siedlecka's honor. Tad Krauze, a professor of sociology and Kosinski's closest friend during the period just before he emigrated to the United States, told me that Kosinski betrayed "a great ideal." Describing him as a man recklessly in pursuit of literary fame and fortune, Krauze recalled Plato's warning to his fellow-Athenians to abjure art forms that may do harm by falsifying reality.

Why would people with personal ties to Kosinski turn on him? And why were so many intellectuals who had never cared for Kosinski now staunchly defending him?

The answers to both these questions are more political than literary. Internationalist and anti-Marxist intellectuals tended to be pro-Kosinski—or, at least, anti-Siedlecka—whereas Polish nationalists and Poles with roots in the Marxist past, whether as former apparatchiks or as believers in the "great ideal," tended to side with Siedlecka. No matter which side you talked to, though, the problem had to do with boundaries between fact and fiction. Kosinski wrote novels that dared you to believe they were true and dared you not to. But nowhere was the boundary between fact and fiction more problematic than in "The Painted Bird." To deny its truth, so it seemed, was to refuse to acknowledge the horror of the German occupation.

The first printing of the book contained an epilogue that appeared to connect the boy in the story to the author: the boy grows up to find that living in the Communist regime of postwar Eastern Europe is every bit as tough as being on the lam from Nazis and degenerate peasants. Still a "painted bird," marked for persecution by the undifferentiated flock, he flies across the ocean and becomes, presumably, the writer of the book.

It is classic Kosinski—the kind of anarchically individualistic statement that made him such a disturbing and interesting man. The Holocaust is described not as an attack on a group but as something even more terrifying: an attack on the integrity of the self. As such, it could reasonably be linked with the totalitarianism of the Communist regime.

In a 1965 review entitled "The Butcher's Helpers," Andrew Field not only treated the novel as an indictment of Polish anti-Semitism and complicity in the Holocaust but went on to say, "Mr. Kosinski found postwar Communism to be but a logical extension of much that he lived through during the war." Kosinski backpedalled furiously, disavowing the epilogue as a misappropriated letter to his editor and writing a letter to the editor of the *Herald Tribune*—where Field's widely syndicated review appeared—denying that "The Painted Bird" referred to any specific nation or ethnic group. The damage, however, had been done: Kosinski was cast as a writer who had libelled the Polish nation.

The Polish response to the book and its reception had the effect of bundling nationalists, Communists, and anti-Semites—none of them in short supply in the Poland of 1965—into an anti-Kosinski coalition. The Communist authorities went blindly on the attack. Journalists were dispatched throughout Poland to track down and expose any discreditable information they could find about Kosinski's wartime experiences—an effort that met with only limited success. Still, between 1966 and 1968 Polish journals came out with a series of scalding critiques of the book and its author. Written in intemperate language and riddled with factual errors, these assaults on a book that had never been available in Polish—and would not be for another twenty years—made the Polish press look ridiculous and hypersensitive. So maladroit were the Polish attacks, in fact, that Kosinski's supporters could cite them as a *defense* when Kosinski came under fire from the *Village Voice.* Such enemies, the argument went, did Kosinski honor.

There the matter stood until Siedlecka began to examine some of those articles from the sixties. She pulled actual names and addresses from one of them—a 1968 article in the Kielce *Slowo Ludu*—and set out to locate persons in the town of Sandomierz who had known the Kosinskis during the war. She quickly hit pay dirt: the Kosinskis had been there. And Siedlecka got the story.

"Czarny Ptasior" reads in places like a tract seeking to vindicate Polish honor in the face of indictments such as Claude Lanzmann's "Shoah." Look, Siedlecka seems to be saying, here's the truth behind one of those tales of Polish anti-Semitism, and it proves that the Poles weren't really so terrible—in fact, Poles saved Jews, yet the Jews turned around and did them harm.

Siedlecka's basic posture was one her critics found all too familiar. To them, her work seemed an extension of the anti-Kosinski campaign conducted by Polish officialdom in the late sixties. Indeed, her project gave off an odor of ideological malice: in her zeal to defend Poland—and condemn Kosinski—she seemed to downplay the presence of Polish anti-Semitism. Although Siedlecka's critics did not rebut her core findings, they took her to be insufficiently skeptical toward much of the evidence she accumulated—especially with respect to her allegations that the elder Kosinski was a collaborator. Finally, the intensity of the debate may owe something to the fragility of the long anti-Marxist evolution known as "the Change"—a passage that is by no means over, and one that has rewarded its progenitors very unevenly. To side against Siedlecka is to affirm one's stance as cosmopolitan, anti-Marxist, and *anti*-anti-Semitic. In this atmosphere, the truth of her claims seems almost unimportant.

One of the few Warsaw intellectuals to attempt a genuinely objective view was Tomasz Mirkowicz, whose Polish translation of "The Painted Bird" was published in 1989. I discussed the Siedlecka controversy with him and his wife, Julita (the translator of Kosinski's "Being There"), during dinner at a restaurant in Warsaw's Old Town.

Dressed causally in jeans, the Mirkowiczes combine, in a manner unfamiliar to Americans, Western countercultural style with Eastern European anti-Marxist politics—the mirror image, politically, of America's nineteen-sixties hippies. Their dissident credentials are impeccable. In 1986, Zbigniew Bujak, then the head of the Solidarity underground, was captured in the Mirkowiczes' apartment, where he was tending their cat while they were away in America.

"Siedlecka *almost* wrote a very interesting book," Tomasz Mirkowicz said. "Kosinski once told me honestly that he drew upon a postwar Polish text, 'Polish Children Accuse.' " He was referring to a compilation of accounts by Polish children of their experiences under the German occupation. "The fact that Kosinski was not separated from his parents, the information on places he stayed and the people he was with—all this is very interesting material for historians and literary scholars." What surprised him, he said, was that, so far, no one had gone to the villages to check on the details for themselves. What if Siedlecka had made it all up? "You'll be going to Sandomierz and Dabrowa," he said. "I'll be interested to hear what you discover."

Early on the morning of June 8th, after a stopover in Lodz, I took the train for Sandomierz, accompanied by Agnieszka Kmin, a graduate student from Lodz, who was serving as my research assistant. For eight hours, the train crept southeast, and, as it did so, the view through our window moved backward in time, to miniature tractors of types I hadn't seen since my rural boyhood, and, finally, to horse-drawn plows and hay wagons. The villages became smaller and farther apart, the vegetation greener and darker, the forests heavier and deeper. "I'm frightened," Agnieszka said, only half in jest, as we changed trains for the last time. "I've never been this far east before."

Sandomierz is a picturesque medieval town set on a hill above the Vistula, eighty-five miles from the Ukrainian border. It has an old church, some grain-storage cellars dug in the hillside, wall towers, and the remnants of a castle, all of which make it a popular destination for Polish school groups. Its most distinctive feature, perhaps, is a series of ravines through which one walks to outlying areas. Gouged deep into heavy forest and brush, and revealing sculptures of gnarled tree roots, the ravines are the natural landscape of fairy tales—places where the passions and terrors of the human heart may assume the shapes of unimaginable beasts.

Our contact in Sandomierz was a tour guide named Zenon Pas, a short, hawklike man in his late forties, who wore tinted sunglasses indoors and out. His movements revealed a relentless impatience and energy, which on this occasion would be put to my service. Before we could begin, however, I had to undergo a ritual of initiation. A second man appeared, identified himself as a local reporter, and asked if I would mind submitting to a brief interview. He had a bulky antique tape recorder, which he could not get to function properly, and I set my microrecorder next to it on Pas's desk. Against these stage props of dueling tape recorders, we interviewed each other, with Kmin translating and Pas interrupting to clarify statements or speed the process along. After ten minutes or so, there came a barrage of questions about my ancestry and origins. Kmin and I exchanged glances. "I think he wants to know if you are Jewish," she said. Feeling complicitous in something sinister, I told him that I was a Scottish Protestant, and the interview was swiftly concluded.

Pas marched us through a tour of the houses in which the Kosinskis had lived while they were in Sandomierz; at one of them, he forced his way in past a sullen teen-ager and compelled the girl's mother to abandon her housework and take us on a guided tour of her cramped rooms, which she did rather sheepishly. Always the tour guide, Pas pointed out landmarks: a house once occupied by the wealthy Salamonowiczes, a building in which the Gestapo had conducted interrogations, a square that had been sealed off as the Jewish ghetto. Then he marched us down a ravine to a cottage where, he said, his own grandmother, quite courageously, had kept the Kosinskis for two summers.

From the cottage, he led us back up another ravine to the Sandomierz State Archive, to examine verifying documents, some of them bearing his grandmother's signature. Pas himself placed the yellowed papers—some referring to the Kosinskis and some using the family's prewar name of Lewinkopf—in my hands. Back outside the archive, which had once been the synagogue (there is, of course, no Jewish community in contemporary Sandomierz), Pas pointed out a bathhouse outside of which his father used to lie in ambush to "touch the Jewish women," and so compel them to return for repurification. "We are not Jew-haters," he said. "He did it because back then they didn't have TV."

By this time, I had learned that Pas's grandmother, Marianna Pasiowa, was the woman Kosinski had transformed into Marta, the superstitious peasant crone to whom the boy is entrusted in the first episode of "The Painted Bird"; in the book, Marta dies while soaking her feet in a bucket of water, and her lifeless body is engulfed in flames when the boy accidentally spills kerosene from a lamp. According to villagers, the real-life Marianna Pasiowa, a humble farmwife who lived in a thatched cottage, had aided not only the Kosinski family but other Jews as well, including an infant she hid in a hillside dugout and nourished on cow's milk.

Pas insisted on showing me the church in Sandomierz, where, I was told, the local priest, with the help of his parishioners, had hidden Jews in the presbytery. His instincts as a docent aroused, he went on to show us the church's distinctive feature—twelve frescoes surrounding the nave, one for each month, in which each day of the year is represented by a graphic and bloody depiction of Christian martyrdom. On a separate panel at the rear was a detailed depiction of the ritual murder of an angelic Christian child by a group of rapacious Jews.

It was a village, clearly, where the iconography of anti-Semitism was so commonplace as to pass beneath consciousness; where the harassment of Jewish women could be presented as recreation. Even today, in the shadow of the Nazi genocide, there seemed to be little self-consciousness about these matters—and no acknowledgment that petty bigotries might relate to a larger atrocity.

The next day, Pas drove us to Dabrowa Rzeczycka, fourteen miles away and now virtually in the shadow of the emerging industrial center of Stalowa Wola. Situated on the west bank of the San River near the Janow forest, Dabrowa—to which the Kosinskis had retreated when the Germans tightened their grip on Sandomierz—rarely appears on maps, and no road sign announces it until the village is almost in sight. In Dabrowa, I spoke with Stefania Woloszyn and Edward Warchol, the daughter and son of the peasant landlord who had rented the Kosinskis a semidetached house for the final two and a half years of the war. They confirmed Siedlecka's story completely, repeating the allegations that after the war the elder Kosinski informed on the villagers to the N.K.V.D.

Warchol, now in his late sixties, lives in a prosperous-seeming two-story farmhouse with an underground garage. A sturdy, short-legged man, he emerged from the house putting on his shirt but never got past the middle button, which struggled to contain an expanse of flesh. He said he could not understand the fuss in Warsaw about Siedlecka, for in his eyes she had told the simple truth. "The Painted Bird," which he had not read until 1989, came as a shock. "We saved their lives," he said, brushing away tears with the back of his hand. "And he turned us into monsters."

Several events in "The Painted Bird" had their prototypes in Dabrowa. Young Jerzy Kosinski was attacked on the surface of the frozen pond by neighborhood toughs, who intended to pull down his pants and inspect his penis; Warchol, who was then seventeen, skated by to save him, and he vowed to me that Kosinski, unlike the boy in the novel, was never pushed below the ice. Similarly, some informants remembered the young Kosinski serving as an altar boy in the church at nearby Wola Rzeczycka, but denied categorically, and convincingly, that his dropping a missal ever led to his being beaten or flung into a latrine.

Before leaving Dabrowa, I had the eerie experience of staring into the face of a literary symbol. The villagers took me to the cottage of Lech Tracz, who had been damaged by "brain fever" in his youth and was now well into his sixties. As a young man, Tracz had the odd hobby of trapping crows, painting them with limewash, and releasing them in order to watch them being attacked by the rest of the flock. Lech Tracz (the fictional spelling "Lekh" is unknown in the region) still lives alone in a cottage festooned with handmade wooden bird traps and cages.

Having been summoned by his niece, Tracz did not appear for about twenty minutes: he had insisted on shaving—a laborious process, apparently—and finding proper clothes in which to meet "the American." Finally, a tall, thin man emerged, wearing baggy trousers, a loose-fitting jacket with a religious medal on the lapel, and an old-fashioned motoring cap. His movements were stiff and awkward, and he had a fixed, childlike smile. He spoke in a loud, affectless monotone, but it was hard to say to whom, because he met no one's eyes; rather, he seemed to stare off in whatever direction his body was facing.

"He apologizes that he can't tell you anything about the boy, but it's been a long time," his niece said. "If you had come while the boy was here, he says, he might have remembered."

In retrospect, two lines of reasoning might have suggested that "The Painted Bird" was something less—and therefore more—than straightforward autobiography. The first argument is simply a matter of statistics. There were about three and a half million Jews in Poland before the war; of those who stayed, roughly thirty-five thousand survived. The odds against survival were about a hundred to one. The odds for a family aided by abundant resources, a sound strategy, and good luck were still steep, but not insuperable. Split the family into two units, living in separate circumstances (as in the book), and the odds against both units' surviving approach ten thousand to one—not impossible, but far less likely.

The second argument has to do with the episodic intensity of the story. Kosinski's protagonist has a knack for riding into town just as the local pot of trouble is about to boil over. He arrives in one village just in time to see the brutal murder of Stupid Ludmila, and at the miller's house just in time to witness the plucking out of eyeballs. Unless one is prepared to believe that a woman is assaulted and eye balls are plucked out at least, say, once every month or two, it follows that the experiences described in the book are heightened to some degree. Why didn't these arguments occur to readers at the time? The answer applies equally to "The Painted Bird" and to "Czarny Ptasior": people hear what they want to hear.

One might, of course, doubt even such seemingly guileless witnesses as the villagers. If they did not intentionally set out to deceive, might they not suffer from a certain selectivity of memory? Common sense would argue so. But the documents and the number of witnesses weigh against the notion of conspiracy. At least in one particular, Siedlecka's version was backed up by Kosinski's postwar friends in Lodz: whatever may have happened to him during the war, they all agree, the young Jerzy Kosinski never lost the power of speech. Siedlecka's basic story was confirmed by more than a dozen informants in Sandomierz, Dabrowa, and Lodz. Kosinski was never separated from his parents for any significant period. The local peasants, living in a culture suffused with anti-Semitism, were scarcely free of its grip, but by all accounts these particular peasants did something brave and good for the Kosinski family during the war. "The Painted Bird" is fiction. Kosinski borrowed the atrocities from other accounts, or made them up.

And yet to say that Kosinski was not abused physically in the dramatic ways depicted in "The Painted Bird" is not to deny the psychological pain he suffered, along with his family, during the German occupation. The banal and unremarkable thuggery of village life was hardly unique to this period, but it could not have failed to leave scars on its victims. The Kosinski family would have needed only a suspicion of what was happening in the country around them to live in mortal dread. Confined to the narrow compass of polemic, Siedlecka shows little appreciation of why the painted bird, emblem of a nearly reflexive persecution of difference, might resonate for the young Kosinski, even in the absence of the outside horrors to which his imagination later gravitated. He was, in a very real sense, both a Holocaust victim and a Holocaust survivor. He was also, as a longtime acquaintance of his from New York's Polish Institute put it, "an uneven man"—or, in the blunter words of Mira Michalowska, who knew Kosinski when she was working as a journalist in New York, "an absolute mythomaniac."

Does the discovery that "The Painted Bird" was a far more fictional work of fiction than Kosinski often suggested it was give readers who were moved by the book just cause for feeling cheated? His real story might have been every bit as compelling, in its way, as "The Painted Bird," but would the world have seized so eagerly upon an account of the less dramatic form of harassment he had to take for granted as a Jew in the Polish countryside? Ironically, Siedlecka's revelations provide a convincing rebuttal to those who have argued that Kosinski is not the author of "The Painted Bird"; indeed, abstracted from its archival pretensions, the work gains in stature as an achievement of the novelistic imagination. Kosinski transmuted his wartime years into a version of the most primal and universal of plots: he was the hero and victim; everybody else was a villain. The trouble came when others took up his script. It served all too conveniently the purposes of various groups in need of a governing myth. It said what *should* have been true about both the German occupation and the Marxist regime. Even the Germans could take comfort in the book's implicit message that genocide was not a uniquely German phenomenon but a manifestation of a universally distributed human depravity.

Maybe it is only the historian's task to reassert the annoying complexity of events against the satisfying simplicity of a storyline. If the novelist trimmed his experiences to accord with a personal myth, the narrative that resulted fell on receptive ears. Certainly it was a myth that the world, demanding purity and innocence of its victims, was all too ready to appropriate. Now all must profess to be shocked—shocked—that a practitioner of the liar's profession, a man who survived the war by living a lie, told lies.

ORIGINAL ESSAYS

♦

Cockpit, Blind Date, and *Passion Play*: Kosinski's Novel Cycle

NORMAN LAVERS

When I published my monograph on Jerzy Kosinski in 1982, a reviewer twitted me with the fact that I had not been honest about how disturbing parts of Kosinski's novels really were. I immediately felt the reviewer was exactly right. With my own sheltered, optimistic, slightly upper-middle-class upbringing, I emphasized the positive fact that Kosinski's characters were survivors and tended to overlook how costly and partial their survival was.

Kosinski himself warned me about this. I wrote that the boy's regaining of his speech at the end of *The Painted Bird* indicated a positive step forward: his return to communication with other human beings. Kosinski suggested that maybe speech had returned to the boy so that he could use it to manipulate others in the huge revenges he was planning for those who had hurt him. I naively maintained that, in that case, he wouldn't really have *been* a survivor. Perhaps I had in mind that the boy in certain ways represented Kosinski, and Kosinski seemed in every sense a survivor: a successful novelist, a friend to celebrities, a celebrity himself. He was quick, bright, witty, incisive; his rich life seemed to be organized just as he wanted it.

But all that may have been part of the mask he presented. James Park Sloan, in his biography of Kosinski, convincingly argues that Kosinski, like so many Holocaust survivors, was in fact badly damaged. Thousands survived concealed in the margins of Europe only by pretending to be someone they were not, by manufacturing a life, and by avoiding close contact with others who might betray them. It was out of this world that the existential philosophers arose, with their existential psychology proclaiming that in any relationship, one must be the subject and the other must be the object: manipulate or be manipulated. In this world where the old virtues had so signally failed, "To possess hate is to possess great power,"[1] and all that made life tolerable was contemplating and executing revenge on one's enemies. Sloan suggests that, even in affluence and safety in the West, Kosinski maintained his carefully manufactured false self, though the pressure of it weighed more and

This essay was written especially for inclusion in this volume and is published here with the permission of the author.

more heavily on him and the cost of being found out grew more and more dire, though it stopped him from being able to love, and though it led him into manipulative relationships, an essential hollowness at the core, an unbearable lightness of being.

Kosinski's novels are indeed autobiographical, but not in the easy way we imagined. The six-year-old boy adrift in Eastern Europe—that was part of the myth. The clever escape from the Communists—also made up. Rather, the real autobiography lies in Kosinski's secret-agent protagonists, who take no side but are nevertheless condemned to secrecy, to disguise, to hollowness, and to transient relationships in which the characters must jockey to be subject and avoid being object.

Kosinski has often said that all his novels are part of a cycle exploring the relationships between the individual and society. No doubt this is true, but the reader most readily perceives the three novels, *Cockpit* (1975), *Blind Date* (1977), and *Passion Play* (1979), as constituting a cycle. The cycle begins with a secret-agent protagonist in *Cockpit* hiding to avoid being hunted down and killed. He is able to have only transient relationships in which he attempts by any means to manipulate the other, and he takes severe revenge against those who seek to resist his control. The novel is deliberately plotless so that reader (and protagonist) will give full attention to the present action rather than see the action in terms of what it will lead to. In the next two novels, these positions are progressively softened, as the protagonists sublimate and moderate the revenge ethic and move toward less exploitative relationships. Perhaps because these developments give the protagonists some chance at a more positive outcome to their lives, the novels move toward more conventional plots with their implied futurity.

In *Cockpit,* the protean narrator Tarden experiences—often creates—various adventures that seem to be tonally or thematically related and that, by slow accumulation, become at last the experience of the novel. Tarden has abandoned the "Service" and, because all defecting agents are hunted down and killed, is forced to live a mobile, anonymous, disguised life, moving from apartment to apartment, constantly on guard. Unable to live a normal life, he has fleeting, generally unsuccessful relationships with women, and, increasingly, enters vicariously into the lives of others as a kind of self-appointed helper of the needy and punisher of evil. His obvious pleasure is in having control over other's lives, and his methods for gaining control—even in a "good" cause—are unscrupulous.

From time to time, the novel flashes back to Tarden's youth in Eastern Europe, to his time as a young immigrant just entering the United States, and to the various jobs he held in this country and abroad to eke out a living before his beautiful Lebanese lover introduced him to the Service. In all the earlier incidents, Tarden already had a strong penchant for disguise and for manipulating the lives of others. For instance, when he is 12 years old, while his parents are away during the day (it is shortly after the war, in a tightly controlled Eastern European country), he phones numbers at random and brilliantly mimics the tone of a government administrator, ordering people to make a long, expensive trip to the capital to get a government permit that will allow them to remain in their present lodgings. When the police come to interrogate him, Tarden brazenly tells one of the officers that he had better release him or kill him outright; otherwise Tarden will one day punish the man's wife and children. "I reminded him how adept I was at affecting the lives of people I did not even know."[2] After a bit of blustering, the policeman sees to it that Tarden and his family are released. These same qualities of ingenuity, mimicry, nerve, and lonely single-mindedness serve him again when he plans his escape from the totalitarian state by inventing four patrons who write letters recommending him for study abroad.

In his work for the Service, Tarden was frequently obligated to adopt other more sophisticated disguises to cover his activity; in Indonesia, for instance, he posed as a member of an international delegation of psychiatrists and anthropologists, and in Europe as an industrial representative. Like the various roles (archaeologist and business representative are particular favorites) of the multipersonaed protagonists of other Kosinski novels, Tarden's work as an agent is, in terms of Kosinski's artistic intention, itself a disguise, a cover for the fact of our own multiple and shifting selves—another reason it is so difficult for anyone to know us, or for us to know another. "I've come to look upon disguise," Tarden says, "as more than a means of personal liberation: it's a necessity. My life depends on my being able to instantly create a new persona and slip out of the past" (*Cockpit,* 129–30). Tarden's words recall Kosinski's comments in *The Art of the Self* that the self must constantly get clear from its past in order to live fully in the present moment. We are, of course, a new person in each moment of our lives, a combination of the person created by that moment and the person we create to meet that moment.

The key to Tarden's jealously guarded independence is his absolute control of himself, which he achieves by disguise so that at each moment, he literally creates himself. In the opening chapter, he speaks of the apartments he keeps in every major city, paid for three years in advance, three-digit combination locks on every door, multiple exits, hiding places, electronic controls to set off small explosives in any room he chooses, and papers kept in vaults in various locations.

His safeguards preserve his existence, but at a great cost. He instinctively probes the inmost heart of all he comes in contact with, just in case they offer a threat to him. But in practical terms, doing so means he cannot have a close human relationship. This is evident with Valerie, the woman in the first chapter whom he tested and challenged until she left him. Another time, he suffers a brief heart seizure while a prostitute is in his apartment. "It wasn't the thought of dying that disturbed me," he says, "but that I might die without leaving a trace" (3). He has devoted himself so thoroughly to anonymity that, he realizes, the only result can be anonymous death.

There are nevertheless limits on his control, such as the autonomy his body asserts. In addition to his seizures, which make his breathing difficult and his heartbeat irregular, there is his body's system of healing wounds: "Although I often tried to keep a wound open and bleeding, it always healed itself overnight, challenging my power over myself. I hated the sense of an autonomous force in my body, determining what would happen to me" (13). Worst of all, though, is his irreducible dependence on other human beings, such as occurs after he experiences a freak reaction to the anesthetic at the dentist's. "I had survived after my heart stopped," he says, "only because the incident had happened in a clinic. . . . Like the elusive substance that had once healed my wound, now the State had saved me without my consent" (14–15). Perhaps it is this occasional powerlessness that makes him believe that even if he cannot control his life, he can at least control his death. When he tries to escape from Eastern Europe, for example, he says, "I sensed freedom only when my fingers stroked the foil-wrapped [cyanide] pellet in my pocket" (16).

There is a definite pattern to Tarden's control. It begins with his controlling himself, then the immediate environment of his apartment, and finally his outer environment, which is to say all the human beings with whom he comes in contact. It is a standard Kosinski theme—the most direct and safest way to preserve oneself as subject is to convert everyone else into objects. Tarden's interference in other people's lives is not always harmful, yet it is always exploitative, and it always occurs for his own satisfaction. Tarden confronts "hundreds of anonymous faces" and then chooses one. "I pick a life and enter it, unobserved" (148).

Even in his very best actions, there is a kind of patronizing meanness. For instance, he likes to find an older, tired-looking saleswoman and give her a very bad time, making her bring out from the storeroom dozens of models of whatever he pretends to want to buy and then saying he has changed his mind. Only if she is unfailingly polite (if Tarden were in the saleswoman's place, and someone treated him like that, he would plot a diabolical revenge) does she earn her reward—a letter to the president of the company saying how courteous she was. Usually, however, his preferred way of being a benefactor is not by helping the needy but rather by punishing the wrongdoer. That way he is able to do good by harming someone.

Kosinski, in an interview with Gail Sheehy, noted that his protagonists are both adventurers and "self-appointed reformers of an unjust world."[3] This notion of the "scourge of God," of someone placed on earth for the purpose of enacting God's justice, is initially mentioned—ironically, to be sure—when the superstitious peasants in *The Painted Bird* feel that the Nazis are God's instruments of revenge against the Jews who killed Christ.[4] It occurs again in a scene in *Steps* when the protagonist causes some soldiers to be blown up because one soldier, apparently just for the pleasure of it, had shot down two civilians.[5]

But it is in *Cockpit* that the idea of the protagonist as scourge of God is first fully worked out. Tarden robs mail sacks to get "a magic passport to another's life" (155). In one of his stolen letters, he reads that a man was arrested and imprisoned in the Eastern European country from which the man had escaped 25 years before, when the airplane he was traveling on made an unscheduled stop there. Tarden carefully investigates the UN ambassador from that country and finds out he is involved in a real-estate kickback deal to rob his country of a great deal of money. Tarden threatens the ambassador with exposure if he does not use his weight to have the other man released and returned to America. On another occasion, Tarden learns through his snooping that a best-selling author who was creating a stir because he had been arrested in East Germany had actually trumped up the whole story just to boost sagging book sales. Tarden intervenes, and the man is found dead in his car, killed by carbon monoxide fumes.

More than Kosinski's other protagonists—those "self-appointed reformers" described in the Sheehy interview—Tarden successfully combines his need for control with his desire for revenge. The revenge, usually highly personal and directed against people who have crossed him or refused to submit to his control, begins on a small scale but accelerates steadily. Early on, he catches his girlfriend with a lover, sneaks up on them while they are sleeping, and photographs them. Later, after he confronts the girl with the pictures and she wonders how he could have taken them, Tarden hints that he and her lover had arranged it together. She storms out, furious with both men. Another time, as Tarden is engineering his escape from Eastern Europe, he arranges for some of his imaginary sponsors to request letters of recommendation from his actual teachers—the letters, of course, all coming to Tarden so that he can dispose of any negative ones. Years later, when one of those professors needs help to stay in America, he turns to Tarden, who then produces the professor's very negative letter. The man leaves, crestfallen. On yet another occasion, Tarden begins photographing a prostitute. When her tough pimp, angry that the photography is taking up so much of the girl's working time, knocks Tarden down one night, Tarden plants in the pimp's car a substance that looks like heroin, and the pimp is killed by the police.

Tarden's acts of revenge for most of the novel are typical of the acts of Kosinski's other protagonists, and Kosinski manages to keep the reader feeling some sympathy for Tarden, distasteful as some of his behavior may be. But Tarden's final, elaborate act goes so far beyond the standard that it turns the reader against him. On the condition that she will always be on call for him, Tarden offers to fix up a beautiful girl with a millionaire businessman; she agrees and is soon married to the man. After the marriage, however, the girl gets her own press agent and begins building her career; she becomes less and less available to Tarden when he calls. So he arranges for her to come to his apartment, where he binds her hand and foot and has three derelicts ("two blacks and a white" [222]), fresh out of a gutter, gang rape her and defecate on her. Untouched by the experience, she takes a shower and shrugs it off. Tarden then discovers she has a boyfriend, searches his apartment, and finds letters suggesting she plans to murder her husband, who is leaving her everything. When Tarden tries to blackmail her with the information, she laughs him away. So he has one last date with her, at an air show, and while she stands in front of a jet plane, he briefly turns on its radar, enough to give her a fatal dose of radiation. By this time, however, the reader is completely on the side of the brazen girl and against Tarden, who appears to be punishing her for the very qualities of nerve, single-mindedness, and control that he himself possesses. But evidently there is no room for admiration in Tarden's desperate struggle for dominance.

I call that struggle desperate because in all the relationships he attempts to establish with other human beings, almost invariably women, he fails. He becomes, to others, the totalitarian State that he could not endure to have over himself, and the women cannot endure it either. For instance, he offers at the beginning of the novel to set up an unconditional trust fund for Valerie, forever liberating her from work, if she will quit her job and come live with him. "I assured her that I did not expect her to love me. She would live with me, but she would be as free as I to see other people." Valerie sees through his offer and tells him that "by appointing myself her liberator, I was actually prohibiting her from shaping her own existence; I was concerned only with my own future and had created an illusion of what I wanted her to be" (6). After she leaves him, he tries other ways to force himself on women, but in each case, they display only contempt for him.

Tarden's most complex struggle is with Theodora, the Lebanese woman who first introduces him to the Service. They become lovers, but she grows possessive of him, and they part. Years later, they meet again. By then she is aged, obese, and barely making a living; nevertheless, she wants to have a baby. Tarden is not interested in servicing her, but when she promises to supply him daily with his choice of companion, the only stipulation being that she can collect his semen at the end, he cannot resist. Although no one believes her, soon Theodora tells everyone that she is pregnant and then that she has given birth to a son.

When Tarden tries to see the child, she explains that because of her bone cancer, she has given the baby to foster parents to raise. Convinced she is lying, Tarden does not see her again until she is in the last days of her terminal illness. She does not speak to him and is dead a few days later. But he notices a Polaroid picture of a child in a playpen. From a nurse, Tarden learns that Theodora indeed had a son and that, each day in the hospital as she waited to die, she had made herself up and waited for Tarden. Because he did not come, she lost interest and let herself go. Only then did Tarden appear, and she did not speak to him.

Tarden tries to trace the child, but no one will disclose the identity of the foster parents, and it is explained to Tarden that the son will never be told he is adopted. In this way, Theodora, who did not want to be simply "an afterthought tacked onto the main part of my existence" (52) but rather its center, has succeeded. By her act, she takes control of Tarden's future, and he in turn falls into the trap he set for Valerie, who had had the prescience to see that "I was actually prohibiting her from shaping her own existence; I was concerned only with my own future" (6).

Tarden is still a young man when Theodora uses him to produce a son. By the time he makes his contractual arrangement with the girl at the end of the novel—the girl who conveniently forgets her obligations to him—he is "a bony old bird." She, with her brash nerve, her ambition to achieve what she wants by any means, and her single-minded perseverance, is like his own youth; he, by contrast, is moving steadily toward old age and death. Although he had given the girl her start, he finds—as with Theodora—that she used him for the sake of her own future. Perhaps this is why he is so unforgiving. Perhaps, as is typical of the Kosinski protagonist who gets revenge on somebody, even if not precisely the person who has injured him, Tarden is paying Theodora back. The blast from the radar equipment, after all, will kill the girl with the same kind of cancer from which Theodora died.

By destroying the girl, Tarden is in a sense destroying his own past, just as Theodora destroyed his ability to have his own future. He is left squarely in the present moment, "one of the few survivors left to contemplate the urban remains" (236), with nothing ahead but anonymous death. If that present is illusionless, at least it is the truth and offers a certain lonely splendor.

The novel ends with two brief, obviously symbolic scenes. In the first, Tarden is trapped in the elevator of his apartment building for eight hours, the elevator constantly going up and down, never pausing, the doors never opening. Weakened and dehydrated, he strips himself naked, vomits, defecates, and shouts and bangs at the doors, but there is no one to hear him until the following morning. The forces that propel his "windowless cell" seem arbitrary and autonomous. "I was completely cut off from my past," he says, "a royal mummy, safely cradled and sealed for the long voyage ahead" (247). It is—in a novel in which control has been so important—a powerful image of the bare truth of existence in the present moment, of the actual lack of control in life.

That image is reinforced by another image, of the collective, in the next scene. As Tarden looks down from his window at night onto a lighted skating rink, the skaters seem to blend safely together, giving up their individuality to the rhythm of the music imposed on them from outside. An odd optical illusion stresses their abnegation of life, their nonliving stance: "Now the rink appears to revolve around the skaters as they stand like frozen sculptures growing out of the ice." Tarden recalls "a great old army tank, hit decades ago by an enemy shell, sunken in a shallow lagoon. . . . Its corroded gun defiantly trains on trenches and machine-gun nests, long buried in the sands of a deserted beach" (248). That is the final image of the book, a lone, dead battler in a lost and forgotten war, meaningless, except for the qualities of dignity and defiance. But in a world where we must choose between the loneliness of the endless elevator ride and the frozen living death of the circling skaters, dignity and defiance are all we are left with—a bleak Nordic vision in which the best we can ask is to be allowed to fight honorably against overwhelming odds until the moment of final defeat.

The spiritual autobiography that begins in *Cockpit* is even more obvious in *Blind Date,* the second novel of the three-novel cycle. *Blind Date* is presented in the standard Kosinski fashion: a series of incidents that find Levanter, the mobile lone-wolf protagonist, a self-described "small investor" and idea man, in various countries, frequently flashing back to the past, moving from adventure to adventure, from woman to woman. Like Tarden, Levanter is growing old; he is unable to ski as well as he used to. Levanter's heart, it seems, beats to its own rhythm. When it is calm, he is calm. When it is agitated, he must perform some adventurous action. When he discovers that the head of internal affairs of some totalitarian country, a man famous for arrests, tortures, and deaths, is skiing incognito at the lodge, he ingeniously manages to blow him up. Afterward, Levanter's heart is calm again.

In *Cockpit,* there were signs that Kosinski's protagonist was moving away from a personal revenge ethic and toward a more impersonal role as self-appointed reformer of an unjust world, a sort of "scourge of God." In *Blind Date* the tendency has gone much further. There is little in the way of personal revenge, but as the impersonal "scourge of God," Levanter is very active, especially—as the scene with the minister of internal affairs reveals—on an international scale.

In another episode, Levanter learns that the desk clerk in an American hotel where Eastern European visitors stay is actually an agent whose job is to gather evidence of disloyalty. Thanks to his work, numerous guests are arrested on their return home. When a man Levanter knows, a world-champion saber fencer, has his arm cripplingly broken and is imprisoned and sentenced to 25 years owing in part to information given by the desk-clerk informer, Levanter finds a pretext to have a clandestine meeting with the informer. In their private stall at a Turkish bath, Levanter overpowers him, ties him to a table, puts a saber into the opening of his anus, and then rams the saber to the hilt up into his body. "Scarcely an hour had passed since the clerk had entered Levanter's room at the baths. But what had taken place there had already receded into a remote corner of his memory."[6]

In each of these cases, Kosinski stresses the impersonality of the actions, as though Levanter were merely a vehicle through which justice is meted out. This is evident again on the ski slope, where he sees some men taking an obviously terrified female novice skier to the highest and most dangerous point. Levanter forces the men to take off their skis and walk the woman back down to a safe position. When one of the men snaps, "In whose name are you doing this?" he replies, "Simple humanity" (*Blind Date,* 28). In *Cock-*

pit, Tarden performed some generous actions, but his motive always seemed to be the pleasure of exerting his will on others. When Levanter says that his motive is simple humanity, we believe him.

Unlike most of Kosinski's other protagonists, Levanter occasionally feels remorse. In one of the few personal revenge actions in the novel, Levanter, wearing his most modish ski attire and carrying the finest equipment that can be bought, overhears three Russian tourists making fun of him. To their amazement, he challenges them in fluent Russian, tells them he is a lieutenant colonel on the Soviet Ski Team, and threatens to report them for disparaging Russian athletes. So far, it is a standard Kosinski scene. But a few minutes later, when he sees the Russians in nervous conference, no doubt preparing for the investigation that would await them at home, "for a moment he felt sorry for them and considered going over to apologize and tell them the truth . . . then he felt ashamed and somehow unnerved by his deception" (21).

Moreover, Levanter is notably less successful at maintaining "control" than previous protagonists have been. When a girl he wants to see calls unexpectedly, he must contact friends to break a prior engagement: "He would apologize: here he was an investor, he joked, who wanted to be master of his fate yet couldn't even master his leisure time" (185). When he achieves his ambition of going out with a glamorous Russian woman he had always dreamed of, he is powerless to make love to her; the Russian language they speak works as a resistless chaperon: how could he make a lewd suggestion to her in the language of Pushkin? When he picks up a girl in a small town and has a brief affair with her, he is forced to remain in the town to testify against her in her divorce trial.

Levanter is very much subject to the chance juxtapositions of the moment. "Chance" had occasionally been a factor in Kosinski's previous novels (it was, after all, the name of the protagonist of *Being There*), but only in *Cockpit,* a novel in which scenes turn on sheer coincidence (e.g., the roundabout but wholly accidental way Tarden locates an agent who has defected), does chance begin to emerge as a thematic statement. By *Blind Date,* chance and coincidence become major themes. At the beginning of the novel, Levanter hears a woman, Pauline, playing on the piano a piece that his mother used to play. He meets Pauline, and it turns out that she had the same teacher his mother did. When he says the teacher was his mother's mistress, Pauline suggests that she too was the teacher's mistress, creating a connection between the two women. The connection is increased when it turns out Levanter and his mother have been lovers. He and Pauline lose touch with each other, but at the end of the novel, by sheer chance, Levanter sees her name on a poster and hears her play, and they come together as lovers, completing the connection suggested at the beginning. In another episode, the young Levanter, at camp, uses his friend Oscar's techniques to rape a girl Levanter admires. By coincidence, he meets the girl the next year; they hit it off and are on the point of becoming lovers. But he unconsciously kisses her in the way he did when he raped her; realizing who he really is, she leaves him in a rage.

We would be patronizing of such pat, often almost sentimental coincidences in a nineteenth-century Victorian novel. But Kosinski, who is so sternly opposed to the falsifications of life suggested by any sort of conventional plot that looks ahead to the foreshadowed conclusion and seduces the reader away from looking at the incident before his or her eyes at the present moment, uses coincidence both to make a philosophical point and, oddly enough, to create something like a plot. It is, however, a plot of blind chance, of "blind dates," and so once more it reminds us that the future is out of our hands, that only the present exists as an arena for our exertions. Jacques Monod, in real life a friend of Kosinski's, is imported into the novel to reinforce this point. As Levanter and Monod are discussing Levanter's friend Romarkin, Monod observes: "Romarkin doesn't dare to admit that blind chance and nothing else is responsible for each random event of his life. Instead, he is searching for a religion that, like Marxism, will assure him that man's destiny is spelled out in the central plot of life. Meanwhile, believing in the existence of an orderly, predetermined life scheme, Romarkin bypasses the drama of each unique instance of his own existence. Yet, to accept a notion of destiny, he might as well believe in astrology, or palm reading, or pulp novels, all of which pretend that one's future is already set and needs only to be lived out" (86).

Although in *Blind Date* Kosinski puts these words into the mouth of a "real" person, a person whose *Chance and Necessity* was an admittedly important influence, in fact they express the underlying philosophy of all of Kosinski's novels. But an equally great influence is *Being and Time* (1927) by the German philosopher Martin Heidegger. *Dasein,* a word Kosinski is fond of (translated into English it became the title of *Being There*), is the term Heidegger uses to refer to *Being,* or selfhood. The important question for Heidegger—as for Kosinski's protagonists—is the quest for being. The *Being* constitutes three fundamental aspects: (1) *facticity:* we are already in a world not of our making; (2) *existentiality:* the act of making my world mine ("Being exists as anticipation of its own possibilities: it exists in advance of itself and grasps its situation as a challenge to its own power of becoming what it may, rather than being what it must be"); and (3) *forfeiture:* the scattering of our essential forward drive through attention to the distracting and disturbing cares of everyday and of the things and people that surround us everyday. Thus, inevitably and continuously, the forward-driving *I* is sacrificed to the persistent and pressing *they*. "If the world is material for our creative energy," noted Heidegger, "it is also the agent by which we are seduced from the essential drive to understand and to create."

What rescues us from forfeiture—the daily routine—and makes us grasp our own being is dread *(Angst),* our sense of our coming death. We authenticate ourselves by recognizing our death, our only unique action. We see our whole self only when we see our past and future (i.e., death) and how they both create the present moment.[7] The idea of using the fear or awareness of approaching death to push aside the daily routine in order to live and experience fully the present moment is basic in all of Kosinski's writing, beginning with the young boy in *The Painted Bird* who lies between the rails while the train thunders overhead and who feels as if "nothing mattered except the simple fact of being alive" (*Painted Bird,* 198).

If facticity—the world we must live in, the body we must inhabit—is a product of pure chance, as Monod scientifically demonstrates, a question arises. Supposing that with our *Angst,* our awareness of our limited and finite future, we are *able* to shove aside the soothing seductions of religion, society, and television, which all insist that death happens only to the other guy—supposing we are *able* to concentrate on the present moment—then how do we existentially create our being, fulfill our possibility, seize control of that part of our life over which we can exercise some control? *Blind Date* provides several examples.

There is the beautiful Foxy Lady, with whom Levanter has an exciting sexual affair—until he learns she is actually a man who just had a sex-change operation. Born in a Moslem country where males are all-important and females are chattel, the Foxy Lady has decided to take her ambiguous destiny into her own hands and create herself, at least superficially, as a female. "And they say only secret agents live in disguise?" (*Blind Date,* 148) she says bitterly, at the same time that she seems to be aligning herself with other marginal Kosinski characters.

The cost to her is great. She is disowned by her wealthy and powerful father, who is able to have her passport revoked, so that she becomes a citizen of no country. (Levanter, pointedly enough, had met her in the "no man's land" between two countries.) She has left herself out of having a normal role in either sex and, with her amputation, even seems to have lost her ability to have orgasm. For *Angst,* she need only go upstairs to a special room in the private club she and her kind frequent. There are the middle-aged transsexuals, looking aged and coarse and bloated from hormone overdoses, their sex drive gone, their looks vanished, sleeping most of the time and staying drugged. Having made her choice, the Foxy Lady must live her entire life in the present moment, for sex, for dancing, for the admiration of the men around her—until she too ends up upstairs. On the other hand, had she opted for the easy way—the sham role of male—she would have had wealth and social acceptance but not even the fulfillment she feels as the Foxy Lady.

Another woman Levanter meets is singularly blasted by fate. She is 26 years old but so deformed from a bone disease that she is legless and has stiff, toadlike appendages for arms and an infant-sized body. Her head, however, is normal sized, expressive, and quite beautiful. Although she requires a nurse to take her around in a pram, she refuses to let fate crush her and lives a rewarding life, attending a university to study art history. She has learned four foreign languages, has a boyfriend she is emotionally committed to, and, most amazingly, spends her holidays hitchhiking about Europe. "Each summer a friend takes me to the main highway and thumbs a ride for me," she explains. "Of course, I always have money and my papers with me. Eventually, someone—a man or woman, a couple, or even a family—comes along who does not mind picking me up. After that, I'm on my own—passed from hand to hand, from car to car" (190).

Where does Levanter fit into this scheme? His "given" is to live in a world of blind chance in which at any moment his heart might stop forever. A small investor, he must make his own life rewarding. But, like the plastic surgeon whom Levanter admires and observes at work, he must also make life better for those around him. Certainly this attitude is a change from Kosinski's earlier protagonists. And although on a more personal level Levanter attempts to find meaning in some of the standard ways past protagonists have—skiing dangerous slopes, putting himself in the way of adventures with new people in new places—he possesses some significant differences: he is softened, more human, more compassionate, less interested in personal revenge, less interested in controlling other human beings. Sex for Levanter is less an act of aggression, so that at least the possibility of love exists for him.

In *Cockpit,* Tarden was capable of forcing his sexual attention on a woman just because she had behaved hostilely toward him, and later in the novel he murders a woman who will not tolerate his advances. In *Blind Date,* Levanter, although he rapes and abuses the woman he calls "Nameless," meets her again and wants to get to know her. "I am afraid of losing you, Nameless," he confesses. "Of losing you again" (*Blind Date,* 75). But when she realizes he is her rapist, she leaves him at once. Levanter knows that, by never really communicating with her, he has missed a real opportunity. Language as a form of necessary communication between lovers, in fact, becomes a complex issue in the novel. After the episode with the girl, Levanter becomes his mother's lover, and their relationship goes on for years. But oddly they never speak about it. Later, when he meets a beautiful Russian actress, he feels hopelessly inhibited by his Russian language and is unable to carry through with his seduction. Levanter's boyhood friend Oscar, perhaps to escape the same sort of language inhibition, invents his own vocabulary of blind dates and breaking eyes.

Levanter's mother had another way of communicating with him: through her music. And it is music that first brings Levanter together with Pauline, who is playing the same piece he heard her play at their first meeting—the same piece his mother played—when he rediscovers her at the end of the novel. As he listens, the music is "pure spirit without words, without gestures" (226). At the conclusion of the performance, he goes to Pauline's dressing room and then invites her to his apartment. She wants to know why. " 'I'm afraid of losing you,' he said. The sound of his words brought him a faint memory, so faint that he dismissed it" (227). They are, of course, the words he had used with Nameless, the girl he had raped. (When Levanter first meets Pauline, she is described as having "thick blond hair" [8], much like Nameless's thick blond braid.) "I want you to fall in love with me," he tells her, and then, in this novel of chance, says, "Somehow, I think you're my last chance" (227).

They begin to make love—records of her piano playing on the phonograph—but somehow she cannot surrender to him until he takes a handful of neckties (this time the softest, smoothest he has) from his closet. Gently but convincingly, he ties her hand and foot (as he had tied Nameless in the woods 30 years before), recreating the scene, but gently this time, with Pauline's permission, face to face, and hears "her whisper, 'Yes!' and, as its sound ebbed, her body softened, freed from its own bondage, no longer struggling against any restraints" (231). The personal violence against others symbolized in his original binding and raping of the girl has been sublimated into social action—the binding and raping (with the saber, or *rapier*) of the desk-clerk informer—leaving him free for the gentle, psychotherapeutic binding and raping of Pauline in love.

Kosinski tries, in the scene, to bring some sort of resolution to another aesthetic and philosophical problem. Memory is both a help and a hindrance in living the full and rich life; memory can trap us, make us an object of history, rather than a subject of the present moment. Pauline, for instance, has been made an object of the rape in her childhood, which has stopped her from having sexual fulfillment. But when Levanter recreates the binding, the rape, he is using the memory of past trauma to heal, to bring her to live in and respond to the present act.

Using his own memory of the past traumatic act to recreate it in the present is essentially what the novelist does when he takes the ingredients of his past to create his fictions. Through her art, her piano playing, Pauline is able to take Levanter back to his original meeting with her, just as at that original meeting she took him back to the memory of his mother. "A good audience," she says after he compliments her on her concert performance. "But the audience is gone now. All that's left is the recording, a memory." Levanter replies, "But it's a memory with feeling, which can be listened to many times." (There is an obvious analogy with the printed novel.) She agrees, "But only as a source of reflection; no more magic of the spontaneous" (226).

In his personal relationship with her, Levanter wants the "spontaneous magic." Memory is not enough. Even memory with feeling is second to living in the actual present moment. So life is better than art, but—and here is the point—art can bring us to the present moment by reminding us, by shocking us, into the necessary *Angst*. In this sense, Kosinski does not separate memory from the imagination: "I think you start by imagining yourself in the very situation which frightens you. Hence, the enormous importance of imagination, our ability to project oneself into the 'unknown'—the very 'blind dates' of our existence. . . . In the moment of such a projection you are at peace with both your own condition and with a change this condition implies. . . . You intensify your joy of the moment . . . and you ready yourself for whatever might be, for the innumerable contingencies you might have to face in your life."[8]

Had *Blind Date* ended with Levanter and Pauline's coming together in the present moment—as a novel of conventional plot and coincidence might end—it would have been false to Kosinski's imaginative vision. Instead the novel concludes with the most inescapable fact of life, which is death. Levanter is on the ski slopes. Spring is approaching, so the cold weather catches him by surprise and without adequate clothing. He gets lost in the fog, and though he fights against it, the cold slowly claims him. "The game was good to him, made him want to play it, yet even a solitary player needs his rest. . . . He sank down and turned his face away from the wind" (*Blind Date,* 235).

Passion Play, the third novel in the cycle, carries even further the themes introduced in *Cockpit* and extended in *Blind Date*. Fabian, the protagonist, is older, more vulnerable, and less vengeful. Whereas Levanter operated on an international scale, trying to make the world slightly better by eliminating enslaving tyrants, Fabian is more parochial. As he says of himself, he is strictly a one-on-one man; if he improves the world, he does so not by eliminating the enslavers but rather by freeing individuals to their full potential—in this case, the young ladies he trains in "horsemanship." A polo player who writes books about what it means to be a rider, Fabian lives in his VanHome, a motor home with room in the back for his two horses. He has never been a team man—the other players blackballed him for not wanting to share the ball; therefore he makes most of his living playing one-on-one for stakes. It is a poor living, especially for an aging man, and from day to day he does not know if he will have enough money to feed his horses or drive his VanHome. Distinctly anachronistic—like a gaunt, ridiculous, but somehow noble Don Quixote—Fabian takes his horses out on a deserted downtown parking lot to practice polo.

For a while, he had been a friend and sort of paid partner to Eugene Stanhope, a millionaire who played polo as a hobby. But after Eugene's girlfriend Alexandra seduced Fabian and claimed that he forced himself on her, Eugene, in a fury, challenged Fabian to a one-on-one match. Fabian, to avoid Eugene's deliberate direct hit on him, with a fluke shot drove the ball into Eugene's head, killing him. A few years later, Fabian is challenged by Alexandra's new boyfriend, a rich South American professional polo player, but Fabian defeats him in similarly rough play.

In addition to writing and playing one-on-one, Fabian teaches riding to beautiful high-school-age girls who have an aptitude for the sport. His lessons, however, are not limited to riding; he initiates the girls sexually as well. The training in riding and the training in sex follow similar philosophies (and are described in similar vocabulary). In both, Fabian aims to bring out the total potential in his students. His best student was Vanessa Stanhope, niece of his former friend Eugene Stanhope. Vanessa came to Fabian with great warmth, but because she was underage, they make it a rule that in all their lovemaking, they will preserve her hymen. But there is another reason for his refraining from taking her virginity: she is special in his life, the only girl he has ever loved. "She never ceased to be, for him, sovereign in her possession of a flame of life."[9] That flame always equated, in Kosinski's writing, with the full Heideggerian "being" in the present moment. Preserving Vanessa's virginity is, for Fabian, an attempt to halt the flow of time, to freeze their relationship in the present moment, to give him a promise to come back to many years later.

When he does see Vanessa again, toward the end of the novel, he is penniless and his body is in decay; she, by contrast, is in the full bloom of her youth, and, as heiress to the Stanhope fortune, a millionairess many times over. Having kept her virginity for Fabian, she now wants him to take it, and when he hesitates, she forces herself on him. Having reluctantly fulfilled his role as teacher, Fabian prepares to move on. Vanessa, however, tries to keep him, even presenting him with a no-strings-attached gift of $1 million so that he will be independent and money will not come between them. But he recognizes that what she is asking for is a kind of possession, a robbing of the stern independence and solitude of his nomadic life. He refuses her gift and leaves.

Fabian's horses, the only other important characters in the novel, are genuine horses, of course, nicely and convincingly realized. But they have a symbolic dimension as well, representing the body, whereas the rider represents the will or spirit. "The union of rider and mount was, at base, a duel of human brain and animal physiology" (*Passion Play,* 24). Fabian's horsemanship is an "attempt at mechanical perfection," an act "of violence committed by the spirit against an unwilling, submissive body" (12). The horse (never "he" or "she," but always "it")—and therefore by extension his own aging body—appears to remain for him at the level of mechanism. He contrasts a New Zealand polo team whose players are rated identically at 9 out of 10 with a South American team, which has two players rated 10 and two rated 8. After tournaments, the New Zealanders bear the expense of bringing their horses home with them. The crowd likes them, likes their "link to an Anglo-Saxon legacy of respecting the horse." The South Americans, by contrast, sell their ponies at auction after the match. They "never staked winning on one horse" but use several in a match, training them mainly for speed, using drugs to stimulate them and anesthetics to keep them from noticing pain. The South Americans' "peculiar vehemence of temperament" (45), which causes them to whip the bloodied flanks of their ponies into a frenzied gallop, turns the crowd against them. But it is for just these reasons Fabian prefers the South Americans, preferring the single star to the even team, and preferring to drive horse and body fiercely and passionately to their greatest heights.

The point is brought out in his relationship with Stella, a seemingly typical blond Southern belle in training for dressage competitions. She claims that her horse is bred to the artificial gaits of dressage, but in fact during training she rigs the horse with complicated weights and braces that virtually cripple it into moving in a very unnatural manner. Fabian accuses her of treating her horse exactly as the Southern masters used to treat their slaves, forcing their wills to unnatural bondage. After Fabian discovers that Stella is herself a black albino who has forced her body unnaturally into the mold of a Southern belle, he frees her to be herself, sexually and otherwise. In the meantime, she sells her horse to Fabian for a third of its market price, and he retrains it for polo, a sport that brings out the horse's true attributes.

Just as there is an advantage to finding a horse while it is still young and before it has been mistrained, so Fabian prefers young and virginal girls. The analogies between training horses and training young virgins are often handled quite humorously, almost with a Nabokovian playfulness. Puns on the genus *Equus* abound. For instance, when Fabian is out to take Stella's virginity, he says he would like "to break her equanimity" (161). As the young girls in lepidopterist Nabokov's books are sometimes described in terms reminiscent of butterflies, the young girls in *Passion Play* are described in what the alert reader can see are horselike terms. The women Fabian likes are "young, tall, slender, long-legged, with large eyes and thick hair, a wide mouth" (110). Vanessa has "expressive eyes, high cheekbones, lush hair, the wide mouth, even teeth" (194). Alexandra sports a "mane of copper-colored hair" (52) and has a "broad mobile mouth, framing wide teeth" (68). There is even the suggestion of a horse's gait when Kosinski describes Stella's conversation, "her aloof manner, the languid rise and fall of her speech" (164).

The purpose of Fabian's training is to take away the last of the girls' inhibitions, to free them from their restraint-filled past, to bring out the fullness of their being, and to make them live solidly in the sensation of the moment. A part of the intensity is the fact that the moment is transitory, that he is a nomad who will soon leave them. But the relationships in *Passion Play* are not always mutually liberating; they can be perilous, as Falsalfa demonstrates. Falsalfa, a Trujillo-like dictator of a Caribbean island who pays Fabian to make him look good at polo, sets him up. Along with an aging journalist critical of Falsalfa's regime and the journalist's attractive wife, he sends Fabian into the jungle interior, where natives insist that all of them sample the local drink. Fabian goes into a dreamlike state during which at one time the wife seems to be dancing lasciviously before him, at another moment the journalist is attacking him with a machete, and at another Fabian is on the floor making love to the woman, with dozens of natives looking on. In the morning, the journalist is dead, allegedly killed by a tarantula, his wife heavily sedated and unconscious. Knowing that somehow Falsalfa is involved, Fabian accuses him of murder, but the dictator merely laughs and reminds him that dozens of witnesses saw him making love to the journalist's wife and the journalist fighting with him. If there were an investigation, Fabian would be found guilty, an argument Fabian cannot deny.

Fabian is being used in the most obvious way, being made an object by Falsalfa. A careful reading of the dreamlike scene suggests that, drugged, he was indeed maneuvered into the woman's arms. But he did in fact make love with her, though had his mind been clear, he probably would not have wanted to come between the man and his wife. The scene spells out the falsity of Fabian's whole relationship with the dictator, suggested already by the name Falsalfa. By denying his own drive to win at polo, Fabian had gained financial security and luxurious surroundings. But he lost his freedom of action.

With Eugene Stanhope, Fabian has a more subtle, but similar, relationship. The millionaire helps Fabian finance his VanHome and buy his horse; though the relationship is ostensibly one of friendship, Stanhope keeps Fabian virtually as a salaried hand. The position is less demeaning than his work for Falsalfa: Fabian can play to win, but it is still a kind of bondage. After Alexandra seduces him, he must ride against Eugene in a final contest, in which—as described earlier—Eugene is killed. Once more, however, for the sake of brief financial stability, Fabian has put himself almost completely in the hands of others.

Fabian encounters Alexandra again when he is trying to jump an extremely tall fence for the championship at a horse show. He hears her shouting at him at a critical moment. The voice from the past distracts him briefly, and he turns, unbalancing the horse, and the fence is toppled. Fabian loses the match and nearly takes a bad fall. Alexandra's actions, on the surface, appear to be based on some vicious, inexplicable hatred she has for Fabian. In fact, her relationship with Fabian is the most complicated relationship in the novel. Even their lovemaking, described in great detail, is complex and marked by many reversals. To begin with, it is she who challenges him, and in terms he cannot resist. Whereas he would have to lure other girls into his VanHome, Alexandra demands entrance. "Could it wait for another time?" he asks, hesitating. "It could. But should you?" (52). It is his own ethic she is challenging him with, that the moment, always unrepeatable, must be seized.

Inside the VanHome, when she invites him to take her, "Fabian felt himself at a crossroads, forced by the will of another to unsettle the harmony he had achieved between his codes and inclinations" (53). It is her will operating, not his. But "to decline Alexandra's challenge, to thwart his instinct toward her, would ratify an indolence or lapse in value. Either would subvert his trust in himself. . . . The balance of his mind restored" (54), he accepts her challenge. As they make love, she continues to hold the position that is usually his. In the horse-riding parallels of the scene, her legs are "upon his chest, her calves girdled around his ribs" (56); she insists on entering all his bodily orifices, and in a final bit of control, she pulls back and refuses to give him his climax, "knowing that, with orgasm, her power over her lover waned" (57). Taking over his role as teacher and liberator, she keeps him rigidly within the present moment, "commanding his gaze, not allowing him . . . even in thought, to withdraw to another world, one that might be entirely his own—or one that he might share, in recollection or fantasy, with another woman" (56).

In their merging, it is finally immaterial to him "what impulses she submitted to in her commitment to his need: whether they were stages in a drama ordered by her and enacted by him, that would permit the revelation of his own nature, his pleasure at the discovery a tribute to her zeal; or whether, provoked by her, he was the one who would disclose what lay hidden in her, what she could not otherwise release, the pleasure she sought most" (57). In a way, her withholding orgasm from him parallels his refraining from taking Vanessa's virginity: in both cases, the act is a way of extending the moment. If indeed Alexandra is to Fabian as Fabian is to the young girls he trains, Kosinski seems to be trying to create that existential impossibility, a relationship in which one is not subject and the other object, but in which each helps create the other as subject without losing subject status him- or herself—in other words, a creative, rather than a destructive, relationship.

In light of their relationship, Alexandra's treachery may appear inconsistent, but it is not. The reader will recall that her nickname is "the centipede"—reminiscent of that other poisonous arthropod in the novel, the tarantula that appears to have killed the journalist. The parallels are instructive. As the dictator's hired man, Fabian was in a false position, faking his game for financial security by making Falsalfa look good. The tarantula is what finally adverts Fabian to his situation, so that he can at last break free of the dictator and leave. Fabian's position with Eugene Stanhope was equally false. Fabian's hesitation to take Alexandra at once was a sign of how Eugene—though certainly not as dictatorial as Falsalfa—had locked him up, subverting his instincts. Through her seeming treachery, Alexandra "the centipede" in fact brought on, just as the tarantula had, the necessary rupture between Fabian and Eugene, so that Fabian would once more be true to himself. When she meets Fabian later, his finances and spirits are at a low ebb. The Stanhope family offers him a new form of financial security, as the television moderator for a series of programs about polo, an attempt to make polo a popular mass-audience sport. Once more it is an unnatural role for him to become spectator, player-at-one-remove, from the real game. But because he has scarcely enough money left to feed his horses, he has little choice. At that moment, Alexandra sets the challenge match with her young boyfriend. It seems as if she is out for revenge, but the upshot is that Fabian makes enough on the match to regain his independence and is able to turn down the television job.

The last meeting between them is the most paradoxical. Fabian has gone to Madison Square Garden to watch the show jumping competition in which Vanessa's horse, Captain Ahab, is competing. But at the last instant, Ahab's rider has a reaction to drugs he had taken to calm himself and there is no time to find a replacement. Fabian wants to help Vanessa, so he decides to ride Ahab himself. The horse is strong, and Fabian does very well with it. At last all competitors have been eliminated except for Fabian and one other, interestingly a woman rider. While Fabian is trying to clear a seven-foot fence in the jump-off, Alexandra shouts, breaking his concentration, and he loses. It is important to note that Fabian is competing for the sake of Vanessa, who is another of the wealthy Stanhopes. Because he himself is a polo player, show jumping is an unnatural sport for him. By having him engage in an unnatural activity, Vanessa, in effect, puts the crippling weights and bindings on him that Stella put on her gaited horse. Immediately after the competition, Vanessa offers Fabian a large monetary gift, ostensibly to make him independent. She has the same motive Eugene had in offering to underwrite Fabian's horsemanship manuals. In practice (as when similar offers were made in *Cockpit* and *Blind Date*), the gift would have bound him to her forever.

When Alexandra shouts, "Take it, Fabian, take it now!" (241), she does not mean for him to take the jump. She certainly does not mean for him to take the $1 million and a lifetime of bondage to Vanessa. Instead, she means for him to take his freedom, and to take it "now," in the moment, the moment fading, the moment followed no doubt by aging and loneliness and death.

I am, however, being unfair to the novel if I do not mention that it is, in the reader's experience of it, not a ruthless combating of wills, a harsh system of shifting philosophical coordinates, but rather a moving love story. Vanessa is indeed possessive; she does indeed—perhaps scarcely realizing it herself—want to hold Fabian in ways probably destructive to him. As more than a teacher, as virtually a father to her, he has set her off in life, and his part is now to withdraw from her youth and let her make her own life. But he loves her, and she loves him. That much the reader feels; their parting, however necessary, is not less sad for that reason.

At this point, we need to look at the distance we have come in this cycle of three novels. In *Cockpit,* the relationship between Tarden and his protégée is destructive: he, as a defected secret agent living in a disguise, cannot have personal relationships; she, after attempting to split from him, suffers a fatal dose of his poison. In *Blind Date,* Levanter's violent rape of the young girl prohibits her from achieving fulfilling relationships with others. Only at the end does Levanter reach the point in his own development where he is able to begin undoing the harm he has done her. And the complex, difficult, and paradoxical relationships in *Passion Play* always push toward selfhood and being—relationships that cannot in the end prevent aging and death, but can fill the preceding moments with drama and meaning.

In beginning to deal with himself as the disguised protagonist of his novels, Kosinski is moving away from protagonists who represent extreme, desperate positions to more moderate, more humanly vulnerable, and ultimately more successful protagonists. Although Kosinski has written these novels to point out the dangers and difficulties of life, perhaps he is also showing how he has negotiated the reefs himself. Having personally been through many of the most traumatic upheavals and disruptions of our recent desperate history, and perhaps having been damaged by his childhood experience in ways that made it difficult or impossible for him to have personal relationships with others, he charts—through the progression of his novels—his own safe arrival. Although his own life seems to have ended as his novels prefigured it would—overcome by his enemies, aging and alone and tired—who can deny him the brilliant moments he had? In these senses, he is a survivor who has not only come through but triumphed. More than most others, he is in a position to be an example to us.

Notes

1. Jerzy Kosinski, *Notes of the Author on The Painted Bird* (New York: Scientia-Factum, 1965), 27.
2. Jerzy Kosinski, *Cockpit* (Boston: Houghton Mifflin, 1975), 118; hereafter cited in the text as *Cockpit.*
3. Gail Sheehy, "The Psychological Novelist as Portable Man," *Psychology Today,* December 1977, 55.
4. Jerzy Kosinski, *The Painted Bird* (Boston: Houghton Mifflin, 1965), 84; hereafter cited in the text as *Painted Bird.*
5. Jerzy Kosinski, *Steps* (New York: Random House, 1968), 31–32.
6. Jerzy Kosinski, *Blind Date* (Boston: Houghton Mifflin, 1977), 161; hereafter cited in the text as *Blind Date.*
7. I have taken my discussion from Marjorie Grene, "Martin Heidegger," in *The Encyclopedia of Philosophy,* ed. Paul Edwards (New York: Macmillan, 1967), 3:459–65.
8. Sheehy, 55.
9. Jerzy Kosinski, *Passion Play* (New York: St. Martin's Press, 1979), 197; hereafter cited in the text as *Passion Play.*

Is There Any History in It? The Fiction of Jerzy Kosinski

THOMAS S. GLADSKY

In *Jerzy Kosinski: A Biography,* James Park Sloan hints at a lucrative way of reading Kosinski. Sloan describes *The Painted Bird* as a "researched 'historical' novel, comparable perhaps to Doctorow's *Ragtime,*" and provocatively suggests that the novel is actually "a liberation from the shackles of historical fact."[1] Sloan also points out that a number of reviewers and readers have regarded *The Painted Bird* as a "quasi-historical document" and that some, such as John Aldridge, have seen other Kosinski novels through the prism of history. For example, Aldridge called *Being There* a novel that "exists simultaneously on the levels of fiction and fact, fantasy and contemporary history" (*Jerzy Kosinski,* 293). With this, Sloan moves on to other of Kosinski's selves, but his notion of Kosinski's fiction as history is intriguing and thought-provoking.

In terms of genre form, Kosinski's novels do not resemble either the traditional historical novel or the new varieties developed by Gore Vidal *(Lincoln, Burr),* Thomas Flanagan (Irish Trilogy), William Kennedy *(Quinn's Book, The Flaming Corsage),* John Updike *(Memories of the Ford Administration),* John Barth, E. L. Doctorow, and others. Even as these writers spoof and stretch the form and wrench traditional notions of history and fiction, they continue to include historical facts and people, to fashion their plots within a recognizable historical frame, and, generally speaking, to adhere to most of the conventions of the historical novel. Not even *The Painted Bird,* however, Kosinski's most outwardly historical novel, can sustain such comparisons. And except for *The Painted Bird* and perhaps *The Hermit of 69th Street,* none of Kosinski's novels appears to be grounded in history in the usual ways.

From another perspective, however, Kosinski's fiction is very much about history without being historical. In one of the obtuse but witty dialogues that typifies *The Hermit of 69th Street,* Norbert Kosky talks about the novel he is writing: "It will be a post-Exodus novel about a modern-day Judah Halevi traveling back into his Ruthenian-Jewish past," he explains. "Is there

This essay was written especially for inclusion in this volume and is published here with the permission of the author.

any real history in it?" Kosky is asked. "There is," he replies, "but not enough to reconstruct history."[2] Although the reader is tempted to dismiss these comments as yet another example of Kosinski's excesses, Kosky inadvertently characterizes Kosinski's attitude vis-à-vis the issue of fact and fiction, history and invention, that has puzzled readers and reviewers from the beginning. From his first novel, *The Painted Bird,* to his last, *Hermit,* Kosinski carried on a sustained dialogue with history. One might say that this dialogue is, in fact, the core of both Kosinski's fiction and the personal nightmare that possessed him all of his life.

At first glance, Kosinski's novels appear to be without any coherent connection to history. *The Painted Bird* is the only one based on a specific recognizable historical event—the German and subsequent Russian invasions of Poland in World War II. In the seven novels that follow, Kosinski places the narrative and plot events outside history. That is to say, the protagonists make a deliberate effort to free themselves of historical time without ultimate success, and despite references to recognizable places and events, the plots have little to do with what most would call "history." In *Hermit,* yet another kind of novel, history returns; or rather Kosinski's protagonist returns to history, thus completing the circle that begins in *The Painted Bird.* In other words, beneath these three radically different kinds of novels, history is the driving force and the principal obsession of his protagonists in much the same way that it was for Kosinski himself.

In addition to James Park Sloan, others have noted Kosinski's struggle with history. Ronald Granofsky and Andrew Gordon suggest that Kosinski's novels function as a way "to gain revenge" on the past.[3] This observation serves well in characterizing the novels in general but does not sufficiently describe Kosinski's fictional development in terms of the novel as history. In this regard, Kosinski's fiction consists of three stages: his initial novel *The Painted Bird* (and opening chapters in *Steps*), in which an intrusive old-world history sweeps over the young protagonist like a storm from sea from which he cannot escape; the novels from *Steps* to *Pinball,* in which Kosinski, having himself stepped out of old-world history, sets his plots in ahistorical new-world time, featuring protagonists who have retreated from history but who ironically must spend a great deal of their time fending off repeated attempts by history to reenter their lives; and finally *The Hermit of 69th Street,* different from the others not only in form but in the degree and extent to which history is itself the subject. As I have argued earlier and in a somewhat different context, what we see over the course of the novels is a reluctant but gradual accommodation with the past on a personal level and on a historical level—from complete rejection to resigned reconciliation to an almost contrite but satisfying acceptance.[4]

For Kosinski, the crucial event in postwar history was the emergence of the deracinated self. Kosinski saw that phenomenon as a direct consequence of World War II and the ensuing political cold war that has dominated the history of the last half century and shaped all other "historical" events great and small. His novels, beginning with *The Painted Bird,* offer a running commentary on the pervasive effects of a half century of cold war history on the individual and collective psyche. To the exclusion of perhaps all his other talents, Kosinski's primary contribution to fiction is the deracinated protagonist, a quintessential ahistorical cultural exile, molded by East-West confrontation, repressing his personal historical past, but facing a history that is always there—and ultimately inescapable.

Kosinski himself did not speak to the question of history in extended form either in his essays or in his fiction. He did, however, make frequent brief comments about history in both. In fact, *Passing By: Selected Essays 1962–1991* begins and ends with references to history that substantiate both Kosinski's preoccupation with the historical past and its centrality to his work. In the 1989 essay "Aleksander and André Wat" that opens the volume, Kosinski introduces history in violent terms—as a record of the greatest "endangerment" of children, as a force that "forbids" present actions, as a "burial ground," and as a monster whose eyes should be "gouged out." He connects Poland's tragic history to these images, suggesting that history is apportioned in different degrees to different peoples. Poland, in effect, has had too much history, which, ironically, becomes for Kosinski Poland's "special gift."[5]

In these essays written over a 30-year period, Kosinski returns frequently to the war and to the Holocaust, making it sufficiently clear that for him the monster that is history and wartime events in Poland are synonymous with each other and with Kosinski's own artistic mission. For example, in "To Touch Minds," he refers to World War II and the Holocaust as a drama "that resides in me," "as something to be narrated" (*Passing By,* 35). He also recounts Aleksander Wat's advice to "touch the reader because the reader will not be touched by history on its own," to regard history as emotion not fact, and to render everything "in verbs, adjectives, nouns, and adverbs" (33). Kosinski recognized the profound effect of this advice on his fictional strategy, and on at least one occasion, he claimed that he regarded his works as historical novels. He refers, for example, to historical documents as the source materials for *The Painted Bird,* unfortunately without identifying any he might have used. He insists nonetheless that the novel is more than memoir, fiction, or document—that it is indeed to be read as "historical" (195). In the final essay, "On Death," Kosinski completes the frame when he reminds us that we are all history students, part of a "whole class learning history" (252).

History to Kosinski was as much an internal construct as the selection and interpretation of external events. In *The Art of the Self,* he implies that the individual lives outside of history until death, then suggests that the past, as James Park Sloan phrases it, is "an almost impalpable entity which could be retained or lost, imposed upon another, owned, or placed in the hands of a caretaker" (415). Consequently, history—the conscious relationship of events to the individual self—is quite simply a usable and reusable object. To an interviewer, Kosinski noted that the "moment carries the essence of our life" and that separate events are connected only by the consciousness of the individual.[6] But in *Hermit,* Kosinski's most direct and extensive engagement with history, Kosinski turns to the rather old-fashioned notion of history as document, although he continues to argue that the past is entirely subjective. In short, Kosinski's dialogue with history in his essays—though prominent and sustained—is at times inconsistent and even cryptic. To understand the importance of history to Kosinski's art, we must depend on the fiction itself.

All of Kosinski's fiction derives from *The Painted Bird,* more specifically from the Holocaust, which stands as the shaping event in the novel. Although none of the later works portrays the Holocaust in dramatic form or includes settings in wartime Poland, the Holocaust reappears frequently. In *Steps,* Kosinski refers to the camps and their ostensibly "hygienic" function. Later, in the preface to the 1976 edition of *The Painted Bird,* he elaborates on this further by including a letter from a camp inmate. Then in *Pinball* (1982), Kosinski returns to the letter again. This time Gerald Osten refers to a copy he keeps under the glass on his desk. In *Hermit,* Holocaust allusions, documents, puns, and crypto-puzzles abound.

Kosinski's attitude and representation of history as it appears in *The Painted Bird* is in many ways at the heart of Kosinski criticism. As Sloan points out, editors and reviewers were puzzled about the manuscript—many believing it to be historically true, that is to say accurately based on real events in the life of Kosinski. The question of credibility that began innocently enough with the reluctance of some to recognize one of the earliest examples of what would become the new historical novel led inexorably to a debate about Kosinski's credibility as a stylist. In its way, *The Painted Bird* belongs to that group of novels appearing within a few years of one another that would dramatically and permanently alter the historical novel: John Barth's *The Sot-Weed Factor* (1960), Doctorow's *Welcome to Hard Times* (1960), Berger's *Little Big Man* (1964), and Vidal's *Burr* (1973). Different from their predecessors, these novels testify to the willingness of American writers to push historical fiction in new directions. Vidal unconventionally employs historical figures as major characters; Barth and Berger work at convincing readers that their fictional protagonists are indeed historical; Doctorow, employing the outline of the traditional western, includes virtually no historical characters or specifics. All, however, challenge history as presented, trespass traditional boundaries between history and fiction, and make history itself the subject of the novel.

To a marked degree, Kosinski does the same in *The Painted Bird.* The young boy's sufferings comprise the thin plot, but the novel is about the plot that is history—the theme that would occupy Kosinski throughout his career. In the novel, Kosinski blurs the lines between history and fiction. For example, although most readers believe that the setting is Poland, Kosinski says so only in an italicized preface. Instead, he writes about wartime events in such a way as to lead readers to believe that the events could be happening almost anywhere in Central or Eastern Europe. No one actually speaks Polish; place names are omitted; the geopolitical world is rarely referred to; and the boy's narration has the ring of improbability.

Even without historical specifics, there is no doubt that the novel is about World War II—a novel of occupation, politics, and historical interpretation. At first glance, the brutalities perpetrated by the peasants overwhelm other events. Even so, almost every chapter makes reference to the historical. At one point, the boy stumbles upon a bunker abandoned at the outset of the war; at another he flees German troops on patrol; then he is ensnared in a German raid on a village. Gradually, it becomes obvious that the villagers' crude behavior is less a threat than the German occupation and warring Partisan groups. Midway through the novel, Kosinski links these dual threats to his protagonist to the larger issue of the Holocaust. In chapter nine, he talks about "trains carrying Jews" that pass near the village. The boy seems to know that these people are heading toward crematories as he describes the many articles that they discard as the trains go by. In the boy's mind, however, these events are not coherently connected because for him time exists only in the present.

The boy takes on an historical perspective for the first time when he overhears the village priest talking about the Germans. He recognizes that he "began to understand the extraordinary success of the Germans" only by referencing their history: "Peace had never appealed to them. They did not want to till the soil, they had no patience to wait all year for the harvest. They preferred attacking other tribes and taking crops from them."[7] The random cruelties by the peasants, the German atrocities, and the appearance of death trains become connected in a coherent pattern. With increasing authority, the novel moves away from the nonhistorical (the boy's personal suffering) to the historical. This occurs with reports of the 1944 advance of the Russian armies, their revenge on German units, and the boy's adoption by sympathetic Russian soldiers. In addition, Kosinski frequently refers to the Red and White Partisan units operating in the area and their political conflicts. Given the limited perspective of his narrator, however, Kosinski is able to educate the reader only sparingly about the Partisan political agenda and, ironically, must depend on the reader's knowledge of history in order to give significance to a development that would eventually dictate Poland's fate and European history for the next 50 years.

Eventually, *The Painted Bird* becomes less a narrative of a child's suffering and more a signifier of historical patterns. The boy meets a Russian soldier, Gavrila, who instructs him about Marxism. Gavrila explains that events have a natural order, not divine; that human history has rules; and that one of these rules is that "a man would from time to time spring up from the vast nameless mass of men . . . who had superior knowledge and wisdom" (*Painted*

Bird, 213). The boy discovers that the past not only exists in a discernible order but can be understood as well. That this understanding is politically biased escapes the boy, but not the reader, as Kosinski's aim is to show that unfortunately the boy's first awareness of history is flawed. Even so, the novel closes with the boy aware that his condition results not from random acts of violence by untutored villagers but from preordained and plotted atrocities emanating from historical forces.

Thus *The Painted Bird* dramatizes the exchange of ahistorical innocence for historical knowledge—a young boy's initiation to the march of folly, his introduction to the facts that human events have a past time as well as a present and that these events are connected in "historical" patterns. In *Steps,* Kosinski's second novel, the protagonist believes, as all Kosinski protagonists with the exception of Norbert Kosky do, that freedom and peace of mind can be found only by stepping out of history, so to speak. Simplistically, they believe that history is Europe and that by fleeing the Old World, they can put aside the burdens of the past and emerge into a New World that has only present and future time. The protagonist of *Steps* speaks for all when he thinks, as he journeys to America, that he is "timeless, unmeasured . . . suspended forever between my past and my future."[8]

The insistence that history can be left behind and the past consciously denied characterizes the protagonists from *Steps* to *Pinball.* In *Being There,* frank Chance "moves in his own time," and another character advises that "a man's past cripples him, his background turns into a swamp."[9] In *The Devil Tree,* Jonathan Whalen masterfully conceals his own past by "tailoring my reminiscences to the person I'm talking to."[10] Despite attempts to stay clear of "the swamp," the Old World, with all its attendant historical baggage, intrudes. Chance meets the Russian ambassador, who mistakenly thinks Chance speaks Russian and reads Russian literature. Whalen is confronted by an older Jewish man with a heavy European accent who suddenly exclaims, "You are a Jew. Millions of your people died poisoned by gas. Why would anyone want to kill Jews?" (*Devil Tree,* 63). What these seeming intrusions make clear is that the Holocaust, Jewishness, the Soviets—Eastern European history—are never far away from Kosinski's "Americanized" protagonists.

Although *Cockpit* (1975), *Blind Date* (1977), and *Passion Play* (1979) continue to feature rootless wanderers whose background is largely mysterious, these novels represent a shift in attitudes toward the past. The protagonists are Eastern European-born immigrants who express alternating feelings of anger and accommodation toward their former countries. In addition, the survival of the self is directly related to the historical past, which recreates itself even as it is destroyed. In *Cockpit,* Tarden believes he exists in "a curious time warp . . . completely cut off from my past."[11] His life depends, he insists, on his ability "to instantly create a new person and slip out of the past" (*Cockpit,* 129). Juxtaposed against this impulse is a contrasting urge to evoke a single memory picture so that "the montage of a past self will emerge" (13). Tarden's compulsion is to hide the past even as he feverishly tries to retrieve it. Frequently, he talks about his former life in Poland, Warsaw landmarks, the socialist government, Ruthenia, the Tatras, postwar resettlement, and Polish-Jewish relations. Tarden never quite understands the relationship of the past to the present, nor does Kosinski fully succeed in developing this theme.

This impulse continues in *Blind Date* and *Passion Play.* Levanter, the protagonist of *Blind Date,* a transplanted Slav escaping totalitarian Eastern Europe, reveals as much as he hides in his struggle with the past. In the process, history repeatedly creeps into the text. Levanter comments on Soviet militarism, Slavic anti-Semitism, the massive resettlement in Poland after the war, and the cold war mentality that resulted in a captive frame of mind. More to the point, history follows him wherever he goes. Moving to Princeton, he is shocked to learn that Svetlana Stalin is his neighbor. In New York City, he meets a cab driver who had delivered groceries in Levanter's boyhood village. In comparison, however, to the brutal portraits of Eastern Europe in previous novels, *Blind Date* betrays a touch of sentiment for the homeland. Levanter fondly remembers boyhood friends, skiing in the Tatras, and Chopin's "Nocturnes." As in *Cockpit,* romantic notions of the past nonetheless give way to the horrors of history. At his death, Levanter returns to his memories of World War II and "dead German soldiers . . . their teeth flashing through the holes in their frostbitten cheeks."[12]

In *Passion Play,* Fabian, another exile, still rankles at the Soviet-style socialism that "diminished one's achievements." Unlike his predecessors, however, he recognizes that history cannot be put aside and that all "the skins that he shed, phases of the body and the mind,"[13] were alive in memory. The striking new turn that Kosinski takes toward history is reflected in the second half of the novel. Once again, Kosinski alludes to the Holocaust as "one of the biggest fires ever" and to his relatives who died in it. In this case, Holocaust history offers a chance of renewal. Riding into a forest clearing, Fabian wonders why he had not searched himself as he had searched the clearing and ultimately understands the "inexorability of the past" and our inability to "thwart its cycle of repetition" (*Passion Play,* 268).

Reconciliation with history—with one's own past—is an even more pronounced theme in *Pinball.* Predictably, Domostroy, an immigrant who grew up in Poland and studied in Warsaw, still bears the scars of World War II. Once again Kosinski offers a study of the deracinated self whose alienation has its origins in the Holocaust. Within this pattern, Kosinski makes crucial changes. Patrick Domostroy is neither a spy nor a self-appointed avenger, nor is he especially preoccupied with totalitarian Eastern Europe in the usual ways. Instead, he concentrates on music because music transcends self: "To compose music was for me to belong to everyone, to speak every language, to convey every emotion."[14] Notably, Kosinski turns for illustration to old-world history—and to Poland's mythopoeic hero, Frederic Chopin.

As an artist, political refugee, fellow Pole, and romantic rebel, Chopin bears certain similarities to Domostroy (and to Kosinski). To Poles, Chopin represents the best of cultural history; in *Pinball,* he is the bridge for Domostroy to reconnect himself to that history. What attracts Domostroy is Chopin's *zal,* "a spiritual enigma—pain and rage, smothered by melancholy—an emotional trademark of Poles or any people oppressed for long periods of time" (109). Domostroy is also afflicted with *zal*—so too is Donna, his protégée. At Domostroy's insistence, Donna journeys to Poland to compete in the prestigious Chopin piano competition, and Domostroy follows her triumph on television. He approves as she plays Chopin's "Seventh Etude in C-sharp Minor," and he is profoundly touched when she notes in her acceptance speech that she shares *zal* "with all the people of Poland" (284). For the first time in his fiction, Kosinski seems more at ease with his own past and with Polish history. Through his surrogate, Domostroy, Kosinski appears to have reconciled his old- and new-world selves and to be ready for a new game. Kosinski's relative silence after the publication of *Pinball* and the nature of his next novel, *Hermit,* are testimony that the seeds of change evident in *Pinball* were fertile.

If Kosinski was unable to live with history in his first eight novels, in *The Hermit of 69th Street,* his last, he frantically rushes to reconnect himself to history in a myriad of ways. Partly essay, document, autobiography, *apologia pro sua vita,* and novel, *Hermit* is difficult to categorize in terms of a single genre. What emerges from the hundreds of quotations, subtexts, references, and personal asides and forms perhaps the core of this "autofiction," as Kosinski calls it, is a sustained, hyperfrenetic dialogue with history. In the text, Kosinski reminds his readers that this "autofiction means inner drama as much as it means history" (*Hermit,* 379). In a broader sense, *Hermit* is Kosinski's response to the seemingly insignificant question, "Is there any history in it?"—a response not only to the "historical/factual" ambiguities in his fiction but also to the allegations that Kosinski was a lightweight, lacking the depth and substance to write the fiction that he published.

The Hermit of 69th Street is history in the best postmodernist tradition of those American writers most concerned with the novel as history. At the outset, Kosinski makes it clear that history is neither nonlinear nor objective but rather the simultaneous interaction of the past with the present and the scientific with the personal. History that matters is a stream-of-consciousness dialogue from the self comprising cultural, literary, political, personal, and imaginative events that matter most to the self. He opens with a quote from Einstein's preface to the theory of relativity and then refers to Bernard Grun's *The Timetables of History: A Horizontal Linkage of People and Events* (*Hermit,* 1–3) to stress the impertinence of historical time. Soon afterward, he introduces the historical complexities that make up the very nature of a book. Any book, he explains, "no matter how ahistorical, has at least a five-year long history"

(64), and then he proceeds to cite as example the making of Thomas Hardy's *Jude the Obscure,* although the reader knows by then that Kosinski is actually referring to *Hermit.* In the first pages, Kosinski does more. He demonstrates that *Hermit* will be a history of all that might be called *Jerzy Kosinski.* As James Park Sloan points out, from the beginning, Kosinski planned that the book following *Pinball* would explore the ambiguous history of Poles and Jews with the aim of reconciling historical tensions as well as personal tensions originating in his own Polish-Jewish background, or the "author's true history" (406). Kosinski does more. He constructs a history of literary and contemporary events that have influenced the historical self that produces the author's true self.

Eager to establish his Jewish, Polish, and American heritage, Kosinski turns to the histories of all three. Having rarely called attention to his Jewish background in his previous works, Kosinski labors to document the Jewish tradition to contextualize the self. He furnishes an impressionistic history of Judaism and the evolution of Jewish thought, drawing on such diverse works as Jacob B. Agus's *The Evolution of Jewish Thought from Biblical Times to the Opening of the Modern Era,* the history of the Hasidim movement by Simon Dubnow, and Gershon Sholem's work on Sabbataism, to name a few. Kosinski's primary and personal interest in Judaism centers in Poland, however. On this topic Kosinski is a revisionist—interpreting 1,000 years of Polish-Jewish history in controversial terms. He describes the Polish invitation to Jews to settle in Poland, the relative peace and the prosperity enjoyed by most Polish Jews during most times, and significant events from Jewish-Polish history. Clearly, he aims to soften contemporary tensions emanating from wartime events and subsequent Communist policy toward Poland's Jews. His quote from Abraham Joshua Heschel is, in effect, his summary of the history of Jews in Poland: "There . . . the Jewish people came into its own. It did not live like a guest in somebody else's house, who must constantly keep in mind the ways and customs of the host. There Jews lived without reservation and without disguise, outside their homes no less than within them" (94).

As he had from the beginning in *The Painted Bird,* Kosinski concentrates on the Holocaust as a singular event in Polish-Jewish history. Early in the text, he constructs a brief chronology to suggest that the Holocaust was, in a real sense, an ongoing event—from retaliation against the Jews during the period of the Black Death in 1349 and the Chmielnicki massacres in 1648 to the Czestochova deportation in 1940, which represents the beginning of Nazi genocide (36). He spends a great deal of time, primarily through citations and textual quotes, on World War II, especially events in Lodz, his boyhood city. Surprising to some, he concludes, as he had done in *Passing By,* that the Holocaust affected everyone in Poland in relatively equal measure, that Polish Christians suffered to the extent of their Jewish neighbors. Even though Kosinski makes it clear that events of World War II are paramount to his own history as well as a watershed in Polish-Jewish history, he also argues that the preservation and reconstruction of Polish-Jewish cultural history are now what matters and that conciliation and compassion matter even more.

Accordingly, Kosinski tries to show that he (and so many others) cannot and should not refute his bicultural heritage. He is forever as much Polish as he is Jewish, as much an Eastern European as an American, and by extension so too are hundreds of thousands of Jews now scattered outside Poland—their cultural home. Once more, he speaks largely through scores of quotations inserted into the narration and scores of references incorporated into the text to document his familiarity with, and his appreciation for, his Polish heritage. He quotes from and refers to distinguished Poles from the fifteenth century to the present but identifies primarily with modernist Polish artists such as Eliza Orzeszkowa, Stanislaus Reymont, Stefan Zeromski, Karol Wojtyla (Pope John Paul II), and especially with Chopin and Conrad. Conrad is a special case with whom Kosinski empathizes as an exile, as a writer relatively unappreciated in Poland during his lifetime, and as a Pole. Citing Conrad perhaps more than anyone in this reference guide to Polish thought, Kosinski's last reference to Conrad pushes the sympathetic comparison toward finality. He recalls Conrad's statement that "wherever he traveled over the seas he was never far away from his own country. . . . The leading principle of my life was to help Poland" (523).

Whether indeed Conrad's claim may be applied to Kosinski (or even to Conrad) is arguable. What is not in question is Kosinski's sincere attempt to correct the historical record in terms of Poles and Jews and to counter current tendencies to indict Poles for wrongs committed by the Nazis. In this case, history is simply wrong, Kosinski boldly argues. There can be no doubt, as witnessed by his enthusiastic attempts to reenter the literary, economic, and intellectual life of Poland in his last years, that Kosinski tried to bring together two histories that had been rendered apart. When he quotes from the commonly held belief that the history of Jews in Poland has had divine guidance and protection, in *Hermit,* his treatment of Poland transcends the exclusivity of Jewish life there. Even his closing quote from Sholem Asch appears designed to extend to all of Poland despite Asch's intention: "In the great future, when the Messiah will come, God will certainly transport Poland with all its settlements, synagogues and Yeshivas to Eretz Yisroel" (525).

Although there is no doubt that the answer to the seemingly rhetorical question asked of the protagonist in *Hermit,* "Is there any history in it?" is an unconditional "yes," the question remains, what kind and whose history is it? To this end, postmodernist historians and fiction writers alike have already provided scholarly and popular answers. The latest responses may be found in works such as *Memory, Narrative, and Identity,* a collection of essays that tries "to put into historical perspective the ahistoricized and commercialized sites and scenes of American conflict."[15] For these scholars and others and for contemporary writers of the American historical novel, history is a construct of documents and the imagination, an amalgam of public record, collective and individual memory, and personal experience—the sum, in effect, of the life lived. The fiction of Jerzy Kosinski may be considered as an integral part of this continuing reassessment and representation of history.

Notes

1. James Park Sloan, *Jerzy Kosinski: A Biography* (New York: Dutton, 1996), 193; hereafter cited in the text as *Jerzy Kosinski.*

2. Jerzy Kosinski, *The Hermit of 69th Street* (New York: Seaver Books/Henry Holt and Company, 1988), 474; hereafter cited in the text as *Hermit.*

3. Ronald Granofsky, "Circle and Line: Modern and Postmodern Constructs of the Self in Jerzy Kosinski's *The Painted Bird,*" *Essays in Literature* 18, no. 2 (1991): 264; Andrew Gordon, "Fiction as Revenge: The Novels of Jerzy Kosinski," in *Third Force Psychology and the Study of Literature,* ed. Bernard J. Paris (Rutherford, N.J.: Fairleigh Dickinson University Press, 1986), 280.

4. In my essay "Jerzy Kosinski's East European Self," *Critique* (Winter 1988): 121–32, I suggested that Kosinski's fiction revealed an increasing desire for reconciliation with his Polish self. Within the year, Kosinski returned to Poland for the first time and began to court his past and his homeland in various ways.

5. Jerzy Kosinski, *Passing By: Selected Essays* (New York: Grove Press, 1992), 3; hereafter cited in the text as *Passing By.*

6. Gail Sheehy, "The Psychological Novelist as Portable Man," *Psychology Today,* December 1977, 52, 55–56, 126, 128, 130.

7. Jerzy Kosinski, *The Painted Bird* (Boston: Houghton Mifflin, 1965), 174; hereafter cited in the text as *Painted Bird.*

8. Jerzy Kosinski, *Steps* (New York: Bantam Books, 1969), 108.

9. Jerzy Kosinski, *Being There* (New York: Harcourt Brace Jovanovich, 1971), 116.

10. Jerzy Kosinski, *The Devil Tree* (New York: Harcourt Brace Jovanovich, 1973), 31; hereafter cited in the text as *Devil Tree.*

11. Jerzy Kosinski, *Cockpit* (Boston: Houghton Mifflin, 1975), 247; hereafter cited in the text as *Cockpit.*

12. Jerzy Kosinski, *Blind Date* (Boston: Houghton Mifflin, 1977), 233.

13. Jerzy Kosinski, *Passion Play* (New York: St. Martin's Press, 1979), 182; hereafter cited in the text as *Passion Play.*

14. Jerzy Kosinski, *Pinball* (New York: Bantam, 1982), 25; hereafter cited in the text as *Pinball.*

15. Amritjit Singh, Joseph T. Skerrett Jr., and Robert E. Hogan, eds., *Memory, Narrative, and Identity: New Essays in Ethnic American Literatures* (Boston: Northeastern University Press, 1994), vii.

Jerzy Kosinski in Fact: A Master Fabricator's Nonfiction

Jerome Klinkowitz

How ironic it is that Jerzy Kosinski's posthumously published collection of essays, *Passing By* (1992), should be a major factor in the rehabilitation of his reputation as a writer. For it was his own blurrings of fact and fiction that prompted the initial discounting of his literary value in the late 1970s and early 1980s, just when he was at the height of his popular fame. Autobiographical ambiguities had motivated much of the appeal of *The Painted Bird,* and with *Steps* and *Being There,* Kosinski had proved himself adept at melding fictive storytelling with his public role as intellectual spokesperson. But as his novels of the next decade became increasingly glitzy and even trashy in their appeal, critics both popular and academic alike began wondering about their investment in this author who was no longer fashionably avant-garde. When the *Village Voice* savaged his good name in a piece of investigative journalism that was as much an attack on his coterie of friends (from the *New York Times*) as on his work, little seemed left of his former premier status as a writer of serious fiction.

In his biography, James Park Sloan has described the literary strategies Kosinski pursued in the last years of his life for books that would raise some needed money and get his writing career back on track:

> In November [1989] he wrote Mort Janklow of the Janklow & Nesbit literary agency seeking representation for three possible projects, which Janklow declined. The first, entitled *Dialoghi d'Amore,* was described somewhat vaguely as a writer's search for the lost dialogues of Leone Ebreo, a work of philosophy devoted to passion, desire, and lovemaking. The second was a novel, *Center-State,* about the elected president-for-life of a newly formed republic, which Kosinski saw as a sort of sequel to *Being There*. The third was *Passing By,* a collection of his essays and incidental writing. Kosinski claimed to have done substantial work on each book and projected completion dates of spring, summer, and fall of 1990.[1]

This essay was written especially for inclusion in this volume and is published here with the permission of the author.

Given how the author failed in his self-professed attempt to write himself out of the clutches of the *Voice* and into stylistic immortality with *The Hermit of 69th Street,* it seems unlikely that either *Dialoghi d'Amore* or *Center-State* would have restored his reputation to the level at which it had been from 1965 to 1971. But in *Passing By,* the only one of these works to see publication, the record exists for both judging Kosinski's spokesmanship and assessing how his work in that role was still developing as late as six months before he died.

It was, of course, as a writer of nonfiction that the author of *The Painted Bird* had first made his literary mark. His pseudonymous studies of collective behavior, *The Future Is Ours, Comrade* and *No Third Path,* are so lyric in character that they deserve to be studied not only in the tradition of similarly personalized sociological works by C. Wright Mills but with an eye toward the revolutionary "New Journalism" replete with the orientation and techniques of fiction that was just then being pioneered by Mills's student Dan Wakefield and others such as Tom Wolfe, Gay Talese, and eventually Hunter S. Thompson. On the other hand, Kosinski the novelist had felt compelled to surround his fictive work in an envelope of commentary, from the controversial afterword to *The Painted Bird* (subsequently dropped from later editions) to the privately printed booklets *Notes of the Author* and *The Art of the Self,* with which the author publicized *The Painted Bird* and *Steps*.

To the objections that Kosinski was beholden to an academic tradition of discursiveness and was in fact trying to stage-manage the reception of his work, one need only consider what would very soon become the tradition of these times: that of novelists not only earning doctorates but publishing literary commentaries contemporaneously with, or even before, their fictive work. Indeed, even writers without Ph.D.'s would soon be logging in with books of essays on both theory and practice. To William Gass's *Fiction and the Figures of Life* and Ronald Sukenick's *Wallace Stevens: Musing the Obscure* would be added Gilbert Sorrentino's *Something Said,* Donald Barthelme's *The Teachings of Don B.,* Raymond Federman's *Critifiction,* Sukenick's later *In Form: Digressions on the Act of Fiction,* and Kurt Vonnegut's three volumes of commentary: *Wampeters, Foma, & Granfalloons; Palm Sunday;* and *Fates Worse Than Death*.[2] With these two sociological books drawn from materials for his unfinished doctoral dissertation and the pair of accomplished studies of his own first two novels, Kosinski was not out of step but merely a bit ahead of his times. By 1991, when he was completing *Passing By,* there existed an important shelf of nonfiction books by serious novelists from which only his similar volume was missing.

The earliest materials in *Passing By* are the *Steps* and *Painted Bird* booklets, yet they conclude the volume rather than begin it. This is the first of several strategies Kosinski uses to reframe his public image. Whereas once the talking about his fiction was virtually coincidental with the text, now it is something he wants read only after other things have been considered. The overall plan of *Passing By* as presented to a prospective literary agent orchestrates a careful rhythm between matters of life and of art, with life always taking prominence. In the book as published, Kosinski's widow acknowledges that at the time of her husband's death, some of the individual selections were still not settled, but even her role in bringing the book to posthumous publication is characterized by an emphasis on the author's life. For example, the cover photograph is one long familiar to the world as credited to Scientia-Factum, Kosinski's personal corporation. Here, for the first time, the photographer is acknowledged as "Kiki von Fraunhofer-Kosinski." Yet the acknowledgments statement that begins the collection is signed in a most unfashionable, politically incorrect way, by "Mrs. Jerzy (Kiki) Kosinski," as if to emphasize her husband's presence even after his passing away.

The manner of that presence is evident in Kosinski's theory of art, a theory that demands a thorough investigation of his way of life before readers can be expected to have full and sympathetic appreciation. Prefacing all else that he wishes to preserve is a motto drawn from Lisa Grunwald's 1977 interview. Here the author sounds a familiar theme, one argued with much greater intellectual ponderousness in the *Steps* and *Painted Bird* commentaries: that the purpose of art is not merely to portray but to evoke. In terms of life, this means pausing rather than passing by. "Bypass"[3] is the term used in 1977, but throughout the pieces that follow, Kosinski will return to the notion of "passing by" in various contexts and different terms of phraseology. For the impressive public sculpture of Rhonda Roland Shearer, his highest accolade as critic is to say of observers that "[t]hey could not pass by it without making a pass at it" (*Passing By,* 65), and in *Notes of the Author,* he reminds readers that "[h]ate can be a machine as functional and regular as a locomotive; it will always pass by, and there will always be some people cheering it as it passes, silently or not" (220). Life with all its qualities goes on, passes by; human attention is what arrests it and makes it special, changing it into something else, which is a work of art (whether of great joy or of deep hatred).

The signal event in Kosinski's life at the time of *Passing By,* however, was his life's end. James Park Sloan has presented ample biographical evidence that his subject was contemplating suicide during his last years—not from depression or disappointment, necessarily, but as a way of keeping in control of events. And as early as 1968, in the booklet accompanying the publication of *Steps,* the author was celebrating suicide as a victory over nature and an affirmation of one's own dignity (231). Thus it is fitting that the first of the sections in *Passing By,* "Reflections on Life and Death," collects essays devoted to the joy of life that is evident even in the bold-faced contemplation of life's end. From this section, which is distinguished by one of Kosinski's most effective pieces of nonfiction prose—his report of Jacques Monod's last days in Cannes, where he had taken himself off medication and blood transfusions in order to accept the death that hemolytic anemia made inevitable—the author proceeds to a longer and more diverse assemblage subtitled "Life and Art." These essays, many of which are familiar from Kosinski's days of literary self-promotion, are now read not just in awareness of the author's death but in terms of what became his almost fatally damaged artistic reputation.

Following these examples are some very brief aesthetic treatments headed "Artists and Eye," in which sculpture, photography, and film are measured for their audience effect. Within each form, Kosinski traces the viewer's response: from concrete to abstract, which is just the opposite direction that fiction takes. "Literary experience starts from *within,*" he reminds us, "with the general, the language, and depends on [the] reader's effort and ability to evoke concrete characters, situations, memories, and feelings" (66). With this principle established, the essayist then proceeds to arrange his most striking personal material under the rubrics of "The Sporty Self," "Talk of New York," and "People, Places, and Me." Here are all the public stunts—polo playing, levitating in water, hobnobbing with movie stars, eventually scripting one film and appearing in another—that so alienated the outsider press as to bring on the most devastating critical attacks. Yet, in the unhappy wake of these trials, Kosinski not only lets the pieces stand but arranges them in a way that justifies the aesthetics behind such behavior. Then come the intellectually serious parts of *Passing By*—"Self vs. Collective," "Jewish Presence," "Time of Life, Time of Art," and two deftly chosen "Afterwords"—which supply the solid underpinnings for both the life Kosinski led and the novels he wrote.

From the very start, most critical commentators recognized that the contrary forces of collectivism and individualism generated much of what was transpiring in *The Painted Bird* and then in *Steps* and *Being There*. The boy of Kosinski's first novel and the young man of his second set themselves in stark opposition to the societal powers so evident in *The Future Is Ours, Comrade* and *No Third Path*. As for the character Chance in *Being There,* a more hilariously wicked satire of collectivism's balmy ineptness is hard to imagine. Between Marxist East and capitalist West, the writer of these early works is able to construct a universe that is very useful for the demonstrations he wants to make: that under conditions of duress, state socialism can be ruthlessly oppressive, whereas in a land of plenty, collectivism exerts its same directive force, albeit with a more comically ludicrous manner. As the author's career progressed, however, the lightness of his American treatments gave way to a darker vision. Not just Europe, with its heavy baggage of history, but the United States itself became the site for some of his protagonists' more hurtful exercises in revenge. At the same time, Kosinski's personal fortunes had risen from the penury of a dispossessed commentator on materialistic American mores, for as such were his very spokesmanlike novels received. Consequently his public pronouncements were taken seriously and given space in the Op-Ed section of the *New York Times* and in the pages of *The American Scholar*. By the early 1980s, just before the *Village Voice* lodged its complaints about his public image and private manner of composition, Kosinski had amassed a considerable body of nonfiction work. Much of it was addressed to the same issues of collectivism and the individual that motivated his novels—heroically in *The Painted Bird* and *Steps,* comically in *Being There,* but with increasing ambiguity and unease in *The Devil Tree* and even more so in the novels following.

Considered as a whole, the body of work that now constitutes *Passing By* stands as a more sophisticated argument than did most of its separately read parts. In its pages, collectivism is not just a Soviet bogeyman or an American lowest-common-denominator of mass-market culture but rather a sophisticated position all the more dangerous for the premier status it is accorded among the defenders of the so-called higher arts. When shallow humanists argue for a universal response, they speak to deep popular yearnings, but as such, the fulfillment of these desires is little other than a "feeling of magic," a "euphoric sense of belonging to others than to oneself" that is in fact a product of "nature as incantation," a most primitively tribal rite (243). The art produced from such a posture is less creative than it is "gestural," something Kosinski considers a "Pavlovian" response (244–45). But the individualistic contrast to such communal rites is not mere autobiography. Instead, the response such work evokes is akin to that accomplished by the action-painting of Jackson Pollock, Willem de Kooning, and Franz Kline, which prompts not a historical understanding but rather "an identification with the aspects of personality strewn and splattered throughout the story" (240).

To make the center of such fictive work the author's autobiography is to be reductively psychological, if not clinically psychoanalytical—two talents that even if he sought them would be out of reach for the historically traumatized author. Analogically, Kosinski sees the practice of such nonautobiographical yet very personal creativity in the sculpture of Rhonda Roland Shearer, where the temptations toward euphoric centrism are discouraged by the medium's intellectual abstraction. As something fashioned in bronze, Shearer's sculpture is solidly what it is. For an artwork whose medium is not paint or metal but words, the challenge is a greater one, but not an impossibility. All the literary artist must do is what Gilbert Sorrentino (in his own *Something Said*) describes as the writer doing his or her work: not contriving ready-made symbols to tell readers what they already know, but working with the materials of the story itself in order to confront the compositional problems at hand.[4] Anything else, as Sorrentino joins Kosinski in saying, is mere gesture.

Kosinski's reference to action-painting is apt, especially for what he has to say in another context about his protagonist in *The Painted Bird*. "In the book the child . . . survives because he cannot do otherwise, because he is a total incarnation of the urge for self-realization and self-preservation" (209). The boy cannot draft an autobiography because he has no power to limit himself, no power to *describe* (in the strictest sense of the word) his own relation to the world around him. Indeed, his narrative action is much like that of the action-painter engaged with the canvas—who is, like the boy of Kosinski's narrative, "equipped only with those powers of nature and instinct which further his ability" to act (209). For such work, there are no hidden meanings, no symbolic agendas. What you see, as such commentators are fond of saying, is what there is. And what there is in *The Painted Bird* and most other of Kosinski's works is a self whose being is involved with doing, with acting against a canvas of life where narrative art involves capturing the energy of experience, the pausing rather than just the passing by.

In undertaking such action, the worst thing is to submit to being defined collectively, from without rather than from within. Among Kosinski's earlier and better-known essays, there are numerous warnings to this effect. In addition to the usual cautions about behavior, such as being subject to the manipulations of advertising and the pressures of herd behavior, the author covers important new topics from the same perspective. One of these is censorship. It is a commonly argued subject in Kurt Vonnegut's books of essays, notably in the "First Amendment" section of *Palm Sunday,* where the case against book banning is presented on constitutional and civil libertarian grounds.[5] As one of Kosinski's vice presidents at the PEN/American Center, Vonnegut would have been allied with his leader on this important issue. Yet in Kosinski's own "Against Book Censorship" (originally written for *Media & Methods* in 1976), he takes a significantly different tack: that censors are not simply banning books they do not like, but mistaking literary works for instructional manuals. A literary work is individually creative, meant to serve as an imaginative projection for which the reader is a mediator; an instructional manual is a vehicle of collectivity, seeking "to control the reader's behavior" (139). Kosinski feels that mistaking the first kind of writing for the second is the book banner's greater crime, a misapprehension akin to conflating fiction with autobiography, as he argues to similar effect in the 10th-anniversary "Afterward" to *The Painted Bird:*

> Autobiography emphasizes a single life: the reader is invited to become the observer of another man's existence and encouraged to compare his own life to the subject's. A fictional life, on the other hand, forces the reader to contribute: he does not simply compare; he actually enters a fictional role, expanding it in terms of his own experience, his own creative and imaginative powers. (188)

Hence it is the same totalitarian force that must be resisted in such autobiographical and instructional misreadings of fiction.

Coincidentally, Kosinski finds the same fault with pronouncements by Alexander Solzhenitsyn, specifically when the famous dissident—at the time availing himself of an exile's refuge in the United States—objects to freedom of the press by challenging the fourth estate's rights. "By what law has it been elected," Solzhenitsyn asks, "and to whom is it responsible?" (115). Kosinski replies that here is the proper First Amendment issue, for it is not a collectively conveyed responsibility that is being defended but a preeminently individual right. Yet the Russian dissident regrets the implied disorder of such rights, just as he complains that "the defense of individual rights has reached such extremes as to make society as a whole defenseless against such individuals" (116). That Kosinski implies such objections reveal a desire for totalitarian order suggests he was far less of a neoconservative than his critics at the *Village Voice* would claim.

Another topic handled with fresh insight within the format of collective versus individual orientations is that of religion. Once again Kosinski argues for the creative dimension of the individual. In relating to God, he claims responsibility for only one life, his own, and worships the beauty of life's individual moments. What obstructs this worship is problematic, almost always so because it is an external imposition. To the familiar argument against one group imposing its notion of religion on another, the author adds a further bit of logic, which, just like his thoughts on censorship, is allied with Kosinski's first principle for fiction. Uninterested in bureaucracy and unwilling to associate himself with any group that tries to "institutionally modify the beliefs and attitudes of others," he prides himself on being a fiction writer because "fiction is a suspension of disbelief—not a statement of belief; and since it deals in imaginary situations, it cannot slander or damage or seduce or convert anyone; it is in no way a 'how to' " (163), a reference to the instructional-manual disorientation of the book banners and literary censors. In this essay, originally a chapter contributed to Terrance A. Sweeney's 1985 volume, *God &. . .*, the author may once again be preaching to the choir. But as with his readership of teachers for the *Media & Methods* piece on censorship of classroom materials, Kosinski is not taking a familiar approach. Instead he redefines personal issues in terms of social pressures that create the problem and then solves the problem by clarifying fiction's superior role.

From the start of *Passing By,* fiction's role has been to pause and celebrate the presence of life even as life strives to pass by on its journey to completion. Presence is the key to understanding what is perhaps Kosinski's finest essay, "Death in Cannes," written for the March 1986 issue of *Esquire* in response to one of the most personally impressive events in the writer's life, his firsthand experience of Jacques Monod's death. More than just a close friend, Monod had been a man of great style and accomplishment; moreover, through a careful interpretation of *Chance and Necessity,* Monod's masterwork in the philosophy of science, Kosinski had been able to employ him as a virtual apologist for the authorial vision informing *The Painted Bird, Steps,* and the theories used to publicize and defend them.

By itself, "Death in Cannes" is a complex interpretation of Monod's final act and Kosinski's observation of it. Throughout the essay's events, the author is not just present but present with his camera—the same camera that in subsequent parts of *Passing By* will be studied for its role in materializing the abstract (as opposed to fiction's abstraction of the material). Indeed, as strong as the essay is, it becomes even stronger within the collection's context. Although written relatively late in the author's career, it appears in the first section of *Passing By,* and although there is much about life to be discussed in the volume, it is death that is most personally foregrounded at the start. Thus what happened in the Jacques Monod piece is a miniaturization of fiction's role in structuring the record of Kosinski's assembled spokesmanship. Within the awareness of death, his volume pauses to appreciate fully life's vital moment. After all, he was not just in Cannes as a friend with a camera. Throughout the experience as recorded, he cannot stop being a fiction writer, especially a very self-conscious fiction writer forever attentive to the role aesthetics plays in his ethics.

Thus it is an aesthetic motive that prompts Kosinski's ultimate choice for what literary history will judge as his legacy. Together with the Monod essay, the first intimations of this choice are presented very early in *Passing By*—not only in the book's first section, "Reflections on Life and Death," but as that part's first essay, "Aleksander and André Wat" as first drafted in late 1989. Here, with his own death less than two years away, Kosinski thinks back to inspirations for *The Painted Bird* but also looks forward to the alternatives his own history offers. Granted, there is enough unhappiness in his past to justify a life memorialized by tragic ill fortune. Yet what quality of life would that be? Life, as it will be defined in later essays on censorship and on religion, is a positive, creative value. And as *Passing By* continues, readers will be treated to the spectacle of Kosinski most vividly and vibrantly alive: playing polo, in which his own theories of control face the balance of nature's power in the horse; levitating in water, in which he learns to accomplish the most by "doing" nothing (70); and reveling in the liveliness and artistic substance of a movie set, admiring both Warren Beatty's cinematic talent and the American film industry's seriousness in being able to produce such a substantial product as *Reds*. Before all this, as if planning out the meaning of his own personal existence, the author asks himself: "Is it going to be a state of mind based on life, or one immersed in shadows that my memory casts on my soul? Every single moment I face the dilemma: Shall I become like Auschwitz or like Kazimierz?" (8).

That Auschwitz has such commonly understood meaning whereas Kazimierz has to be footnoted suggests Kosinski's point even before he makes his argument, the case for which waits to be presented until much later in *Passing By*. Just mentioning the concentration camp where so many died conjures up the Holocaust as the signal event in twentieth-century Judaism, certainly the major fact about the Jewish condition during Kosinski's lifetime. But this is precisely the view that he wishes to counter. Just as he could so easily have let his life be swallowed up by negatives, so too has much of Jewish life as a whole been dominated not just by the Holocaust but by Holocaust consciousness. In "Hosanna to What?" (1990), he describes this consciousness as "a second Holocaust: a well-meaning, though often inadvertently Jew-demeaning activity, leading to the most aggravated persecution complex in recent Jewish history" (165).

Kazimierz stands in opposition to Auschwitz for several reasons. The old Jewish quarter adjacent to Kraków, Kazimierz is the site not of uncountable deaths and atrocities but of the flourishing of Polish-Jewish culture—a rich culture that for centuries gave so much to a greater Poland of which Jewish citizens were made to feel a part. As an area now in need of repair and restoration, Kazimierz serves as a model for creative, rather than simply regretful, memorializing. A revitalized Kazimierz would serve as a reminder of how Poland was for so many centuries a true home of Jewish life and culture. On the other hand, letting one's energies be wholly directed to mourning the Holocaust trivializes the present strength of Jewish contributions to the sciences, to the arts, and to the quality of life in general. "Hosanna to What?" presents facts and figures to show that although Holocaust museums and monuments spring up almost everywhere, forums for the presentation and support of contemporary Jewish art wither and die for lack of funds and interest.

Even more damning is the argument Kosinski makes from his own ethical and aesthetic convictions. In the continual battle between the individual and the collective, between the self and the larger world, the worst condition possible is to be defined from without rather than from within. The Holocaust was of course such a condition. But so is the second Holocaust, Kosinski claims, inferring that the Nazis are still killing off Jewish culture in the 1990s, thanks to the style of Holocaust fixation that neglects the present in favor of the past. In the even larger contest between life and time, Kosinski accords his deepest respect to human efforts that enhance a sense of presence. Yet he sees no sense of that at all in present-day Jewish American life: "While Jews of North America remain fixated upon Jewish absence from history—absence, as typified by the Holocaust—this continent lacks, for instance, a single national Jewish Presence Center devoted to Jewish invention and imagination, which have profoundly enriched the human mind" (168).

Not that the author of *The Painted Bird* could ever be accused of slighting our memory of the Holocaust. But the existence and arrangement of *Passing By* make very clear that Kosinski handled both his history and his art in a remarkably successful manner. This volume takes great care in organizing his aesthetics and reviewing the ethics of his life before restating, for one last time, the arguments he advanced in the 1960s for those strange new novels being written by such an exotic, challenging young man. Now, in the context of his flourishing and decline, and in full awareness of both his seemingly trendy notes on polo, skiing, and swimming and his more thoughtful commentaries on censorship, religion, and Jewish culture, he asks his readers to redigest his thoughts, circa 1965 and 1968, about *The Painted Bird* and *Steps,* the last full essays in this canonical posture for his prose.

Here lies the statement of his contribution to serious American fiction from 1965 to 1990, an era of great innovation and authorial self-consciousness. At a time when writers from Vonnegut to Sukenick were privileging the imagination as a generative force in fiction, Kosinski was making the additional point that in such endeavors, memory and the imagination were virtually the same. Consider the very first paragraph he ever published as a spokesperson for his life and work, the beginning of his *Notes of the Author on The Painted Bird:*

> The most essential stage of the writing process, it is often argued, is the process whereby the writer comes to stand outside the experience he intends to mirror in his book. The chief element of this "alienation" is the conscious desire to examine oneself and the experience from "without," from a standpoint at which both the writer himself and his surroundings lose their concrete features, and separate themselves from everyday reality after a long period of struggle and uncertainty to enter a fluid and less rigidly limited dimension. This new dimension exists only in the writer's consciousness; within it the elements of reality no longer obey the earthbound laws of gravitation; the minutiae of time and place cease to be important. (201)

From what Kosinski says elsewhere in *Passing By,* in the professional lifetime of commentary that followed these words from 1965, it is evident that terms such as "alienation" and "without" deserve to be in quotes, for the author is using them somewhat ironically. From the experience of reading his collected commentary, one knows that the fiction writer is not really alienated from his material but simply abstracted from its abrasively concrete dimensions—and that abstraction is due not to alienation but rather to memory's function as the good artistic editor. "Individual little fictions" (204) are what Kosinski calls the compensatory devices of memory, the patterns that we quite naturally, if unconsciously, use to clarify our thoughts. The properly empowered fiction writer—the novelist no longer bound by dead conventions and presumptions for serving the signs of discourse—is able to make conscious use of this fiction-making memory.

As such, imagination triumphs over history and, in doing so, conquers death. This is so because, with Jacques Monod's help, Kosinski is able to reconstrue destiny as something being written concurrently with the event and not prior to it. Such an orientation frees the fiction writer to valorize the present without discounting history's effect—for history itself becomes, for all practical purposes, a creature of memory. Even suicide can be construed as a positive act, at least in an artistic sense. Consider these words from the 1968 *Steps* essay: "Man dies because the human condition both wills and allows it. The definitive act of defiance and of superiority over the human condition is to defeat Nature with her own weapon, to bring about death at will (truly, one's *last will*)" (230–31).

"Time of Life, Time of Art"—this concluding section of *Passing By* draws its title from the Dutch edition of the combined *Painted Bird* and *Steps* essays Kosinski prepared in 1970 and defines the poles of its author's existence. For him, the two times were the same, but only because he made them so. *Passing By* stands as the conscious record of that accomplishment—a lonely but not necessarily alienating one. Although dedicated in the months before his death to restoring Kazimierz, it is doubtful that Kosinski could ever have lived there. One of his most convincing arguments in this collection is that he was happy only in New York, that self-made capital of such abstract pursuits as finance and communications. "Now you know why New York is my spiritual fatherland," he concludes a 1979 essay for *Paris Match* that even by page 99 in *Passing By* will be making greater sense to the thoughtful reader: "here in the city of solitude, we—the refugees of the spirit—we get together to become vagabonds of our mutual utopias. And because here we are so many of our species, each finds his own kind. You see, in this city of solitude nobody feels the only solitary one, and thus nobody is really alone."

Notes

1. James Park Sloan, *Jerzy Kosinski: A Biography* (New York: Dutton, 1996), 436–37.
2. William Gass, *Fiction and the Figures of Life* (New York: Knopf, 1970); Ronald Sukenick, *Wallace Stevens: Musing the Obscure* (New York: New York University Press, 1967); Gilbert Sorrentino, *Something Said* (San Francisco: North Point Press, 1984); Donald Barthelme, *The Teachings of Don B.* (New York: Turtle Bay Books/Random House, 1992); Raymond Federman, *Critifiction: Postmodern Essays* (Albany: State University of New York Press, 1993); Ronald Sukenick, *In Form: Digressions on the Act of Fiction* (Carbondale: Southern Illinois University Press, 1985); Kurt Vonnegut, *Wampeters, Foma, & Granfalloons* (New York: Delacorte Press/Seymour Lawrence, 1974); Kurt Vonnegut, *Palm Sunday* (New York: Delacorte Press, 1981); Kurt Vonnegut, *Fates Worse Than Death* (New York: Putnam, 1991).
3. Jerzy Kosinski, *Passing By* (New York: Random House, 1992), xiii; hereafter cited in the text as *Passing By*.
4. Sorrentino, *Something Said,* 25–26.
5. Vonnegut, *Palm Sunday,* 1–17.

Index

◆

The Volume Editor

Barbara Tepa Lupack, formerly academic dean at Empire State College/ SUNY and Fulbright professor of American literature in Poland and France, directs a small literary press and edits *The Round Table.* Her recent books include *Insanity as Redemption in Contemporary American Fiction: Inmates Running the Asylum* and *Plays of Passion, Games of Chance: Jerzy Kosinski and His Fiction.* She is editor of a series of books on film and fiction, including *Take Two: Adapting the Contemporary American Novel to Film* and *Vision/Re-Vision: Adapting Contemporary American Fiction by Women to Film.*

The General Editor

Dr. James Nagel, J. O. Eidson Distinguished Professor of American Literature at the University of Georgia, founded the scholarly journal *Studies in American Fiction* and edited it for 20 years. He is the general editor of the Critical Essays on American Literature series published by Macmillan, a program that now contains more than 130 volumes. He was one of the founders of the American Literature Association and serves as its executive coordinator. He is also a past president of the Ernest Hemingway Society. Among his 17 books are *Stephen Crane and Literary Impressionism, Critical Essays on "The Sun Also Rises," Ernest Hemingway: The Writer in Context, Ernest Hemingway: The Oak Park Legacy,* and *Hemingway in Love and War,* which was selected by the *New York Times* as one of the outstanding books of 1989 and has been made into a major motion picture. Dr. Nagel has published more than 50 articles in scholarly journals and has lectured on American literature in 15 countries. His current project is a book on the contemporary short story cycle.